Palgrave Studies in European Union Politics

Following on the sustained success of the acclaimed European Union Series, which essentially publishes research-based textbooks, Palgrave Studies in European Union Politics publishes cutting edge research-driven monographs. The remit of the series is broadly defined, both in terms of subject and academic discipline. All topics of significance concerning the nature and operation of the European Union potentially fall within the scope of the series. The series is multidisciplinary to reflect the growing importance of the EU as a political, economic and social phenomenon.

More information about this series at
http://www.palgrave.com/gp/series/14629

Christian Hagemann

EU Funds in the New Member States

Party Politicization, Administrative Capacities, and Absorption Problems after Accession

palgrave
macmillan

Christian Hagemann
Technical University Munich
Munich, Germany

Additional material to this book can be downloaded from http://extras.springer.com.

Palgrave Studies in European Union Politics
ISBN 978-3-030-02091-0 ISBN 978-3-030-02092-7 (eBook)
https://doi.org/10.1007/978-3-030-02092-7

Library of Congress Control Number: 2018959727

This Palgrave Macmillan imprint is published by the registered company Springer Nature Switzerland AG
The registered company address is: Gewerbestrasse 11, 6330 Cham, Switzerland

To Madlene

Acknowledgements

This book is based on research conducted during my PhD studies until early 2016 at the Ludwig Maximilian University in Munich. Finalizing this book was only possible thanks to the support of many people and institutions. First of all, Petra Stykow supported my academic and professional development both as doctoral supervisor and employer at the Chair of Comparative Political Systems for many years. She was always available for discussions on progress of my work, offered important comments on ideas collected in papers or presentations at the colloquium, and would even be ready to help out when a grant application would not turn out well. Most importantly, she did always signal trust in my abilities to eventually find the right solution. It is hard to express how much I have learned from her when it comes to research and applying critical thinking. I am also grateful to Berthold Rittberger who gave his support as doctoral supervisor. His sharing of knowledge on writing dissertations, publishing articles, and working in academia was invaluable. Also, his and Bernhard Zangl's weekly International Relations Colloquium offered the most rigorous and productive discussions of papers a PhD candidate could ever hope for. Equally, I thank Klaus H. Goetz as member of my dissertation committee for his insights, ideas, and support.

My colleagues at the Geschwister Scholl Institute of Political Science deserve gratitude for their helpful comments and ideas and sharing our fate as PhD candidates and teaching fellows. In this regard, I especially thank Wiebke Anton, Anna Michels-Boger, Fabian Burkhardt, Nina Guerin, Stefan Jagdhuber, Andreas Kruck, Ingrid Mauerer, Hilde van Meegdenburg, Bartek Pytlas, Nele Quecke, Karina Shyrokykh, Dorothea Traupe, Moritz Weiß, and Florian Wittmann. Benjamin Brast deserves special thanks for dedicated methodological and theoretical discussions, Tim Korver for sharing his approach of writing with me. Our students Christian Emmerich, Darija Fabijanić, Susanne Maslanka, and Theresa Weiß always offered crucial assistance.

Also, several institutions supported my work: I am grateful to the *Univerzita Karlova* in Prague and *Vilniaus Universitetas* for welcoming me as a visiting researcher, and the DAAD and ERASMUS programmes for supporting both conference participations and field trips. None of the field trips, conferences, and workshops would have been useful without the people willing to share their knowledge on Central and Eastern European Politics and EU Cohesion Policy with me. I would especially like to thank in this regard: Jiří Blažek, Miloš Brunclík, Aron Buzogány, Cristian Cercel, Antoaneta Dimitrova, Mažvydas Jastramskis, Robert Leonardi, Lukáš Linek, Klaudijus Maniokas, Vitalis Nakrošis, and Oto Potluka. Also, I am grateful to all civil servants from the new member states who participated in interviews and shared with me their knowledge and expertise, as well as the European Commission and especially Lewis Dijkstra for data support. Last but not least, the book benefited much from Palgrave's and its series editors' excellent reviewing, comments and editing that helped to make it more concise and deliver its message more clearly. Parts of the fsQCA presented in this book were already published in an article in the *Journal of European Public Policy* were it also received excellent comments from three reviewers (see Hagemann 2017 and Sect. 4.5). While I am thankful for all these people's contribution to my work, the remaining mistakes are, of course, my own responsibility.

Last but not least, I am thankful to my family for years of patience and encouragement, especially my parents, sisters, and friends for keeping up with me despite of my limited time for them. Still, the greatest support throughout all of this time was my incredible wife Madlene. She was a constant source of inspiration for this book, always willing to invest her precious time into discussing ideas and hypotheses, sharing with me her deep knowledge of the post-communist region. She bravely tolerated the years of field trips, conferences during holiday times, working late and on weekends, and often having a husband with his mind set on something else. Her support was the essential contribution to finalize this work.

Munich
June 2018

Contents

Acronyms and Abbreviations

AA	Audit Authority
AIR	Annual Implementation Report
AoI	Area of Intervention
ANO	Action of Dissatisfied Citizens (Czech Republic) (*Akce nespokojených občanů*)
BSP	Bulgarian Socialist Party (*Balgarska Sotsialisticheska Partiya*)
CA	Certifying Authority
CEE(Cs)	Central and Eastern Europe(an Countries)
CFR	Romanian National Railroad Company
CM	Centralized Management
CNADNR	National Company for Motorways and National Roads (Romania)
ČSSD	Czech Social Democratic Party (*Česká strana sociálně demokratická*)
CZK	Czech Crowns
DeSUS	Democratic Party of Pensioners in Slovenia (*Demokratična stranka upokojencev Slovenije*)
DG	Directory General
DIGV	Citizen's List of Gregor Virant (Slovenia) (*Državljanska lista Gregorja Viranta*)
DP	Labour Party (Lithuania) (*Darbo Partija*)
DPS	Movement for Rights and Freedoms (Bulgaria) (*Dvizhenie za Prava i Svobodi*)
EC	European Commission
ECJ	European Court of Justice
EEN	Expert Evaluation Network
EFSF	European Financial Stability Facility

EIB	European Investment Bank
ERDF	European Regional Development Fund
ESF	European Social Fund
EU	European Union
FDI	Foreign Direct Investment
FPA	Frequent Party Alternation
FSN	National Salvation Front (Romania) (*Frontul Salvării Naţionale*)
FsQCA	Fuzzy-Set Qualitative Comparative Analysis
GAD	Grant Award Decision
GDP	Gross Domestic Product
GERB	Citizens for a European Development of Bulgaria (*Grazhdani za Evropeysko Razvitie na Balgariya*)
GNI	Gross National Income
HZDS	Movement for a Democratic Slovakia (*Hnutie za demokratické Slovensko*)
IB	Intermediate Body
IMF	International Monetary Fund
IoE	Islands of Excellence
IRL	Pro Patria and Res Publica Union (Estonia) (*Erakond Isamaa ja Res Publica Liit*)
ISPA	Instrument for Structural Policies and Pre-Accession
JL	New Era Party (Latvia) (*Jaunais Laiks*)
KDH	Christian Democratic Movement (Slovakia) (*Kresťanskodemokratické hnutie*)
KDNP	Christian Democratic People's Party (Hungary) (*Kereszténydemokrata Néppárt*)
KDU-ČSL	Christian and Democratic Union—Czechoslovak People's Party (*Křesťanská a demokratická unie—Československá strana lidová*)
KeE	Centre Party (Estonia) (*Eesti Keskerakond*)
KSČM	Communist Party of Bohemia and Moravia (*Komunistická strana Cech a Moravy*)
KzB	Coalition for Bulgaria (*Koalitsiya za Balgariya*)
L	Equal Rights Movement (Latvia) (*Līdztiesība*)
LC	Latvia's Way (*Latvijas Ceļš*)
LDDP	Lithuanian Democratic Labour Party (*Lietuvos demokratinė darbo partija*)
LDS	Liberal Democracy of Slovenia (*Liberalna demokracija Slovenije*)
LEC	Low Executive Capacity
LiCS	Liberal and Centre Union (Lithuania) (*Liberalų ir centro sąjunga*)
LIDEM	Liberal Democrats (Czech Republic) (*Liberální demokraté*)
LLRA	Electoral Action of Poles in Lithuania (*Lietuvos lenkų rinkimų akcija*)

LPP/LC	Latvia's First Party/Latvian Way (*Latvijas Pirmā partija/Latvijas Ceļš*)
LPR	League of Polish Families (*Liga Polskich Rodzin*)
LSDP	Lithuanian Social Democratic Party (*Lietuvos socialdemokratų partija*)
LS-HZDS	People's Party—Movement for a Democratic Slovakia (*Ľudová strana—Hnutie za demokratické Slovensko*)
LVLS	Lithuanian Peasant Popular Union (*Lietuvos valstiečių liaudininkų sąjunga*)
LZJ-PS	Zoran Jankovic's List—Positive Slovenia (*Lista Zorana Jankovića—Pozitivna Slovenija*)
MA	Managing Authority
MC	Monitoring Committee
MDF	Hungarian Democratic Forum (*Magyar Demokrata Fórum*)
MSZP	Hungarian Socialist Party (*Magyar Szocialista Párt*)
N.Si	New Slovenia/Christian People's Party (*Nova Slovenija—Krščanska ljudska stranka*)
NCA	National Coordination Authority (Czech Republic)
NCCSI	National Coordination Committee for Structural Instruments (Romania)
NDA	National Development Agency
NDSV	National Movement Simeon II (*Natsionalno Dvizhenie Simeon Vtori*)
NGO	Non-Governmental Organization
NS	New Union (Lithuania) (*Naujoji sąjunga*)
NSRF	National Strategic Reference Framework
NUTS	Nomenclature of Territorial Units for Statistics
ODS	Civic Democracy Party (Czech Republic) (*Občanská demokratická strana*)
OECD	Organization for Economic Co-Operation and Development
OP	Operational Programme
OPE	Operational Programme Environment
OPT	Operational Programme Transport
OSCE	Organization for Security and Co-Operation in Europe
PA	Priority Axis
PC	Conservative Party (Romania) (*Partidul Conservator*)
PCTVL	For Human Rights in a United Latvia (*Par cilvēka tiesībām vienotā Latvijā*)
PD	Democratic Party (Romania) (*Partidul Democrat*)
PD-L	Democratic Liberal Party (*Partidul Democrat-Liberal*)
PDP	Civic Democracy Party (Lithuania) (*Pilietinės demokratijos partija*)
PDSR	Party of Social Democracy in Romania (*Partidul Democraţiei Sociale in România*)

PHARE	Poland and Hungary: Assistance for Restructuring their Economies
PiS	Law and Justice (Poland) (*Prawo i Sprawiedliwość*)
PNL	National Liberal Party (Romania) (*Partidul Național Liberal*)
PNȚ-CD	Christian Democratic National Peasants' Party (Romania) (*Partidul Național Țărănesc Creștin Democrat*)
PO	Civic Platform (Poland) (*Platforma Obywatelska*)
PS	Civic Union (Latvia) (*Pilsoniskā savienība*)
PSD	Social Democratic Party (Romania) (*Partidul Social Democrat*)
PSL	Polish Peasent Party (*Polskie Stronnictwo Ludowe*)
PUR	Romanian Humanist Party (*Partidul Umanist Român*)
QCA	Qualitative Comparative Analysis
RE	Estonian Reform Party (*Eesti Reformierakond*)
SaS	Freedom and Solidarity (Slovakia) (*Sloboda a solidarita*)
SC	Severe Crisis
SCP	Society for Different Politics (Latvia) (*Sabiedrība citai politikai*)
SD	Social Democrats (Slovenia) (*Socialni demokrati*)
SDE	Social Democratic Party of Estonia (*Sotsiaaldemokraatlikakond*)
SDKH	Christian Democratic Party (Slovakia) (*Slovenské kresťansko-demokratické hnutie*)
SDKU-DS	Slovak Democratic and Christian Union—Democratic Party (*Slovenská demokratická a kresťanská únia—Demokratická strana*)
SDL	Party of the Democratic Left (Slovakia) (*Strana demokratickej ľavice*)
SDS	Social Democratic Party of Slovenia (*Socialdemokratska stranka Slovenije*)/later: Slovenian Democratic Party (*Slovenska demokratska stranka*)
SEF	State Environmental Fund
SGI	Sustainable Governance Indicators
SLD	Democratic Left Alliance (Poland) (*Sojusz Lewicy Demokratycznej*)
SLS	Slovenian People's Party (*Slovenska ljudska stranka*)
Smer-SD	Direction—Social Democracy (Slovakia) (*Smer—sociálna demokracia*)
SNS	Slovak National Party (*Slovenská národná strana*)
SRP	Self-Defence (Poland) (*Samoobrona*)
SZ	Green Party (Czech Republic) (*Strana zelených*)
SZDSZ	Alliance of Free Democrats—Hungarian Liberal Party (*Szabad Demokraták Szövetsége*)
TB/LNNK	For the Fatherland and Freedom (Latvia) (*Tēvzemei un Brīvībai/LNNK*)
TEN-T	Trans-European Transport Network
TOP 09	Tradition Responsibility Prosperity
TP	People's Party (Latvia) (*Tautas Partija*)

TPP	National Resurrection Party (Lithuania) (*Tautos prisikėlimo partija*)
TS	Homeland Union (Lithuania) (*Tėvynės Sąjunga*)
TS-LKD	Homeland Union—Lithuanian Christian Democrats (*Tėvynės sąjunga—Lietuvos krikščionys demokratai*)
TSP	People's Harmony Party (Latvia) (*Tautas Saskaņas Partija*)
TT	For Order and Justice (Lithuania) (*Tvarka ir teisingumas*)
UDMR	Democratic Union of Hungarians in Romania (*Uniunea Democrată Maghiară din România*)
UNPR	National Union for Romania's Progress (*Uniunea Naţională pentru Progresul României*)
V	Unity (Latvia) (*Vienotība*)
VV	Public Affairs Party (Czech Republic) (*Věci veřejné*)
ZRP	Zatler's Reform Party (Latvia) (*Zatlera Reformu partija*)
ZZS	Union of Greens and Farmers (Latvia) (*Zaļo un Zemnieku savienība*)

List of Figures

List of Tables

CHAPTER 1

EU Funds in the New Member States

The enlargement of the European Union (EU) towards the East was the biggest ever expansion in its history. The EU became bigger in the course of enlargement, but it also became more heterogeneous, welcoming countries with an average GDP per capita of less than 40% of the EU's average (Vachudova 2005: 123). Most of the poorest regions of the community would be located in the new member states after accession. Enlargement would thus not only stabilize Central and Eastern European (CEE)[1] countries' post-communist transformation process to democracy and market economy, but also redirect most EU transfer schemes from the old member states towards the new ones. It comes as no surprise that the discussion about the desirability of eastern enlargement among the old member states was thus as much centered on honoring historical promises to the region, as it was focused on future access to billions from Brussels (Schimmelfennig 2001). At the same time, the funds were among the most important incentives for the candidates to take up the burdensome road to membership (Buzogány and Korkut 2013: 1555). However, almost a decade later the biggest obstacle in the way of many CEE countries receiving their fair share of EU

[1]CEE is usually used referring to Hungary, Poland, Slovakia, Slovenia, and the Czech Republic, but is here also set to comprise the Baltic states (Estonia, Latvia, Lithuania) and the Southeast European or 'Balkan' states (Romania and Bulgaria), thus all post-communist EU member states of the 2004 and 2007 enlargements (Lewis 2002: 4).

C. Hagemann, *EU Funds in the New Member States*, Palgrave Studies in European Union Politics,
https://doi.org/10.1007/978-3-030-02092-7_1

money was not old member states' reluctance to grant them access. Rather, it was their own inability to use the money.

Many CEE countries had hardly used their EU funds at the end of their first full financing period in 2013, the European Commission's (EC) seven-year budgetary cycle. A high number of programmes implementing cohesion policy stood at an absorption rate of a third or even less of their total allocation. This was a significant problem in the face of EU financing rules: funds that are not used in time are decommitted, thus entirely lost for the countries with low absorption rates. Accordingly, the EC stressed in 2013 the risk that "by not mobilising the available EU funds promptly, a significant volume of them will be lost and the intended objectives not achieved" (European Commission 2013: 10). In a similar vein, journalists across the region started to wonder why "billions in EU funds may go up [.] [the] chimney" (Česká Pozice 2011), why their countries were building "roads to nowhere" (Ilie 2011), or would ultimately "starve with money in their pockets" (SAR 2011). Thus, especially against the backdrop of old member states' pre-accession fears and candidates' motivation, one central question looms large: Why did some CEE countries struggle to use their EU funds?

It could be argued that these problems come as no surprise. Many observers of the accession process were convinced that the candidate countries would become troublesome new member states. Upon achieving accession, the EC's leverage towards the region would vanish and new member states could soon start dismantling the earlier changes in a region-wide 'backsliding' (Mungiu-Pippidi 2007). However, this expectation seems ill-founded with regard to cohesion policy and the high desirability of EU funds. Even Euro-sceptic parties in CEE argued for their absorption, and electoral contenders often criticized incumbents for their failure to use EU funds. Thus, against the backdrop of a strong wish to use the money, the EC's weakened enforcement capacity after accession is an implausible explanation for the low absorption rates in the region.

Alternatively, it could also be argued that absorption problems result from the region's low absorption capacities. The inability of CEE countries to handle the complex implementation procedures or to provide the necessary co-financing for EU projects could account for the failure to use EU funds in time. While capacities are indeed crucial for absorption problems, this argument fails to account on its own for much of the variation in the region. For example, it fails to explain why some new member states feature both successful and struggling programmes implementing EU funds. Thus, a purely managerial perspective on the process reveals only half the puzzle of poor absorption.

1.1 Politicization and Absorption Problems: The Argument

This study argues that the so far neglected role of politics and especially the politicization of the implementation process and EU fund's management structures are crucial for understanding absorption problems. In the study of bureaucracy, politicization refers to a process in which "the appointment and career of civil servants [is subject] to political will" (Rouban 2003: 313). Political parties often have great leeway to appoint staff to all levels of the state bureaucracy, trying to either achieve political control or access to resources (similar Meyer-Sahling 2008: 8; Kopecký and Mair 2012: 4). These appointments and changes of staff then naturally also influence the success and direction of policy implementation, with two most likely effects.

First, the practice of politicization of the state bureaucracy by political parties holds the potential to strongly affect administrative capacity. Politicization results in the regular exchange of core staff in the state bureaucracy upon the advent of a new government, party, or minister in office. Changes lead to a loss of knowledge and experience, and often also a lack of human resources. Politicization thus goes beyond the mere assessment of low administrative capacity. Rather, it can possibly result in a sudden lowering of well-functioning existing capacity, or systematically impede adaptation in the case of capacity problems. It means that no linear process of improvement is to be expected, not for a lack of resources, but for the very logic of political competition in a member state.

Second, the effect from politicization might well go beyond the weakening of capacities. The desire to politicize the state bureaucracy is often seen as a means to establish control over policy implementation by an incoming new minister or party (Kopecký and Mair 2012; Meyer-Sahling 2006: 275–276). The changes of staff are thus often only a first step in a general drive of an incumbent to implement policy preferences. Following staff changes, policy changes will thus further impact the implementation of cohesion policy. If new incumbents are more inclined to realizing own preferences than assuring absorption in general, changes can quickly result in delays of the absorption process, low absorption rates, and subsequently even a loss of funds due to a failure to use them.

Politicization was already found to matter in several ways for the use of EU funds. It features most prominently in allocation studies: Evidence for a distribution of funds following parties' interests was found in Bulgaria and Latvia (Bloom and Petrova 2013: 1600), but also in Germany (Dellmuth and Stoffel 2012: 427; Schraff 2014: 286) and Italy (Piattoni and Smyrl 2003: 144–145). In contrast to our broad knowledge on the influence of politicization on the allocation process, only two comparative case studies have so far highlighted its effect on the absorption of EU funds. Milio stresses for Italian regions that frequent changes are "detrimental to [...] administrative capacity because they undermine the continuity, consistency and coherence required for the successful implementation of a long term programme" (Milio 2008: 923). This means that politicization lowers administrative capacity and impacts absorption via the fluctuation of important staff. In a similar vein, Surubaru reports from Bulgaria and Romania that political stability was seen by funds' administrators as crucial for the absorption process (Surubaru 2017a: 850). Absorption improved during phases of stable government and thus more limited changes of core administrative staff as witnessed during the Borisov (Bulgaria) and Ponta (Romania) administrations (Surubaru 2017a: 850). However, when political control shifted, not only core staff but even "middle managers (Heads of Unit) or even operational staff (administrators)" (Surubaru 2017b: 114) were changed, again harming the absorption process.

Politicization of the bureaucracy has been reported in many different countries, but is a crucial characteristic of the post-communist context. In general, politicization matters in many countries of the world and is a phenomenon often linked to the question of whether bureaucratic autonomy has become entrenched before the mobilization of masses into politics took place (Shefter 1994: 31). This was not the case for most of the post-communist countries: Before transition to democracy, communist rule was characterized by a high level of politicization of the state bureaucracy. The communist parties of the region controlled the state through the application of political selection criteria for administrative staff, and the concentration of policy-making authority within the party-bureaucracy (Goetz and Wollmann 2001: 865). The end of communist party hegemony then could have ended the practice of 'over-politicization'. However, the practice was retained as it was useful for post-communist parties who could use discretionary appointments to establish control over institutions (Meyer-Sahling 2004: 81), or use officially non-political positions to reward loyal party supporters (O'Dwyer 2004: 529; Kopecký 2006: 258). Politicization was transformed from its function for a single party to control the state to a practice used by all parties with access to the spoils of government. It makes thus sense to test for the influence of politicization on the absorption process in the new member states as these feature mostly rather high levels of politicization, while it is possible to control for their roughly similar experience with the management of EU funds.

1.2 Testing the Role of Politicization for Absorption Problems

What are absorption problems and how can they be identified? Absorption problems refer to a member states inability to access its allocation of EU funds. The easiest way to detect absorption problems is to look at member states' share of interim payments received from the EC: If a country has only claimed a low share, for example less than half of its allocation of funds at the end of the financing period, this is a very strong sign of problems using the money. Still, to be sure that low absorption rates are not misinterpreted, they should go along with other characteristics to be seen as imminent expressions of absorption problems. For example, countries struggling to use their EU funds will witness criticism and warnings mentioned in evaluation reports provided by the EC or policy experts; often, they will try to save the money via reallocations from weak to better performing programmes within the country; or try to negotiate with the EC extensions of deadlines and exemptions from decommitment rules. Ultimately, some member states might also just lose some of their allocation due to belated spending. How can these absorption problems be explained?

Most existing studies stress the relevance of absorption capacities and especially administrative capacities for successful absorption, but there are further aspects to be considered. Overall, there are several different context factors adding to or also influencing administrative capacity that are potentially relevant for CEE countries' absorption performance during the 2007–2013 financing period. Integrating the different literatures on post-communist politics and economic reform, as well as insights on countries' pre-accession preparations for EU membership into the existing frameworks for cohesion policy analysis serves to offer a more dynamic and detailed picture of the causes and consequences of absorption problems.

In general, the quality of capacities and the extent of politicization of the central state bureaucracy are the most crucial factors. The EU accession process acknowledged CEE countries' problems in both areas and aimed at the professionalization and de-politicization of the civil service, but mostly failed in its endeavor of broad horizontal reform (Dimitrova 2005: 81; Meyer-Sahling 2011: 238–239). Its criteria for civil service professionalization and the development of administrative capacity were underspecified and introduced only late into the accession process (Verheijen 1999: 85; Buzogány and Stuchlík 2010: 276). Also, the prescribed civil service legislation was not part of the EU *acquis*, and the rules were also not consistently followed in the old member states. It was thus neither possible to enforce them at the European Court of Justice (ECJ), nor was demanding them considered very legitimate. The EU thus mostly failed to achieve broad horizontal reform in the candidate countries, and could rather increase sectoral capacity in some areas by means of direct support, creating so-called 'islands of excellence' (Goetz 2001). Still, in cohesion policy implementation their development was most likely only an outcome of the shortened post-accession financing period which was the first encounter of CEE countries with cohesion policy proper.

In 2009, implementation of cohesion policy became even more difficult due to the global financial and economic crisis. The coinciding of the crisis with the start of the financing period made it the single most important impact on CEE countries' economies in the period under scrutiny. Still, its effect varied widely and again depended on the domestic context and pathways of post-communist reform, namely countries' social contracts (Bohle 2011), their attractiveness for investments, their taste for 'financialized' growth during the 2000s (Myant and Drahokoupil 2012), and their degree of integration reached within the EU monetary union (Åslund 2010).

Against the backdrop of this implementation context, the analysis tests general levels of capacities, changes of political control over programmes, prior quality of EU fund management structures from the 2004–2006 financing period, the effect of the financial and economic crisis, and the structure of the implementation system for their ability to account for member states' absorption performance. This framework is applied in a set-theoretic multi-method research design (Schneider and Rohlfing 2013; Beach and Rohlfing 2018), combining a fuzzy-set Qualitative Comparative Analysis (fsQCA) (Ragin 1987, 2000) with two detailed process tracing case studies.

The fsQCA is ideal for comparing the mid-sized number of cases available, and its foundation in set-theory matches very well with the assumptions of existing research that all facets of absorption capacity must be jointly present to assure the use of EU funds. The analysis compares a total of 17 programmes implementing cohesion policy in all ten CEE member states. These programmes are among the largest in the region, implement mainly big infrastructure projects in the areas of transport and environment, and make up half of all convergence funds allocated to the region. The analysis is based on an original data set, assembling both existing measures of capacity as well as newly collected data, for example an own comprehensive collection of all instances of party alternation in operational programme's implementation systems for the entire financing period (2007–2013). The empirically most relevant result of this analysis is that the combination of poor capacities with frequent changes of political control in a context without centralized management structures for EU funds leads to absorption problems. This conjunction is then further tested in the process tracing analysis.

The fsQCA is complemented by two process tracing case studies of 'typical cases' for the detected combination of conditions (George and Bennett 2005; Beach and Pedersen 2013). The chapter starts by formulating a causal mechanism on the basis of the results of the prior analysis, and then specifies testable hypotheses for its presence. Evidence for testing the causal mechanism in the two typical cases is derived from regular implementation reports, evaluation studies, and numerous interviews conducted with ministerial officials, experts, and NGO representatives in three member states (Czech Republic, Lithuania, Romania) in the course of five field trips in 2014 and 2015. The analysis of cases in the Czech Republic and Romania reveals that there is a similar politicization mechanism working in both cases, leading to the outcome of absorption problems. While politicized changes of staff in the Czech Ministry of Environment interrupted the implementation process and made absorption more difficult, in the Romanian Ministry of Transport regularly alternating ministers kept changing strategies as well as staff on key positions, thereby making it difficult to improve the nascent EU fund management system. The analysis thus supports the findings from the fsQCA, but also offers further insights into the actual mechanism connecting the conditions to the outcome.

1.3 Plan of the Book

Following the introduction, the second chapter presents the puzzle of absorption problems in some of the new member states. It outlines in detail how the absorption process works and links the different stages of using EU funds to concepts from other fields of EU implementation research. It then discusses in detail the outcome, that is the patterns of absorption problems visible in the operational programmes under scrutiny. This look at the data is followed by a discussion of the two most prominent explanations for EU policy implementation failures in the new member states, that is the EU's lack of enforcement power after accession, and the lack of absorption capacity for EU funds. The chapter explains why these two strands of argument fail to account convincingly for absorption problems and why the analysis has thus to cast the net wider for potentially relevant variables.

The third chapter builds the framework for analysis. The focus rests initially on the domestic context of post-communist politics and the role of party politicization. It offers a comprehensive overview of parties in the transformation process and an answer to the question why the politicization of the central state administration remained widespread in the region despite of the introduction of democracy and market economy. It then summarizes existing knowledge on the EU accession process and its influence on both the professionalization of the civil service as well as the creation of capable EU fund management capacities. Finally, the process of post-communist economic reform and the diverging trajectories and growth models in the region are discussed as a background for countries' varying suffering during the global financial and economic crisis. While the three subchapters discuss the relevant domestic and international political as well as economic context conditions for the use of EU funds, the final sub-chapter summarizes the insights gathered as distinct conditions, explains their potential impact on the use of EU funds, and presents them as the framework for analysis.

The fourth chapter contains the first part of the empirical analysis. It starts with a detailed description and justification of the selection of the 17 operational programmes compared in this study. This is followed by a comprehensive discussion and presentation of the data used for the QCA, including: the general level of capacities in a member state and the quality of EU fund management capacities before 2007; the structure of the management and control system responsible for EU funds;

the extent of financial and economic crisis experienced in 2009; and a distinct characterization of every new member state's party system and the alternations of party control over ministries responsible for EU fund management during the financing period. The discussion of the operationalization and also calibration of the data concludes with a calibrated data matrix that summarizes all empirical information used in the comparative analysis. This analysis is then conducted focussing on the detection of necessary and sufficient (combinations of) conditions for absorption problems and its complement (that is, successful absorption). This comes with an explanation of the results and robustness tests conducted alongside the analysis. The findings are then summarized in the final sub-chapter of part four.

The fifth chapter builds directly on the findings from the comparative analysis and complements the QCA with two detailed case studies of operational programmes in the Czech Republic and in Romania. The chapter explains the rational of case selection and then formulates a testable causal mechanism to link the detected combination of conditions from the comparative analysis to the outcome. The goal is thus to shed light on the process of how the combination of low administrative capacities, frequent party alternation in control of EU funds, and the lack of a centralized management and control system lead to absorption problems. The causal mechanism is tested in the case of the Czech investment programme for the environment, and the Romanian programme supporting the transport sector. The case studies support the findings of the comparative analysis and offer further insights into the effect of politicization on the implementation process. The chapter concludes again with a summary of the results and the distinct insights gathered from the case studies.

Finally, the conclusion summarizes all results of this analysis, links them to relevant literatures, and discusses future perspectives of EU fund research.

References

Åslund, A. (2010). *The Last Shall Be the First: The East European Financial Crisis*. Washington, DC: Peterson Institute for International Economics.

Beach, D., & Pedersen, R. B. (2013). *Process-Tracing Methods: Foundations and Guidelines*. Ann Arbor: University of Michigan Press.

Beach, D., & Rohlfing, I. (2018). Integrating Cross-Case Analyses and Process Tracing in Set-Theoretic Research Strategies and Parameters of Debate. *Sociological Methods & Research, 47*(1), 3–36.

Bloom, S., & Petrova, V. (2013). National Subversion of Supranational Goals: 'Pork-Barrel' Politics and EU Regional Aid. *Europe-Asia Studies, 65*(8), 1599–1620.

Bohle, D. (2011). East European Transformations and the Paradoxes of Transnationalization. In J. DeBardeleben & A. Hurrelmann (Eds.), *Transnational Europe: Promise, Paradox, Limits* (pp. 130–151). Basingstoke: Palgrave Macmillan.

Buzogány, A., & Korkut, U. (2013). Administrative Reform and Regional Development Discourses in Hungary. Europeanisation Going NUTS? *Europe-Asia Studies, 65*(8), 1555–1577.

Buzogány, A., & Stuchlík, A. (2010). Wandlungen in Kafkas Schloß? Verwaltungsreform und -Modernisierung in Mittel- und Osteuropa. In H. Hill (Ed.), *Verwaltungsmodernisierung 2010* (pp. 255–281). Nomos: Baden-Baden.

Česká Pozice. (2011). *Billions in EU Funds May Go Up Dobeš's Chimney (Published 5 April 2011).* Available at http://ceskapozice.lidovky.cz/billions-in-eu-funds-may-go-up-dobes-s-chimney-fn4-/tema.aspx-?c=A110404_121659_pozice_10614. Accessed 13 Feb 2016.

Dellmuth, L. M., & Stoffel, M. F. (2012). Distributive Politics and Intergovernmental Transfers: The Local Allocation of European Union Structural Funds. *European Union Politics, 13*(3), 413–433.

Dimitrova, A. L. (2005). Europeanization and Civil Service Reform in Central and Eastern Europe. In F. Schimmelfennig & U. Sedelmeier (Eds.), *The Europeanization of Central and Eastern Europe* (pp. 71–90). Ithaca, NY and London: Cornell University Press.

European Commission. (2013, April 18). Cohesion Policy: Strategic Report 2013. *COM(2013) 210 final.* Brussels: European Commission. Available at http://ec.europa.eu/regional_policy/how/policy/doc/strategic_report/2013/strat_report_2013_en.pdf. Accessed 15 Mar 2017.

George, A. L., & Bennett, A. (2005). *Case Studies and Theory Development in the Social Sciences.* Cambridge, MA: MIT Press.

Goetz, K. H. (2001). Making Sense of Post-communist Central Administration: Modernization, Europeanization or Latinization? *Journal of European Public Policy, 8*(6), 1032–1051.

Goetz, K. H., & Wollmann, H. (2001). Governmentalizing Central Executives in Post-communist Europe: A Four-Country Comparison. *Journal of European Public Policy, 8*(6), 864–887.

Ilie, L. (2011). *Romania's Roads to Nowhere* (Special Report). Bucharest: Reuters. Available at http://www.reuters.com/article/us-romania-infrastructure-idUSTRE74P0ZK20110526. Accessed 12 Feb 2016.

Kopecký, P. (2006). Political Parties and the State in Post-communist Europe: The Nature of Symbiosis. *Journal of Communist Studies and Transition Politics, 22*(3), 251–273.

Kopecký, P., & Mair, P. (2012). Party Patronage as an Organizational Resource. In P. Kopecký, P. Mair, & M. Spirova (Eds.), *Party Patronage and Party Government in European Democracies* (pp. 3–16). Oxford: Oxford University Press.

Lewis, P. (2002). *Political Parties in Post-communist Eastern Europe*. London: Routledge.

Meyer-Sahling, J.-H. (2004). Civil Service Reform in Post-communist Europe: The Bumpy Road to Depoliticisation. *West European Politics, 27*(1), 71–103.

Meyer-Sahling, J.-H. (2006). The Rise of the Partisan State? Parties, Patronage and the Ministerial Bureaucracy in Hungary. *Journal of Communist Studies and Transition Politics, 22*(3), 274–297.

Meyer-Sahling, J.-H. (2008). The Changing Colours of the Post-communist State: The Politicisation of the Senior Civil Service in Hungary. *European Journal of Political Research, 47*(1), 1–33.

Meyer-Sahling, J.-H. (2011). The Durability of EU Civil Service Policy in Central and Eastern Europe After Accession. *Governance, 24*(2), 231–260.

Milio, S. (2008). How Political Stability Shapes Administrative Performance: The Italian Case. *West European Politics, 31*(5), 915–936.

Mungiu-Pippidi, A. (2007). Is East-Central Europe Backsliding? EU Accession is no 'End of History'. *Journal of Democracy, 18*(4), 8–16.

Myant, M., & Drahokoupil, J. (2012). International Integration, Varieties of Capitalism and Resilience to Crisis in Transition Economies. *Europe-Asia Studies, 64*(1), 1–33.

O'Dwyer, C. (2004). Runaway State Building: How Political Parties Shape States in Postcommunist Eastern Europe. *World Politics, 56*(4), 520–553.

Piattoni, S., & Smyrl, M. (2003). Building Effective Institutions: Italian Regions and the EU Structural Funds. In J. Bukowski, S. Piattoni, & M. Smyrl (Eds.), *Between Europeanization and Local Societies: The Space for Territorial Governance* (pp. 133–156). Lanham et al.: Rowman & Littlefield.

Ragin, C. C. (1987). *The Comparative Method: Moving Beyond Qualitative and Quantitative Strategies*. Berkeley et al.: University of California Press.

Ragin, C. C. (2000). *Fuzzy-Set Social Science*. Chicago: University of Chicago Press.

Rouban, L. (2003). Politicization of the Civil Service. In B. G. Peters & J. Pierre (Eds.), *Handbook of Public Administration* (pp. 310–320). London et al.: Sage.

SAR. (2011). Morti de foame, cu banii in buzunar. *Raport SAR*. Bucharest: Societatea Academica din Romania. Available at http://sar.org.ro/morti-de-foame-cu-banii-in-buzunar-autoritatile-romane-sunt-depasite-de-sarcina-de-a-cheltui-15-milioane-euro-pe-zi/. Accessed 12 Feb 2016.

Schimmelfennig, F. (2001). The Community Trap: Liberal Norms, Rhetorical Action, and the Eastern Enlargement of the European Union. *International Organization, 55*(1), 47–80.

Schneider, C. Q., & Rohlfing, I. (2013). Combining QCA and Process Tracing in Set-Theoretic Multi-method Research. *Sociological Methods & Research, 42*(4), 559–597.

Schraff, D. (2014). Buying Turnout or Rewarding Loyalists? Electoral Mobilization and EU Structural Funding in the German Länder. *European Union Politics, 15*(2), 277–288.

Shefter, M. (1994). *Political Parties and the State: The American Historical Experience*. Princeton: Princeton University Press.

Surubaru, N.-C. (2017a). Administrative Capacity or Quality of Political Governance? EU Cohesion Policy in the New Europe, 2007–13. *Regional Studies, 51*(6), 844–856.

Surubaru, N.-C. (2017b). Revisiting the Role of Domestic Politics: Politicisation and European Cohesion Policy Performance in Central and Eastern Europe. *East European Politics, 33*(1), 106–125.

Vachudova, M. A. (2005). *Europe Undivided: Democracy, Leverage, and Integration After Communism*. Oxford: Oxford University Press.

Verheijen, T. (1999). Civil Service Systems in EU Candidate States: Introduction. In T. Verheijen & A. Kotchegura (Eds.), *Civil Service Systems in Central and Eastern Europe* (pp. 85–91). Cheltenham: Edward Elgar.

CHAPTER 2

The Puzzle of Absorption Problems in Central and Eastern Europe

2.1 Absorption: A Process of EU Policy Implementation

Cohesion policy is the EU's development policy, focusing especially on the union's poorest regions. Its major goal is to reduce imbalances within the union "by promoting economic growth, job creation, and competitiveness" (Bache 2015: 244). These goals are realized mainly through investments in transport and environment infrastructure, but also by supporting job training and the adaptability of workers and businesses (European Commission 2007: 6).

In its current form, the policy came into effect alongside the Single European Act and the establishment of the single market (Leonardi 2005: 35). It was expected that further market liberalization would mean a burden for poorer regions lacking the ability to adjust to increased competition, particularly in the southern member states of Greece, Spain, and Portugal (Bache 2015: 246). The general idea behind cohesion policy is thus that an integrated market only works if all member states can participate effectively, and if the benefits of integration are not concentrated within a narrow group of countries (McCann 2015: 49). The importance of this 'balancing' of market forces for the EU is underlined by cohesion policy's share of the total budget, which at 35%, is just in line with that of the Common Agricultural Policy (McCann 2015: 62). Cohesion Policy is thus financially one of the EU's two biggest policies.

C. Hagemann, *EU Funds in the New Member States*, Palgrave Studies in European Union Politics,
https://doi.org/10.1007/978-3-030-02092-7_2

The objectives of cohesion policy have their roots already in the Treaty of Rome, but a concrete regional policy started to take shape only after the foundation of the European Regional Development Fund (ERDF) in 1975 (Bachtler and Mendez 2007: 537). Still, it was not before 1988 that cohesion policy developed as a distinct EU policy which was no longer only a support for national interventions (Bache 2015: 245). During the period under investigation, the instruments for financing cohesion policy apart from the ERDF were the European Social Fund (ESF) and the Cohesion Fund (European Commission 2007: 10). These funds supported the three objectives implementing cohesion policy in the 2007–2013 financing period (European Commission 2007: 13–20) as follows:

- The Convergence Objective supports the EU's poorest regions, defined as those with a GDP per capita of less than 75% of the EU average. These regions can benefit both from the ERDF as well as the ESF, and usually also receive support from the Cohesion Fund if their gross national income (GNI) per capita is below 90% of the EU average (European Commission 2007: 13).
- The Regional Competitiveness and Employment Objective is aimed at all regions that do not benefit from convergence support. It receives funds from both the ERDF and the ESF (European Commission 2007: 10).
- Finally, the European Territorial Cooperation Objective supports cross-border cooperation (border regions are eligible), transnational cooperation (all regions are eligible), and interregional cooperation (all regions are eligible) in all member states. This objective is funded by the ERDF only.

The emphasis in cohesion policy clearly lies with the Convergence Objective, which receives by far the biggest amount of funds: Four out of five Euro spend in cohesion policy were spend on convergence (EUR 281 billion or 81.5%) (European Commission 2007: 24–25). As CEE members feature most of the EU's poorest regions, they benefit strongly from cohesion policy and funding under the convergence objective. In the 2007–2013 period, they received roughly half of all cohesion policy funds available, even though only one fifth of the population of the EU lives in the post-communist countries (McCann 2015: 59). Thus, even though the allocation of funds was adjusted prior to enlargement in order to accommodate net-contributors' and EU 15 recipients' interests (Beichelt 2004: 42), CEE countries are now among the main beneficiaries of the policy.

Cohesion policy is implemented by the member states, but it is not to be confused with a purely domestic support policy. Implementation of the policy is based on several principles set at the supranational level. The 'additionality' principle stresses that EU finance should not replace, but rather supplement domestic spending (European Commission 2007: 27). 'Concentration' stresses the importance of allocating the funds to the poorest regions of the Union (Bache 2015: 247). 'Programming' focuses on the multi-annual planning of implementation, and 'partnership' stresses the fact that cohesion policy is implemented by national governments and regional or local governments, together with the EC (Bache 2015: 247). Thus, while the implementation takes place at the level of the member states who also develop implementation plans, the EC still has a considerable say in what the money is used for, not least because of the territorial eligibility criteria described above (Bachtler and Mendez 2007: 556).

The study of the absorption of EU funds is thus part of the broader subfield of EU policy implementation studies (Milio 2010b: 3). Most of the studies in this field focus on the transposition of directives, a process markedly different from the process of cohesion policy implementation (which is governed by regulation, not directive). Still, it makes sense to apply the terminology of EU policy implementation, as both directives and absorption are, after all, processes of putting EU policies into effect at the level of the member states. The following paragraph therefore offers an introduction to the most important concepts of EU policy implementation research. The concepts are then related to the different stages of the absorption process, thus cohesion policy implementation.

2.1.1 Absorption as a Process of EU Policy Implementation

To measure a member state's success in cohesion policy implementation, many studies have used the absorption of EU funds as the outcome (Noetzel and Stumm 1997: 13–14; Milio 2007: 430; Markovic Hribernik et al. 2008: 1223; Milio 2008: 916; Huszák 2010: 26; Milio 2010a: 26–28; Lackowska-Madurowicz and Swianiewicz 2013; Bachtler et al. 2014; Tosun 2014: 373–374). Absorption is a useful measure, because it is the endpoint of all stages of the cohesion policy implementation process. In order to reclaim funds from the EC, one must comply formally with institutional requirements, apply EU rules during the implementation of projects, and finally enforce these rules on beneficiaries. Obviously, absorption does not necessarily mean that funds are used efficiently or effectively, or that they contribute to the goals of the policy.[1] Still, absorption signals that EU money is spent on projects aiming at the implementation of the EC's priorities; that projects are developed and executed by beneficiaries in the member states; and that they are managed in line with EU prescribed rules and procedures. Absorption is therefore not a sufficient condition, but still a necessary one for cohesion policy to have any impact at the level of the member states.

Policy implementation is interested in the process and the concrete actions taken to put a policy into effect (Joachim et al. 2008: 6; Treib 2014: 5). The process of implementation of EU policies is usually separated into three distinct phases (Treib 2004: 61; Falkner et al. 2005: 6; Hartlapp and Falkner 2009: 282–283; Toshkov et al. 2010: 16–17; Treib 2014: 6). First, the policy is formally adopted, usually in parliament. Then, the practical implementation starts, and the new rules are applied by both the administration and private actors who have a stake in a certain policy area (citizens, enterprises) (Treib 2014: 6). Enforcement of the policy is guaranteed by the state through its administration and courts, possibly supported by independent agencies or social partner organizations as well as the infringement procedure of the European Court of Justice (ECJ) (Hartlapp and Falkner 2009: 284; Treib 2014: 6). Implementation can only be conceived of as complete if all three steps have been accomplished. Rules which are formally adopted but not enforced will remain as 'dead letters' (Falkner et al. 2008) or 'empty shells' (Dimitrova 2010) without much practical influence. The next paragraph explains what the stages of the implementation process mean in the process of absorption.

[1]The funds' impact on convergence is controversial anyway (Bachtler and Gorzelak 2007: 313–315).

2.1.2 The Process of Absorption: Formal Adoption, Application, and Enforcement

Cohesion policy implementation in the 2007–2013 financing period is regulated by Council Regulation (EC) No. 1083/2006 (Council of Ministers 2006).[2] The regulation sets the general provisions for the use of the ERDF, the ESF, and the Cohesion Fund during the financing period. It specifies in detail how formal adoption, application, and enforcement of its rules can be observed in the course of the absorption process.

Before the official start of implementation, member states must submit necessary planning documents to the EC and create the institutional framework required for policy implementation. These two tasks are essential to achieve formal implementation of cohesion policy. The member states must present their implementation strategy in a national strategic reference framework (NSRF) (CR Art. 28, 2). It contains an analysis of development disparities and potentials within the member state (CR Art. 27, 4a), formulates a development strategy (CR Art. 27, 4b), and ultimately operationalizes this strategy in the form of thematic operational programmes (OPs) (CR Art. 27, 4c). The NSRF contains an outline of programmes as well as their annual allocation of funds (CR Art. 27, 4e). Thus, the NSRF states in which areas money will be spent and how much of the available money will be used for each topic area. It is not only a manifestation of the multi-annual vision of cohesion policy implementation in a country, but also ensures that policy planning is aligned with broader EU strategies (Bache 2015: 249).

Formal implementation proceeds with the creation of an institutional framework for the proper handling of funds and the application process. This so-called management and control system includes four bodies (CR Art. 58b): a managing authority (MA), a certifying authority (CA), an audit authority (AA), as well as a monitoring committee (MC). Each operational programme requires all of these bodies, but the same bodies can serve several or even all programmes. The system manages projects, takes care of auditing (CR Art. 58f, g), and secures regular reporting and monitoring (CR Art. 58e). It also detects irregularities (resulting from cases of fraud) and is responsible for the recovery of funds spent in such

[2] The Council Regulation will be in the following referred to as 'CR', together with the respective article quoted.

cases (CR Art. 58e, h). Overall, the system's goal is to ensure the use of funds in accordance with EU rules. The different tasks of the management and control system are in CEE member states mostly performed by ministries at the central level acting as MAs, but often also as intermediary bodies (IBs),[3] or CAs (mostly ministries of finance).

Proper formal implementation has been achieved at the latest when the first monies are reimbursed to a member state. This reimbursement is conditional on delivering the NSRF prior to the start of the financing period (CR Art. 28, 2) and the EC's agreement to the plans (CR Art. 28, 3). The EC's endorsement of both the NSRF and the management and control system is thus a necessary precondition for any payments beyond pre-financing[4] (CR Art. 71, 1).[5] Thus, as soon as interim payments are made, it is clear that the EC regards the formal structure to be correctly in place. The process of formal implementation can be regarded as complete at the latest at this point.

Following formal implementation, subsequent application and enforcement of cohesion policy rules is the task of the member states and the beneficiaries of EU funds. The different bodies of the management and control system are at the centre of this task during the implementation process:

[3]The MA can outsource some of its tasks to so-called intermediary bodies. These IBs then perform the tasks for the MA, however, the MA still remains ultimately responsible for implementation.

[4]There are three different types of payments: pre-financing payments, interim payments, and the payment of the final balance. Pre-financing is spread over the first years of the financing period and set at a fixed level. The share of funding to be received differs between new and old member states as well as funds. For the new member states, pre-financing from the structural funds was set at 2% in both 2007 and 2009, and 3% in 2008 (CR Art. 82, 1b). The same accounts for the cohesion fund at 2.5% in 2007, and 4% in both 2008 and 2009 (CR Art. 82, 1e). The interim payments are usually studied when it comes to absorption. Interim payments are those funds reimbursed on the basis of actual implementation. They are therefore of prime interest to this study as they mean actual implementation on the ground. The final balance is 5% of the total allocation and is only paid after programme-closure (CR Art. 89).

[5]They are not sufficient, however, as interim payments also depend on transmitting correct applications for reimbursement to the EC which need prior projects to be implemented.

- The MA informs potential beneficiaries of their chances to apply for EU funds, and then guarantees that projects for co-financing are selected and implemented on the basis of EU rules (CR Art. 60a, d). It also verifies the delivery of the co-financed activities (CR Art. 60b). The MA is thus at the centre of practical implementation of an OP.
- The CA is responsible for the proper accounting of expenditures. Beneficiaries from EU funds send their requests for payments to the CA for certification, which is a confirmation that the applicant's statement of expenditure is in order, based on the necessary and accurate documentation, and in line with the respective rules set for project selection (CR Art. 61b). The CA also keeps account of recoverable or withdrawn funds and ensures their repayment to the EU budget if support for an operation is cancelled (CR Art. 61f).[6]
- The AA monitors the proceedings in both the CA and MA (CR Art. 62, 1a). It ensures the application of high audit standards, and checks on third parties' functional independence to conduct audits whenever they are assigned such tasks (CR Art. 61, 2, 3).
- Finally, the MC acts as an advisory body. Its major task is to oversee the "effectiveness and quality of the implementation of the operational programme" (CR Art. 65, a). It approves the selection criteria for projects (CR Art. 65a), discusses the development of OP implementation in regular meetings (CR Art. 65b, c), and also controls the communication of this development to the EC (CR Art. 65d). In contrast to the other three bodies, the MC is less involved in the actual management of an OP, but rather observes progress and adaptation.

The concrete process of cohesion policy implementation focuses on the generation and implementation of projects. The MA usually starts a call for applications and then examines the submitted projects. Successful applicants sign a financing contract and can start to implement their projects, usually by initiating a public procurement procedure. Beneficiaries reclaim the cost of implementation either continuously during the execution or in total once a project is completed. After the CA accepts these claims for reimbursement, it sends them to the EC and first compensates

[6]Tasks of both the MA and CA may also be transferred partially to so-called intermediate bodies to perform their tasks. These intermediate bodies work, however, still under the general authority of the specific MA or CA (CR Art. 59, 2).

the beneficiaries from national coffers. The EC verifies the expenditure and pays the money back to the member state. Applications are usually not sent immediately to the EC, but are often collected by the CA and sent in bundles at different times of the year. If applications are in order, applicants should receive the interim payments at the latest two months after the EC receives the application (CR Art. 87). Only after the EC has reimbursed the money, is it recognized as absorbed. This process of project development, implementation, and reimbursement is repeated until 95% of the total funds allocated have been disbursed.

How can the enforcement and application of EU rules be verified during the actual implementation process? Member states are responsible for the correct application and enforcement of EU rules, but their conduct is closely controlled by the EC. If it detects irregularities, it has means at its disposal to ensure clarification and correction of the errors. Besides the verification of claims for reimbursement, the EC follows the implementation of every OP on the basis of annual reports (CR Art. 67, 1). In these reports, the MA summarizes the progress of implementation (CR Art. 67, 2) as well as the "steps taken by the managing authority or the monitoring committee to ensure the quality and effectiveness of implementation" (CR Art. 67, 2d). The MA reports the most important problems posing a challenge to the implementation process as well as measures taken to overcome these problems (CR Art. 67, 2d). The delivery of the latest annual report by the MA is again a necessary condition for the continued reimbursement of interim payments (CR Art. 86, 1c).

If the EC detects irregularities at the system or at the project level, it has several instruments of rule enforcement at its disposal. Initially, the payment deadline is interrupted for up to six months (CR Art. 91). If member states fail to respond adequately to the EC's criticism within a two-month period, payments will be suspended (CR Art. 92). Such a suspension is only lifted if corrective measures are taken by the member state, and might even be extended across the entire OP if it fails to do so (CR Art. 92, 3). If the then following investigation of projects or the management and control system result in an actual detection of non-compliance, the EC can impose financial corrections on the member state (CR Art. 99, 1). Financial corrections are "withdrawals of funding that take place when payments to EU-backed projects have been made in error due to irregularities such as fraud" (Regional Policy Glossary 2015). They mean "cancelling all or part of the community contribution to an operational programme" (CR Art. 99, 1). Member states are able to comment on EC criticism up to two months before the final decision is taken to impose a correction (CR Art. 100, 1). If the EC and the member state agree on the problems detected and the extent of steps to be taken, member states are allowed to reuse the respective funds as if they had detected the fraud themselves (CR Art. 100, 4). Even if a financial correction was ordered against a member state, funds, which have been spent on the irregular activity still have to be recovered by the member state (CR Art. 101).

In sum, oversight during application and enforcement is quite close and, if neglected by the member state, subsequently conducted by the EC. The system is therefore closer to a 'police-patrol' mechanism of oversight than a mere 'fire-alarm' policy as in the transposition of directives (McCubbins and Schwartz 1984: 166). The EC is capable of stopping payments at any time against the backdrop of suspicions of problems with the domestic management and control system, or if the member state does not meet its reporting obligations. Still, money is not only lost due to irregularities. Beyond suspension, there is also the $N+2/+3$ rule. If member states fail to send an application for reimbursement of funds by the end of the second or third year following the commitment of funds, they will be permanently decommitted and the funds are thus lost for the member state (CR Art. 93). It is thus not only important to spend the money correctly, but also to spend it on time in order to make use of the full allocation. Decommitments are overall the biggest danger for countries to lose money they were allocated in cohesion policy.

What does all of this mean for the use of the absorption rate as the outcome? The high level of EC control signals that conformity or compliance with EU rules is a necessary condition for using the funds. Thus, whenever absorption works well, this should be a sign for compliance with EU rules on spending the funds. A high absorption rate usually shows that a member state applies EU rules correctly and that it is able to create and implement eligible projects for EU support. The rate of funds absorbed by a member state can thus be seen as a valid indicator of the degree of successful practical implementation of cohesion policy by a member state. The terms absorption of EU funds and implementation of cohesion policy will therefore be used interchangeably in the following chapters.

Still, one important caveat must be stressed: effectiveness as the actual achievement of cohesion policy's goals of convergence and economic growth is not part of this study. The implementation of projects and the spending of EU funds are necessary conditions for the effectiveness of cohesion policy, but they are not necessarily sufficient. At least in theory (and probably also often in practice) the money could be wasted on projects that have little impact. Research on the effectiveness of cohesion policy is often conducted by economists and resembles an independent branch of cohesion policy research.[7] It is therefore not within the scope of this study, which instead focuses on the implementation process itself. However, only if absorption is successful there is any chance of an impact of cohesion policy. The absorption rate is thus nonetheless important for the practical effects of cohesion policy, though it should not be confused with its impact.

2.2 Absorption Problems in the CEE Member States

After focusing mostly on the EU's democratizing power and specific policy sectors like environmental policy or minority rights, the analysis of the new member states' performance in cohesion policy gained only slowly more attention (more recent exemptions are Bloom and Petrova 2013; Bachtler et al. 2014; Tosun 2014; Surubaru 2017). The new member states are studied here as a group[8] because the 2007–2013 programming period, that is the EC's seven-year budgetary cycle for cohesion policy implementation, was the first experience with cohesion policy for these countries in the usual multi-annual framework.[9] Cohesion policy is an especially interesting policy area in the new member states. The prospect of benefitting from structural and cohesion funds was often highlighted as one of the main motivations for CEE countries to accept the strict pre-accession conditionality formulated by the EC for membership (Scherpereel 2010: 46; Buzogány and Korkut 2013: 1555). Their first full financing period meant more time for implementation as well

[7] See McCann (2015: 64–65) for an overview of probably all existing studies of cohesion policy's effectiveness.

[8] Cyprus and Malta are (just like in most other post-accession studies) not considered in this analysis. Overall, the two island-nations are difficult to compare to the CEE countries when it comes to the challenges they face, especially with regard to their historical trajectories. In addition, Cyprus does not even receive convergence support from the EU, and is thus anyway no possible case.

[9] The 2004 entrants to the EU could already participate for two years in the earlier financing period from 2004–2006.

as a much higher allocation of funds than in the shortened 2004–2006 period or in comparison to pre-accession support (Baun and Marek 2008: 13). In 2007–2013, CEE countries were allocated just below two-thirds of all funds available for the convergence objective (60.4%), the EU's support for its poorest regions. This is impressive, taking into account that the convergence objective receives the bulk of all funds available for cohesion policy (81.5%) (European Commission 2007: 24–25).

However, many of the new member states encountered serious problems with policy implementation during the financing period, and at the end of 2013 absorption of the funds was often very low. The situation soon drew the attention of the media, and journalists started to ask why the often needy CEE countries would "starve with money in their pockets" (SAR 2011); were building "roads to nowhere" (Ilie 2011); or why "billions in EU funds may go up [.] [the] chimney" (Česká Pozice 2011). This alarmism in the media was echoed by regional experts on cohesion policy. They stressed that if absorption would not increase substantially soon, some countries would "need a near miracle to access the entire allotted amount" (Gyorine Szabo 2014: 22) by the end of the period. For example, it was stressed that the Slovak programme for transport projects was facing "serious problems" (Frank 2013: 11) in implementation. Programmes in Romania were found to be generally "far behind the initial planning" (Lucaciu 2012: 13). The Hungarian OP Environment and Energy was "at high risk of de-commitments" (Balas et al. 2013: 4), thus of losing funds due to late spending.

But apart from these snapshots, what is the actual situation on site? Figure 2.1 presents an overview of absorption rates of the 17 biggest OPs in the region, covering almost half of all funds available for CEE countries (45.6%).[10] It shows that six of these programmes had barely used a third of their funds during the seven-year period. Three of the programmes managed to use around 40%, which is still not only below the EU 15 average (the line), but also well below the region's average for the spending of convergence money. Thus, the

[10]Cohesion policy is implemented in distinct thematic operational programmes at the level of the member states. See Sect. 4.2 for a detailed discussion of why these 17 programmes were selected for analysis, and Sect. 4.3 on how the differentiation between successful and less successful programmes is established on the basis of qualitative and quantitative criteria.

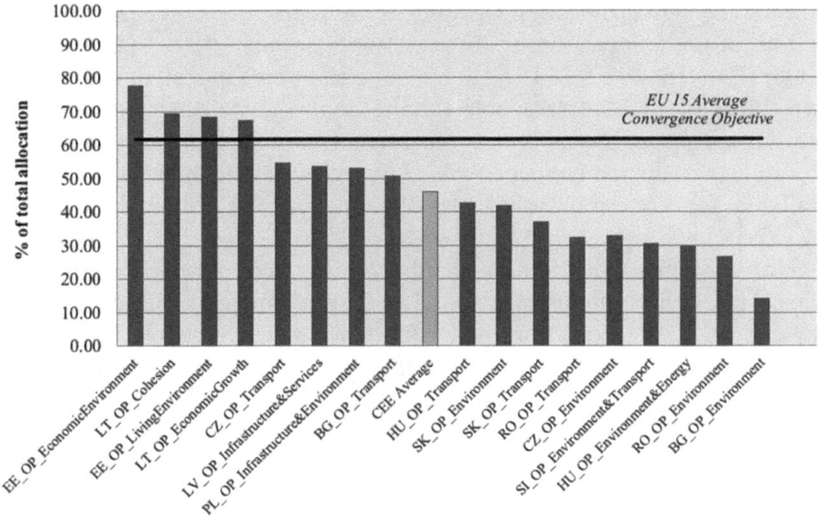

Fig. 2.1 Absorption rates in CEE as at 31 December 2013 (*Source* The author's compilation based on data provided by the EC [the data can be found online in Appendix III])

majority of huge programmes located in the poorest regions of the EU was long unable to use billions of available funds.

Still, the data shows further interesting (non-)variation at the level of policy areas, member states, and also within countries. First, there is no clear pattern of variation when it comes to policy areas and accession rounds. There are both programmes aiming mainly at environmental as well as transport projects among the poor performers (e.g. Slovak OP Transport, Romanian OP Environment) as well as the high flyers (e.g. Bulgarian OP Transport, Estonian OP Living Environment, which mainly focuses on environmental projects). At the same time, the typical pattern of 'leaders and laggards' (Noutcheva and Bechev 2008) of the region seems to be not entirely reflected when it comes to absorption. Probably as expected, the Baltic states are among the most successful users of EU money, while a Romanian and a Bulgarian programme are at the end of the line. Still, the chart also shows that absorption problems equally concern Hungary, one of the champions of post-communist reform and an early candidate country (Vachudova 2005: 20). Hungary's OP Environment and Energy is with regard to absorption one of the weakest programmes in the whole region. In contrast, there is a well-performing Bulgarian OP which is even close to the Polish programme, one of the most successful countries of this financing period (*The Economist* 2014). In sum, the expected patterns of variation among member states and policy areas are not entirely reflected when it comes to their absorption performance. This also draws attention to the most interesting variation: that is variation within member states.

Second, the focus on distinct programmes reveals that there are also cases of successful and unsuccessful use of EU funds within the same member state. Many of the countries are not very relevant in this regard as they have only one OP in this sample (Poland, Latvia, Slovenia), or have similarly performing OPs (Estonia, Lithuania, Romania, Slovakia). In contrast, Hungary has seen more success in using transport than environmental funds. Nevertheless, this difference is rather one in degree than in kind, as both programmes are still below the region's average and rather low-performing. However, Bulgaria and the Czech Republic feature both a successful programme and an unsuccessful one. Especially Bulgaria is interesting in this regard with the poorest-performing OP of all, and at the same time a reasonably successful transport programme. The OPs from the Czech Republic follow a similar pattern. Thus, it is seemingly not only country-level factors influencing the success of absorption in the new member states.

What was ultimately the effect of the observed absorption problems on OPs' ability to deliver and Cohesion Policy's effectiveness in the new member states? As discussed in Sect. 2.1, the most direct effect of belated spending of EU funds is their decommittment if spending deadlines are not met. Overall, some of the OPs under scrutiny lost a large amount of funds, but eventually the sums were lower than could have been expected at the end of 2013. Instances of decomittment occurred in the Bulgarian OP Environment (EUR 71 Mio./5% of the total allocation to the OP), the Romanian OP Transport (EUR 137 Mio./3%), and especially the Czech OP Environment (EUR 274 Mio./5.6%) (European Commission 2016: 49–50). These lost funds would thus not benefit the affected member states. Still, OPs avoided much higher decommittment rates not because of the limited relevance of absorption problems, but because of the EC's approach of rather supporting than punishing countries failing to absorb their EU funds. Instead of only invoking its enforcement instrument, the EC applied several support measures to help low absorbing member states. For example,

Romania and Slovakia received extended time for using their allocations for 2011 and 2012 (Ferry and Kah 2017: 30). Furthermore, direct help was extended to struggling OPs through a 'Task Force for Better Implementation' created by Commissioner Crețu. This task force engaged in Bulgaria, Croatia, the Czech Republic, Hungary, Italy, Romania, Slovakia, and Slovenia (Grzebieluch 2017: 4), thus in all countries whose OPs are below the CEE average in Fig. 2.1. The task force helped to modify more than 40 OPs and 120 major projects to increase their ability of spending (Grzebieluch 2017: 4). In this way, for example Romania avoided a loss of around EUR 4.3 billion (European Commission 2017: 10), that is 20% of its total allocation.

Despite of avoiding the worst possible outcome, absorption problems did nevertheless leave their mark on OPs' implementation performance. First, OPs under pressure of spending did often fail to pursue its originally planned agenda as the focus shifted from policy goals towards spending goals. When absorption pressure increased with approaching programme closure, in some instances quantity was given precedence before quality. For example, in its own evaluation report the EC found that a large proportion of MA officials interviewed agreed that in project selection "in-depth assessment of the quality of project proposals was less important than ensuring absorption" (European Commission 2017: 5). Also, OPs strategic priorities became less important: in case of slow or lacking project development, money was sometimes spent for already existing public projects which had normally been paid for from national coffers and were not originally foreseen in the OP (so-called "retrospection") (Ferry and Kah 2017: 32). Finally, low absorption rates at the end of the financing period also meant a much higher burden on administrations who needed both to finish a large share of implementation of the former and handle in the meantime the start of the next financing period, creating huge problems especially in contexts of low capacities.

Overall, absorption problems posed a serious challenge no only to the quantity but also to the quality of EU fund spending in many OPs in the new member states. The question for EU funds' absorption problems thus poses a central puzzle: Why do some member states (or their programmes) fail to use their funds, even though access to them was one of the main incentives for accession? The following chapters deal with this puzzle in detail. I argue that neither the enforcement-based explanations derived from post-accession research (Sect. 2.3), nor the management-based perspective from absorption-research (Sect. 2.4) can properly account for the low absorption rates in CEE presented above. Thus, it is proposed to consider absorption in the regional context of post-communist politics and pre-accession reforms as well as the crisis, in order to account for absorption problems.

2.3 Lack of Enforcement: An Implausible Explanation for Absorption Problems

The inability of the EC to enforce EU policy implementation is highlighted as a major threat for post-accession compliance in CEE member states, but it is not the problem underlying absorption problems. The worries about post-accession compliance are linked to the prior use of accession conditionality. The importance of conditionality to achieve a transfer of EU rules to the CEE candidate countries was perceived as a double-edged sword. It worked successfully to achieve rule transfer during the accession process, but also meant that there was later no guarantee for the preservation of these rules.

The fading of accession conditionality was referred to as a change of CEE countries' incentive structure (Epstein and Sedelmeier 2008: 797). After accession, the EU had lost its major tool of enforcement. The general expectation derived from both practical experience as well as theoretical analysis was thus a drop in CEE countries' willingness to comply with EU rules, or even a 'backsliding' (Mungiu-Pippidi 2007) behind the state achieved prior to accession. CEE countries would reverse EU policies to avoid high implementation costs, and a lack of societal mobilization would mean that the EC's decentralized monitoring system could not work properly in the region (Sedelmeier 2008: 808–809). This expectation resulted in a considerable number of studies that overall disagree on CEE countries' subsequent performance.

The early studies on post-accession compliance using mostly quantitative data often reject the 'backsliding'-hypothesis and underline that since accession "virtually all of the EU8 outperform virtually all of the EU15" (Sedelmeier 2008: 807) member states (see also Schwellnus et al. 2009: 18; Sedelmeier 2009: 8; Ram 2012; Börzel and Sedelmeier 2017). In constrast, more qualitative accounts stress that despite of successful formal adoption of EU rules, there is a "huge gap between the law on the books and the practice on the ground" (Falkner and Treib 2008: 303), thus a lack of application and enforcement of EU rules (see also Falkner and Treib 2008: 308; Falkner 2010; Dimitrova and Steunenberg 2013: 260; Sasse 2008; Brosig 2010: 400). Interestingly, however, while the former group of studies tends to focus too much on the formal adoption of EU rules, the second group seems to suffer from a certain selection bias for potentially problematic policy areas, making poor policy implementation results more likely.

More convincing are those studies painting a more differentiated picture of EU policy implementation in the new member states. These studies highlight that the process is not that different from that in the old member states. They stress that the performance of CEE countries in EU policy implementation varies (Michelsen 2008: 128; Knill and Tosun 2009: 10), and that domestic politics and thus preferences play an important role in either supporting or impeding compliance (Dimitrova and Toshkov 2009: 12; Maniokas 2009: 11; Sedelmeier 2012: 35). Compared to other policy areas, the "dead letters" in social policy implementation proved to be the exemption rather than the rule (Zhelyazkova et al. 2017: 231). As Grabbe stresses, what "is remarkable about EU influence is not so much that countries sought to renege on hotly contested commitments, but rather that they continued to comply in many other fields" (Grabbe 2014: 43).

Overall, it seems that the new member states behave pretty much like old member states when it comes to the implementation of EU policies. There seems to be no systematic rejection or even reversal of the EU *acquis* after accession, but rather occasional instances of non-compliance in highly contested or costly areas. The same goes for differentation between old and new member states, which is found to be very low (Schimmelfennig and Winzen 2017: 256). Domestic actors weigh policy implementation against the backdrop of their preferences—this generally appropriate finding from EU compliance research (see e.g. Mastenbroek and Keulen 2006; Mastenbroek and Kaeding 2007) can thus be sustained for the new member states. Is the EC's lack of enforcement power after accession thus a potential explanation for absorption problems?

2.3.1 A Lack of Enforcement Does Not Matter for Absorption Problems

CEE countries mostly continued to comply with EU policies after accession, but domestic politics started to play a bigger role in contested or costly areas. Against the backdrop of these results, a failure to absorb EU funds would only be expected if the new member states' governments entirely rejected the use of EU funds. Still, this is obviously not the case and the focus on a lack of enforcement on the side of the EC is not a plausible argument to account for low absorption rates.

The absorption of EU funds is clearly in the interest of CEE member states. This can be derived both from the goals of cohesion policy as well as actors' treatment of EU funds. First, EU funds mean a high amount of financial support for a region in need of investment. In the 2007–2013 financing period, the post-communist member states were the main recipients of convergence funds (60.4%), thus the recipients of those funds supporting the development of the EU's poorest regions (European Commission 2007: 24–25). At the country level, this resulted in a contribution as high as the equivalent of 4% of GDP in Lithuania, Bulgaria, or Hungary (Popa 2012: 163). The money focuses on investments in environment and transport infrastructure, thus supporting two areas which have long been neglected. For example, in 2007 Romania had only 228 km of motorway (RO 2007: 10). Traffic safety was very low, with a rate of road accident fatalities per car that is three times higher than the EU average (RO 2007: 22). In addition, even the Czech Republic as a comparably affluent new member state could make good use of EU funds for the modernization of its water supply systems or for dealing with ecological burdens from the past (CZ 2007: 89, 116). Access to EU funds thus provided a chance to benefit from EU membership, rather than being an EU-imposed scheme.

The availability of EU funds was generally perceived as an attractive opportunity in the region. Haughton puts it rather drastically when he claims that all "politicians in these net recipient states tend to see the EU as a 'cash cow' to be milked" (Haughton 2014: 80). Interestingly, this statement is supported by other evidence, which finds that even Eurosceptic parties like the Polish PiS (Law and Justice) supported the use of EU funds in their country (Gwiazda 2013: 237). More recent studies even find a positive effect from EU spending on parties' positions towards European integration (Gross and Debus 2018). Absorption of EU funds is thus not a contested topic at the national level. Rather, parties used it as ammunition in electoral contests against incumbents who were failing to absorb the money (Haughton 2014: 80). Thus, parties did not promise their voters that they would end the absorption of EU funds, but rather that they would be more capable managers of the funds, thereby increasing the intake.

This preference for EU money above party lines was also acknowledged in the discussion of post-accession compliance. Several authors stress that the threat of withholding EU funds could be a useful replacement for the now lacking accession conditionality to influence CEE countries (Pridham 2007: 186; Levitz and Pop-Eleches 2010: 471). The most prominent example generally quoted is the freezing of Bulgarian pre-accession assistance in 2008. Back then, the EC revoked the accreditation of EU fund managing bodies due to suspected fraud, and Bulgaria lost a total of EUR 220 million (Gateva 2013: 435). Thus, withholding access to EU funds is generally perceived as a threat to CEE countries' preferences, rather than the other way around.

In sum, external enforcement by the EC to demand implementation is not relevant for cohesion policy as member states have both an interest in the use of funds as well as the implementation of the very projects the funds are intended to finance. Thus, on the basis of the post-accession literature, a high level of absorption in all CEE countries and all OPs can be expected. As this is not the case, preference-based accounts are not useful to explain the low absorption performance in many CEE countries.

2.4 Lack of Absorption Capacity: An Incomplete Explanation for Absorption Problems

Studies accounting for different levels of absorption success in member states have stressed mainly managerial factors related to their ability to use EU funds, and not their willingness. This ability is referred to as member states' absorption capacities, three of which are crucial. First, administrative absorption capacity referring to domestic authorities' skill to manage and implement EU funds (Boeckhout et al. 2002: 2). Then, macro-economic absorption capacity as the amount of funds a member state's economy is able to digest. Finally, financial absorption capacity asking for a country's ability to provide the necessary amount of co-financing to use EU funds (Horvat 2005: 9).

Especially administrative and financial capacities are prominent variables in accounting for member states' absorption performance. Interestingly, studies on CEE have stressed that especially the lack of administrative capacity has caused or could cause a problem for EU policy implementation in general (Sedelmeier 2008: 809) and the absorption of EU funds in particular (Ederveen et al. 2003: 4; Leonardi 2006: 161; Marek and Baun 2008: 252; Falkner 2010: 113). Still, the exclusive focus on absorption capacities is of limited use to account for absorption problems.

There are three limits to the sole focus on absorption capacities. First, absorption capacities struggle to account for variation of absorption within member states. Second, it is hard to explain why capacities did not only fail to improve, but sometimes apparently even deteriorated over time, while both the EC and the CEE countries had a strong interest in absorption. Third, the focus on purely managerial factors neglects our knowledge of the political dimensions of the implementation process such as the use of EU funds for political purposes and the detrimental effect of changes of government on the implementation process.

2.4.1 Absorption Capacity in the Literature

Absorption capacities is broadly defined as the sum of member states' administrative, financial, and macroeconomic capacities. First, administrative capacity is the most prominent variable studied in its effect on member states' absorption performance. The focus on administrative capacity was especially triggered by the experience of absorption problems of EU funds in the early financing periods. After the 1988 reform of structural funds, it was found that especially the poorest regions with low administrative capacity in Greece, Portugal, and Spain made the least use of their fund-allocation (Bailey and De Propris 2002b: 305). The problem was also pervasive in southern Italy: "Certain Mezzogiorno regions had to return ECU 518 million of funds, and the Integrated Mediterranean Programmes [...] had a failure rate in Southern Italy of 32.6%, with rates of 56% in Sicily and 50.3% in Calabria" (Bailey and De Propris 2002b: 306). Thus, these regions were entitled to EU support and desperately needed investments, but in fact they could not benefit from the funds due to their inability to manage them (Bailey and De Propris 2002a: 409).

Administrative capacity refers to the organizational and human resources as well as the rules available in public administrations and government agencies to deal with the implementation of cohesion policy (Bachtler et al. 2014: 748). Administrative capacity therefore addresses the very ability of member states to practically implement cohesion policy and make use of EU funds. The main tasks to be fulfilled by the bureaucracy to use EU funds are:

- programming,
- project preparation and selection,
- financial management,
- monitoring and reporting,
- and evaluation (Šumpíková et al. 2004: 4–8; Horvat 2005: 12; Milio 2007; Huszák 2010: 46; see similar Milio 2010b: 38; Bachtler et al. 2014: 748; Terracciano and Graziano 2016: 304–308).

Programming refers to the prior planning of an operational programme before the beginning of the financing period. Then, project preparation and selection start the implementation process. During this process, financial management of reimbursement claims, monitoring and reporting of the progress of implementation, and the compliance with EU financing rules have to be ensured. Finally, evaluations make sure that constant mistakes can be eliminated and that processes can be adapted appropriately to achieve an improvement of the implementation process.

Studies that evaluate the influence of administrative capacity usually fail to specify its effect in terms of a mechanism and fail to go beyond the conceptualization and operationalization of capacity. Nevertheless, all studies follow the implicit assumption that a low level or a lack of administrative capacity will lead to poor absorption results (Šumpíková et al. 2004; Milio 2007: 439; Cace et al. 2010: 98; Bachtler et al. 2014: 736; Tosun 2014), especially in the CEE countries (Ederveen et al. 2003: 4; Leonardi 2006: 161; Marek and Baun 2008: 252). But how is administrative capacity actually studied?

One strategy to assess administrative capacity is to focus on the way in which countries manage to accomplish the tasks mentioned above (Milio 2007: 437; Šumpíková et al. 2004: 4–8). The level of capacity is then assessed as the quality of this performance. In contrast, another strategy is to consider the dimensions of administrative capacity necessary to achieve high performance at all steps of the implementation process. In order to excel at all of these levels, three elements of capacity are mentioned as necessary: an appropriate level of and highly motivated staff

(Horvat 2005: 12); well-functioning organizational structures and management and control systems (Horvat 2005: 12; Bachtler et al. 2014: 748); and the ability to adapt processes and structures where necessary during the implementation period (Bachtler et al. 2014: 748). Overall, this strategy pursues a direct measurement of capacity, while the former focus on the tasks is rather indirect (considering performance and not structures).

Most studies based on these approaches conduct a qualitative analysis and provide a handful of in-depth case studies (Bachtler et al. 2014: 748; see similar Horvat 2005: 12; Huszák 2010: 46; Milio 2010b: 38). Milio (2007), for example, only covers two Italian regions, while Horvat (2005) assesses five CEE states prior to accession. The only comprehensive endeavor in this regard is a recent project by Bachtler and others (2014) who have collected this kind of data in a collaborative project for all eight 2004 CEE entrants to the EU.

In contrast, a much broader, quantitative analysis is provided by Tosun (2014). In her study of the absorption performance of all EU member states in the 2004–2006 financing period, the author uses the 'Government Effectiveness' indicator to determine government capacities (Tosun 2014: 377). This indicator captures:

> perceptions of the quality of public services, the quality of the civil service and the degree of its independence from political pressures, the quality of policy formulation and implementation, and the credibility of the government's commitment to such policies. (World Bank 2015: 1)

It is an aggregate measure of secondary, perception-based sources estimating the underlying concept, thus it is a rather indirect measure of capacity. The main advantage of this indicator is its availability for a high number of countries and territories (215) and coverage of a period of many years (1996–2011), thereby enabling broad cross-country comparisons. While the use of 'Government Effectiveness' is rather exotic in the study of absorption performance, it is the measure most widely used in other fields of EU policy implementation, for example in transposition research (see e.g. Berglund et al. 2006: 704; Siegel 2006: 15; Thomson 2007: 997; Toshkov 2007: 339; Thomson 2009; Steunenberg and Toshkov 2009: 960). Still, the (major) downside is that its scope is very broad as its conceptualization offers no distinction between technical and political problems. In addition, it often lacks the ability to make meaningful distinctions between countries.[11]

In sum, even though operationalization differs strongly, both qualitative and quantitative studies agree in their results: Administrative Capacity is central in accounting for different absorption performances of member states (Tosun 2014: 379; Bachtler et al. 2014; Milio 2007; Horvat 2005: 21).[12] The centrality of capacity is thus one of the main findings of absorption research so far.

Second, also macroeconomic and financial absorption capacities have to be considered for member states' implementation performance (Horvat 2005: 9; Popa 2012: 168). It might seem absurd that financial capacities are beneficial for the implementation of a development policy targeting especially the poorest regions of the EU. These regions are to benefit from financial inflows for the very reason that they are cash-strapped, so all of them should have low levels of financial capacities. Still, it is important to take them into consideration. On the one hand, macroeconomic absorption capacity refers to the economic performance of a member state. Its effect is mainly related to the allocation of funds. If a certain amount is surpassed, a member state's economy is no longer able to use the additional funds. A higher level of funds will thus not necessarily result in a stronger developmental effect. This limit is generally seen at 4% of GDP (Popa 2012: 168). On the other hand, financial absorption capacity refers to a member state's ability to provide the necessary amount of co-financing for projects (Horvat 2005: 9). CEE countries must finance 15% of projects realized in the realm of cohesion

[11] Spendzharova and Versluis criticize, for example, that it is not possible to make a distinction between Spain and Bulgaria, even though qualitative evidence would strongly recommend doing so (Spendzharova and Versluis 2013: 1508).

[12] Support for administrative capacities was also found in other fields of EU implementation studies. The expectation of a positive influence of high capacities on implementation success is (at least among other variables) confirmed by the majority of studies for transposition (Berglund et al. 2006: 706; Kaeding 2006: 244; Haverland and Romeijn 2007: 776; Toshkov 2007: 346; Spendzharova and Versluis 2013: 1512), practical implementation (Falkner et al. 2004: 459; Falkner et al. 2005: 302), and infringements (Mbaye 2001: 274; Perkins and Neumayer 2007: 198; Börzel et al. 2010: 1379; Börzel et al. 2012: 465), even if not always significant (König and Maeder 2013: 53; König and Mäder 2014: 257) or sufficient (but see Siegel 2006: 20; Thomson 2007: 1002; Milio 2008; Dimitrova and Toshkov 2009: 12; Steunenberg and Toshkov 2009: 964; Thomson 2010: 591 for no or negative results).

Table 2.1 EU assistance to CEE during the 2007–2013 financing period

Country	*Total assistance (billion Euro)*	*Assistance per capita (Euro)*	*% of GDP*
Czech Republic	26.686	2627	3.5
Estonia	3.393	2555	4.1
Hungary	25.307	2561	3.9
Latvia	4.001	1751	3.9
Lithuania	6.775	2041	4.2
Poland	67.284	1773	3.6
Slovakia	11.507	2102	3.9
Slovenia	4.102	2082	2.0
Bulgaria	6.674	901	4.0
Romania	19.668	911	3.2
Total	*175.397*	*1930*	*3.6*

Source DG Regio, quoted after Popa (2012: 163)

policy themselves (Council of Ministers 2006: Annex III), meaning that the money is a necessary condition for the implementation of projects.

Overall, macroeconomic absorption capacity should have less of an effect on a member state's absorption performance because it is considered during the allocation of funds, thus before the beginning of the financing period and the implementation process. This ensures that member states do not receive funds only on the basis of their needs, but also against the backdrop of a realistic estimate of what they are able to use effectively. Table 2.1 presents data on the allocation of EU funds for the 2007–2013 financing period. It shows that the allocation varies between EUR 901 per capita in Bulgaria and EUR 2627 per capita in the Czech Republic, as well as 2% of GDP in Slovenia and 4.2% of GDP in Lithuania. The critical level for macroeconomic absorption capacity is thus usually not surpassed as the allocation of funds is strongly adjusted to the economic capabilities of the member states.

In contrast, financial absorption capacity is more likely to vary during the financing period and is a much more dynamic factor. The literature identifies two important obstacles for access to sufficient financial resources. First, especially regional authorities responsible for implementation can lack the ability or authority to generate their own revenues. The institutional structure and formal authority of regional actors in charge of managing and implementing structural funds is important, even as most studies agree that the level of decentralization has no effect on the absorption performance (Glusman 2010: 173; Huszák 2010: 252; Milio 2010b: 20). Still, studies stress that co-financing is more likely to be guaranteed if the bodies managing and implementing OPs have their own financial means and/or financial autonomy (Noetzel and Stumm 1997: 97). For example, Baun and Marek stress that limited financial resources made the implementation process more difficult in the 2004–2006 period in regions that were able to participate in cohesion policy implementation in Poland, the Czech Republic, and Hungary (Marek and Baun 2008: 254). If implementing actors depend on other actors to mobilize the necessary amount of co-financing, for example at the central level, the implementation process will generally be more difficult.

Second, external shocks can limit the financial capacities of a member state as a whole. Most importantly, economic and financial crises will have this effect (Cace et al. 2010; Tosun 2014: 378). Such crises can limit member states' access to financial markets and increase their borrowing costs. At the same time, a slump in the economy will cause tax revenues to decrease and can also lead to a rise in social spending, thereby increasing the general financial burden on the state. Interestingly, Tosun finds that there is no effect of the 2007–2008 crisis on the absorption performance of 25 member states in the 2004–2006 financing period (Tosun 2014: 383). Still, this result is most probably related to her operationalization of the variable.[13]

Overall, absorption capacities determine a member state's ability to access EU funds. Especially administrative capacity has been heralded as the major influence on absorption. While these results are important for the study of absorption in the 2007–2013 financing period, their ability to account for absorption problems in the new member states is limited.

2.4.2 *The Limitations of Absorption Capacities to Account for Absorption Problems in CEE*

Absorption capacities are a plausible influence on the absorption performance, but they are only of limited use when trying to account for

[13]Tosun uses the percentage-change in GDP between 2007 and 2008 (Tosun 2014: 378). However, the crisis hit CEE countries most strongly in 2009. It is therefore likely that the crisis had not reached all countries yet and had only later an effect on their financial capacities (see Sect. 3.3 on this matter).

absorption problems in CEE. There are three blank spots left by absorption capacities: the variation of absorption performance within member states; the apparent deterioration of capacity from the earlier period; and the influence of politics on cohesion policy implementation mentioned in many studies and evaluation reports.

First, absorption capacity is usually assumed to vary among countries, but not within them. Capacities for absorption are usually measured at the level of the member state (Bachtler et al. 2014; Tosun 2014) or, when it comes to regional programmes, at the very level of the unit implementing a programme (Milio 2007). Still, Fig. 2.1 shows absorption-variation also within member states. Two countries feature both successful and less successful OPs at the end of 2013. Bulgaria has a well-performing OP Transport, which has already used more than half of its funds at this point. In contrast, the country's environmental programme is the weakest performer of all OPs considered, and with an absorption rate of 14.05%, absorption has seemingly barely even started at the end of the financing period. Then, in the Czech Republic, the situation is similar when comparing the successful OP Transport and the low-absorbing OP Environment. It is not possible to account for such differences with a variance in national absorption capacity. At the same time, it is also doubtful how a pure focus on capacity would account for the successful Bulgarian programme, considering that Bulgaria has notoriously low administrative capacities (see also Sect. 4.4).

It could be argued that in contrast to the general assumption in the literature, capacity varies at the sectoral level and thereby causes these differences. Still, this fails to explain why programmes, which are implemented at the same (national) level by the same government, display different absorption capacities. Why should a government invest in one programme but not in another, even though all OPs hold the same threat of possible decommitment as a result of delays?

The ability of absorption capacity to account on its own for absorption problems decreases even further when considering the results of the earlier 2004–2006 financing period. Eight of the ten countries considered in this study could gain first experience of cohesion policy implementation during this shortened financing cycle. In their assessment of administrative performance in the region, Bachtler and colleagues find that many of the countries performed rather well, some even better than old member states (Bachtler et al. 2014: 747). Nevertheless, the EC mentioned Slovakia, a country credited with reasonably well-developed capacity 2004–2006, as being severely threatened by decommitment in 2013 (European Commission 2013: 10; Bachtler et al. 2014: 751). Absorption capacity alone is unable to account for this apparent change in fortunes. Administrative capacity is most often described in the literature as weakly developed in countries lacking adequate resources or experience for building it (Bailey and De Propris 2002a: 417; 2002b: 305). Capacity can thus be weak if not sufficiently supported, and the management approach would suggest overcoming such a situation through the offer of capacity-building measures (Chayes et al. 2000: 52). However, this reasoning leaves no space to account for a weakening of capacity, which had already been stronger earlier.

Furthermore, it also seems puzzling that the adaptation of capacity over time fails even though the EC closely follows the process and member states have a clear interest in absorption. Nevertheless, the Czech OP Environment reported that problems related to the rules for project-contracting discovered early in the period could only be solved at the end of 2013 (CZ 2014: 39). In a similar vein, the Romanian OP Transport stressed a lack of human resources, both at the beginning (RO 2009: 18–19) as well as the end of the financing period (RO 2013: 28). If such capacity problems are known early on, why are they not simply overcome? The pure focus on capacity can accommodate these observations as 'low capacity', but the fact that 'low capacity' develops in unexpected ways should caution a sole focus on this factor.

This is also related to those factors left out by the 'technical' discourse on absorption as an administrative process, and the emphasis on capacity and capital for implementation. This focus entirely neglects the role of politics in the process. In contrast, many evaluation reports and a few studies on the allocation of EU funds suggest that politics do play an important role in absorption. For example, the change of government in Hungary from the socialist party MSZP to the conservative Fidesz resulted in a large change of staff in the management and control system as well as in changes of programme priorities (Buzogány and Korkut 2013: 1572–1573). A similar development was reported in the Czech Republic, where a newly incoming government resulted in a "dramatic scale of fluctuation even of professional staff" (Blažek 2011: 4). Other studies have stressed that parties might use EU funds at their own discretion, as a sort of pork-barrel politics for their electoral constituencies (Bloom and Petrova 2013: 1613). Still, using funds as a political resource makes likely a reorientation of spending after a political alternation. Such changes, however, will result in delays and a possible interruption of the implementation process. A purely managerial look at the implementation process is unable to account for such 'voluntary' lowering of absorption capacity.

Overall, the focus of absorption capacity on purely managerial factors cannot account for variation in the ability to use funds among different ministries in the same country and over time, as well as the sudden deterioration of capacity or the lack of adaptation. Furthermore, it entirely neglects political factors, which nevertheless seem very relevant for implementation. This study thus stresses the importance of considering the context of implementation. Especially patterns of domestic (post-communist) politics as well as the experience of the EU accession process are likely to affect member states' ability to use EU funds. In addition, also the global financial and economic crisis might have affected the process of absorption. The following chapter therefore discusses possible influences on absorption related to the regional (Sects. 3.1 and 3.2) as well as global context (Sect. 3.3) at that time. It also details how the theoretical propositions can be tested empirically (Sect. 3.4).

References

Bache, I. (2015). Cohesion Policy: A New Direction for New Times? In H. Wallace, M. Pollack, & A. R. Youn (Eds.), *Policy-Making in the European Union* (pp. 243–262). Oxford: Oxford University Press.

Bachtler, J., & Gorzelak, G. (2007). Reforming EU Cohesion Policy: A Reappraisal of the Performance of the Structural Funds. *Policy Studies, 28*(4), 309–326.

Bachtler, J., & Mendez, C. (2007). Who Governs EU Cohesion Policy? Deconstructing the Reforms of the Structural Funds. *JCMS: Journal of Common Market Studies, 45*(3), 535–564.

Bachtler, J., Mendez, C., & Oraže, H. (2014). From Conditionality to Europeanization in Central and Eastern Europe: Administrative Performance and Capacity in Cohesion Policy. *European Planning Studies, 22*(4), 735–757.

Bailey, D., & De Propris, L. (2002a). The 1988 Reform of the European Structural Funds: Entitlement or Empowerment? *Journal of European Public Policy, 9*(3), 408–428.

Bailey, D., & De Propris, L. (2002b). EU Structural Funds, Regional Capabilities and Enlargement: Towards Multi-level Governance? *Journal of European Integration, 24*(4), 303–324.

Balas, G., Kiss, G., & Borbas, G. (2013). Hungary. *Expert Evaluation Network*. Budapest: HEFTA Centre for Analyses. Available at http://ec.europa.eu/regional_policy/sources/docgener/evaluation/pdf/eval2007/2013_een_task2_hu.pdf. Accessed 29 May 2017.

Baun, M., & Marek, D. (2008). EU Cohesion Policy and Sub-national Authorities in the New Member States. *Contemporary European Studies*. Olomouc: Palacký University. Available at http://www.4europartners.cz/prezentace/Baun_Marek_EU_Cohesion_Policy_and_Sub-National_Authorities_in_the_New_Member_States.pdf. Accessed 12 Feb 2016.

Beichelt, T. (2004). *Die Europäische Union nach der Osterweiterung*. Wiesbaden: VS Verlag.

Berglund, S., Gange, I., & Van Waarden, F. (2006). Mass Production of Law. Routinization in the Transposition of European Directives: A Sociological-Institutionalist Account. *Journal of European Public Policy, 13*(5), 692–716.

Blažek, J. (2011). Czech Republic. *Expert Evaluation Network*. Prague: Charles University. Available at http://ec.europa.eu/regional_policy/index.cfm/en/policy/evaluations/ec/2007-2013/#1. Accessed 29 May 2017.

Bloom, S., & Petrova, V. (2013). National Subversion of Supranational Goals: 'Pork-Barrel' Politics and EU Regional Aid. *Europe-Asia Studies, 65*(8), 1599–1620.

Boeckhout, S., Boot, L., Hollanders, M., Reincke, K.-J., & De Vet, J. M. (2002). *Key Indicators for Candidate Countries to Effectively Manage the Structural Funds* (Principal Report). Rotterdam: NEI Regional and Urban Development. Available at http://www.evaluace.cz/dokumenty/hodnot_zpr_eu/souhrnna_studie.pdf. Accessed 12 Feb 2016.

Börzel, T. A., Hofmann, T., & Panke, D. (2012). Caving in or Sitting It Out? Longitudinal Patterns of Non-compliance in the European Union. *Journal of European Public Policy, 19*(4), 454–471.

Börzel, T. A., Hofmann, T., Panke, D., & Sprungk, C. (2010). Obstinate and Inefficient: Why Member States Do Not Comply with European Law. *Comparative Political Studies, 43*(11), 1363–1390.

Börzel, T. A., & Sedelmeier, U. (2017). Larger and More Law Abiding? The Impact of Enlargement on Compliance in the European Union. *Journal of European Public Policy, 24*(2), 197–215.

Brosig, M. (2010). The Challenge of Implementing Minority Rights in Central Eastern Europe. *European Integration, 32*(4), 393–411.

Buzogány, A., & Korkut, U. (2013). Administrative Reform and Regional Development Discourses in Hungary. Europeanisation Going NUTS? *Europe-Asia Studies, 65*(8), 1555–1577.

Cace, C., Cace, S., & Nicolaescu, V. (2010). Management of the Structural Funds Within the Context of the Global Economic Crisis. *Review of International Comparative Management, 11*(1), 87–101.

Česká, Pozice. (2011). *Billions in EU Funds May Go Up Dobeš's Chimney (Published 5 April 2011).* Available at http://ceskapozice.lidovky.cz/billions-in-eu-funds-may-go-up-dobes-s-chimney-fn4-/tema.aspx?c=A110404_121659_pozice_10614. Accessed 13 Feb 2016.

Chayes, A., Chayes, A. H., & Mitchell, R. B. (2000). Managing Compliance: A Comparative Perspective. In E. B. Weiss (Ed.) *Engaging Countries: Strengthening Compliance with International Environmental Accords* (pp. 39–62). Cambridge, MA: MIT Press.

Council of Ministers. (2006, July 11). *Laying Down General Provisions on the European Regional Development Fund, the European Social Fund and the Cohesion Fund and Repealing Regulation (EC) No. 1260/1999* (Council Regulation (EC) No. 1083/2006). Brussels: Council of the European Union. Available at http://eur-lex.europa.eu/legal-content/EN/ALL/?uri=CELEX%3A32006R1083. Accessed 17 Mar 2014.

CZ. (2007). OP Environment 2007–2013. *National Strategic Reference Framework.* Prague: Ministry of Environment, Czech Republic. Available at http://en.opzp2007-2013.cz/ke-stazeni/515/5060/detail/the-operational-programme-environment—for-the-period-2007-2013/. Accessed 12 Feb 2016.

CZ. (2014). Annual Report for 2013. *Annual Implementation Report.* Prague: Ministry of Environment, Czech Republic. Available at http://en.opzp2007-2013.cz/ke-stazeni/515/15731/detail/annual-report-op-environment-for-2013-incl-annexes/. Accessed 12 Feb 2016.

Dimitrova, A. L. (2010). The New Member States of the EU in the Aftermath of Enlargement: Do New European Rules Remain Empty Shells? *Journal of European Public Policy, 17*(1), 137–148.

Dimitrova, A. L., & Steunenberg, B. (2013). Living in Parallel Universes? Implementing European Movable Cultural Heritage Policy in Bulgaria. *JCMS: Journal of Common Market Studies, 51*(2), 246–263.

Dimitrova, A. L., & Toshkov, D. (2009). Post-accession Compliance Between Administrative Co-ordination and Political Bargaining. *European Integration Online Papers, 13*, Article 19. http://eiop.or.at/eiop/texte/2009-019a.htm. Accessed Jan 2016.

Ederveen, S., Gorter, J., de Mooij, R., & Nahuis, R. (2003). *Funds and Games: The Economics of European Cohesion Policy* (Occasional Paper No. 3). Brussels: ENEPRI. Available at http://aei.pitt.edu/1965/1/ENEPRI_OP3.pdf. Accessed 29 May 2017.

Epstein, R. A., & Sedelmeier, U. (2008). Beyond Conditionality: International Institutions in Postcommunist Europe After Enlargement. *Journal of European Public Policy, 15*(6), 795–805.

European Commission. (2007). Cohesion Policy 2007–13: Commentaries and Official Texts. *European Union Regional Policy.* Brussels: European Commission, Directorate-General for Regional Policy. Available at http://

ec.europa.eu/regional_policy/en/information/publications/legislation/2007/cohesion-policy-2007-13-commentaries-and-official-texts. Accessed 29 May 2017.

European Commission. (2013, April 18). Cohesion Policy: Strategic Report 2013. *COM(2013) 210 final.* Brussels: European Commission. Available at http://ec.europa.eu/regional_policy/how/policy/doc/strategic_report/2013/strat_report_2013_en.pdf. Accessed 15 Mar 2017.

European Commission. (2016). *Analysis of the Budgetary Implementation of the Structural and Cohesion Funds in 2016* (Commission Staff Working Paper). Brussels: European Commission, Directorate-General Budget. Available at http://ec.europa.eu/budget/library/biblio/publications/2016/AnalysisOfTheEuropeanStructuralAndInvestmentFundsIn2016_en.pdf. Accessed 20 June 2018.

European Commission. (2017). *Document for the Committee on Budgetary Control, European Parliament* (Commission Staff Working Paper). Brussels: European Commission, Directorate-General Regional and Urban Policy. Available at http://www.europarl.europa.eu/cmsdata/124722/Hearing%20Briefing_Absorption%20of%20funds%20July%202017%20resized%20with%20Adobe.pdf. Accessed 29 May 2017.

Falkner, G. (2010). Institutional Performance and Compliance with EU Law: Czech Republic, Hungary, Slovakia and Slovenia. *Journal of Public Policy, 30*(1), 101–116.

Falkner, G., Hartlapp, M., Leiber, S., & Treib, O. (2004). Non-compliance with EU Directives in the Member States: Opposition Through the Backdoor? *West European Politics, 27*(3), 452–473.

Falkner, G., & Treib, O. (2008). Three Worlds of Compliance or Four? The EU-15 Compared to New Member States. *JCMS: Journal of Common Market Studies, 46*(2), 293–313.

Falkner, G., Treib, O., Hartlapp, M., & Leiber, S. (2005). *Complying with Europe: EU Harmonisation and Soft Law in the Member States.* Cambridge, MA: Cambridge University Press.

Falkner, G., Treib, O., & Holzleithner, E. (2008). Introduction: The Challenge of Implementation Research in the New Member States. In G. Falkner, O. Treib, & E. Holzleithner (Eds.), *Compliance in the Enlarged European Union: Living Rights or Dead Letters* (pp. 1–26). Aldershot: Ashgate.

Ferry, M., & Kah, S. (2017). *Research for REGI-Lessons Learnt from the Closure of the 2007–13 Programming Period.* Brussels.

Frank, K. (2013). Slovakia. *Expert Evaluation Network.* Bratislava: Slovak Academy of Sciences. Available at http://ec.europa.eu/regional_policy/sources/docgener/evaluation/pdf/eval2007/2013_een_task2_sk.pdf. Accessed 29 May 2017.

Gateva, E. (2013). Post-accession Conditionality—Translating Benchmarks into Political Pressure? *East European Politics, 29*(4), 420–442.

Glusman, J. (2010). The Impact of Policy Implementation in Poland: Centralisation, Decentralisation and Recentralisation. In S. Milio (Ed.), *From Policy to Implementation in the European Union: The Challenge of a Multi-level Governance System* (pp. 149–174). London and New York: Tauris Academic Studies.

Grabbe, H. (2014). Six Lessons of Enlargement Ten Years On: The EU's Transformative Power in Retrospect and Prospect. *JCMS: Journal of Common Market Studies, 52*(Annual Review), 40–56.

Gross, M., & Debus, M. (2018). Does EU Regional Policy Increase Parties' Support for European Integration? *West European Politics, 41*(3), 594–614.

Grzebieluch, B. (2017). The Absorption of Structural and Cohesion Funds Under 2007–2013 Programming Period. *European Parliament Briefing*. Brussels: European Parliament, Policy Department D—Budgetary Affairs. Available at http://www.europarl.europa.eu/cmsdata/124722/Hearing%20Briefing_Absorption%20of%20funds%20July%202017%20resized%20with%20Adobe.pdf. Accessed 20 June 2018.

Gwiazda, A. (2013). The Europeanisation of Regional Policy in Poland: Did Political Parties Make a Difference? *East European Politics, 29*(2), 226–244.

Gyorine Szabo, G. (2014). How the Institutional System Charged with Regional Development Policy Actually Impact the Use of Cohesion Funds as Reflected by a Comparative Analysis of Poland and Hungary. *European Scientific Journal, 10*(19), 20–31.

Hartlapp, M., & Falkner, G. (2009). Problems of Operationalization and Data in EU Compliance Research. *European Union Politics, 10*(2), 281–304.

Haughton, T. (2014). Money, Margins and the Motors of Politics: The EU and the Development of Party Politics in Central and Eastern Europe. *JCMS: Journal of Common Market Studies, 52*(1), 71–87.

Haverland, M., & Romeijn, M. (2007). Do Member States Make European Policies Work? Analysing the EU Transposition Deficit. *Public Administration, 85*(3), 757–778.

Horvat, A. (2005). *Why Does Nobody Care About the Absorption? Some Aspects Regarding Administrative Absorption Capacity for the EU Structural Funds in the Czech Republic, Estonia, Hungary, Slovakia and Slovenia Before Accession* (WIFO Working Papers). Wien: Österreichisches Institut für Wirtschaftsforschung. Available at http://www.wifo.ac.at/jart/prj3/wifo/resources/person_dokument/person_dokument.jart?publikationsid=25750&mime_type=application/pdf. Accessed 29 May 2017.

Huszák, L. (2010). *Der Wettbewerb der Regionen: regionale Unterschiede in der Absorption der EU-Fördermittel: Eine empirische Analyse*. Frankfurt: Peter Lang.

Ilie, L. (2011). *Romania's Roads to Nowhere* (Special Report). Bucharest: Reuters. Available at http://www.reuters.com/article/us-romania-infrastructure-idUSTRE74P0ZK20110526. Accessed 12 Feb 2016.

Joachim, J., Reinalda, B., & Verbeek, B. (2008). International Organizations and Implementation: Pieces of the Puzzle. In J. Joachim, B. Reinalda, & B. Verbeek (Eds.), *International Organizations and Implementation: Enforcers, Managers, Authorities?* (pp. 1–18). London: Routledge.

Kaeding, M. (2006). Determinants of Transposition Delay in the European Union. *Journal of Public Policy, 26*(3), 229–253.

Knill, C., & Tosun, J. (2009). Post-accession Transposition of EU Law in the New Member States: A Cross-Country Comparison. *European Integration Online Papers, 13*, Article 18. http://eiop.or.at/eiop/pdf/2009-018.pdf. Accessed Jan 2016.

König, T., & Mäder, L. (2013). Non-conformable, Partial and Conformable Transposition: A Competing Risk Analysis of the Transposition Process of Directives in the EU 15. *European Union Politics, 14*(1), 46–69.

König, T., & Mäder, L. (2014). The Strategic Nature of Compliance: An Empirical Evaluation of Law Implementation in the Central Monitoring System of the European Union. *American Journal of Political Science, 58*(1), 246–263.

Lackowska-Madurowicz, M., & Swianiewicz, P. (2013). Structures, Procedures and Social Capital: The Implementation of EU Cohesion Policies by Subnational Governments in Poland. *International Journal of Urban and Regional Research, 37*(4), 1396–1418.

Leonardi, R. (2005). *Cohesion Policy in the European Union: The Building of Europe*. Basingstoke: Palgrave Macmillan.

Leonardi, R. (2006). Cohesion in the European Union. *Regional Studies, 40*(2), 155–166.

Levitz, P., & Pop-Eleches, G. (2010). Monitoring, Money and Migrants: Countering Post-accession Backsliding in Bulgaria and Romania. *Europe-Asia Studies, 62*(3), 461–479.

Lucaciu, L. O. (2012). Romania. *Expert Evaluation Network*. Bucharest: LIDEEA. Available at http://ec.europa.eu/regional_policy/sources/docgener/evaluation/pdf/eval2007/expert_innovation/2012_een_task2_ro.pdf. Accessed 12 Feb 2016.

Maniokas, K. (2009). Conditionality and Compliance in Lithuania: The Case of the Best Performer. *European Integration Online Papers, 13*, Article 20. http://eiop.or.at/eiop/pdf/2009-020.pdf. Accessed 5 Jan 2016.

Marek, D., & Baun, M. J. (2008). Conclusion. In M. J. Baun & D. Marek (Eds.), *EU Cohesion Policy After Enlargement* (pp. 248–269). Basingstoke: Palgrave Macmillan.

Markovic Hribernik, T., Kirbiš, M., & Vek, U. (2008). Institutional Regulation and the Effectiveness of Absorbing EU Funds: The Experiences of Ireland, Estonia and Slovenia. *Društvena istraživanja, 17*(6), 1219–1239.

Mastenbroek, E., & Kaeding, M. (2007). Transcending the Goodness of Fit. *Comparative European Politics, 5*(3), 342–343.

Mastenbroek, E., & Keulen, M. (2006). Beyond the Goodness of Fit: A Preference-Based Account of Europeanization. In R. Holzhacker & M. Haverland (Eds.), *European Research Reloaded: Cooperation and Integration Among Europeanized States* (pp. 19–42). Wiesbaden: Springer.

Mbaye, H. A. D. (2001). Why National States Comply with Supranational Law: Explaining Implementation Infringements in the European Union, 1972–1993. *European Union Politics, 2*(3), 259–281.

McCann, P. (2015). *The Regional and Urban Policy of the European Union: Cohesion: Results-Orientation and Smart Specialisation.* Cheltenham and Northampton: Edward Elgar.

McCubbins, M. D., & Schwartz, T. (1984). Congressional Oversight Overlooked: Police Patrols Versus Fire Alarms. *American Journal of Political Science, 28*(1), 165–179.

Michelsen, J. (2008). A Europeanization Deficit? The Impact of EU Organic Agriculture Regulations on New Member States. *Journal of European Public Policy, 15*(1), 117–134.

Milio, S. (2007). Can Administrative Capacity Explain Differences in Regional Performances? Evidence from Structural Funds Implementation in Southern Italy. *Regional Studies, 41*(4), 429–442.

Milio, S. (2008). How Political Stability Shapes Administrative Performance: The Italian Case. *West European Politics, 31*(5), 915–936.

Milio, S. (2010a). Multi-level Governance and Implementation Performance: Lessons from Italy. In S. Milio (Ed.), *From Policy to Implementation in the European Union: The Challenge of a Multi-level Governance System* (pp. 59–122). London and New York: IB Tauris.

Milio, S. (2010b). The Struggle to Implement European Union Policies: Political and Administrative Factors in the Member States. In S. Milio (Ed.), *From Policy to Implementation in the European Union: The Challenge of a Multi-level Governance System* (pp. 1–57). London and New York: IB Tauris.

Mungiu-Pippidi, A. (2007). Is East-Central Europe Backsliding? EU Accession is no 'End of History'. *Journal of Democracy, 18*(4), 8–16.

Noetzel, R., & Stumm, T. (1997). *Factors Influencing the Spending of Structural Money. A Discussion at the European and Member State Level, with Special Regard to the European Regional Policy.* Regional Policy Series. Luxembourg. Available at http://bookshop.europa.eu/en/factors-influencing-the-spending-of-structural-funds-money-pbQAREGIW24/. Accessed 9 Feb 2016.

Noutcheva, G., & Bechev, D. (2008). The Successful Laggards: Bulgaria and Romania's Accession to the EU. *East European Politics & Societies, 22*(1), 114–144.

Perkins, R., & Neumayer, E. (2007). Do Membership Benefits Buy Regulatory Compliance? An Empirical Analysis of EU Directives 1978–99. *European Union Politics, 8*(2), 180–206.

Popa, A. (2012). The Impact of the Structural Funds in the Transformation Process of the New EU Member States. *L'Europe en Formation* (Vol. 364, pp. 161–179). Brussels: Centre International de Formation Européenne, No. 364.

Pridham, G. (2007). Romania and EU Membership in Comparative Perspective: A Post-accession Compliance Problem?—The Case of Political Conditionality. *Perspectives on European Politics and Society, 8*(2), 168–188.

Ram, M. H. (2012). Legacies of EU Conditionality: Explaining Post-accession Adherence to Pre-accession Rules on Roma. *Europe-Asia Studies, 64*(7), 1191–1218.

Regional Policy Glossary. (2015). *Financial Corrections.* Available at http://ec.europa.eu/regional_policy/en/policy/what/glossary/f/financial-corrections. Accessed 11 July 2015.

RO. (2007). OP Transport 2007–2013. *National Strategic Reference Framework.* Bucharest: Ministry of Transport, Romania. Available at http://old.fonduri-ue.ro/res/filepicker_users/cd25a597fd-62/Doc_prog/prog_op/5_POST/2_POST_Eng.pdf. Accessed 12 Feb 2016.

RO. (2009). Raportul Anual de Implementare 2008. *Annual Implementation Report.* Bucharest: Ministry of Transport, Romania.

RO. (2013). Raportul Anual de Implementare 2012. *Annual Implementation Report.* Bucharest: Ministry of Transport, Romania.

SAR. (2011). Morti de foame, cu banii in buzunar. *Raport SAR.* Bucharest: Societatea Academica din Romania. Available at http://sar.org.ro/morti-de-foame-cu-banii-in-buzunar-autoritatile-romane-sunt-depasite-de-sarcina-de-a-cheltui-15-milioane-euro-pe-zi/. Accessed 12 Feb 2016.

Sasse, G. (2008). The Politics of EU Conditionality: The Norm of Minority Protection During and Beyond EU Accession. *Journal of European Public Policy, 15*(6), 842–860.

Scherpereel, J. A. (2010). EU Cohesion Policy and the Europeanization of Central and East European Regions. *Regional and Federal Studies, 20*(1), 45–62.

Schimmelfennig, F., & Winzen, T. (2017). Eastern Enlargement and Differentiated Integration: Towards Normalization. *Journal of European Public Policy, 24*(2), 239–258.

Schwellnus, G., Balázs, L., & Mikalayeva, L. (2009). It Ain't Over When It's Over: The Adoption and Sustainability of Minority Protection Rules in New EU Member States. *European Integration Online Papers, 13*, Article 24. http://eiop.or.at/eiop/pdf/2009-024.pdf. Accessed Jan 2016.

Sedelmeier, U. (2008). After Conditionality: Post-accession Compliance with EU Law in East Central Europe. *Journal of European Public Policy, 15*(6), 806–825.

Sedelmeier, U. (2009). Post-accession Compliance with EU Gender Equality Legislation in Post-communist New Member States. *European Integration Online Papers, 13*, Article 23. http://eiop.or.at/eiop/texte/2009-023a.htm. Accessed Jan 2016.

Sedelmeier, U. (2012). Is Europeanisation Through Conditionality Sustainable? Lock-in of Institutional Change After EU Accession. *West European Politics, 35*(1), 20–38.

Siegel, S. N. (2006). *Law and Order in the European Union: Explaining Variations in Compliance with the European Community Treaty* (Discussion Paper SP IV 2006-303). Berlin: Wissenschaftszentrum Berlin für Sozialforschung. Available at http://www.ssoar.info/ssoar/bitstream/handle/document/11351/ssoar-2006-siegel-law_and_order_in_the.pdf?sequence=1. Accessed 12 Feb 2016.

Spendzharova, A., & Versluis, E. (2013). Issue Salience in the European Policy Process: What Impact on Transposition? *Journal of European Public Policy, 20*(10), 1499–1516.

Steunenberg, B., & Toshkov, D. (2009). Comparing Transposition in the 27 Member States of the EU: The Impact of Discretion and Legal Fit. *Journal of European Public Policy, 16*(7), 951–970.

Šumpíková, M., Pavel, J., & Klazar, S. (2004, May 14). *EU Funds: Absorption Capacity and Effectiveness of Their Use, with Focus on Regional Level in the Czech Republic*. Paper presented at the The 12th NISPAcee Annual Conference 'Central and Eastern European Countries Inside and Outside the European Union: Avoiding a New Divide', Vilnius.

Surubaru, N.-C. (2017). Administrative Capacity or Quality of Political Governance? EU Cohesion Policy in the New Europe, 2007–13. *Regional Studies, 51*(6), 844–856.

Terracciano, B., & Graziano, P. R. (2016). EU Cohesion Policy Implementation and Administrative Capacities: Insights from Italian Regions. *Regional & Federal Studies, 26*(3), 293–320.

The Economist. (2014). *Poland's Second Golden Age: Europe's Unlikely Star (Published 28 June 2014)*. Available at http://www.economist.com/news/leaders/21605910-poland-just-had-best-25-years-half-millennium-its-transformation-remains. Accessed 20 Jan 2016.

Thomson, R. (2007). Time to Comply: National Responses to Six EU Labour Market Directives Revisited. *West European Politics, 30*(5), 987–1008.

Thomson, R. (2009). Same Effects in Different Worlds: The Transposition of EU Directives. *Journal of European Public Policy, 16*(1), 1–18.

Thomson, R. (2010). Opposition Through the Back Door in the Transposition of EU Directives. *European Union Politics, 11*(4), 577–596.

Toshkov, D. (2007). Transposition of EU Social Policy in the New Member States. *Journal of European Social Policy, 17*(4), 335–348.

Toshkov, D., Knoll, M., & Wewerka, L. (2010). *Connecting the Dots: Case Studies and EU Implementation Research* (Working Paper No. 10/2010). Vienna: Institute for European Integration Research (EIF). Available at https://eif.univie.ac.at/downloads/workingpapers/wp2010-10.pdf. Accessed 12 Feb 2016.

Tosun, J. (2014). Absorption of Regional Funds: A Comparative Analysis. *JCMS: Journal of Common Market Studies, 52*(2), 371–387.

Treib, O. (2004). *Die Bedeutung der nationalen Parteipolitik für die Umsetzung europäischer Sozialrichtlinien*. Frankfurt and New York: Campus Verlag.

Treib, O. (2014). Implementing and Complying with EU Governance Outputs. *Living Reviews in European Governance, 9*(1). http://www.europeangovernance-livingreviews.org/Articles/lreg-2011-1/ (cited version from August 2014).

Vachudova, M. A. (2005). *Europe Undivided: Democracy, Leverage, and Integration After Communism*. Oxford: Oxford University Press.

World Bank. (2015). *World Bank Governance Indicators: Government Effectiveness*. Available at http://info.worldbank.org/governance/wgi/pdf/ge.pdf. Accessed 20 Dec 2015.

Zhelyazkova, A., Kaya, C., & Schrama, R. (2017). Notified and Substantive Compliance with EU Law in Enlarged Europe: Evidence from Four Policy Areas. *Journal of European Public Policy, 24*(2), 216–238.

CHAPTER 3

Absorption of EU Funds in a Post-communist and Post-accession Context

The following chapter builds the framework for analysis. I argue that in order to account for absorption problems in the new member states, it is crucial to take the domestic context and especially the role of politics seriously. While the general concept of absorption capacity is relevant for the use of EU funds also in the new member states, it still neglects some important aspects, especially the role of politicization, that are characteristic of these countries' domestic contexts.[1] By taking these contextual factors into account, it is possible to reach a more dynamic and complete explanation for absorption problems.

In order to illuminate the implementation context, the following chapter discusses CEE countries' absorption capacity against the backdrop of the literature on post-communist politics and pre-accession reforms. Especially the prevailing practice of politicization and patronage of the state bureaucracy (Sect. 3.1) and the pre-accession support offered for sectoral capacity building (Sect. 3.2) are influences that could be crucial for absorption capacity in the region. These factors influenced the level of capacities initially available for implementation, and they had the potential to further affect the success of EU fund management during the financing period. Finally, also the global financial and economic crisis could be a major impact, which must be accounted for (Sect. 3.3). After a detailed discussion of these influences and their possible impact on

[1] These aspects are at the same time also important in some old member states (see the conclusion for a further discussion).

C. Hagemann, *EU Funds in the New Member States*, Palgrave Studies in European Union Politics,
https://doi.org/10.1007/978-3-030-02092-7_3

absorption, Sect. 3.4 summarizes the framework for analysis and introduces the methods used in the empirical applications in Chapters 4 and 5.

3.1 Politicization and Party Patronage in Post-communist Countries

Administrative capacity is the core variable in research on EU-fund absorption (cf. Sect. 2.4). The presence of low capacity in many CEE member states is therefore a central obstacle to the use of EU funds. However, low capacity is not the only feature that might limit absorption. In order to understand the role of capacity in CEE, it is important to take into account the complex relationship between politics and the state bureaucracy in the region.

The state bureaucracy can be defined as the "set of nonelected, publicly funded positions of administration of the central government and its branch offices" (O'Dwyer 2004: 523). Appointment practices to these positions were strongly politicized during the communist regime. After democratization, however, the practice was not abolished but rather adapted to the new circumstances. The politicization of the state bureaucracy by one party was replaced by the same practice conducted by several parties competing for access to state resources and eager to establish control. This results in constant changes of administrative staff every time a political change occurs in a ministry.

The role of patronage and politicization is understood here not in 'culturalist' or 'developmentalist' terms that would deem it a trait only of a certain set of societies at certain stages of socio-economic development, but as a strategy based on a rational cost-benefit calculation, and thus in rather 'economistic' terms (Piattoni 2001: 9). In order to understand the ongoing relevance of patronage and politicization, it is thus crucial to explore the contextual circumstances making it a viable strategy (Piattoni 2001: 11). Even though there was after transition to democracy room for "creative choices of political leaders" (Piattoni 2001: 24), it turned out that continuing party politicization of the bureaucracy was still regularly the most viable strategy even in the post-communist context.

The following paragraphs therefore discuss in detail how the communist practice of party politicization and patronage was adapted to the new circumstances of competitive politics. It is ultimately argued that the continued systematic interference of the political sphere with the bureaucracy has an important effect on absorption, the dynamic of which is not adequately captured by the sole focus on general levels of administrative capacity.

3.1.1 Party Politicization and Patronage

Before discussing politicization and patronage in the communist and post-communist context, it is necessary to define these concepts with regard to the public administration. The terms refer to different processes and motivations of staff appointment to the state bureaucracy. Nevertheless, they are also often used interchangeably in the literature (Meyer-Sahling 2006: 275; Kopecký and Spirova 2011: 902–903; Nakrošis and Gudžinskas 2012: 89).

On the one hand, politicization of the state bureaucracy involves "activities that subject the appointment and career of civil servants to political will" (Rouban 2003: 313). It is often associated with the installation of a new minister or party in office, and it is common practice in many liberal democracies (Kopecký and Mair 2012a: 367). Politicization is motivated by the desire to control state institutions (Kopecký and Spirova 2011: 902; Meyer-Sahling and Veen 2012: 14). Staff that used to work for a previous government or appointed by that previous government might impede the implementation of policies formulated by incoming parties, often from the opposite camp (Meyer-Sahling 2004: 77). The desire to exchange staff is thus rooted in a lack of trust between political competitors, and the mistrust in bureaucrats appointed by preceding governments (Meyer-Sahling 2004: 76).

On the other hand, patronage is often referred to as the provision of state jobs by political actors to supporters in the realm of a clientelist relationship (O'Dwyer 2004: 521; Kitschelt and Wilkinson 2007: 7). It is thus the result of parties' desire for resources. Appointing loyal supporters to positions in the bureaucracy results in the inflation of staff numbers, with the parallel stagnation of capacity-levels because resources are wasted on staff often lacking adequate professional experience (O'Dwyer 2006b: 15–16).

Even though politicization and patronage follow different paths of logic and can potentially result in different outcomes, they also have much in common. Both processes assume changes of staff working in a ministerial bureaucracy when there are changes in political control. Politicization studies especially stress the occurrence of shifts at the highest levels (Meyer-Sahling 2006: 281, 2008: 13), but also account for more comprehensive changes as the 'range' (the number of positions affected by politicization) and 'intensity' (the career-background of a candidate in the state bureaucracy or the party organization) of politicization increase (Meyer-Sahling and Veen 2012: 9). Thus, party staff appointed to a lower level of the ministerial bureaucracy might still be referred to as party politicization even though the process would be empirically indistinguishable from party patronage as defined above. This observation is acknowledged by a distinct definition of party patronage as an organizational resource[2] in the literature, stressing both a desire to control the bureaucracy and/or rewarding party supporters as possible motivations behind appointment practices (Kopecký and Mair 2012b: 9–10). Thus, even though party politicization and party patronage can be studied as distinct processes, it also makes sense to combine both understandings.

In this study both party politicization and party patronage are understood as the power of parties to appoint staff with either professional or party background to all levels of the state bureaucracy, following the desires of either achieving political control or access to resources (similar Meyer-Sahling 2008: 8; Kopecký and Mair 2012b: 4). This understanding can also be justified by the observation that it is often difficult to discriminate empirically between the motivations for this practice or that both motivations can be at the same time the driver of politicization (Kopecký et al. 2016: 424). Also, the assertion of control may equally result from a desire to achieve access to state resources, meaning a sequential relationship. Thus, leaving the definition open for both motivations seems to be the most plausible strategy.

3.1.2 Politicization of the Bureaucracy During Communism

The development of administrative capacity was a crucial part of the transformation and reform process of the CEE countries during the last two decades. It soon became clear that all of the post-communist successor states had to engage in a process of capacity-building or even state-building to adapt to the new requirements of democracy and market economy (Grzymala-Busse and Luong 2002: 530). Despite the

[2] In contrast to patronage as an electoral resource and a distinct party-voter linkage strategy (Kitschelt and Wilkinson 2007: 7).

omnipotence and omnipresence of the state in communist societies, the size of the civil service of CEE countries was rather on par with the average or even small in comparison to the mostly highly developed members of the Organization for Economic Co-Operation and Development (OECD) (Nunberg 2000: 198). Besides this quantitative measure of capacity shortage, the qualitative side of capacity building was generally seen as even more important.

In order to understand the problems of post-communist bureaucracies, it is useful to recall the communist system of governance and the central role the communist party played in this system. The formal state institutions of communist countries resembled more or less those of liberal democracies, with the Council of Ministers taking up the task of the government (Dimitrov et al. 2006: 6). Still, this formal structure was far less important and powerful than its Western counterpart, as it was doubled by the communist party's bureaucracy, which held the monopoly on political power (Kornai 1995: 36).

The dominance of the communist party and the doubling of structures led to a situation in which the central state bureaucracy was both over- and under-politicized (Goetz and Wollmann 2001: 865): On the one hand, the government structures remaining after the separation of the state and the party were 'under-politicized' with regard to their ability to formulate and design policies. In the past, the "discussion of policy alternatives, arbitration among contending interests, and authoritative decision making were mostly the preserve of the party bureaucracy" (Dimitrov et al. 2006: 6). The centre of government was in fact the Politburo of the communist party (Nunberg 2000: 191) and not the office of the prime minister or a similar institution. The separation of party and state, which took place in all CEE countries upon democratization, thus resulted in the removal of the institution which had until then provided both for coordination among ministries as well as for policy planning. On the other hand, the central state apparatus was also 'over-politicized' as staffing policy was more influenced by political criteria than by merit. Most importantly, candidates had to be politically reliable in order to be appointed (König 1992: 152), even as the importance of political criteria varied over time (Wasilewski 1990). Still, while the extent of and motivation for appointments to the bureaucracy differed among the communist countries, political loyalty and reliability were generally a precondition for staff selection (Goetz and Wollmann 2001: 868; Meyer-Sahling 2004: 79). In sum, CEE countries were left to democratization with a central bureaucracy largely inexperienced in political planning and often filled with political appointees from the communist *nomenklatura* of questionable qualification, especially for the new situation of democracy and market economy.

Still, the broadly similar practice of politicization did not result in a convergence of the quality of capacities in the region. Rather, the practice of politicization during communism and its effect on the quality of capacity depended much on the quality of capacity prior to the installation of communism. The use of patronage appointments to the central administration to co-opt citizens as party supporters was most prevalent in those countries where the professionalization of the bureaucracy was very low upon the advent of communism (Kitschelt 1999: 23–24). Here, the communist party used the state apparatus to reward loyalty. In contrast, in those countries where a professional bureaucracy existed prior to communism, the new regime depended instead on its professionalism in order to secure its rule (Kitschelt 1999: 26). The quality of administrative capacities thus varied among CEE countries upon democratization, just as it had already varied during the interwar period.

The different levels of administrative capacity in the pre-communist and communist period naturally resulted in different levels of capacity in the post-communist period. A quarter-century after democratization, two trends are visible. The first trend shows that capacities have increased, but that the CEE region remains heterogeneous. The CEE countries are on average still somewhat behind the old member states when it comes to the overall level of capacity. Table 3.1 presents CEEC's scores on 'Executive Capacity', which is relevant for measuring capacities to implement cohesion policy.[3] It determines in how far the executive has sufficient steering capacities (strategic capacity, interministerial coordination, evidence-based instruments, societal consultation, policy communication), whether or not effective policy implementation is guaranteed, and in how far institutional learning is provided (SGI 2014b: 13).

The comparison of average values with the EU 15 (6.66) shows that CEE countries (5.74) are only one point behind the old member states on the 10-point-scale. Even more interesting, CEE countries have a standard deviation of 1.18, which is only slightly higher than that of the EU 15 (1.14). Thus, the countries have not only been rather successful

[3] The selection of the SGI 'executive capacity' indicator is discussed in greater detail in Sect. 4.4.

Table 3.1 Administrative capacity and politicization in CEE countries

Country	*Executive capacity*	*Politicization in CEE (turnover in %)*
Latvia	7.42	<10
Poland	7.19	70–89
Lithuania	7.12	<10
Estonia	6.42	<10
Slovakia	5.39	70–89
Hungary	5.25	30–49
Czech Republic	5.11	30–49
Bulgaria	4.85	*high*
Romania	4.43	*"largely personalistic and patronistic"*
Slovenia	4.37	50–69
Average/standard deviation		
EU 10 (CEE)	5.74/1.18	–
EU 15 average	6.66/1.14	–
EU 27	6.12/1.35	–

Note The third column refers to appointment practices of staff in the ministerial bureaucracy in the ten post-communist member states. For the 2004 entrants to the EU, the data is based on an expert survey on the average turnover of staff in the ministerial bureaucracy after elections. Bulgaria and Romania were not included in this survey, but Bulgaria was covered in another project, and information on Romania was provided in a case study on patronage in the country

Source The author's compilation and calculation based on SGI data 'executive capacity' (SGI 2014a: 17), Meyer-Sahling and Veen (2012: 9, on 2004 entrants), Kopecký and Spirova (2011: 908 on Bulgaria), and Roper (2006: 371, on Romania)

on average with regard to capacity building, but the differences within the group are nowadays very comparable with the heterogeneity of the old member states. For example, the difference between Lithuania (7.12) and Romania (4.43) is comparable to the difference between the United Kingdom (7.22) and Greece (4.31) (SGI 2014a: 17). It is therefore hardly possible to take CEE countries as a homogenous group when it comes to their general level of capacity, or to speak of an 'eastern problem' similar to the 'Mediterranean syndrome' expression made famous during the 1990s (Börzel 2000). Intra-group heterogeneity was perpetuated in the region after the end of communist rule. Depending on the measurement, authors either argue that the difference of capacities between the post-communist countries mostly remained the same (Fortin 2010: 675, also including the post-Soviet states), or that some countries have changed pace since the early years (with the Baltic countries exceeding expectations, and Hungary and Poland falling somewhat behind [Meyer-Sahling 2009b: 516–517]). Still, it is overall agreed that

CEE countries have very heterogeneous levels of capacity and thus one can expect varying abilities in dealing with EU funds.

In contrast, party politicization is still an important issue in the whole region, making it more homogeneous in this regard. The politicized staff working nowadays in the central state bureaucracy are, however, not those remaining from the communist *nomenklatura*, but mostly new appointees of changing governments since the early 1990s. After the introduction of political competition, it is now no longer one, but rather several parties or camps competing for the staffing of the central state apparatus.

Civil servants used to rely on the communist party for their career in a certain sector of the state administration, but now civil servants often link their careers to different party camps, and spend their time in other fields such as academia or private business when 'their' party is out of office (Meyer-Sahling 2008: 18). In Hungary, for example, generally perceived as a frontrunner of civil service reform (Camyar 2010: 149), a regular pattern of staff changes at the highest level of the ministerial administration could be observed after changes of government. It is impressive that "the tenure of nominally professional, permanent civil servants was therefore only slightly longer than that of their political masters" (Meyer-Sahling 2008: 15), i.e. of ministers. Further empirical evidence suggests that this practice is also widespread in the other post-communist countries. Column three of Table 3.1 provides recent information from expert surveys and a case study on politicization practices. Overall, the authors of the most comprehensive study including all 2004 entrants to the EU stress that despite of rather low levels of staff turnover in all Baltic states, only Estonia features a largely depoliticized bureaucracy according to some measurements (Meyer-Sahling and Veen 2012: 9). In contrast, the remaining five 2004 entrants to the EU still show high or extremely high levels of regular turnover of senior civil service, especially Poland and Slovakia (Meyer-Sahling and Veen 2012: 9). Similar evidence for such patterns also exists among the 2007 entrants Bulgaria (Kopecký and Spirova 2011: 908) and Romania (Roper 2006: 371). Politicization is therefore still a widespread phenomenon.

But why was politicization continued despite democratization and the end of the communist system? The following section deals with this question in more detail. It is argued that while politicization of the state apparatus was a core feature of the communist system, the legacies of this very system made the perpetuation of the practice more likely in the post-communist period. The possible mechanisms linking both periods are both a lack of trust between core political actors as well as a need for resources to engage in party-building after democratization.

3.1.3 *Post-communism: Politicization as a 'Leninist Legacy'*

The central question now is why levels of politicized changes to the central state administration with the goal of achieving political control or access are still high in the region. The observation that politicization was ubiquitous under the rule of the communist parties, as mentioned above, does not count much as evidence for this. The following paragraphs thus present a detailed argument as to how the characteristics of communist rule created the conditions under which the perpetuation of practices of politicization became more likely. It is argued that the continuation of politicization practices in CEE can be explained by the low level of trust between political contenders on both sides of the 'regime divide', and the newly formed parties' lack of resources due to the previous system of single-party rule.

3.1.3.1 The First Argument: Ongoing Politicization as a Result of Low Trust

The previous high level of politicization of the bureaucracy and the lack of trust between the former communist party and the anti-communist opposition made the continuation of politicization more likely. Meyer-Sahling stresses the importance of the different constellations of transition in the region for the continuation of politicization.

In those countries where the former communist party itself managed the transition process, a high level of politicization prevailed in the early years as it had no incentive to exchange the staff it had appointed earlier through political criteria (Meyer-Sahling 2004: 82).

In contrast, if the former anti-communist opposition succeeded in the founding elections, they were likely to replace senior bureaucrats perceived as 'politically contaminated' and/or incompetent (Meyer-Sahling 2004: 84). The change of power was thus likely to lead to a high level of changes of staff in the state bureaucracy and the replacement of staff appointed following political criteria (most probably again using political criteria). Still, as newly incoming anti-communist governments were, for practical reasons, unable to exchange all senior bureaucrats, they had an interest in maintaining their ability to exercise political discretion and would therefore not opt for a strict civil service law banning future changes of staff (Meyer-Sahling 2004: 86).

Thus theoretically, the only likely scenario of a decision for the institutionalization of de-politicization was in the case of a pacted transition. During round-table meetings the democratic opposition could learn about the policy preferences of communist party appointed bureaucrats and soft-line communists, increasing mutual trust (Meyer-Sahling 2004: 86–87). Still, the number of politicians taking part in such meetings was limited, and so was its effectiveness as a trust-building exercise (Meyer-Sahling 2004: 87). Civil service de-politicization was therefore often not institutionalized until the end of the 1990s (Meyer-Sahling 2004: 73), and even then the influence of these civil service acts was limited as they were prone to changes, or concerned only a low number of people actually working in the state bureaucracy (Meyer-Sahling 2009a: 7, 20; Goetz 2001: 1045).

It is possible to use the argument of mutual distrust further when accounting for the 'lock-in' (Meyer-Sahling 2004: 92) of high levels of civil service politicization in most CEE countries. Trust between political camps is assumed to result from the experience of cooperation, usually in government coalitions. However, if governments regularly alternate wholesale after an election, the felt need to exchange staff in order to establish political control will be higher (Meyer-Sahling and Veen 2012: 15).

Cooperation experience was difficult to obtain in most CEE countries as political camps remained deeply polarized. In the early years of political competition, the central competitive line in most CEE party systems was the 'regime divide', referring to the roots of post-communist parties in either the former anti-communist opposition or the former communist regime (Grzymala-Busse 2001: 87). These historical roots could account for a stunning 86% of coalitions formed in the region during the first post-communist decade (Grzymala-Busse 2001: 91). The importance of the regime-divide is maintained by several different studies (Druckman and Roberts 2007: 24; see also Grotz and Weber 2011: 204). Parties fought fiercely on this historical divide and often treated each other like enemies rather than competitors (Segert 2008: 25–27). Overall, polarized competition meant that parties hardly ever crossed camp lines for coalition formation.

After the regime divide had faded in the region, it was often replaced by other divides which were not less fierce and often involved the same competitors (Kiszelly 2008: 128). Cooperation experience beyond the

Table 3.2 Alternation of parties in power after elections (1990–2014)

Election no.	*2*	*3*	*4*	*5*	*6*	*7*	*8*
Bulgaria	1995	1997	2001	2005	2009	2013	2014
Czech Rep.	1996	1998	2002	2006	2010	2014	–
Estonia	1995	1999	2003	2007	2011	–	–
Hungary	1994	1998	2002	2006	2010	2014	–
Latvia	1995	1998	2002	2006	2010	2011	2014
Lithuania	1992	1996	2000	2004	2008	2012	–
Poland	1993	1997	2001	2005	2007	2011	–
Romania	1992	1996	2000	2004	2008	2012	–
Slovakia	1994	1998	2002	2006	2010	2012	–
Slovenia	1996	2000	2004	2008	2011	2014	–

Note Parties' strength is calculated against the backdrop of their share of parliamentary seats as a share of the government's total number of seats in parliament. More than 90% seat continuity or change between governments formed directly after consecutive elections is coloured grey. The grey spaces thus cover (almost) wholesale alternations and re-elections

Source The author's calculation, based on data from the ParlGov database (Döring and Manow 2014) (see Appendix III for the calculation)

boundaries of important divides is thus still rare, and the continuation of politicization remains likely due to a lack of trust between the central political actors. The lack of cooperation experience across camp divides is clearly illustrated by the data presented in Table 3.2. I calculated the differences between the party compositions of governments formed following each parliamentary election since democratization for all countries of the region. Those cells colored grey represent elections where either 90% of parties in government were new or remained the same in comparison to the government formed after the elections. The table shows that wholesale alternations or (more rarely) re-elections occurred in the vast majority of cases (37 out of 62 elections). In fact, only Latvia and Slovenia never saw a change or persistence of more than 90% of its governmental parties, whereas Poland and Hungary never experienced a partial alternation during the entire period.

In sum, the high level of distrust and the inability of both political camps to agree on a depoliticization of the civil service directly after the end of the communist regime made the continuation of the practice more likely. The fact that camps remained highly polarized in most of the region and low trust between them resulted in a lock-in of the situation. This can also be seen in the fact that even though the EU demanded a law that would institutionalize depoliticization, it was usually changed after accession or not even adopted at all (as in the Czech Republic) (cf. Sect. 3.2).

3.1.3.2 The Second Argument: Ongoing Politicization Because of a Need for Resources

There is another important argument why politicization continued in the post-communist period. This argument refers to the legacy of the communist state as a single-party system, which made it more likely for parties to use state resources for their party building exercises. Parties were generally interested in resources as usually only the former communist party had a developed organization in place.[4] In addition, as the state was delegitimized due to its high degree of politicization during the former regime, it was an easy target for resource-seeking parties.

In order to understand how communist legacies contributed to the need of post-communist parties to seek patronage appointments in the central state bureaucracy, it is useful to recall the differences between the introduction of liberal democracy in Western Europe and in CEE. The special feature about the formation of party systems in Western Europe is that the "decisive sequences of party formation took place at the early stage of competitive politics, in some cases well before the extension of the franchise" (Lipset and Rokkan 1967: 34). The introduction of the general suffrage after the First World War therefore often met an already organized and stratified society (van Biezen 2005: 155). The process was thus mostly about the inclusion of already existing, externally created organizations into political competition.

These already existing mass parties had high incentives to build strong linkages to society. On the one hand, the existence of a strong organization linking the parties with their respective segments of society secured their survival even in the context of an exclusion from the political system (Lipset and Rokkan 1967: 34). In addition, in the absence of party financing from the state, most party resources came from civil society donors and membership fees. A mass-membership was therefore necessary in order to secure a party's supply with resources (Duverger 1990: 41; van Biezen 2003: 22). On the other hand, the party organization was important to be able to communicate with the electorate. The logic

[4] Minor exceptions are block parties such as the Polish PSL (Bingen 2008: 81).

of party competition at that time meant that a success at the ballot box depended mostly on the mobilization of a party's core electorate, rather than a party's general appeal (Katz and Mair 1995: 7). The only way to mobilize this electorate was via party newspapers or party meetings at the local level, which were also seen as a means to educate voters (Duverger 1990: 41). A highly developed party structure was thus necessary in order to reach out to voters and be electorally successful.

In contrast, the situation was markedly different upon the introduction of the general suffrage in the CEE countries. The communist systems were either hegemonic or single-party systems dominated by the communist party (Kornai 1995: 36). Therefore, it was usually the only party with a vast membership and organizational structure at its disposal at the end of the communist regime. All other parties, especially those from the former anti-communist opposition, had to engage in a process of party building in order to compete in the newly emerging party systems. Still, the contextual situation faced by these parties was very different from that of the mass parties in Western Europe. The new parties did not only lack an earlier developed organization they could draw on, it was also much more difficult to create such an organization.

On the one hand, CEE societies were "undernourished and inchoate" (Mair 1997: 177), and often shied away from politics altogether (O'Dwyer 2004: 528). Some link the rather "individualized social structure" (Kopecký 2006: 252) with a leveling of societal divides during the communist period (Tiemann 2008: 37–38). This argument makes sense against the backdrop of the four-decade long rule of a political regime with a strong claim to societal change (van Biezen 2003: 36). However, one should be cautioned against the expectation of a *tabula rasa* situation in the region upon democratization in which the past had lost its importance for the present (Kitschelt 1995: 450–451; Whitefield 2002: 197). Rather, it is also important to note that some societal cleavages were much less developed in CEE because the respective groups had not yet been mobilized nor had they even existed prior to the advent of communism (e.g. workers were a rare commodity everywhere except in Czechoslovakia prior to communism) (Kitschelt 2001: 308–309). Overall, the societal situation meant that party-builders could not easily connect with existing societal groups they would just have to organize and mobilize for political success. Thus, society played a very different role upon democratization in CEE than upon the extension of the suffrage in Western Europe. Mair describes the difference in a very intriguing manner:

> [D]emocratization in early twentieth-century Europe involved the extension of the right to participate in regimes in which the principle of contestation had already been established, whereas the democratization of the former communist regimes has involved establishing the principle of contestation in regimes which were already participant. (Mair 1997: 179)

This observation has important repercussions for parties' development and organizational strategies. In the 'first-wave' democracies, parties had to overcome high thresholds during their struggle for representation (Lipset and Rokkan 1967: 27). In contrast, parties in post-communist countries "almost immediately exceeded the threshold of executive power, which for many parties in the early Western European democracies was usually the final step in a protracted process of organizational development" (van Biezen 2003: 31). Thus, while the old mass parties of Western Europe had strong incentives to build their organizations to achieve political participation, the post-communist parties had no such incentive for party-building as they had already achieved access to political decision-making without the backing of a well-organized segment of society.

On the other hand, the building of mass parties was also much less attractive in the post-communist context for another reason. The evolution of mass media made local party structures and own newspapers redundant for communication with the electorate (Mainwaring and Zoco 2007: 166–167). Access to state television was ubiquitous and the communication of one's message via TV channels was much cheaper than the creation of own media. In addition, connecting with the electorate via mass media also better matched the requirements of a now less mobilizational, but rather competitive style of electoral competition in which parties competed for the same voters (Katz and Mair 1995: 18; van Biezen 2003: 44). TV was thus also the suitable instrument for reaching out to all voters, and not only to certain societal groups.

In sum, the contextual situation strongly shaped the organizational choices of party-builders, making it unlikely that mass party structures would evolve like those developed upon democratization in Western Europe (Mainwaring and Zoco 2007: 166–167; Mair 1997: 186). In contrast, most scholars agree that it is even more likely that West European parties will develop into the direction of CEE parties' slim membership structures and professionalized campaigning than the other way round, because these are much better adapted to the current requirements of party competition (van Biezen 2005: 169; Bos and Segert 2008).

These observations have two important repercussions for party building in CEE. First, the professionalized logic of campaigning meant that the lack of volunteers from party branches (available for local agitation) only caused limited headaches for party executives (van Biezen 2005: 156). Second, the professional staff who would organize the campaigns instead needed to be paid for, and the lack of broad membership meant that the funds to pay for this staff would not come from society. Therefore, the most promising resource left to reward merited party-workers after electoral success was the state and their provision of jobs in the state bureaucracy (Kopecký 2006: 258–259; O'Dwyer 2006b: 20; Grzymala-Busse 2007: 6–7).

O'Dwyer underlines that this strategy was comparatively easy to realize in the post-communist context. The earlier high level of politicization of the bureaucracy and the memory of poorly functioning public services had strongly delegitimized the state (Holmes 1997: 17; O'Dwyer 2004: 529–530). This made replacements and new appointments of staff especially easy as politicians had an "extraordinary license to reform the state" (O'Dwyer 2004: 530).[5] As a result of this combination of factors, some CEE countries experienced more than a doubling (Slovenia, Lithuania, Poland), some even a quadrupling (Latvia, Czech Republic, Bulgaria) of employment in the state bureaucracy during the first post-communist decade (Grzymala-Busse 2007: 5). Most importantly, even as employment sky-rocketed, the level of capacity available stagnated or even suffered (O'Dwyer 2004: 524).

But were post-communist parties not saturated after years of patronage and building a viable party machine? This seems unlikely.

[5]The phenomenon of weakening party-society linkages and parties' subsequent turn to the state for resources is also stressed as a development in West European party systems (Katz and Mair 1995). Still, these parties have most often still strong organizational legacies from their time as mass parties, and tend to seek support through official state party finance, resulting rather in "inter-party collusion" (Katz and Mair 2009: 755). In contrast, the presence of a delegitimized state, a strongly antagonizing party competition, and the necessity to build parties from scratch make extensive party politicization and patronage in the post-communist region much more likely and intense. I agree that the phenomenon can be studied for Europe as a whole (see also the conclusion on this), but I argue that the communist legacy makes the CEE countries especially prone to this practice, a fact which is also underlined by the comparative findings gathered in studies taking a European perspective (where no CEE country is below the European average of politicization) (Kopecký and Mair 2012a: 367).

A saturation effect over time does not only assume that there is no need for a regular inflow of new party workers, but also that the composition of the early party systems did not change. Still, a weak membership makes parties also much more likely to vanish if they lose representation, as the 'party in public office' is much more important than the 'party on the ground' (Mair 1997: 184). Also, splits and mergers entail fewer risks for elites as party identities carry little weight (Mair 1997: 188).

Thus, another reason for the continuous need for resources is the low level of institutionalization of most CEE party systems. Institutionalization in the context of party systems is defined as the degree to which "actors develop expectations and behaviour based on the premise that the fundamental contours and rules of party competition and behaviour will prevail into the foreseeable future" (Mainwaring and Torcal 2006: 206). Institutionalization is generally an important aspect of party systems of so-called 'third-wave democracies' (Mainwaring and Torcal 2006: 205; Mainwaring 1999), most of which did not stabilize over time but rather started out stable or maintained high levels of volatility since democratization (Mainwaring and Zoco 2007: 170). Table 3.3 shows that even in rather stable contexts, existing party systems in CEE usually experienced a blow to their level of institutionalization at some point.

Party system institutionalization is usually measured using the Pedersen index of electoral volatility (Pedersen 1979; Mainwaring and Torcal 2006: 207). Column two of Table 3.3 indicates that CEE party systems feature very different degrees of institutionalization. While the Czech Republic with an average of 17.3% comes close to unstable West European cases such as the Netherlands or Italy (Jungerstam-Mulders 2006: 16), Latvia and Lithuania seem to have suffered from extreme turnover with almost half of the votes changing between parties on average. However, the average volatility does not necessarily provide the full picture on the development of the party system. While competition can be stable for some time, 'electoral earthquakes' (Deegan-Krause and Haugton 2010: 227) can cause fundamental shake-ups of the party system that change the face of the party system and its constituent parts at regular intervals.

In column two, I therefore added the number of fundamental shake-ups that party systems experienced during the last two decades. Following the idea that an institutionalized party system shows some stability both in its constituent parts (i.e. the parties) as well as their

Table 3.3 Stability of CEE party systems (1990–2013)

Country (sorted by volatility)	*Average volatility*[a] *(first two decades) (%)*	*Party system shake-ups*[b]
Czech Republic	17.3	2013 (newcomer 2nd)
Hungary	20.7	1998 (Fidesz becomes major force on the centre-right) 2010 (MSZP suffers electoral collapse)
Romania	22.3	2000 (PNŢ-CD leaves parliament) 2005 (PD changes colours to centre-right)
Slovenia	25.8	2004 (end of LDS dominance) 2011 (newcomer 1st)
Estonia	29.1	2003 (newcomer 1st)
Bulgaria	35.5	2001 (newcomer 1st) 2009 (newcomer 1st)
Slovakia	36.2	2002 (Smer-SD takes over centre-left)
Poland	36.1	2005 (realignment around centre-right—right competition)
Latvia	51.9	1995 (newcomer 1st) 1998 (newcomer 1st) 2002 (newcomer 1st) 2011 (newcomer 2nd)
Lithuania	54.6	2000 (newcomers 1st and 2nd) 2004 (newcomer 1st)

Note A shake-up of the party system was counted every time a new party became strongest or second strongest force in an election, or the position of relative strength or ideological orientation between existing parties was changed fundamentally
Source [a]Volatility as reported by O'Dwyer (2014: 520). [b]The author's compilation based on a review of the party politics literature and EJPR country reports (Enyedi 2006: 184–185; Fink-Hafner 2006: 212–213; Mikkel 2006: 30; Pabriks and Stokenberga 2006: 60–61; Ramonaite 2006: 71–74; Rybar 2006: 159; Autengruber 2008: 136; Bingen 2008: 85; Olteanu 2008: 153, 158; Spirova and Kolarova 2010: 910; Varnagy 2011: 991; Fink-Hafner 2012: 290; Ikstens 2012: 175, 181; Linek 2014: 97)

interrelationship (Mainwaring and Torcal 2006: 205), a 'fundamental shake-up' was counted every time a party system was fundamentally changed in this regard. The results in column three indicates that fundamental changes of party competition did take place in all of the countries, and that even the most stable cases such as the Czech Republic and Hungary experienced a challenge to the existing order at some point. Especially following the first post-communist decade, the advent of highly successful newcomers, often as 'unorthodox parties' (Pop-Eleches 2010), shook the foundations of post-communist party systems.

It is thus not convincing to assume that post-communist parties' taste for patronage will generally have been satisfied after some years of their existence. This is not only because there is an ongoing need for resources, but also because they might well have been replaced by other parties starting from scratch and still in need of rewards for their supporters. The practice of the use of civil service jobs to reward supporters does therefore not necessarily have to end after a few years into the post-communist period, as party systems are still prone to changes.

But what if the former communist party did not leave office immediately and newcomer parties thus had no access to state resources? Unsurprisingly, this situation did not improve the levels of patronage. The former communist party had a discredited ideology and thus faced a painful process of reform to become a social democratic party that was attractive for voters. This reform usually resulted in the loss of the majority of former party members as well as highly divisive discussions within the party (Grzymala-Busse 2006: 429–432). The generally preferred practice of former communist parties was therefore to use clientelist linkages to voters based on state resources instead of ideological reform (Kitschelt 2001: 311; Grzymala-Busse 2006: 426). In those cases where the party succeeded in this endeavor (Bulgaria, Romania), levels of patronage remained thus high for the party to sustain its dominant position.

In sum, the distinct character of the communist system as a system of one-party rule confronted all other political competitors with the task of party-building upon democratization. Still, the contextual conditions of weakly-stratified societies and possible access to mass media present in all liberal democracies made the creation of mass parties as in Western Europe unlikely upon the extension of the suffrage. Newly emerging parties could therefore not draw on funds from society to compete in elections, but rather turned to the state for resources and reward their party workers with jobs in the central state administration following electoral victory. It was therefore the very situation of post-communist party formation that would make patronage practices more likely, and it was the general contextual conditions of late twentieth century party competition that would possibly lock-in the practice (via low societal linkages and therefore low institutionalization).

3.1.4 How Do Party Politicization and Patronage Impact Absorption?

Politicized changes in the bureaucracy have the potential to lower administrative capacity as experienced staff is replaced and knowledge lost. The effect is even stronger if the achieved control over the state bureaucracy is then used to alter programme priorities and to enhance political discretion across the implementation process.

The importance of politicized changes in CEE for absorption was hinted at by some authors (Horvat 2005: 15; Buzogány 2012: 125), but rarely tested directly. Still, several empirical accounts provide first anecdotal evidence for the effect of party politicization on the use of EU funds in CEE. When it comes to staff changes, Buzogány and Korkut (2013) report excessive party politicization of the EU fund implementation structures after the landslide victory of Fidesz in the Hungarian elections in 2010. Changes included

> [...] not only the upper echelons of bureaucracy, but also administrators at the desk level, prompting the European Commission to voice criticism of such restructuring by pointing to the potential shortcomings that may affect the absorption capacity of the [National Development] Agency. (Buzogány and Korkut 2013: 1572–1573)

In a similar vein, Olejniczak found that the adaptation of the Polish implementation system suffered from instability at the ministerial level (Olejniczak 2013: 1659). In the context of frequent changes, it was rather natural for bureaucrats to focus on the day-to-day business without considering adaptation or frequent problems: "Since the institutions were not sure of their future, they were not interested in planning beyond the policy cycle" (Olejniczak 2013: 1659). Bachtler and McMaster add to this observation that changes of Polish regional governments regularly resulted in "major turnover of staff" (Bachtler and McMaster 2008: 417).

So far only two comparative case studies go beyond the focus on capacity and highlight the effect of such staff changes on absorption. In Sicily and Puglia, politicization is formalized as the head of the administration has to leave office with her political patron (Milio 2008: 927). Milio stresses that frequent changes are "detrimental to the region's administrative capacity because they undermine the continuity, consistency and coherence required for the successful implementation of a long term programme" (Milio 2008: 923). This means that politicization lowers administrative capacity and impacts absorption via the fluctuation of important staff. In a similar vein, Surubaru reports from Bulgaria and Romania that political stability was seen by funds' administrators as crucial for the absorption process (Surubaru 2017a: 850). Absorption improved during phases of stable government and thus more limited changes of core administrative staff as witnessed during the Borisov (Bulgaria) and Ponta (Romania) administrations (Surubaru 2017a: 850). However, when political control shifted, not only core staff but even "middle managers (Heads of Unit) or even operational staff (administrators)" (Surubaru 2017b: 114) were changed. Overall, party politicization and patronage made implementation in all these cases more difficult as capacities were lowered and the implementation process disturbed.

In addition, political discretion in the use of funds might be an equally important influence on absorption. Many studies stress the fact that it is not necessarily economic trends that determine allocations (Dotti 2013: 612) and that fund distribution can "easily lead to a pork barrel logic" (Rynck and McAleavey 2001: 546). This is especially likely in CEE. On the one hand, EU prerogatives for the policy are often rather broad and vague and can therefore be adapted to domestic actors' preferences in the course of the implementation process (Blom-Hansen 2005: 625). On the other hand, and more importantly, the politicized allocation of funds does not break EU spending rules, but may easily happen within the realm of eligible regions (Rynck and McAleavey 2001: 547; Dellmuth and Stoffel 2012: 427). Especially in CEE where virtually all regions are formally eligible for convergence funding, political actors can make strongly discretionary choices for the allocation of these funds. Evidence for an effect of party preferences on the allocation of EU funds was early detected in the new member states Latvia and Bulgaria: EU funds went to the regions which had supported the incumbent political parties in the last national elections (Bloom and Petrova 2013: 1600). As a result, "[w]ealthier regions, rather than those with economic need, were the recipients of EU aid" (Bloom and Petrova 2013: 1612).[6]

[6]This finding is supported by other studies that find that funding increases with congruence between the leading regional party and the leading national party (Chalmers 2013: 826). In their analysis of sub-state governments in Germany, Dellmuth and Stoffel found that "there is robust and strong evidence that recipient sub-state governments provide

Nevertheless, everything remained within the scope of official EU spending rules (see also further evidence for politicized allocations (Muraközy and Telegdy 2016: 340; Banaszewska and Bischoff 2016: 20; Medve-Bálint 2017: 233; Dotti 2016: 12).

Political preferences in allocation decisions make also changes of direction more likely after political shifts, potentially impacting the absorption process beyond changes of staff. In Slovakia, Šipikal finds that evaluation procedures take considerably longer following a change of government, indicating "political influence on the evaluation of the projects" (Šipikal 2014: 7). Also in Hungary following an alternation of government, OPs were reportedly "halted and reframed according to the new government priorities" (Buzogány and Korkut 2013: 1572–1573). Milio underlines for the Italian regions that the politically discretionary decision-making for EU fund implementation disturbed the implementation process further, as the continuous revision of programming documents resulted in "the accumulation of long delays" (Milio 2008: 929).

In sum, these observations from CEE together with the theoretical literature discussed above highlight two important points. On the one hand, politicization is very likely to be an important influence on the absorption performance of the new member states. On the other hand, politicization only affects the use of EU funds when it is actually conducted. It is not the general existence of politicization that is the problem, but rather the (frequent) occurrence of the practice, leading to an interruption of the implementation process. A similar effect is stressed by Frye (2002: 313–316, 2010), who finds in his study on post-communist economic reform that not the political discretion exerted by the winners of political struggles hampered economic development in the region, but rather the frequent changes of direction resulting from undecided political battles. Thus, a dismal effect on absorption of EU funds is expected when parties in charge of OPs alternate frequently in office.

more funds to districts [...] in which they already have high electoral support" (Dellmuth and Stoffel 2012: 427, and also a high turnout, according to Schraff 2014: 286 working with the same data). In Italy, the regional governments of Abruzzo and Puglia were found "to allocate funds with an eye to the electoral return that they may bring" (Piattoni and Smyrl 2003: 144–145). In a similar vein, other studies found also a positive effect in the allocation of funds for regions with many swing voters (Bodenstein and Kemmerling 2011: 17; similar Bouvet and Dall'Erba 2010, but see Dellmuth 2011: 1029). Still, these studies never report 'all-or-nothing'-fundamental changes upon the advent of a new government in office.

These alternations will lead to interruptions of these OPs' implementation processes, because staff is exchanged and programme priorities possibly altered. Party alternation in office during the financing period is therefore seen as the core trigger of the impeding influence of politicization on absorption.[7]

3.2 The EU Accession Process: 'Islands' and Central Coordination

The adaptation of administrative capacity was also an important topic on the EU's accession agenda. However, while a de-politicization and professionalization was demanded from all candidate countries, rules were neither clear, nor were incentives or threats for exclusion credible in the case of non-fulfilment of these criteria. The influence of the EU on horizontal administrative reform was thus rather weak during the accession process and unable to alter the general post-communist trajectory. Still, the EU's influence was often stressed as more successful at the sectoral level. In many areas, selective EU support (in contrast to conditional horizontal demands) has fostered the emergence of so-called 'islands of excellence' in CEE bureaucracies, making the implementation of some policies more likely than an overall level of weak capacity would suggest. Still, the following chapter argues that also the creation of such 'islands' in the realm of EU fund management was rather doubtful due to limited support in this area, differences between pre-accession and post-accession funds, and a much higher allocation of funds after accession. In contrast, it seems more likely that the immediate post-accession financing period proved more helpful to build the necessary sectoral

[7] Support for the assumed importance of the occurrence of politicization in contrast to its presence as a phenomenon is also stressed in different studies. While political changes go hand in hand with low absorption levels, this is not necessarily confirmed for party politicization (Buzogány and Korkut 2013: 1558) or even corruption per se (Beugelsdijk and Eijffinger 2005: 50). Use of funds with an eye on the electoral return can work well if the focus is not too narrowly on a few particularistic groups (Piattoni and Smyrl 2003: 145). Evidence for Poland suggests that 'bonding social capital', that is the rather inward-looking type of social capital focussing on one's own kinship (in contrast to generalized trust in the society), is beneficial for a stringent absorption of funds (Lackowska-Madurowicz and Swianiewicz 2013: 1410). Thus, it is most likely rather the competition of special interests, in contrast to their existence causing absorption problems.

capacities. Also, implementation of cohesion policy might benefit from the centralization of the implementation process, just as the example of the adoption of EU rules in the pre-accession period has shown. The following paragraphs elaborate on these aspects in greater detail.

3.2.1 The Accession Process and the Capacity-Criterion

The EU was well aware of the low level of administrative capacity in many CEE candidate countries. However, an explicit demand for capacity building had never been on the agenda of earlier accession rounds, and was also only later integrated in the realm of the eastern enlargement. The famous Copenhagen Criteria for EU accession were formulated in 1993 dealing with the existence of a functioning democracy, market economy, and the adoption of the EU's *acquis*, and yet it did not make explicit reference to a capacity-criterion, which was added only later (Verheijen 1999: 85).

Drawing on Schimmelfennig and Sedelmeier's 'external-incentive model' to account for the rule adoption of candidate countries, it is easy to see why the EU's influence in this area was only weak. The authors stress that for conditionality to be effective its requirements have to be formulated clearly, standards must be ideally the same in the old member states (legitimacy), and the withholding of incentives must be credible (Schimmelfennig and Sedelmeier 2005b: 12–13). All of these conditions where only vaguely fulfilled by the EU's administrative criterion. On the one hand, the EU had no administrative *acquis* of its own to export as an institutional template to the candidate countries, and practices in the old member states also vary widely (Dimitrova 2002: 180). The EC was even described as insecure in how far it should go in providing templates. For example, its central document referring to specific necessary structures and best practices from member states was initially only assigned the status of an 'unofficial paper' (Grabbe 2001: 1023). An administrative capacity criterion was first mentioned during the European Council of Madrid in 1995, and only further specified in the Commission Opinions on the candidate countries in 1997 ('Agenda 2000') (Verheijen 1999: 87). Demands became more clear when the EC asked SIGMA, an OECD body, to formulate EU standards of civil service against the backdrop of existing practice and law in the EU (Dimitrova 2005: 81). Overall, the demands can be summarized under three main headings:

- *the separation of politics and administration* (adoption of a civil service law (to ensure impartiality, accountability and legal predictability; protect civil servants from political or discretional dismissal); the separation of politics and administration within the senior ranks of the administration);
- *the creation of necessary infrastructures for the professionalization of the civil service* (training infrastructure for civil servants; creation of a central management body for civil service); and
- *the creation of transparent and impartial rules governing the civil service* (transparent and predictable salary system, transparent and fair performance evaluation, regulation of rights and duties to ensure professional integrity, political neutrality, impartiality; the introduction of open competition for entry to civil service (compulsory advertisement of vacancies) with clear requirements (standardized written examinations)) (Meyer-Sahling 2011: 238–239).

Still, even despite this clarification, experts remained sceptical and raised criticism that specific demands were vague and capacity was overall an "elusive concept" (Dimitrova 2002: 178; Buzogány and Stuchlík 2010: 276).

On the other hand, conditionality in this area was also not necessarily credible. It was generally understood that a refusal of accession only on the basis of the administrative capacity criterion was unlikely (Verheijen 1999: 88), especially for the big countries such as Poland, Hungary, and the Czech Republic (Dimitrova 2005: 86). The Czech Republic for example, made it to accession without ever adopting a civil service law. While the EC reportedly expected that the Czechs would 'deliver' upon accession (Meyer-Sahling 2011: 240), the ODS (Civic Democratic Party) government of the Czech Republic explicitly stated that it did not see any necessity for a civil service law (Dimitrova 2002: 186). Therefore, even though the de-politicization of the civil service was subject to conditionality, it was not necessarily implemented.

As discussed in Sect. 3.1, civil service reform had a very weak domestic constituency. Those reforms actually undertaken were generally adopted in a very short period of time, showing that external conditionality and not domestic efforts was the driver behind it (Dimitrova 2005: 89). Experts generally assign low trust to the importance of externally induced civil service legislation in altering levels of politicization. These legislation demands usually do not trigger a domestic debate on civil service policy, but rather result in formal compliance (Verheijen 2000: 29).

In the case of EU conditionality, the combination of a lack of a domestic reform constituency and the status of civil service legislation outside of the general EU *acquis* made it a prime candidate for 'backsliding' (Mungiu-Pippidi 2007) after accession. While there were most often no domestic veto players to lock-in pre-accession change (Sedelmeier 2012), there was no possibility to start infringement procedures as civil service legislation is not based in EU law.

Thus, it comes as no surprise that a reform reversal is reported for all CEE countries, with the exception of Hungary ('reform reorientation') and partly the Baltic states (Meyer-Sahling 2009a: 7, 2011: 234). Still, also the Baltic states do not seem to be entirely shielded against a possible backsliding, as the Lithuanian government adopted a law allowing for higher politicization in 2009 (Nakrošis and Gudžinskas 2012: 108). In a similar vein, a high number of changes of staff was reported upon the electoral win of the Fidesz party in Hungary in 2010 (Buzogány and Korkut 2013). These observations are in line with the empirical results of other studies finding a continuously high level of politicization and party patronage in almost all CEE countries (Kopecký and Spirova 2011; Meyer-Sahling and Veen 2012: 10). Thus, as the major interest of this study is in de facto and not de jure politicization, the EU's endeavour for sustainable horizontal administrative reform was at best only limited in its success.

3.2.2 The Focus on Sectoral Reform: Creating 'Islands of Excellence'?

Still, the EU's focus on administrative capacity in the region was not necessarily lacking in effect. Even though horizontal reform of the civil service was demanded, the accession process mostly focussed on sector specific capacity building in order to enhance candidate countries' abilities to enforce EU law (Grabbe 2001: 1027). The importance of this area of capacities is stressed by the fact that all pre-accession assistance towards institution-building in the realm of the PHARE[8] pre-accession assistance programme went to this area (Dimitrova 2002: 179). The biggest beneficiary of PHARE (30% of total funds) was the twinning exercise. Twinning is the deployment of civil servants from the member states to candidate countries' administrations to share knowledge.

[8] PHARE stands for 'Poland and Hungary: Assistance for Restructuring their Economies' (Beichelt 2004: 40).

It could thus not necessarily be expected from the start that the accession process would lead to an overall professionalization of the administration, but rather that some parts of the administration would become more professionalized, while the rest would remain the same. This phenomenon is known from the Latin American context as the emergence of so-called ‘islands of excellence’. These highly professional ‘islands’ can exist concurrently with inefficient parts of the bureaucracy and do not necessarily emanate a positive (good example) or negative (drawing talent from other branches) effect on general capacities (Goetz 2001: 1044–1046; Goetz and Wollmann 2001: 883). Thus, while the overall level of capacity might be mediocre or even low, the existence of such ‘islands’ can facilitate the execution of certain policies more efficiently than is generally the case within the state bureaucracy.

Such a development is clearly illustrated in the realm of the high transposition rates of CEE member states, which, after accession, were even higher than in the old member states, sometimes had surprising champions (Bulgaria in 2008 [Trauner 2009: 8]), and were referred to as an indicator illustrating the sustainability of accession conditionality (Sedelmeier 2008: 822). Still, the new member states had gained much experience in the formal adoption of EU law during the enlargement process, adopting all 80,000 or so pages of the whole EU *acquis*. Lithuania, for example, developed distinct structures only for the rapid adoption of EU law which were kept in place even after accession (Maniokas 2009: 6). This facilitated the ongoing quick adoption of EU rules, also in other new member states (Sedelmeier 2008: 821). However, qualitative case studies suggest that this highly successful process of formal compliance might be detached from the application and enforcement of rules, which was often found to be lacking (see for example Dimitrova and Steunenberg 2013; Falkner and Treib 2008). The ongoing high rate of transposition is thus probably rather an example for well-developed capacities in this area, and not necessarily for effective implementation of EU rules.

The adaptation of capacities for the use of EU funds was also an important aspect of the enlargement process. The preparation for the use of structural funds was more demanding than the simple transposition of EU rules and also proved more difficult for the candidate countries (Verheijen 2007: x). The EU demanded in negotiation of Chapter 21 that the candidate countries create

> mechanisms for interministerial communication; capacity for multiyear programming; capacity for monitoring and implementing policy; the adoption of a national development plan; and the adoption of the EU's NUTS territorial units for statistical classification and Structural Funds implementation. (O'Dwyer 2006a: 227)[9]

On the one hand, this resulted in a need for legal compliance, which was not fully achieved in some areas before enlargement. Upon accession, there were still some areas left where compliance with the *acquis* on cohesion policy was incomplete, for example in the area of public procurement legislation (Leonardi 2005: 172). On the other hand, a much more demanding task was the creation of the necessary administrative structures. The EC started out with a rather maximalist approach and demanded the creation of subnational units for fund administration, while leaving it open as to whether these units would also wield political functions (Grabbe 2001: 1019). However, this plan was gradually abandoned as the EC was more concerned about poor regional capacities in handling the funds in the late stages of the enlargement process. Accordingly, they empowered more reliable central ministries with the task of fund administration (Hughes et al. 2004: 539). The EC finally distanced itself from initial support for decentralization and supported a centralized approach for cohesion policy implementation, at least for the 2004–2006 period (Leonardi 2005: 165). However, this did not mean that implementation was especially easy, as capacities were lacking also at the central level. In general, the fear of limited benefits from structural funds due to poor capacities was widespread before and also after enlargement (Bailey and De Propris 2004: 91; Horvat 2005).

Capacity building for structural funds was also seen as crucial against the backdrop of the experience of the 'southern enlargement', and therefore this time it was tackled before accession (Drevet 2000: 352). The EC responded to candidate countries' need for preparation with two measures. First, it channelled a substantial amount of money via the PHARE programme towards the issue of institution-building, mainly in the form of so-called 'twinning' projects in which civil servants from the old member states would work in candidate countries' administrations and share knowledge and best practices. Within PHARE's

[9] NUTS refers to the 'Nomenclature of Territorial Units for Statistics', thus the subdivision of member states into smaller units, for example for purposes of fund allocation.

institution-building priority, a special focus was introduced for the preparation of candidate countries in the future management of structural funds since 1997 (Drevet 2000: 351). Second, the EC modelled the pre-accession funds on the EU funds. This means that PHARE would provide preparation for handling the structural funds, whereas ISPA (Instrument for Structural Policies and Pre-Accession) was an exercise for dealing with the cohesion fund (Bailey and De Propris 2004: 83).

Even though these measures were important for CEEC's preparation, they still had their limitations. For example, preparations for the use of EU funds could benefit only from few twinning projects. Data presented by the EC shows that in the period 1998–2002, only 10% of twinning projects took place in the realm of regional development and the preparation for the structural funds, which is only half of the projects taking place, for example, in the area "Justice and Home Affairs" (Bailey and De Propris 2004: 87). Another important argument for the limits of pre-accession preparation concerns the still limited comparability of pre-accession and post-accession funds. After all, pre-accession funds are different from the structural funds with regard to their rules and also their total amount. PHARE was criticized for its annual planning procedures, which did not very much resemble the multi-annual procedures of cohesion policy (Bachtler et al. 2000: 373; Allen 2008: 21). Projects under ISPA were implemented strongly under EC supervision, "rather than by national administrative structures operating on their own" (Leonardi 2005: 166). The third and final limitation of pre-accession experience concerns the amount of funds to be handled. During the pre-accession period only an annual EUR 2.5 billion were available for all candidate countries (Bailey and De Propris 2004: 83),[10] whereas Poland alone received annually almost EUR 10 billion in the 2007–2013 period (European Commission 2007: 25). Thus, even if pre-accession funds had been perfectly modeled on structural funds regarding their rules and procedures, it could still be expected that the experience of a full financing period and an increased amount of funds are an entirely different process to be mastered.

Considering the limitations of pre-accession preparation, it was thus most likely the learning experience with cohesion policy proper right after accession 2004 that helped most new member states of that accession

[10] ISPA and PHARE combined, 2000–2006 period.

round to handle the funds. Rather surprisingly, the results of the first and shortened financing period 2004–2006 were very promising. When it comes to absorption, new member states used their (limited amount of) money even faster than the old member states (Tosun 2014: 382). In addition, Bachtler and colleagues (2014) find that EU fund management capacities developed well in most new member staes during that period, with highest capacities in Estonia and Lithuania (rated B, thus 'developing'), followed by Slovakia, the Czech Republic, Poland, Latvia, and Hungary (rated between B and C ('basic')). In contrast, only Slovenia's capacity did not supass the rating 'Basic' (C). Overall, according to the authors capacities after accession "developed faster and better than policy-makers and academic commentators predicted" (Bachtler et al. 2014: 752). Taking into account that new member states perform here rather consistently well in contrast to their still varying overall capacities (see Table 3.1), it is underlined that especially in those new member states with overall low capacities the well performing EU funds units should be the result of the successful building of 'islands of excellence' most likely in the course of post-accession adaptation.

3.2.3 The Influence of Central Coordination on Implementation

Apart from the quality of sectoral capacities, there is also an organizational aspect that can possibly make a difference for implementation. Studies on the enlargement process have stressed that the existence of central bodies of control and oversight have facilitated the implementation of EU rules. In general, a high number of involved ministries can cause implementation problems, as more resources have to be invested in coordination (Haverland and Romeijn 2007: 774; Haverland et al. 2011: 277). A possible remedy for this is the establishment of 'watchdog' units monitoring ministries' performance in implementation (Falkner et al. 2005: 24). While they were found to be less important in the old member states (Falkner et al. 2005: 301), many new member states from CEE used central coordination bodies for the transposition of EU law prior to accession (Dimitrova and Toshkov 2007: 969).

Zubek stressed the importance of centralized incentives and monitoring in the process of pre-accession transposition of EU law in Poland. Ministers were unwilling to take both the opportunity and coordination costs in cases of EU law transposition where they would not be able to take individual credit for the adoption of rules (Zubek 2005: 593).

Successful transposition became only more likely against the centralized offer of selective incentives and the provision of monitoring from the core executive (Zubek 2005: 611–613). In general, the task of such centralized bodies is to coordinate different parts of the government involved in implementation (facilitate the flow of information, settle conflicts), provide technical assistance for implementation, and monitor the performance of different parts of the executive (Dimitrova and Toshkov 2009: 3; see also for Lithuania Maniokas 2009: 6). The advantage of such co-ordination structures is that they can act as "separate actors with a focus on and vested interest in the smooth compliance with EU law" (Dimitrova and Toshkov 2009: 3). This makes implementation more likely, because both involuntary (these bodies can offer technical assistance) and voluntary (they can enforce implementation even if other actors try to avoid it) sources of non-compliance can be tackled. Bodies responsible for coordination of EU policies can take various forms and be assigned to the office of the prime minister, the ministry of foreign affairs, or the council of ministers (Dimitrova and Toshkov 2009: 5).

3.2.4 How Does Pre-accession Experience Impact Absorption?

Over a quarter century after the end of communism, levels of administrative capacity are rather heterogeneous in CEE. Still, while neither domestic will nor external incentives could decisively lead to a horizontal reform in all cases and could barely ever lead to a depoliticization of the civil service in any, the sectoral influence of the EU could still have made a difference. On the one hand, technical assistance during the enlargement process together with learning during the first, shortened financing period (2004–2006) in CEE member states seem to have created 'islands of excellence', which are administrative clusters facilitating the implementation of cohesion policy, in some new member states. Support for the possible existence of such 'islands' is provided by Bachtler and colleague's data on 2004–2006 cohesion policy capacity. Their possible effect will be taken into account in the form of the level of administrative capacity available in the management and control system during the earlier financing period. 'Islands' could thus offer a useful backdrop or starting platform for the creation of the management and control system in the period under scrutiny.

On the other hand, also centralized management structures were found to be beneficial for the implementation of EU policies during the enlargement process. It might thus well be that the absorption of EU funds is not only supported by high overall capacities or highly professionalized clusters in the bureaucracy, but also by central bodies offering oversight and advice, and which have a strong stake in the implementation of EU policies. The implementation of cohesion policy is conducted within member states' management and control systems. EU rules stipulate necessary bodies for these systems, but the assignment of tasks to domestic institutions is the decision of the member state. The core actor within the management and control system is the MA. While every OP needs an MA, a single MA can be responsible for all OPs in a country (see Sect. 2.1 for more details). Thus, a centralized management structure boils down to a system in which only one ministry or other institution is assigned the role of MA, responsible for all OPs. In contrast to this centralized design, it is also possible that MAs are located directly at the sectoral level and that every OP has its own distinct MA, thus forming a decentralized system of implementation.

It is expected that those systems with one single MA will benefit from the advantages of centralized monitoring, technical support, and if necessary, also steering. For example, a strong central actor could threaten underperforming OPs with a reallocation of funds to other programmes, a decision which is within the authority of the MA. The presence of centralized management structures might also weaken the influence of politicization. If authority rests with a centralized body that holds a stake in EU fund absorption, it could well be that ministerial discretion and therefore also the politicization of both staff and priorities is limited with regard to incoming new ministers.[11] Finally, access to many different OPs could turn the single MA into a hub for learning processes and therefore a platform for sharing useful lessons-learned between otherwise separated programmes. Overall, the existence of a single MA structure in the management and control system should result in a higher rate of absorption.

[11]For example, the Lithuanian Labour Party, a populist newcomer, tried to alter the countries' management and control system for the 2007–2013 financing period in order to have complete control over programme implementation at the level of the ministries it controlled at that time. Still, an insider from the centralized MA in Lithuania stressed that when the Labour Party tried to push for this decentralization "we convinced them that they are not able to do that" (LT4 2014).

3.3 The Global Financial and Economic Crisis in the New Member States

Financial capacities are important for absorption as all member states have to provide a certain amount of co-financing for their projects.[12] The EC takes into consideration member states' financial and macroeconomic absorption capacities prior to the financing period in the process of allocation. The amount committed by the EC in 2007 should thus have been a sum that could be reasonably digested by CEE member states during the financing period against the backdrop of the state of their economies. Nevertheless, these capacities might be subject to fluctuations depending on national as well as global economic prospects. Especially big departures from the earlier financial development will therefore have a constraining effect on member states' ability to use their EU funds (Tosun 2014: 377).

The biggest effect on new member states' access to financial resources in the period under investigation was arguably the global financial and economic crisis beginning in September 2008, thereby almost coinciding with the start of the financing period. As its name already implies, the crisis hit almost all countries irrespective of their recent post-communist or post-enlargement background. Still, some of the new member states suffered more than others, mostly according to their reliance on external financial resources and trade as well as high amounts of foreign currency denominated debt (Connolly 2010: 264, 2012: 36, 41).

New member states were predisposed to suffer from a financial crisis for two reasons. First, the hardships of the early transition period were followed by the welcome advent of cheap transnational finance during the 2000s. In some countries this money then fueled consumption-lead growth and real-estate bubbles that were already "accident[s] waiting to happen" (Åslund 2010: 27). Second (the prospect of) EU membership had increased lenders' confidence in CEECs' reform trajectories and their perceived trustworthiness. However, this led to an unhealthy

[12] They are set for member states whose GDP per capita was below 85% of the EU 25 average between 2001 and 2003 at 85% for both the structural funds as well as the cohesion fund, and for both the convergence and the competitiveness and employment objective (Annex III to Council Regulation (General Regulation)). This provision includes all central and eastern European member states as well as Greece, Cyprus, Malta, and Portugal.

growth in short-term foreign currency denominated credit that would pose a huge problem for some countries when access to liquidity to re-finance these credits dried up in autumn 2008.

The biggest problem was therefore visible in those countries that had not only been offered high amounts of mostly foreign currency denominated debt, but had also taken up this debt. The following paragraphs explain in detail why the combination of the post-communist economic transformation context and the status as accession candidates made the countries of the region more likely victims of shifts in the global economic and financial development.

3.3.1 *The Process of Post-communist Economic Reform*

The process of post-communist transformation, known as the 'third wave of democratization' (Huntington 1993), was in many important respects different from the earlier transitions to democracy in Latin America and southern Europe. In these countries, the process of change was limited to the political regime, keeping all other important aspects of state and society (especially property rights) as they had been before. In contrast, in the post-communist countries there was a lack of any 'non-contingent givens', i.e. all basic questions of nation, territory, and political regime were at stake (Offe 2004: 508). When it comes to economic liberalization, the situation was especially difficult as the prevalence of central planning made large-scale reforms necessary. This process of economic liberalization was unprecedented in history, as its goal was nothing less than the creation of an entrepreneurial class by political decree (Offe 2004: 504).

The challenging character of the necessity of concurrent political and economic liberalization was described by Claus Offe as the 'dilemma of simultaneity' (Offe 2004: 519–520). On the one hand, the process of economic liberalization follows the rationale that short-term hardships for the population are put up with in the hope of expected long-term benefits of reform. Still, this process of reform is likely to be halted at the ballot box as soon as newly enfranchised voters realize that their economic fortunes decrease, while other parts of society apparently benefit much quicker from reforms. The process of economic reform is thus unlikely to be successful under conditions of political competition. On the other hand, this very political competition, which is likely to impede the process of economic liberalization, is also a necessary condition for its success. If privatization starts without prior political liberalization, unaccountable elites will design the process to their own benefit (Offe 2004: 520). The result of liberalization is then likely to be based on "nomenklatura buyouts", changing the structure of the economy only from "plan to clan" (Stark 1990: 365, 374). Thus, proper economic liberalization and also political liberalization are unlikely under these circumstances.

The intriguing formulation of this dilemma by Offe was echoed by other scholars' skepticism on the likelihood of stable democratic transformation in the face of parallel economic and political reform (e.g. Crawford 1995: 4; Przeworski 1995: 10–11; Stone 2002: 5). Focusing on this 'breakdown-literature', Greskovits noted that there were much more elaborate theories provided on how democracy was eventually going to break down in the post-communist countries than anything which had ever been on offer before to account for the breakdown of communism in the region (Greskovits 1998: 2). Still, the feature that both events eventually came to share was not the outcome (i.e. breakdown), but rather the lack of a prior existing theory to account for it. A quarter century after the beginning of transformation (and the writing of Offe's original piece in 1991), all countries in CEE have turned into reasonably stable liberal market economies and democracies. How can this development be accounted for despite the 'dilemma'? How did CEE voters develop the unexpected high levels of 'patience' Offe deemed necessary for the processes to work?

The necessity of voters' 'patience' in capitalist democracies is not a distinct feature of the post-communist transformation process. The literature on political economy stresses that there is an inherent tension between the instability of the market and "citizen's demands for security and predictability in their lives" (Crouch 2008: 476). This security and predictability is usually provided by some form of social contract, most prominently exemplified by the welfare state in Western Europe. Starting from this very point of departure when formulating his 'dilemma', Offe (2004: 523–526) also highlighted that similar procedures could support the success of transformation, such as the provision of support by international actors (e.g. from the EU, the Organization for Security and Co-Operation in Europe (OSCE), or the International Monetary Fund (IMF)), the establishment of social policies offering relief to the pains of reform, or the involvement of large intermediary actors (such as unions) into processes of reform to enhance their legitimacy.[13] Was the external support offered by the EU thus ultimately the decisive factor to create the necessary 'patience' for reform?

Taking into account the development of a 'post-communist divide' (Way and Levitsky 2007) between a democratic CEE and a mostly non-democratic former Soviet Union during the last few decades, it seems to make sense to tie the different trajectories of the regions to their varying exposure to western leverage and linkage. In this scenario, external actors managed to successfully stabilize democracy in CEE through various processes, ranging from external pressure up to cultural and economic transnational linkages between the countries of the region and other liberal democracies (Way and Levitsky 2007: 55–61). Still, the sole focus on external actors helping to achieve patience in the difficult phase of multiple processes of transformation offers only a partial explanation for the outcome. For example, Schimmelfennig and Sedelmeier find that the EU only made a difference for successful democratic transformation in the case of weak democracies such as Romania or Slovakia which were at the threshold between democratization and continued authoritarian rule (Schimmelfennig and Sedelmeier 2005a: 214). However, it did not account for the success of frontrunner cases such as Poland, Hungary, the Czech Republic and Slovenia, who had already democratized on their own at the beginning of the 1990s and apparently did not need the push from an external actor (Schimmelfennig and Sedelmeier 2005a: 214).

Other authors offer the thus necessary specification of the argument. They stress the temporal variance of the importance and selective use of external support to achieve voter's 'patience'. Drawing on Offe's prior work, Bohle (2011: 131) proposes the idea of what she calls temporary solutions to the 'dilemma'. While CEE elites have to build support for their reforms and have to keep the population at bay (Offe's 'patience'), they have several means at their disposal to achieve (temporary) support for the new political and economic order. The author explains her idea by following the examples of Hungary and Latvia. On the one hand, the Hungarian post-communist government secured popular support by maintaining a high level of social security spending ('goulash

[13] On such use of social policies see similar 'Compensation as a Government Tactic' as presented by Greskovits (1998: 137–154) or 'Strategic Social Policies' by Vanhuysse (2006: 136).

post-communism' [Kornai 1996: 944]). It was thereby possible to keep voters at bay while introducing liberalizing reforms. On the other hand, Latvia used the legitimacy evolving from its nation-building project after independence from the Soviet Union, and engaged in a 'nationalist social contract' (Bohle 2011: 135–137), the symbol of which became the *lats* as the re-introduced national currency.

Both types of domestically founded social contracts however, wore out rather quickly and were no longer feasible in the mid-1990s when also Hungary had to implement budget cuts, and Latvians started to get tired of the economic hardships resulting from reform (Bohle 2011: 143–145). Thus, both countries' populations were becoming increasingly dissatisfied with the situation, and both countries were in need of financial resources to overcome this dissatisfaction.

The advent of the EU and the prospect of accession offered then the next 'temporary solution' for the stabilization of the system via two mechanisms (Bohle 2011: 138). First, it offered governments legitimacy as they suddenly had to negotiate their 'return to Europe', a desired goal for most people in the region. Second, the engagement with the EU towards accession provided further credibility for the countries' reform processes, making them also more attractive for transnational capital flows.

This is the very point when the development becomes relevant for the later effect of the financial crisis. The first Orban government in Hungary (1998–2002) had learned from the pitfalls of fiscal prudency experienced earlier by the Socialists and used the new situation to engage heavily in spending policies (Bohle 2011: 138). The Latvian government, in contrast, remained true to its course of fiscal solidity, but private households made strong use of the access to cheap foreign-currency denominated loans in order to maintain or improve their standard of living, also fueling a growing real-estate bubble (Bohle 2011: 142). The inflow of transnational finance secured political stability during the following years as well as economic growth in many countries of the region. However, it also created massive incentives for moral hazard. Åslund summarizes this situation as follows:

> With cheap credits and sharply rising real estate prices, all borrowing made sense but saving did not. Consequently, the locals reduced their saving. The banks did not finance themselves through deposits but through loans from the old, stagnant European Union. […] The consequence was that

> commercial banks in Eastern Europe as well as their customers exposed themselves to massive currency risks because of currency mismatches. (Åslund 2010: 69)

In great part, West European economies were lending their money to the east so that CEE consumers could buy their goods (as well as real estate) (Connolly 2010: 244). Quite naturally however, this type of social contract as "financialized growth" (Myant and Drahokoupil 2012: 31) proved to be unsustainable, because productivity gains in the region often did not keep up with the new spending habits. When external debt and current account deficits rose ever stronger, some of the countries already started to experience difficulties even before the start of the crisis (Connolly 2012: 41). Its advent then put an end to the social contracts in the region that were based on cheap capital available on the international market.

3.3.2 The Financial and Economic Crisis in CEE

The collapse of Lehman Brothers Bank on 15 September 2008 started a panic reaction, leading to a standstill of international financial markets. The ensuing financial crisis resulted in the collapse of several European banks and extensive government rescue operations (Kickert and Randma-Liiv 2015: 7–8). The new member states were termed by some observers the "epicenter for the World Financial Crisis" (Sagemann and Reese 2011: 60). One of the main problems of the region was its exposure to high levels of foreign currency denominated credit (mainly Euro and Swiss Franc) which was issued only for the short term. Credits in foreign currencies were popular in the region as they had lower interest rates than those in domestic currencies, but they also transferred exchange rate risks to borrowers (Myant and Drahokoupil 2012: 14–15). Two problems then resulted from the suddenly lacking availability of financial resources. First, there was a lack of finance available to pay for construction and consumption (Myant and Drahokoupil 2012: 25). Second, of the $1.7 trillion borrowed by the CEECs from West European Banks, as much as $400 billion had to be repaid or refinanced as early as 2009 (Åslund 2010: 70): "The outbreak of the global financial crisis in autumn 2008, finally pulled the rug from under the existing social contracts" (Bohle 2011: 143).

Still, the impact on the countries was differential. The main effect of the crisis was felt in 2009 when the Baltic states had double-digit negative growth rates and Latvia and Lithuania were seen as the worst affected by the crisis, even on a global scale (Connolly 2010: 245). In contrast, other countries were hit less hard and Poland weathered the whole period, including 2009, with positive growth figures. The differential impact of the crisis was eventually linked to both the way the international financial conditions had played out at the domestic level during the boom years, and the institutional structures in the member states at the point of the slump.

The international conditions leading to the financial crisis in the region were the same for all countries: the broad availability of liquidity on international markets, CEECs' offer of an attractive investment environment, and exchange rate policies that helped to boost domestic money supply with external sources (Åslund 2010: 4). Still, these external conditions had not produced the same result in all new member states. In contrast to Bohle's rather pessimistic scenario of the sustainability of CEE economic transformation, many of the countries had developed rather stable economic foundations during the 1990s. Growth was not in all countries and not only consumption driven, but also for a long time "accompanied by transformations of economic structures, including substantial upgrading of the composition, quality and technological sophistication of manufactured exports" (Bideleux 2011: 340). It was therefore not in all places and not all the time only a bubble building up that would finally burst. The accumulation of high external debt depended, among others, on countries' exchange rate policy and domestic regulation. While the extent of the crisis was mainly the result of accumulation of debt and countries' dependence on trade (Connolly 2010: 264; 2012: 36, 41), the way in which this could play out in the end to create a financial crisis was again mitigated by factors such as Eurozone membership, the level of debt, and the dependence on exports (Åslund 2010: 16, 43, 53–59). Overall, the global financial crisis had a differential effect on the CEE region, but was surely the single most important event affecting new member states' financial absorption capacity during the 2007–2013 financing period.

3.3.3 How Did the Crisis Impact Absorption?

The overall level of economic development of a state is less important for absorption because it is already taken into account upon the allocation of funds (macroeconomic absorption capacity). This understanding is substantiated by different levels of allocation unrelated to the 'neediness' of member states (Popa 2012: 163) as well as the empirical finding of a negative correlation between absorption rates and income levels (Tosun 2014: 383). It is thus more important to account for possible shifts of financial absorption capacity during the financing period.

CEECs were especially susceptible to a change in global economic fortunes due to the context of post-communist transformation as well as the status as candidate countries and new member states. Transnational finance was welcome in order to achieve societal 'patience' for economic reform, and the prospect of accession made the countries attractive destinations for abundantly available cash in the world economy. Nevertheless, this development played out differently in the region, and only some countries saw the creation of unsustainable levels of debt, while others made more substantial progress in their economic transformation. It is thus necessary to pay special attention to the different extent of crises in the countries in the aftermath of the global downturn.

In order to account for this differing extent, it does not seem adequate to measure the crisis only in terms of decline of GDP. While this is a useful overall measure of economic strength, it does not do justice to the severity of the crisis in particular countries. For example, Hungary's GDP shrank only by 6% between 2008 and 2009, which is a far cry from the 18% experienced in Latvia. However, both countries were considered as equally desperately affected by the crisis and both were among the three that ultimately turned to the IMF for support (Åslund 2010: 31–51; Bideleux 2011: 355–356; Connolly 2012: 44–45). Therefore, also other factors must be considered such as countries' Eurozone membership, their level of (foreign currency denominated) debt, and their dependence on exports (Åslund 2010: 16, 43, 53–59), in order to understand to what extent the crisis meant a blow to these countries' economies and finances, making EU fund absorption more difficult. Only those member states deeply affected by the crisis were likely to experience problems raising the necessary amount of co-finance for their projects, resulting in a lower level of absorption.

3.4 Summary: Framework for Analysis and Methods

3.4.1 The Framework for Analysis

The framework for analysis consists of five factors that may be important to account for absorption problems in CEE. Two of these factors are related to the general idea of absorption capacity (administrative capacity, financial crisis), while the remaining three factors (party politicization and patronage, 'islands of excellence', and centralized management) are derived from the literature on post-communist and post-accession developments.

- *Administrative Capacity*: There is a strong stress in the literature on the importance of administrative capacity for absorption. It is thus expected that an overall low administrative capacity will lower CEE countries' ability to manage and access their EU funds.
- *Financial Crisis*: In contrast to administrative capacity, the other two dimensions of absorption capacity are already taken into account upon the allocation of funds. Thus, macroeconomic and financial absorption capacities in a member state should be appropriate to allow for absorption. Still, the financial and economic crisis strongly limited the access of CEE countries to finance. A country severely affected by the crisis will thus suffer from absorption problems.
- *Party Politicization and Patronage*: The exchange of staff and programme priorities following political preferences interrupts the implementation process and causes delays. These delays could well result in the decommitment of funds as countries fail to meet their initial schedules. Still, party politicization and patronage are only relevant when they take place on a regular basis, and not only by a single party subsequently remaining in power. Absorption problems are thus expected in countries with a frequent alternation of parties in charge of ministries controlling OPs.
- *'Islands of Excellence'*: The existence of management structures for cohesion policy implementation with better than average administrative capacity will facilitate absorption. The shortened 2004–2006 financing period offered a good starting point for building the 2007–2013 implementation system in this regard. If earlier capacities were well developed, this could have a supportive effect on the capacity available for the following financing period.
- *Centralized Management*: A centralized management and control system holds several advantages for implementation. OPs are then not only subject to the influence of (changing) ministers, but can benefit from constant technical support and also control from a central body charged with supervision. This supervision might not only facilitate adaptation of administrative capacity, but could also limit the politicization of the implementation process by parties controlling OPs. Thus, the presence of a centralized system facilitates the absorption of EU funds.

3.4.2 *Combining FsQCA and Process Tracing in Set-Theoretic Multi-method Research*

The theoretical propositions developed above are tested in Chapters 4 and 5 using two different qualitative methods. The first application of the framework for analysis is an fsQCA. On the basis of the results of this fsQCA, two cases are selected for process tracing case studies. This study is thus an instance of 'set-theoretic multi-method research' (Schneider and Rohlfing 2013, 2016).

Qualitative comparative analysis (QCA) was developed by Charles Ragin as an attempt to bridge the gap between qualitative and quantitative analysis (Ragin 1987, 2000). The central feature of QCA is its basis in a set-theoretic understanding of causation. It does not seek mean causal effects of variables, but focuses on the detection of necessary and sufficient conditions for an outcome (Berg-Schlosser et al. 2009: 10). QCA is not only a technique for data analysis, but also and maybe even most importantly an approach for analysis with a distinct interest in the cases under study. At the centre of this approach is the process of careful case selection as well as operationalization and calibration of causal factors (sets) considered in the analysis. In contrast, the 'analytic moment' when the data is actually analyzed is usually rather short in comparison to the prior processes (Schneider and Wagemann 2012: 11).

QCA as a data analysis technique is based on the use of truth tables. These tables display all logically possible combinations of conditions considered in an analysis. The analysis of a truth table yields distinct patterns of superset and subset relationships, thus necessary and sufficient conditions for the outcome under study. These results have certain features. First, QCA is open to 'conjunctural causation', implying that a combination of conditions rather than a single factor can be sufficient for the outcome (Ragin 1987: 26–30; Berg-Schlosser et al. 2009: 8). Furthermore, it is also possible that instances of 'multiple conjunctural causation' emerge, thus different combinations of conditions or 'causal recipes' (Ragin 2008b: 124) leading to the same outcome. The existence of multiple causal paths leading to the same outcome is usually referred to as equifinality (George and Bennett 2005: 157; Ragin 2008b: 63).

The ability to account for conjunctural causation makes QCA a good match with the existing theorization on absorption. On the one hand, the idea of absorption capacity is in essence a set-theoretic argument. Research on absorption has so far looked for patterns of regular association, and tested single dimensions of absorption capacity as independent variables (Tosun 2014; Milio 2007). Still, the idea of absorption capacity is that well-developed administrative capacity, financial capacity, and macroeconomic capacity must all be present in order to achieve absorption of EU funds (see e.g. Boeckhout et al. 2002: 2; Horvat 2005: 9; Popa 2012: 168). The very logic of this statement suggests that the absence of any one of these different capacities will lead to a low level of absorption. Thus, in set-theoretic terms, all of these three capacities are at least INUS conditions for absorption.[14] Existing theories of absorption thus fulfil the most important prerequisite for the application of QCA: The "phenomenon of interest is best understood in terms of set relations" (Schneider and Wagemann 2012: 12).

Process tracing is then an ideal supplement to the application of QCA. The method's main goal is to identify the 'path' between an independent and dependent variable (George and Bennett 2005: 206). This can be pursued by applying the same deterministic, set-theoretic understanding of causality just as in QCA (Rohlfing 2012; Beach and Pedersen 2013: 33). At the centre of a process tracing analysis is the formulation and testing of a causal mechanism (George and Bennett 2005: 206). At the most general level, causal mechanisms can be understood to be "the pathway or process by which an effect is produced or a purpose is accomplished" (Gerring 2008b: 178). Thus, process tracing does not seek to determine which independent variable (*x*) is connected to a certain dependent variable (*y*), but rather how they are connected. Causal mechanisms are understood here as systems of interlocking parts transmitting causal forces from an independent to a dependent variable (Rohlfing 2012: 35–36; Beach and Pedersen 2013: 29), or from a sufficient combination of conditions to an outcome. The understanding of a mechanism as a system of interlocking parts entails the necessity to formulate clearly every part of the mechanism, and ideally to display it as a detailed path diagram (Beach and Rohlfing 2018: 8). The parts can then be tested, collecting evidence from the case and comparing it with the expected empirical manifestations (Van Evera 1997: 64).

[14] "INUS conditions are […] neither individually necessary nor individually sufficient for an outcome of interest. Instead, they are essential (i.e. non-redundant) components of an overall configuration of variable values that is sufficient for the outcome" (Mahoney and Goertz 2006: 24–25).

The QCA benefits from the process tracing analysis as the interpretation of QCA results "does not follow automatically from the demonstration of the subset relation" (Ragin 2008a: 99; see also Beach and Rohlfing 2018: 5). Process tracing is stressed as an especially adequate choice for a second empirical application because it offers insights on the cases going beyond the detection of mere patterns of regular association (Schneider and Wagemann 2012: 308–309; Beach and Rohlfing 2018: 5). It both helps to show that a detected sufficient combination of conditions is plausible for an outcome, but also reveals how the combination actually leads to the outcome. The result of process tracing in a 'cross-case-analysis-first design' in qualitative multi-method research (Beach and Rohlfing 2018: 15) is therefore not only further support for the earlier finding, but rather another contribution of distinct theoretical value.

References

Allen, D. (2008). Cohesion Policy Pre- and Post-enlargement. In M. Baun & D. Marek (Eds.), *EU Cohesion Policy After Enlargement* (pp. 15–33). Basingstoke: Palgrave.

Åslund, A. (2010). *The Last Shall Be the First: The East European Financial Crisis.* Washington, DC: Peterson Institute for International Economics.

Autengruber, C. (2008). Bulgarien: Zwischen anfänglichen Konsolidierungstendenzen und aktuellen Umbrüchen. In E. Bos & D. Segert (Eds.), *Osteuropäische Demokratien als Trendsetter? Parteien und Parteiensysteme nach dem Ende des Übergangsjahrzehnts* (pp. 133–146). Opladen and Farmington Hills: Verlag Barbara Budrich.

Bachtler, J., Downes, R., & Gorzelak, G. (2000). Transition, Cohesion and Regional Policy in Central and Eastern Europe: Conclusions. In J. Bachtler, R. Downes, & G. Gorzelak (Eds.), *Transition Cohesion and Regional Policy in Central and Eastern Europe* (pp. 355–378). Aldershot et al.: Ashgate.

Bachtler, J., & McMaster, I. (2008). EU Cohesion Policy and the Role of the Regions: Investigating the Influence of Structural Funds in the New Member States. *Environment and Planning C: Government and Policy, 26*(2), 398–427.

Bachtler, J., Mendez, C., & Oraže, H. (2014). From Conditionality to Europeanization in Central and Eastern Europe: Administrative Performance and Capacity in Cohesion Policy. *European Planning Studies, 22*(4), 735–757.

Bailey, D., & De Propris, L. (2004). A Bridge Too Phare? EU Pre-accession Aid and Capacity-Building in the Candidate Countries. *JCMS: Journal of Common Market Studies, 42*(1), 77–98.

Banaszewska, M., & Bischoff, I. (2016). *The Political Economy of EU-Funds in Poland: Evidence for the Period 2007–2013* (Joint Discussion Paper Series in Economics). Available at http://www.uni-marburg.de/fb02/makro/forschung/magkspapers. Accessed May 2016.

Beach, D., & Pedersen, R. B. (2013). *Process-Tracing Methods: Foundations and Guidelines*. Ann Arbor: University of Michigan Press.

Beach, D., & Rohlfing, I. (2018). Integrating Cross-Case Analyses and Process Tracing in Set-Theoretic Research Strategies and Parameters of Debate. *Sociological Methods & Research, 47*(1), 3–36.

Beichelt, T. (2004). *Die Europäische Union nach der Osterweiterung*. Wiesbaden: VS Verlag.

Berg-Schlosser, D., De Meur, G., Rihoux, B., & Ragin, C. C. (2009). Qualitative Comparative Analysis (QCA) as an Approach. In B. Rihoux & C. C. Ragin (Eds.), *Configurational Comparative Methods: Qualitative Comparative Analysis (QCA) and Related Techniques* (pp. 1–18). London et al.: Sage.

Beugelsdijk, M., & Eijffinger, S. C. (2005). The Effectiveness of Structural Policy in the European Union: An Empirical Analysis for the EU-15 in 1995–2001. *JCMS: Journal of Common Market Studies, 43*(1), 37–51.

Bideleux, R. (2011). Contrasting Responses to the International Economic Crisis of 2008–10 in the 11 CIS Countries and in the 10 Post-communist EU Member Countries. *Journal of Communist Studies and Transition Politics, 27*(3–4), 338–363.

Bingen, D. (2008). Polen: Wie ein labiles Parteiensystem zu einer Stabilisierung der Demokratie beiträgt. In E. Bos & D. Segert (Eds.), *Osteuropäische Demokratien als Trendsetter? Parteien und Parteiensysteme nach dem Ende des Übergangsjahrzehnts* (pp. 77–90). Opladen and Farmington Hills: Verlag Barbara Budrich.

Blom-Hansen, J. (2005). Principals, Agents, and the Implementation of EU Cohesion Policy. *Journal of European Public Policy, 12*(4), 624–648.

Bloom, S., & Petrova, V. (2013). National Subversion of Supranational Goals: 'Pork-Barrel' Politics and EU Regional Aid. *Europe–Asia Studies, 65*(8), 1599–1620.

Bodenstein, T., & Kemmerling, A. (2011). Ripples in a Rising Tide: Why Some EU Regions Receive More Structural Funds Than Others. *European Integration Online Papers, 16*(1). http://eiop.or.at/eiop/texte/2012-001a.htm. Accessed Jan 2016.

Boeckhout, S., Boot, L., Hollanders, M., Reincke, K.-J., & De Vet, J. M. (2002). *Key Indicators for Candidate Countries to Effectively Manage the Structural Funds* (Principal Report). Rotterdam: NEI Regional and Urban Development. Available at http://www.evaluace.cz/dokumenty/hodnot_zpr_eu/souhrnna_studie.pdf. Accessed 12 Feb 2016.

Bohle, D. (2011). East European Transformations and the Paradoxes of Transnationalization. In J. DeBardeleben & A. Hurrelmann (Eds.), *Transnational Europe: Promise, Paradox, Limits* (pp. 130–151). Basingstoke: Palgrave Macmillan.

Börzel, T. A. (2000). Why There Is No 'Southern Problem': On Environmental Leaders and Laggards in the European Union. *Journal of European Public Policy, 7*(1), 141–162.

Bos, E., & Segert, D. (2008). Osteuropa als Trendsetter? Parteiensysteme in repräsentativen Demokratien unter mehrfachem Druck. In E. Bos & D. Segert (Eds.), *Osteuropäische Demokratien als Trendsetter? Parteien und Parteiensysteme nach dem Ende des Übergangsjahrzehnts* (pp. 323–336). Opladen and Farmington Hills: Verlag Barbara Budrich.

Bouvet, F., & Dall'Erba, S. (2010). European Regional Structural Funds: How Large Is the Influence of Politics on the Allocation Process? *JCMS: Journal of Common Market Studies, 48*(3), 501–528.

Buzogány, A. (2012). Accelerating or Back-Pedalling? *L'Europe en Formation* (Vol. 364, pp. 111–127). Brussels: Centre International de Formation Européenne.

Buzogány, A., & Korkut, U. (2013). Administrative Reform and Regional Development Discourses in Hungary: Europeanisation Going NUTS? *Europe–Asia Studies, 65*(8), 1555–1577.

Buzogány, A., & Stuchlík, A. (2010). Wandlungen in Kafkas Schloß? Verwaltungsreform und -Modernisierung in Mittel- und Osteuropa. In H. Hill (Ed.), *Verwaltungsmodernisierung 2010* (pp. 255–281). Baden-Baden: Nomos.

Camyar, I. (2010). Europeanization, Domestic Legacies and Administrative Reforms in Central and Eastern Europe: A Comparative Analysis of Hungary and the Czech Republic. *Journal of European Integration, 32*(2), 137–155.

Chalmers, A. W. (2013). Regional Authority, Transnational Lobbying and the Allocation of Structural Funds in the European Union. *JCMS: Journal of Common Market Studies, 51*(5), 815–831.

Connolly, R. (2010). The EU Economy: Member States Outside the Euro Area in 2009. *JCMS: Journal of Common Market Studies, 48*(Annual Review), 243–266.

Connolly, R. (2012). The Determinants of the Economic Crisis in Post-socialist Europe. *Europe–Asia Studies, 64*(1), 35–67.

Crawford, B. (1995). Post-communist Political Economy: A Framework for the Analysis of Reform. In B. Crawford (Ed.), *Markets, States, and Democracy: The Political Economy of Post-communist Transformation* (pp. 3–42). Boulder: Westview Press.

Crouch, C. (2008). What Will Follow the Demise of Privatised Keynesianism? *Political Quarterly, 79*(4), 476–487.

Deegan-Krause, K., & Haugton, T. (2010). A Fragile Stability. The Institutional Roots of Low Party System Volatility in the Czech Republic, 1990–2009. *Czech Journal of Political Science (Politologický časopis), 17*(3): 227–241.

Dellmuth, L. M. (2011). The Cash Divide: The Allocation of European Union Regional Grants. *Journal of European Public Policy, 18*(7), 1016–1033.

Dellmuth, L. M., & Stoffel, M. F. (2012). Distributive Politics and Intergovernmental Transfers: The Local Allocation of European Union Structural Funds. *European Union Politics, 13*(3), 413–433.

Dimitrov, V., Goetz, K. H., & Wollmann, H. (2006). *Governing After Communism: Institutions and Policymaking*. Lanham et al.: Rowman & Littlefield.

Dimitrova, A. L. (2002). Enlargement, Institution-Building and the EUs Administrative Capacity Requirement. *West European Politics, 25*(4), 171–190.

Dimitrova, A. L. (2005). Europeanization and Civil Service Reform in Central and Eastern Europe. In F. Schimmelfennig & U. Sedelmeier (Eds.), *The Europeanization of Central and Eastern Europe* (pp. 71–90). Ithaca, NY and London: Cornell University Press.

Dimitrova, A. L., & Steunenberg, B. (2013). Living in Parallel Universes? Implementing European Movable Cultural Heritage Policy in Bulgaria. *JCMS: Journal of Common Market Studies, 51*(2), 246–263.

Dimitrova, A. L., & Toshkov, D. (2007). The Dynamics of Domestic Coordination of EU Policy in the New Member States: Impossible to Lock In? *West European Politics, 30*(5), 961–986.

Dimitrova, A. L., & Toshkov, D. (2009). Post-accession Compliance Between Administrative Co-ordination and Political Bargaining. *European Integration Online Papers, 13*, Article 19. http://eiop.or.at/eiop/texte/2009-019a.htm. Accessed Jan 2016.

Döring, H., & Manow, P. (2014). *Parliament and Government Composition Database (ParlGov): An Infrastructure for Empirical Information on Parties, Elections and Governments in Modern Democracies*. Version 14/12–29 December 2014. Available at http://parlgov.org/. Accessed 27 Jan 2015.

Dotti, N. F. (2013). The Unbearable Instability of Structural Funds' Distribution. *European Planning Studies, 21*(4), 596–614.

Dotti, N. F. (2016). Unwritten Factors Affecting Structural Funds: The Influence of Regional Political Behaviours on the Implementation of EU Cohesion Policy. *European Planning Studies, 24*(3), 530–550.

Drevet, J.-F. (2000). Regional Policy in Central and Eastern Europe: The EU Perspective. In J. Bachtler, R. Downes, & G. Gorzelak (Eds.), *Transition Cohesion and Regional Policy in Central and Eastern Europe* (pp. 345–353). Aldershot et al.: Ashgate.

Druckman, J. N., & Roberts, A. (2007). Communist Successor Parties and Coalition Formation in Eastern Europe. *Legislative Studies Quarterly, 32*(1), 5–31.

Duverger, M. (1990). Caucus and Branch, Cadre Parties and Mass Parties. In P. Mair (Ed.), *The West European Party System* (pp. 37–45). Oxford: Oxford University Press.

Enyedi, Z. (2006). The Survival of the Fittest: Party System Concentration in Hungary. In S. Jungerstam-Mulders (Ed.), *Post-communist EU Member States: Parties and Party Systems* (pp. 177–202). Farnham and Burlington, VT: Ashgate.

European Commission. (2007). Cohesion Policy 2007–13: Commentaries and Official Texts. *European Union Regional Policy.* Brussels: European Commission, Directorate-General for Regional Policy. Available at http://ec.europa.eu/regional_policy/en/information/publications/legislation/2007/cohesion-policy-2007-13-commentaries-and-official-texts. Accessed 29 May 2017.

Falkner, G., & Treib, O. (2008). Three Worlds of Compliance or Four? The EU-15 Compared to New Member States. *JCMS: Journal of Common Market Studies, 46*(2), 293–313.

Falkner, G., Treib, O., Hartlapp, M., & Leiber, S. (2005). *Complying with Europe: EU Harmonisation and Soft Law in the Member States.* Cambridge, MA: Cambridge University Press.

Fink-Hafner, D. (2006). Slovenia: Between Bipolarity and Broad Coalition-Building. In S. Jungerstam-Mulders (Ed.), *Post-communist EU Member States: Parties and Party Systems* (pp. 203–231). Farnham and Burlington, VT: Ashgate.

Fink-Hafner, D. (2012). Slovenia. *European Journal of Political Research Political Data Yearbook, 51*(1), 288–296.

Fortin, J. (2010). A Tool to Evaluate State Capacity in Post-communist Countries, 1989–2006. *European Journal of Political Research, 49*(5), 654–686.

Frye, T. (2002). The Perils of Polarization: Economic Performance in the Postcommunist World. *World Politics, 54*(3), 308–337.

Frye, T. (2010). *Building States and Markets After Communism: The Perils of Polarized Democracy.* Cambridge: Cambridge University Press.

George, A. L., & Bennett, A. (2005). *Case Studies and Theory Development in the Social Sciences.* Cambridge, MA: MIT Press.

Gerring, J. (2008). The Mechanismic Worldview: Thinking Inside the Box. *British Journal of Political Science, 38*(1), 161–179.

Goetz, K. H. (2001). Making Sense of Post-communist Central Administration: Modernization, Europeanization or Latinization? *Journal of European Public Policy, 8*(6), 1032–1051.

Goetz, K. H., & Wollmann, H. (2001). Governmentalizing Central Executives in Post-communist Europe: A Four-Country Comparison. *Journal of European Public Policy, 8*(6), 864–887.

Grabbe, H. (2001). How Does Europeanization Affect CEE Governance? Conditionality, Diffusion and Diversity. *Journal of European Public Policy, 8*(6), 1013–1031.

Greskovits, B. (1998). *The Political Economy of Protest and Patience: East European and Latin American Transformations Compared*. Budapest: Central European University Press.

Grotz, F., & Weber, T. (2011). Regierungskoalitionen: Bildung und Dauerhaftigkeit. In F. Grotz & F. Müller-Rommel (Eds.), *Regierungssysteme in Mittel- und Osteuropa* (pp. 194–216). Wiesbaden: VS Verlag.

Grzymala-Busse, A. (2001). Coalition Formation and the Regime Divide in New Democracies: East Central Europe. *Comparative Politics, 34*(1), 85–104.

Grzymala-Busse, A. (2006). Authoritarian Determinants of Democratic Party Competition: The Communist Successor Parties in East Central Europe. *Party Politics, 12*(3), 415–437.

Grzymala-Busse, A. (2007). *Rebuilding Leviathan: Party Competition and State Exploitation in Post-communist Democracies*. Cambridge: Cambridge University Press.

Grzymala-Busse, A., & Luong, P. J. (2002). Reconceptualizing the State: Lessons from Post-communism. *Politics & Society, 30*(4), 529–554.

Haverland, M., & Romeijn, M. (2007). Do Member States Make European Policies Work? Analysing the EU Transposition Deficit. *Public Administration, 85*(3), 757–778.

Haverland, M., Steunenberg, B., & van Waarden, F. (2011). Sectors at Different Speeds: Analysing Transposition Deficits in the European Union. *JCMS: Journal of Common Market Studies, 49*(2), 265–291.

Holmes, L. (1997). *Post-communism: An Introduction*. Durham, NC: Duke University Press.

Horvat, A. (2005). *Why Does Nobody Care About the Absorption? Some Aspects Regarding Administrative Absorption Capacity for the EU Structural Funds in the Czech Republic, Estonia, Hungary, Slovakia and Slovenia Before Accession* (WIFO Working Papers). Wien: Österreichisches Institut für Wirtschaftsforschung. Available at http://www.wifo.ac.at/jart/prj3/wifo/resources/person_dokument/person_dokument.jart?publikationsid=25750&mime_type=application/pdf. Accessed 29 May 2017.

Hughes, J., Sasse, G., & Gordon, C. (2004). Conditionality and Compliance in the EU's Eastward Enlargement: Regional Policy and the Reform of Subnational Government. *JCMS: Journal of Common Market Studies, 42*(3), 523–551.

Huntington, S. P. (1993). *The Third Wave: Democratization in the Late Twentieth Century*. Norman: University of Oklahoma Press.

Ikstens, J. (2012). Latvia. *European Journal of Political Research Political Data Yearbook, 51*(1), 175–186.

Jungerstam-Mulders, S. (2006). Parties and Party Systems in Post-communist EU Member States: Comparative Aspects. In S. Jungerstam-Mulders (Ed.), *Post-communist EU Member States: Parties and Party Systems* (pp. 1–22). Farnham and Burlington, VT: Ashgate.

Katz, R. S., & Mair, P. (1995). Changing Models of Party Organization and Party Democracy: The Emergence of the Cartel Party. *Party Politics, 1*(1), 5–28.

Katz, R. S., & Mair, P. (2009). The Cartel Party Thesis: A Restatement. *Perspectives on Politics, 7*(4), 753–766.

Kickert, W., & Randma-Liiv, T. (2015). *Europe Managing the Crisis: The Politics of Fiscal Consolidation*. London: Routledge.

Kiszelly, Z. (2008). Ungarn: Auf dem Weg zum Kartellparteiensystem. In E. Bos & D. Segert (Eds.), *Osteuropäische Demokratien als Trendsetter? Parteien und Parteiensysteme nach dem Ende des Übergangsjahrzehnts* (pp. 121–132). Opladen and Farmington Hills: Verlag Barbara Budrich.

Kitschelt, H. (1995). Formation of Party Cleavages in Post-communist Democracies: Theoretical Propositions. *Party Politics, 1*(4), 447–472.

Kitschelt, H. (1999). *Post-communist Party Systems: Competition, Representation, and Inter-Party Cooperation*. Cambridge: Cambridge University Press.

Kitschelt, H. (2001). Divergent Paths of Postcommunist Democracies. In L. Diamond & R. Gunther (Eds.), *Political Parties and Democracy* (pp. 299–323). Baltimore and London: Johns Hopkins University Press.

Kitschelt, H., & Wilkinson, S. I. (2007). Citizen–Politician Linkage: An Introduction. In H. Kitschelt & S. I. Wilkinson (Eds.), *Patrons, Clients and Policies: Patterns of Democratic Accountability and Political Competition* (pp. 1–49). Cambridge: Cambridge University Press.

König, K. (1992). The Transformation of a 'Real-Socialist' Administrative System into a Conventional Western European System. *International Review of Administrative Sciences, 58*(2), 147–161.

Kopecký, P. (2006). Political Parties and the State in Post-communist Europe: The Nature of Symbiosis. *Journal of Communist Studies and Transition Politics, 22*(3), 251–273.

Kopecký, P., & Mair, P. (2012a). Conclusion: Party Patronage in Contemporary Europe. In P. Kopecký, P. Mair, & M. Spirova (Eds.), *Party Patronage and Party Government in European Democracies* (pp. 357–374). Oxford: Oxford University Press.

Kopecký, P., & Mair, P. (2012b). Party Patronage as an Organizational Resource. In P. Kopecký, P. Mair, & M. Spirova (Eds.), *Party Patronage and Party Government in European Democracies* (pp. 3–16). Oxford: Oxford University Press.

Kopecký, P., Meyer-Sahling, J.-H., Panizza, F., Scherlis, G., Schuster, C., & Spirova, M. (2016). Party Patronage in Contemporary Democracies: Results from an Expert Survey in 22 Countries from Five Regions. *European Journal of Political Research, 55*(2), 416–431.

Kopecký, P., & Spirova, M. (2011). 'Jobs for the Boys'? Patterns of Party Patronage in Post-communist Europe. *West European Politics, 34*(5), 897–921.

Kornai, J. (1995). *Das sozialistische System: Die politische Ökonomie des Kommunismus.* Baden-Baden: Nomos.

Kornai, J. (1996). Paying the Bill for Goulash Communism: Hungarian Development and Macro Stabilization in a Political-Economy Perspective. *Social Research, 63*(4), 943–1040.

Lackowska-Madurowicz, M., & Swianiewicz, P. (2013). Structures, Procedures and Social Capital: The Implementation of EU Cohesion Policies by Subnational Governments in Poland. *International Journal of Urban and Regional Research, 37*(4), 1396–1418.

Leonardi, R. (2005). *Cohesion Policy in the European Union: The Building of Europe.* Basingstoke: Palgrave Macmillan.

Linek, L. (2014). Czech Republic. *European Journal of Political Research Political Data Yearbook, 53*(1), 92–103.

Lipset, S. M., & Rokkan, S. (1967). Cleavage Structures, Party Systems, and Voter Alignments: An Introduction. In S. M. Lipset & S. Rokkan (Eds.), *Party Systems and Voter Alignments: Cross-National Perspectives* (pp. 1–64). New York: The Free Press.

LT4. (2014). *Interview in Vilnius with Lithuanian Official on 7 May 2014.*

Mahoney, J., & Goertz, G. (2006). A Tale of Two Cultures: Contrasting Quantitative and Qualitative Research. *Political Analysis, 14*(3), 227–249.

Mainwaring, S. (1999). *Rethinking Party Systems in the Third Wave of Democratization: The Case of Brazil.* Stanford: Stanford University Press.

Mainwaring, S., & Torcal, M. (2006). Party System Institutionalization and Party System Theory After the Third Wave of Democratization. In R. S. Katz & W. J. Crotty (Eds.), *Handbook of Party Politics* (pp. 204–227). London et al.: Sage.

Mainwaring, S., & Zoco, E. (2007). Political Sequences and the Stabilization of Interparty Competition: Electoral Volatility in Old and New Democracies. *Party Politics, 13*(2), 155–178.

Mair, P. (1997). *Party System Change: Approaches and Interpretations.* Cambridge: Cambridge University Press.

Maniokas, K. (2009). Conditionality and Compliance in Lithuania: The Case of the Best Performer. *European Integration Online Papers, 13*, Article 20. http://eiop.or.at/eiop/pdf/2009-020.pdf. Accessed 5 Jan 2016.

Medve-Bálint, G. (2017). Funds for the Wealthy and the Politically Loyal? How EU Funds May Contribute to Increasing Regional Disparities in East Central Europe. In J. Bachtler, P. Berkowitz, S. Hardy, & T. Muravska (Eds.), *EU Cohesion Policy: Reassessing Performance and Direction*. Abingdon: Routledge.

Meyer-Sahling, J.-H. (2004). Civil Service Reform in Post-communist Europe: The Bumpy Road to Depoliticisation. *West European Politics, 27*(1), 71–103.

Meyer-Sahling, J.-H. (2006). The Rise of the Partisan State? Parties, Patronage and the Ministerial Bureaucracy in Hungary. *Journal of Communist Studies and Transition Politics, 22*(3), 274–297.

Meyer-Sahling, J.-H. (2008). The Changing Colours of the Post-communist State: The Politicisation of the Senior Civil Service in Hungary. *European Journal of Political Research, 47*(1), 1–33.

Meyer-Sahling, J.-H. (2009a). *Sustainability of Civil Service Reforms in Central and Eastern Europe Five Years After EU Accession* (Sigma Paper No. 44). Paris: OECD. Available at http://www.oecd-ilibrary.org/governance/sustainability-of-civil-service-reforms-in-central-and-eastern-europe-five-years-after-eu-accession_5kml60pvjmbq-en. Accessed 12 Feb 2016.

Meyer-Sahling, J.-H. (2009b). Varieties of Legacies: A Critical Review of Legacy Explanations of Public Administration Reform in East Central Europe. *International Review of Administrative Sciences, 75*(3), 509–528.

Meyer-Sahling, J.-H. (2011). The Durability of EU Civil Service Policy in Central and Eastern Europe After Accession. *Governance, 24*(2), 231–260.

Meyer-Sahling, J.-H., & Veen, T. (2012). Governing the Post-communist State: Government Alternation and Senior Civil Service Politicisation in Central and Eastern Europe. *East European Politics, 28*(1), 4–22.

Mikkel, E. (2006). Patterns of Party Formation in Estonia: Consolidation Unaccomplished. In S. Jungerstam-Mulders (Ed.), *Post-communist EU Member States: Parties and Party Systems* (pp. 23–47). Farnham and Burlington, VT: Ashgate.

Milio, S. (2007). Can Administrative Capacity Explain Differences in Regional Performances? Evidence from Structural Funds Implementation in Southern Italy. *Regional Studies, 41*(4), 429–442.

Milio, S. (2008). How Political Stability Shapes Administrative Performance: The Italian Case. *West European Politics, 31*(5), 915–936.

Mungiu-Pippidi, A. (2007). Is East-Central Europe Backsliding? EU Accession Is No 'End of History'. *Journal of Democracy, 18*(4), 8–16.

Muraközy, B., & Telegdy, Á. (2016). Political Incentives and State Subsidy Allocation: Evidence from Hungarian Municipalities. *European Economic Review, 89*, 324–344.

Myant, M., & Drahokoupil, J. (2012). International Integration, Varieties of Capitalism and Resilience to Crisis in Transition Economies. *Europe–Asia Studies, 64*(1), 1–33.

Nakrošis, V., & Gudžinskas, L. (2012). Party Patronage and State Politicisation in the Post-communist Countries of Central and Eastern Europe: A Game Theory Approach. *NISPAcee Journal of Public Administration and Policy, 5*(2), 89–120.

Nunberg, B. (2000). *Ready for Europe: Public Administration Reform and European Union Accession in Central and Eastern Europe* (World Bank Technical Paper No. 466). Washington, DC: World Bank. Available at http://documents.worldbank.org/curated/en/2000/05/437136/ready-europe-public-administration-reform-european-union-accession-central-eastern-europe. Accessed 12 Feb 2016.

O'Dwyer, C. (2004). Runaway State Building; How Political Parties Shape States in Postcommunist Eastern Europe. *World Politics, 56*(4), 520–553.

O'Dwyer, C. (2006a). Reforming Regional Governance in East Central Europe: Europeanization or Domestic Politics as Usual? *East European Politics & Societies, 20*(2), 219–253.

O'Dwyer, C. (2006b). *Runaway State-Building: Patronage Politics and Democratic Development.* Baltimore: Johns Hopkins University Press.

O'Dwyer, C. (2014). What Accounts for Party System Stability? Comparing the Dimensions of Party Competition in Postcommunist Europe. *Europe-Asia Studies, 66*(4): 511–535.

Offe, C. (2004). Capitalism by Democratic Design? Democratic Theory Facing the Triple Transition in East Central Europe. *Social Research, 71*(3), 501–528.

Olejniczak, K. (2013). Mechanisms Shaping an Evaluation System—A Case Study of Poland 1999–2010. *Europe–Asia Studies, 65*(8), 1642–1666.

Olteanu, T. (2008). Rumänien: Vom Einparteiensystem zum Einheitsbrei. In E. Bos & D. Segert (Eds.), *Osteuropäische Demokratien als Trendsetter? Parteien und Parteiensysteme nach dem Ende des Übergangsjahrzehnts* (pp. 147–166). Oplanden and Farmington Hills: Verlag Barbara Budrich.

Pabriks, A., & Stokenberga, A. (2006). Political Parties and the Party System in Latvia. In S. Jungerstam-Mulders (Ed.), *Post-communist EU Member States: Parties and Party Systems* (pp. 51–67). Farnham and Burlington, VT: Ashgate.

Pedersen, M. N. (1979). The Dynamics of European Party Systems: Changing Patterns of Electoral Volatility. *European Journal of Political Research, 7*(1), 1–26.

Piattoni, S. (2001). Clientelism in Historical and Comparative Perspective. In S. Piattoni (Ed.), *Clientelism, Interests, and Democratic Representation: The European Experience in Historical and Comparative Perspective* (pp. 1–30). Cambridge: Cambridge University Press.

Piattoni, S., & Smyrl, M. (2003). Building Effective Institutions: Italian Regions and the EU Structural Funds. In J. Bukowski, S. Piattoni, & M. Smyrl (Eds.), *Between Europeanization and Local Societies: The Space for Territorial Governance* (pp. 133–156). Lanham et al.: Rowman & Littlefield.

Pop-Eleches, G. (2010). Throwing Out the Bums: Protest Voting and Unorthodox Parties After Communism. *World Politics, 62*(2), 221–260.

Popa, A. (2012). The Impact of the Structural Funds in the Transformation Process of the New EU Member States. *L'Europe en Formation* (Vol. 364, pp. 161–179). Brussels: Centre International de Formation Européenne.

Przeworski, A. (1995). *Sustainable Democracy*. Cambridge: Cambridge University Press.

Ragin, C. C. (1987). *The Comparative Method: Moving Beyond Qualitative and Quantitative Strategies*. Berkeley et al.: University of California Press.

Ragin, C. C. (2000). *Fuzzy-Set Social Science*. Chicago: University of Chicago Press.

Ragin, C. C. (2008a). Qualitative Comparative Analysis Using Fuzzy Sets (fsQCA). In B. Rihoux & C. C. Ragin (Eds.), *Configurational Comparative Methods: Qualitative Comparative Analysis (QCA) and Related Techniques* (Vol. 51, pp. 87–121). London et al.: Sage.

Ragin, C. C. (2008b). *Redesigning Social Inquiry: Set Relations in Social Research*. Chicago: University of Chicago Press.

Ramonaite, A. (2006). The Development of the Lithuanian Party System: From Stability to Perturbation. In S. Jungerstam-Mulders (Ed.), *Post-communist EU Member States: Parties and Party Systems* (pp. 69–90). Farnham and Burlington, VT: Ashgate.

Rohlfing, I. (2012). *Case Studies and Causal Inference: An Integrative Framework*. Basingstoke: Palgrave Macmillan.

Roper, S. D. (2006). The Influence of Party Patronage and State Finance on Electoral Outcomes: Evidence from Romania. *Journal of Communist Studies and Transition Politics, 22*(3), 362–382.

Rouban, L. (2003). Politicization of the Civil Service. In B. G. Peters & J. Pierre (Eds.), *Handbook of Public Administration* (pp. 310–320). London et al.: Sage.

Rybar, M. (2006). Old Parties and New: Changing Patterns of Party Politics in Slovakia. In S. Jungerstam-Mulders (Ed.), *Post-communist EU Member States: Parties and Party Systems* (pp. 147–176). Farnham and Burlington, VT: Ashgate.

Rynck, S. D., & McAleavey, P. (2001). The Cohesion Deficit in Structural Fund Policy. *Journal of European Public Policy, 8*(4), 541–557.

Sagemann, B., & Reese, P. (2011). The Great Subprime Credit Crisis and Its Impact on Eastern Europe. In J. Jungmann & B. Sagemann (Eds.), *Financial Crisis in Eastern Europe* (pp. 21–63). Wiesbaden: Gabler Verlag.

Schimmelfennig, F., & Sedelmeier, U. (2005a). Conclusions. The Impact of the EU on the Accession Countries. In F. Schimmelfennig & U. Sedelmeier (Eds.), *The Europeanization of Central and Eastern Europe* (pp. 210–228). Ithaca, NY: Cornell University Press.

Schimmelfennig, F., & Sedelmeier, U. (2005b). Introduction. Conceptualizing the Europeanization of Central and Eastern Europe. In F. Schimmelfennig & U. Sedelmeier (Eds.), *The Europeanization of Central and Eastern Europe* (pp. 1–28). Ithaca, NY: Cornell University Press.

Schneider, C. Q., & Rohlfing, I. (2013). Combining QCA and Process Tracing in Set-Theoretic Multi-method Research. *Sociological Methods & Research, 42*(4), 559–597.

Schneider, C. Q., & Rohlfing, I. (2016). Case Studies Nested in Fuzzy-Set QCA on Sufficiency: Formalizing Case Selection and Causal Inference. *Sociological Methods & Research, 45*(3), 526–568.

Schneider, C. Q., & Wagemann, C. (2012). *Set-Theoretic Methods for the Social Sciences: A Guide to Qualitative Comparative Analysis*. Cambridge: Cambridge University Press.

Schraff, D. (2014). Buying Turnout or Rewarding Loyalists? Electoral Mobilization and EU Structural Funding in the German Länder. *European Union Politics, 15*(2), 277–288.

Sedelmeier, U. (2008). After Conditionality: Post-accession Compliance with EU Law in East Central Europe. *Journal of European Public Policy, 15*(6), 806–825.

Sedelmeier, U. (2012). Is Europeanisation Through Conditionality Sustainable? Lock-in of Institutional Change After EU Accession. *West European Politics, 35*(1), 20–38.

Segert, D. (2008). Parteien und Transformation in Osteuropa nach dem Ende des Übergangsjahrzehnts. In E. Bos & D. Segert (Eds.), *Osteuropäische Demokratien als Trendsetter? Parteien und Parteiensysteme nach dem Ende des Übergangsjahrzehnts* (pp. 11–32). Opladen and Farmington Hills: Verlag Barbara Budrich.

SGI. (2014a). Policy Performance and Governance Capacities in the OECD and EU. *Sustainable Governance Indicators*. Gütersloh: Bertelsmann Stiftung. Available at https://www.bertelsmann-stiftung.de/fileadmin/files/BSt/Publikationen/GrauePublikationen/Policy_Performance_and_Governance_Capacities_SGI2014_Overview.pdf. Accessed 29 May 2017.

SGI. (2014b). *Sustainable Governance Indicators 2014 Codebook*. Available at http://www.bertelsmann-stiftung.de/bst/en/media/xcms_bst_dms_37442__2.pdf. Accessed 24 Sept 2014.

Šipikal, M. (2014). *Political and Administrative Barriers of Cohesion Policy Implementation in Slovakia*. Paper Presented at the Conference of the Regional Studies Association 4 June 2014, Prague, 05.06.2014.

Spirova, M., & Kolarova, R. (2010). Bulgaria. *European Journal of Political Research, 49*(7–8), 909–918.

Stark, D. (1990). Privatization in Hungary: From Plan to Market or From Plan to Clan? *Eastern European Politics and Societies, 4*(3), 351–392.

Stone, R. W. (2002). *Lending Credibility: The International Monetary Fund and the Post-communist Transition*. Princeton: Princeton University Press.

Surubaru, N.-C. (2017a). Administrative Capacity or Quality of Political Governance? EU Cohesion Policy in the New Europe, 2007–13. *Regional Studies, 51*(6), 844–856.

Surubaru, N.-C. (2017b). Revisiting the Role of Domestic Politics: Politicisation and European Cohesion Policy Performance in Central and Eastern Europe. *East European Politics, 33*(1), 106–125.

Tiemann, G. (2008). Cleavages' oder, Legacies'? Die Institutionalisierung und Struktur des politischen Wettbewerbs im postsozialistischen Osteuropa. In E. Bos & D. Segert (Eds.), *Osteuropäische Demokratien als Trendsetter? Parteien und Parteiensysteme nach dem Ende des Übergangsjahrzehnts* (pp. 33–53). Opladen and Farmington Hills: Verlag Barbara Budrich.

Tosun, J. (2014). Absorption of Regional Funds: A Comparative Analysis. *JCMS: Journal of Common Market Studies, 52*(2), 371–387.

Trauner, F. (2009). Post-accession Compliance with EU Law in Bulgaria and Romania: A Comparative Perspective. *European Integration Online Papers, 13*, Article 21. http://eiop.or.at/eiop/pdf/2009-021.pdf. Accessed Jan 2016.

van Biezen, I. (2003). *Political Parties in New Democracies: Party Organization in Southern and East-Central Europe*. Basingstoke: Palgrave Macmillan.

van Biezen, I. (2005). On the Theory and Practice of Party Formation and Adaptation in New Democracies. *European Journal of Political Research, 44*(1), 147–174.

Van Evera, S. (1997). *Guide to Methods for Students of Political Science*. Ithaca, NY: Cornell University Press.

Vanhuysse, P. (2006). *Divide and Pacify: Strategic Social Policies and Political Protests in Post-communist Democracies*. Budapest: Central European University Press.

Varnagy, R. (2011). Hungary. *European Journal of Political Research, 50*(7–8), 991–998.

Verheijen, A. J. G. (2000). *Administrative Capacity Development: A Race Against Time?* (Working Documents W 107). The Hague: Scientific Council for Government Policy. Available at http://www.wrr.nl/fileadmin/nl/publicaties/DVD_WRR_publicaties_1972-2004/W107_Administrative_capacity_development.pdf. Accessed 12 Feb 2016.

Verheijen, T. (1999). Civil Service Systems in EU Candidate States: Introduction. In T. Verheijen & A. Kotchegura (Eds.), *Civil Service Systems in Central and Eastern Europe* (pp. 85–91). Cheltenham: Edward Elgar.

Verheijen, T. (2007). *Administrative Capacity in the New EU Member States: The Limits of Innovation?* (World Bank Working Paper No. 115). Washington, DC: World Bank. Available at http://elibrary.worldbank.org/doi/abs/10.1596/978-0-8213-7155-8. Accessed 12 Feb 2016.

Wasilewski, J. (1990). The Patterns of Bureaucratic Elite Recruitment in Poland in the 1970s and 1980s. *Soviet Studies, 42*(4), 743–757.

Way, L. A., & Levitsky, S. (2007). Linkage, Leverage, and the Post-communist Divide. *East European Politics & Societies, 21*(1), 48–66.

Whitefield, S. (2002). Political Cleavages and Post-communist Politics. *Annual Review of Political Science, 5*(1), 181–200.

Zubek, R. (2005). Complying with Transposition Commitments in Poland: Collective Dilemmas, Core Executive and Legislative Outcomes. *West European Politics, 28*(3), 592–619.

CHAPTER 4

The Conditions for Absorption Problems in Central and Eastern Europe

4.1 Overview: The Conditions for Absorption Problems

The first empirical application of the theoretical framework is a fuzzy-set Qualitative Comparative Analysis (fsQCA). QCA excels in testing regular patterns of necessity and sufficiency between causal conditions and an outcome. These take the form of a distinct superset–subset-relationship between a condition and the outcome (necessity), and the outcome and a combination of conditions (sufficiency). In order to conduct the analysis, it is essential to select comparable cases, to operationalize and calibrate the conditions and the outcome in a transparent manner, and finally proceed to minimization (Schneider and Wagemann 2007: 64).

A total of 17 Operational Programmes (OPs) in all ten CEE member states of the EU are identified as relevant cases. The selected programmes share important traits (large allocation of funds, managed at the central level, mainly public beneficiaries, realizing large infrastructure projects) and cover almost half of all funds allocated to CEE (45.6%) during the financing period.[1] The programmes are thus both reasonably comparable as well as empirically relevant (see Sect. 4.2 for a detailed discussion of case selection). OPs are here the selected unit of analysis because cohesion policy implementation is managed at the programme-level, and absorption levels vary not only among, but also within countries at this level.

[1] Own calculation based on EC data, see Appendix III.

C. Hagemann, *EU Funds in the New Member States*, Palgrave Studies in European Union Politics,
https://doi.org/10.1007/978-3-030-02092-7_4

Calibration and operationalization are then important to create a data matrix and a truth table for analysis. The explanatory factors derived from the literature are firstly turned into conditions, thus sets with a distinct membership threshold. In order to define membership in these sets, it must be clear as to how they are measured (operationalization), and at what threshold cases are considered members of a set (e.g. Rihoux and De Meur 2009: 42). The process of assigning membership values in the causal conditions to the cases studied is called calibration (Schneider and Wagemann 2012: 32). The causal conditions considered in this analysis are 'low executive capacity', 'islands of excellence', 'centralized management structures', 'frequent party alternation', and 'severe crisis'.

The complexity of measuring the conditions varies strongly. In order to determine management structures, it was merely necessary to take a look at OPs' programming documents. Measuring capacity as 'low executive capacity' or 'islands of excellence' requires a well-founded choice of indicator, but data is then readily available in the form of the Sustainable Governance Indicator's (SGI) Executive Capacity measure (SGI 2014a, b) and Bachtler and colleagues' (2014: 741) review of capacity in the earlier financing period. In contrast, measuring the trigger of politicization as 'frequent party alternation' at the level of ministries is more complex. First, it must be established from the programming documents which ministries were actually involved in the management and control systems of the OPs. Then, all changes of parties at the level of these ministries are traced for the whole 2007–2013 period. Changes are counted for every party alternation and standardized by the number of ministries involved, where applicable.[2] The same process of detailed operationalization and calibration based on quantitative and qualitative sources was also conducted for the outcome 'absorption problems' (Sect. 4.3).

Overall, operationalization and calibration decisions are discussed in detail in Sects. 4.3 and 4.4. I decided to apply a 'qualitative' or 'conservative' strategy of calibration with a four-value fuzzy scale (0, 0.33, 0.67, 1) (Ragin and Rihoux 2008: 90; Emmenegger 2011). Calibration decisions are based on a triangulation of external information combined with observations of the empirical distribution of cases and prominent

[2] This means that the number of changes in a particular year was divided by the total number of ministries involved in the programme in cases where more than one ministry was involved in OP implementation.

gaps highlighting qualitative differences between them (Schneider and Wagemann 2012: 33–35). The result of this process is displayed in the data matrix in Table 4.6.

Ultimately, the data matrix is converted into a truth table and all conditions are tested for necessity and sufficiency for the outcome of absorption problems (Sect. 4.5). It is found that 'low executive capacity' comes close to but ultimately fails the test of being a necessary condition for 'absorption problems'. This finding thus agrees with the literature's general stress on capacity for absorption. Nevertheless, the importance of capacity is limited in this study, as it is also not sufficient for the outcome. It further needs 'frequent party alternation' and the absence of 'centralized management' to result in absorption problems. It is thus concluded from the fsQCA that the most relevant impact on absorption problems in CEE stems from capacities as well as domestic politics.

4.2 Case Selection: A Comparison of the Region's Largest Operational Programmes

Many studies have already used the absorption rate as the outcome of the cohesion policy implementation process (Noetzel and Stumm 1997: 13–14; Milio 2007: 430; Markovic Hribernik et al. 2008: 1223; Milio 2008, 2010a; Huszák 2010: 26; Lackowska-Madurowicz and Swianiewicz 2013: 1403; Tosun 2014: 373–374). Still, the question is, which absorption rate should be used, because different temporal, spatial, and programmatical choices are possible. The next paragraph elaborates in detail why the absorption rate at the end of 2013 at the level of OPs was selected as the outcome. It is then further explained why the focus of this fsQCA rests on those OPs in CEE focusing on the implementation of big transport and environmental infrastructure as cases of the analysis.

4.2.1 How Is the Outcome Measured?

The outcome is measured as the absorption rate at the end of the financing period on 31 December 2013 at the level of OPs. This measurement has distinct advantages in comparison to alternative points in time or levels of analysis.

There are at least three different ways of how paid funds can be used as the outcome. First, one can take the annual absorption rate of every member state during the financing period as the outcome. This makes it possible to trace both variances between member states as well as variation over time. In addition, there is clearly variance over time in member states' absorption records, showing especially that many of them are more successful towards the end of the period. Still, this does not necessarily ensure that success in policy implementation varies along these lines. For many programmes, development and execution begin much earlier than the moment the actual payment takes place. A particular year might look extremely successful, even though the previous year was the one when the project was executed, but no payment made. The amount of interim payments received is furthermore not only dependent on the claims from the member states, but also dependent on the financial resources within the EC. If funds are used up for one year, payments will be made only in the following year (Bubbico and De Michelis 2011: 2). As a third critical aspect, the EC stresses that there are also cyclical elements in the absorption of funds that can be detected in every financing period:

> [T]he first years of 2000-2006 featured low absorption rates followed by increasing yearly expenditure in the central and final years of implementation. This stage is followed by the closure of the programmes, with significantly lower absorption due to closure procedures. (Bubbico and De Michelis 2011: 3)

Thus, an increase in absorption does not necessarily mean that programmes are performing better than at an earlier point in time, as payments are not "real-time or pertinent indicators" (Bubbico and De Michelis 2011: 1).

A second possibility to construct the outcome is to take member states as the unit of analysis and the absorption rate at the end of 2013 to measure the outcome. On the one hand, this has the advantage that it omits the possible problem of period effects or extensive projects as it presents a single snapshot of implementation success. On the other hand, however, it conceals variation of programme success at the level of the member states. Some member states feature programmes that resemble considerable outliers in both success and failure in the context of their country (see Sect. 4.3). This stresses the fact that there might be factors at the level of single programmes that have a strong influence on implementation success and failure. In addition, it stresses the possible importance of equifinality in the context of cohesion policy implementation. This means that there could be different conditions or combinations of conditions that could account for the same result of successful implementation.

Therefore, to be able to detect possible explanations for variance at the programme level, I chose a third strategy of comparing the absorption rates at the level of OPs at the end of 2013. In this way, both problems of non-comparability of intertemporal variance as well as the occurence of intra-country variance are accounted for. Still, one caveat has to be stressed: The end of the financing period is not equivalent to the end of the absorption period, funds could still be used until the end of 2015. Nevertheless, the focus on implementation in the CEE member states after the seven-year period until 2013 offers a reasonable timeframe to establish qualitative differences between their performance levels and detect those cases with absorption problems. This is also in line with practices in other studies comparing absorption rates before the payment of the final balance and the end of the absorption period (Huszák 2010; Tosun 2014).

4.2.2 *How Are Comparable Cases Selected?*

A thematical differentiation between OPs was made in order to select the cases. The OPs considered as cases in this study are all in the area of environmental and transport policy. These OPs share a range of characteristics making them suitable for a comparison. In set-theoretic terms, all of these programmes lie at the intersection of the sets of big programmes, programmes that aim at the creation of big infrastructure, programmes with a majority of public beneficiaries, and programmes that are centrally managed (see Table 4.1).

First, programmes are considered to be big if they cover a major share of funds available to a member state. As the number of OPs differs strongly between member states, the coverage of funds by a specific OP also varies. In the Baltic states, a coverage of almost half of all funds is rather the norm (resulting in an overall number of 2–3 OPs). In contrast, the biggest programmes in Romania cover hardly a quarter of all funds each (which is still a lot when considering seven programmes overall). Thus, the definition of 'big programmes' is rather broad here, but they all cover at least 20% of the general allocation to a country. Overall,

Table 4.1 Characteristics of OPs considered as cases in the analysis

Case	*OP's share of total convergence funding*[a] *(%)*	*Share invested in large infrastructure*[b] *(%)*	*National programme(MA)*[c]
ESTEE	42.99	43.5	Ministry of Finance
LTC	39.41	42.6	Ministry of Finance
ESTLE	45.51	48.24	Ministry of Finance
LTEG	45.42	54.1	Ministry of Finance
CZT	28.1	98.6	Ministry of Transport
LVIS	71.76	47.58	Ministry of Finance
PLIE	42.18	92.1	Ministry of Regional Development
BGT	24.34	96.5	Ministry of Transport
HUT	29.2	98.6	National Development Agency
SKE	20.93	93.44	Ministry of Environment
SKT	36.35	98.5	Ministry of Transport, Post, and Communication
ROT	22.5	98	Ministry of Transport
CZE	23.74	82.8	Ministry of Environment
SIET	38.1	98.18	Government Office for Local Self-Government and Regional Policy
HUEE	23.15	88.49	National Development Agency
ROE	23.15	87.3	Ministry of Environment
BGE	21.97	91.3	Ministry of Environment and Water

Note [a]Most countries receive only convergence funding and for all it is by far the biggest share of the total allocation. Thus, these numbers are also mostly representative of the total share of funds available. [b]These include railway infrastructure, road infrastructure (TEN-T and others), maritime infrastructure, intermodal transport infrastructure, public transport, water management infrastructure (drinking water supply and wastewater treatment), waste management infrastructure, energy efficiency and renewable energy sources, flood protection and water reserves
Source [a,b]Own calculation based on EC data (see Appendix III). [c]See Table 4.3 for sources

the 17 programmes considered in this study cover almost half of all convergence funds (45.6%) available for the CEE countries in the 2007–2013 period.

Second, the projects to be funded are very similar among these programmes, making implementation patterns more comparable. Both environmental and transport interventions most often require the creation of large infrastructure. These mostly major projects often take much longer to develop and implement than smaller ones, making a comparison with another programme, for example supporting business futile. Thus, the types of projects covered by the OPs under scrutiny are comparable among the OPs considered in this analysis.

Still, the share of large projects varies among OPs. Column 2 in Table 4.1 presents the share of funds of an OP covered by priority axes (PAs) that include mainly investments in big infrastructure. The pattern shows that while the pure transport programmes devote almost all available funds to such projects (the remaining small share is usually assigned to technical assistance), the programmes in the Baltic states are much more heterogeneous and also focus on smaller or different projects. One possibility for dealing with this issue would be to exclude the Baltic programmes altogether as they are qualitatively different from their counterparts. Still, such an extreme measure does not make sense until it is clear whether the infrastructure measures included in the OPs perform in any way differently from the general OPs. It is thus worth considering the progress of these OPs at the level of their different PAs in order to determine whether or not there are large differences between these PAs and the general absorption rate that would justify an exclusion of the Baltic cases. Overall, it seems that there is hardly any difference.

Considering the progress at the level of PAs, all three Baltic states are equally successful in the absorption of funds for big projects as suggested by their overall success. Estonian OP Economic Environment features high rates both in PA3 'Transport Investments of Strategic Importance' (64.9%) and PA4 'Development of Regional Transport Infrastructure' (80.7%), with both values already reached in May 2013 (Kalvet 2013: 36). The same is true for Estonian OP Living Environment, where PA1 'Development of Water and Waste Management Infrastructure' (55%), PA2 'Development of Infrastructure and Support Systems for Sustainable Uses of the Environment' (68.7%), and PA3 'Development of the Energy Sector' (93%) all show high absorption rates, also already in May 2013 (Kalvet 2013: 36). Lithuanian OP Cohesion also succeeds in the absorption of funds in PA3 'Environment and Sustainable Development' (57% by Ministry of Environment that receives the bulk of funds), whereas the Lithuanian OP 'Economic Growth' used its funds well in the PA4 'Basic Economic Infrastructure' (83% by Ministry of Transport) and PA5 'Development of Trans-European Transport Network' (53%). Both Lithuanian programmes achieved these levels already at the end of 2012 (Maniokas and Miseliuniene 2013: 40).

Considering Latvia, the latest data available at the level of PAs is only on 31 July 2012. The two relevant PAs in the OP Infrastructure and Services, PA3 'Development of Transport Network of European Significance' and PA5 'Promotion of Environmental Infrastructure' reached both 37.4 and 54.5%, respectively, with equally large shares of the total sum. This falls around the general Latvian absorption rate at of 47% at this point in time (Vanags and Skruzkalne 2012: 26–27), and therefore also does not point towards a completely different development than in the rest of the OP. In sum, the well-performing PAs including big infrastructure projects are broadly in line with the generally successful absorption performance of the Baltic states. Thus, they are considered as cases in this analysis.

Third, the projects considered here mainly have public beneficiaries. This means that the question of capacity is also relevant for beneficiaries, as projects will be developed mainly by public actors. Also, the access to financing will be much more homogenous in contrast to OPs featuring only private beneficiaries.

Finally, all of these OPs are managed at the central level. The responsible MA is usually a sectoral ministry, or a ministry responsible for all OPs (mostly a Ministry of Finance or a Ministry of Regional Development). The list of respective ministries acting as MAs can be found in the fourth column of Table 4.1. The management of OPs is thus homogenous enough to be reasonably comparable, as it does not include programmes which are managed at the regional level.[3]

Overall, the focus on programmes sharing the mentioned characteristics yields a total of 17 cases, selected from all 47 convergence OPs in the region. The total list of convergence OPs and their allocation of funds is displayed in Appendix III. The selected OPs are:

- OP Environment (Bulgaria) (BGE)
- OP Transport (Bulgaria) (BGT)
- OP Environment (Czech Republic) (CZE)
- OP Transport (Czech Republic) (CZT)
- OP for the Development of the Economic Environment (Estonia) (ESTEE)

[3] Such programmes are rare in CEE anyway.

- OP for the Development of the Living Environment (Estonia) (ESTLE)
- OP Environment and Energy (Hungary) (HUEE)
- OP Transport (Hungary) (HUT)
- OP Infrastructure and Services (Latvia) (LVIS)
- OP for the Promotion of Cohesion (Lithuania) (LTC)
- OP for Economic Growth (Lithuania) (LTEG)
- OP Infrastructure and Environment (Poland) (PLIE)
- OP Environment (Romania) (ROE)
- OP Transport (Romania) (ROT)
- OP Environment (Slovakia) (SKE)
- OP Transport (Slovakia) (SKT)
- OP Environment and Transport Infrastructure Development (Slovenia) (SIET)

4.3 Operationalization and Calibration of the Outcome 'Absorption Problems'

The outcome is measured as the share of interim payments received by an OP at the end of the financing period in 2013 (as elaborated in detail in Sect. 4.2). The question of which OP can be considered a successful absorber of EU money is then first of all a quantitative question. Bachtler et al. (2014: 743) stress three quantitative indicators for performance: the absorption rate, the correspondence between planned and de facto implementation, and the occurrence of decommitments. Still, this quantitative data is ideally substantiated with more qualitative information such as expert evaluations of OPs' performance in order to reach a meaningful calibration of the outcome.

First, when it comes to the quantitative data, the amount of interim payments absorbed by a respective OP is the central criterion for membership in the set 'absorption problems'. It is difficult to determine what level of absorption should be considered successful at the end of the financing period (2013), but not at the end of the absorption period (2015). Taking into account the official plans of member states provides little help, as generally 100% of funds are allocated until 31 December 2013 (e.g. BG 2007b: 132–133; SK 2007a: 133). The difference between the absorption rate at this point in time and the planned allocation would therefore always be the difference between the current absorption rate and the total allocation of funds, i.e. as such not include more information than the absorption rate on its own. Therefore, another strategy seems more promising: that of putting the absorption rates of the cases considered here into the context of the general performance of member states.

This strategy considers what could be reasonably expected to be absorbed until the end of the financing period. It therefore safeguards against unreasonably high expectations which could not be fulfilled by any member state. Overall, the EU27 average rate of interim payments within the convergence objective is 56.23% at the end of 2013. This is quite close to the overall EU27 average rate of interim payments which is 57.92%.[4] The average performance of all EU member states was thus between 50 and 60%. Applying this average to our selected OPs, only those in Estonia and Lithuania manage to perform above this average. A second group, however, formed by Czech OP Transport, Latvian OP Infrastructure and Services, Polish OP Infrastructure and Environment, and the Bulgarian OP Transport is rather close to this rate, all featuring more than 50% funds absorbed. The next OP below this is the Hungarian OP Transport with a rate of 42.82%, which is already a large gap compared to the Bulgarian OP Transport (50.83%). I thus use this empirical gap between OPs' absorption rates as a relevant qualitative difference for calibration (for a similar justification of calibration decisions see for example Emmenegger 2011).

This decision must be substantiated by the other characteristics of successful absorption mentioned above. In general, decommitments are the ultimate measure of OP failure. The *N*+rule entails that funds can only be spent in the next two or three years following the year they were committed (see Sect. 2.1 for a detailed discussion). If a member state fails to use the money in this time frame, it is ultimately lost. Until the end of 2013, the Romanian OP Transport and Czech OP Environment were the programmes included in the sample losing the highest amount of funds. The Romanian OP Transport lost a hefty EUR 137.8 million in 2013 (European Commission 2013a: 54), while Czech OP Environment lost EUR 274 million in the same year (CZ6 2015), which is even a lot taking into account a total allocation of around EUR 4000 million. In a similar vein, also the Bulgarian OP Environment suffered from losses (see Table 4.2 and Sect. 2.2).

[4] Own calculation based on EC data, see Appendix III.

Table 4.2 Calibration of 'absorption problems' in 17 operational programmes

Case	*Absorption rate*	*Implementation problems*[a]	*Expert evaluation*	*EC strategic report 2013*	*Set 'absorption problems'*
ESTEE	77.90	–	Positive	Positive mentioning	0
LTC	69.35	–	"Lithuania among the best absorbers in the EU"	Positive mentioning	0
ESTLE	68.50	–	Positive	Positive mentioning	0
LTEG	67.50	–	"Lithuania among the best absorbers in the EU"	Positive mentioning	0
CZT	54.61	–	"risky"	Risky/positive outlier	0.33
LVIS	53.49	–	"good progress overall"	Not mentioned	0.33
PLIE	53.20	–	"In line with plans except for railways"	Not mentioned	0.33
BGT	50.83	–	"largest value of contracted and paid funds"	Risky/positive outlier	0.33
HUT	42.82	2011 (reallocation)	"slowed down by irregularities, high contracting but slow implementation"	Risky	0.67
SKE	41.85	2011, 2012 (exemption)	"difficulties with procurement"	Risky	0.67
SKT	37.04	2011, 2012 (exemption)	"serious problems"	Risky	0.67
ROT	32.24	2011, 2012 (exemption) 2013 (decomm.)	"far behind planning, decommitment risk high"	Risky	1
CZE	32.90	2013 (attempt. realloc.) 2013 (decomm.)	"poor performance, loss expected, anti-crisis taskforce"	Risky	1
SIET	30.51	2011 (reallocation)	"still not satisfactory, loss of funds likely"	Not mentioned/negative outlier	1

(continued)

Table 4.2 (continued)

Case	*Absorption rate*	*Implementation problems*[a]	*Expert evaluation*	*EC strategic report 2013*	*Set 'absorption problems'*
HUEE	29.83	–	"most critical in terms of payments"	Risky	1
ROE	26.69	2011, 2012 (exemption)	"far behind planning, decommitment risk high"	Risky	1
BGE	14.05	2013 (decomm.)	"delayed implementation, danger of decommitment"	Risky	1

Note [a]'Implementation problems' refers to reallocations of funds to save money from decommitment, the granting of an official exemption from decommitment by the EC for a certain year, and finally the occurrence of decommitment in a certain year

Source The author's compilation based on EC reports (European Commission 2013a: 10, 2013b: 54, 2014: 57) and the Expert Evaluation Network's Annual Evaluation Reports (Balas and Kiss 2011: 16; Balas et al. 2012: 9, 11; Blažek 2012: 8–11; Frank 2012: 12; Kalvet 2012: 3; Lucaciu 2012: 12–13; Maniokas and Miseliuniene 2012: 3; Minena et al. 2012: 9; Vanags and Skruzkalne 2012: 7; Blažek 2013: 11; Frank 2013: 11; Kavas 2012: 8; Shalov and Stefanov 2013: 4; Gorzelak and Kozak 2013: 13; Kavas 2013: 4, 15)

Still, the occurrence of decommitments before the complete end of the absorption period at the end of 2015 was overall rather unlikely. Member states could try to avoid decommitments by reallocating funds from a problematic OP to one whose absorption performance was better. This refers to Bachtler et al.'s third quantitative indicator, the match between planned and de facto implementation. Column three in Table 4.2 shows that reallocations with the intention to save funds occurred in three of the eight OPs with an absorption rate below 50%. In contrast, none of those OPs above this threshold faced any attempts of reallocation to save funds.[5] The fact that not all underperforming OPs experienced reallocations is most likely linked to the fact that reallocations only make sense if a programme is an outlier in a member state. If this is not the case, for example because all OPs are underperforming,

[5]The only further reallocation mentioned in the EEN reports concerned the Estonian OP Living Environment. This reallocation, however, was not a measure to save funds from decommitment, but rather aimed to tackle the changed demand for funds for enterprise support (Kalvet 2011: 8).

it is unlikely that reallocations take place as the money wouldn't be saved through this move anyway.

Furthermore, the likelihood of decommitments was also reduced by the EC itself. It granted some member states exemptions from the *N+2* rule in order to enable them to make use of all of their funds (Romania and Slovakia) (Frank 2013: 9; RO 2014: 35). It is thus also less likely to find decommitments in these cases, which were granted more time to absorb the money. Still, an exemption from the decommitment rules should nevertheless be seen as another sign of weak performance of an OP. Overall, at least one of the aspects indicating absorption problems was found in every OP considered as member of the set 'absorption problems' (below the 50% threshold) but in the Hungarian OP Environment and Energy, which was still mentioned as "at high risk of de-commitments" (Balas et al. 2013: 4). In contrast, these characteristics were conspicuously absent in the other, successful cases. All three indicators (decommitment, reallocation, exemption from *N+2*) for absorption problems are displayed in column 2 of Table 4.2.

Second, in order to further substantiate the calibration decision, I used qualitative information in the form of expert evaluations on the performance of the OPs. On the one hand, I decided to include the regular evaluations provided by the EC's country experts on cohesion policy (Expert Evaluation Network, or EEN). Every time an OP from the sample was mentioned in these reports, for example as 'underperforming', 'risky', or 'behind schedule', this information was collected and included in the table. The same was done with positive characterizations of OPs. In addition, there is also information from the EC itself on absorption problems. The Commission stressed in its Annual Activity Report 2013 that some member states were seriously endangered by the loss of funds (European Commission 2013b). This is equally useful information; however, it must be qualified as it is not provided at the level of the OPs but the member state in general. Whereas it is likely that most OPs in a 'risky' member state will face absorption problems, there is a chance that positive or negative outliers at the level of OPs will have more or less problems than the respective country's average. The information of the EC that a certain country is in danger of losing funds must thus be brought in line with the performance of the given OP in its domestic context.

Columns three and four of Table 4.2 summarize the qualitative information. Overall, the expert and EC evaluations almost perfectly match the cut-off point at 50% of absorbed funds. All but one negative Expert Evaluation Network (EEN) statement focus on the OPs below the 50% absorption threshold. At the same time, none of the OPs below this threshold is evaluated positively by the country experts. Furthermore, also the EC's evaluation of member states' absorption status as 'risky' clearly falls into the two camps. Most importantly, those cases which do not match the divide at the country level can be sorted out easily at the OP level (i.e. at the level which is relevant here). The only deviation from this in a positive sense are the Czech and Bulgarian transport programmes, which are members of the more successful group, even though these countries were criticized for their low absorption rate (European Commission 2013b: 10). Taking a closer look at the implementation rate of these programmes in contrast to their national average, however, reveals that they are outliers in their national contexts, as their absorption rates are 12.11 (Czech OP) and 8.13 (Bulgarian OP) percentage points above their national rate. It therefore makes sense to assume that these OPs are not endangered in the same way as the other programmes in these countries are, as they are way above these countries' averages. Still, there is also a negative example. The Slovenian OP Environment and Transport Infrastructure has one of the lowest absorption rates in the sample (30.51%), even though Slovenia was not mentioned in a critical way by the EC. Again, taking a closer look at the status of this programme in comparison to its national peers reveals that it is an outlier in a negative sense, underperforming the national average absorption rate by 22.89 percentage points (see Appendix III). Thus, also the EC's evaluation matches the calibration threshold very well.

In sum, the calibration of the set 'absorption problems' at the cut-off point of 50% of funds absorbed matches rather well both quantitative and qualitative indicators of absorption performance. Still, it nevertheless makes sense to further differentiate the groups as there are also intra-group differences. In the group of rather successful absorbers, there is a gap between those cases with an absorption rate of above 60%, which are thus full non-members (0), and those below 60%, which are assigned partial non-membership (0.33). Also, the members of the set absorption problems can be further differentiated. The Hungarian OP Transport and two Slovak programmes are rather close together and cluster around an absorption rate of 40%. They are therefore partial members of the set 'absorption problems' (0.67). In contrast, the other programmes have all absorbed just around 30% of their funds, sometimes even dramatically less. These programmes are thus all full members of the set 'absorption problems' (1). Fuzzy set-membership values are summarized in column five in Table 4.2. Overall, nine cases are (partial) members of the set 'absorption problems', while the remaining eight cases are (partial) non-members.

4.4 Operationalization and Calibration of Five Causal Conditions

4.4.1 *The Condition 'Executive Capacity'*

Measuring administrative and government capacity for absorption has focussed mostly on the detailed assessment of the very structures in place for implementation, usually in a handful of cases (Bachtler et al. 2014: 748; see similar Milio 2010b: 38; Huszák 2010: 46; Horvat 2005: 12). Only one study so far applied an analysis based on a general measure of capacity, the 'Government Effectiveness' indicator provided by the World Bank (Tosun 2014: 377). Using a readily available measure of capacity also seems most adequate in this study, as the relatively high number of cases makes a detailed assessment of administrative capacity on site almost impossible. Still, the question is which of the available indices is best for covering the concept of administrative capacity applied here.

Despite notable exceptions (Falkner et al. 2004: 459), the use of general measures of government or administrative capacity is the norm in EU policy implementation and transposition research. The 'Government Effectiveness' indicator is the most prominent measure for capacity in transposition studies (see e.g. Berglund et al. 2006: 704; Siegel 2006: 15; Thomson 2007: 997; Toshkov 2007: 339; Thomson 2009; Steunenberg and Toshkov 2009: 960). Still, as it also covers political aspects, a few studies rather rely on measures that focus solely on the bureaucracy, for example 'Bureaucracy Quality' created for the 'International Country Risk Guide' (it takes into account both the quality of the bureaucracy and its independence of political pressure [PRSG 2001: 7]). It thereby differentiates more clearly between government and the central bureaucracy, but the indicator is only rarely used (Perkins and Neumayer 2007: 195). In contrast to indicators measuring capacity directly by asking for their quality, some studies rely on factors that might influence capacity or factors that are seen as crucial for the efficiency of the bureaucracy. On the one hand, corruption is generally seen as detrimental to government capacity. It is measured using Transparency International's 'Corruption Perception Index' (Kaeding 2006: 241; Spendzharova and Versluis 2013: 1506) or the Internet Center for Corruption Research's corruption index (Mbaye 2001: 270). Corruption is mostly seen to lower the motivation of civil servants as they depend on connections and not performance to keep their positions (Kaeding 2006: 249). Still, this argument entails a very indirect measurement of capacity. Other measures equally stress the importance of civil servants' motivation for work, but take into account different sources of motivation. Auer and colleagues created an indicator of bureaucratic efficiency taking into account civil servant's incentives for high performance (performance-related pay, permanent tenure positions, and competitive tenders for positions) (used by Börzel et al. 2010: 1376). The indicator does not measure the actual quality of the bureaucracy, but expects the quality to be higher under conditions motivating civil servants to work better (see also Mbaye 2001: 270; Haverland and Romeijn 2007: 772; Linos 2007: 553).

Overall, all of these measures have their flaws. First, government effectiveness is conceptually very broad. Empirically, it offers only a rather crude differentiation between countries, as it is, for example, unable to make a distinction between countries like Bulgaria and Spain, even though qualitative evidence would strongly recommend doing so (Spendzharova and Versluis 2013: 1508). Both 'Government Effectiveness' and 'Bureaucracy Quality' are rather opaque in their underlying concepts, consisting either of a broad number of different measures (World Bank 2015), or referring only to a general "strength and expertise" (PRSG 2001: 7) of the bureaucracy. Corruption, on the other hand, is a rather different concept from administrative capacity and cannot necessarily be equated with low capacity.

A viable alternative to these measures is the 'executive capacity' indicator from the SGI offered by the Bertelsmann Foundation (SGI 2014a). 'Executive capacity' refers to the general level of administrative and government capacity available at the level of CEE central governments, thus at the very level where cohesion policy is administered. It is based on the evaluation of eight different categories by two country experts, operationalized as 24 different indicators and presented in detailed country reports (SGI 2014b: 51–67). It is therefore not a perception-based measure, drawing on survey results, but rather one that is based on hands-on evaluation of the actual performance of the central state bureaucracy. As these evaluations took place in the course of 2013, the reports by the country experts can be seen as the latest data available for the 2007–2013 financing period (SGI 2014b: 15). 'Executive capacity' covers three main dimensions:

- It determines in how far the executive has sufficient steering capacities (strategic capacity, interministerial coordination, evidence-based instruments, societal consultation, policy communication),
- whether or not effective policy implementation is guaranteed,
- and in how far institutional learning is provided for (SGI 2014b: 13).

These dimensions are very similar to how Bachtler and colleagues define administrative capacity for cohesion policy implementation on the dimensions of organizational structures, human resources, and administrative adaptability (Bachtler et al. 2014: 748). Both concepts comprise effective coordination and adaptability as core features of administrative capacity. Furthermore, while Bachtler and others ask for the functioning of the management and control system ("Allocation of Competencies and Responsibilities") (Bachtler et al. 2014: 741), the dimension G6 'Effective Implementation' of 'executive capacity' stresses the government's ability to achieve policy objectives, ministerial compliance with decisions, and effective monitoring of the bureaucracy and agencies (SGI 2014b: 60). This means that both 'executive capacity' as well as administrative capacity defined by Bachtler et al. focus on the very ability of a government to implement policies, either at the general governmental level or at the lower level of the management and control system. The measures are naturally not completely alike, however, it still makes sense to assume that both rely on the same underlying concept. Due to its lesser focus on aspects of human resources, it is also possible to refer to 'executive capacity' in a broader sense as 'government capacity', like Tosun does using 'Government Effectiveness' in her study on absorption performance (Tosun 2014: 376). Overall, it seems that 'executive capacity' is a reasonable choice to measure the general capacity available for cohesion policy implementation at the central level which is relevant in this study.

But how to establish a qualitative difference between groups? It is again noteworthy that there is already a rather clear empirical gap of one point between the rating of Estonia (6.42) and Slovakia (5.39) (see Table 4.3). Above Estonia, there are only Lithuania (7.12), Poland (7.19), and Latvia (7.42). Below Slovakia, there are Hungary (5.25), the Czech Republic (5.11), Bulgaria (4.85), as well as Slovenia (4.37) and Romania (4.43). The gap matches rather well with qualitative assessments from the literature putting especially the Baltic states ahead of their new member peers, while seeing the 2007 entrants Bulgaria and Romania as laggards (Noutcheva and Bechev 2008: 115–116; Meyer-Sahling 2009: 7). The low rating of Slovenia is also in line with its low rating in administrative capacity for cohesion policy implementation 2004–2006 ('C', see Table 4.3). Using the gap between Estonia and Slovakia as the cut-off point can also be justified against the EU27 average score of 6.12 on 'executive capacity'.[6] This average is just between the two countries' scores, making it an even more convincing choice for a qualitative distinction. Thus, it is used to establish (non-)membership of the cases in the set 'low executive capacity'. Membership in this set is regarded as detrimental to a country's absorption performance. Further differences are established around this cut-off point. While every case below five points is regarded a full-member of 'low executive capacity' (1), those countries above five points but below or equal to Slovakia were rated partial members (0.67). Estonia is the only country between six and seven points on the scale and thus the only partial non-member of the set (0.33). All other countries scoring seven points or even higher are full non-members of 'low executive capacity' (0).

4.4.2 *The Condition 'Islands of Excellence'*

So-called 'islands of excellence' refer to parts of the bureaucracy which are better than average developed and thus capable of efficient EU fund management, even despite low overall capacity. As explained in detail in Sect. 3.2, it is unlikely that such capacities developed straight from pre-accession preparation for structural funds. The planning procedures for pre-accession funds are very different and the amount allocated much lower than the later convergence support, and also the financial support for capacity building in this area was limited (Bachtler et al. 2000: 373; Bailey and De Propris 2004: 87; Allen 2008: 21). Thus, it is more likely that a distinct professionalization of sectoral capacities for cohesion policy implementation has evolved against the backdrop of the 2004–2006 financing period. It makes sense to assume that only those bodies which

[6]The threshold also fits well the EU 10 (post-communist new member states) average score (5.74) and the EU 15 average score (6.66) (see Table 3.1).

Table 4.3 Administrative capacity and management structures in the 2007–2013 period

Case	*Executive capacity*[a]	*Islands of excellence*[b]	*Management and control system*[c]
ESTEE	6.42	B	Single MA/Ministry of Finance
LTC	7.12	B	Single MA/Ministry of Finance
ESTLE	6.42	B	Single MA/Ministry of Finance
LTEG	7.12	B	Single MA/Ministry of Finance
CZT	5.11	B-C	Multiple MAs/Ministry of Transport
LVIS	7.42	B-C	Single MA/Ministry of Finance
PLIE	7.19	B-C	Single MA/Ministry of Regional Development
BGT	4.85	*NA*	Multiple MAs/Ministry of Transport
HUT	5.25	B-C	Single MA/National Development Agency
SKE	5.39	B-C	Multiple MAs/Ministry of the Environment
SKT	5.39	B-C	Multiple MAs/Ministry of Transport, Construction, and Regional Development
ROT	4.43	*NA*	Multiple MAs/Ministry of Transportation and Infrastructure
CZE	5.11	B-C	Multiple MAs/Ministry of Environment
SIET	4.37	C	Single MA/Government Office for Development and European Cohesion Policy
HUEE	5.20	B-C	Single MA/National Development Agency
ROE	4.43	*NA*	Multiple MAs/Ministry of Environment and Forests
BGE	4.85	*NA*	Multiple MAs/Ministry of Environment and Water

Source The author's compilation based on [a]Sustainable Governance Indicators data 'executive capacity' (SGI 2014a: 17), [b]Data provided by Bachtler et al. (2014: 751), [c]Own compilation based on programming documents (BG 2007a: 78, 2007b: 145; CZ 2007a: 161, 2007b: 126; EE 2007a: 139, 2007b: 155; HU 2007: 99–100, 2013: 130; LT 2007a: 121; 2007b: 137; LV 2007: 269; PL 2007: 184–187; RO 2007a: 104, 2007b: 88; SK 2007a: 136, 2007b: 91; SI 2007: 137)

have had experience with EU fund implementation during the earlier financing period and those who have developed a high level of capacity can make a difference for absorption in the period 2007–2013, because "the creation of institutional capability requires time and learning" (Bailey and De Propris 2002: 304). Thus, only the 2004 entrants to the

EU possibly qualify for 'islands of excellence', as Romania and Bulgaria had no proper previous experience with cohesion policy prior to 2007.

In order to measure the quality of these structures in the earlier financing period, I used data provided by Bachtler and others (2014). The authors gathered qualitative information on the very administrative capabilities dealing with cohesion policy implementation in the 2004–2006 financing period (organizational structures, human resources, administrative adaptability) and rated their quality on a scale from A to D (Consolidated/Strong (A), Developing (B), Basic (C), Absent/ Rudimentary (D)) (Bachtler et al. 2014: 741, 751). The data (displayed above in column four of Table 4.3) provides a clear impression of how well these countries' capacities were developed and from which level they could start into the 2007–2013 financing period.

That the earlier developed capacity was potentially relevant for absorption in the new financing period also makes sense against the backdrop of widespread continuity of bodies participating in the implementation process. In order to establish in how far continuity exists, I evaluated the relevant programming documents for the two financing periods 2004–2006 and 2007–2013 to establish whether or not the ministries responsible for policy implementation in the period of interest were already involved, and whether they could gain experience from earlier exercises of cohesion policy implementation in the same field. This is not about whether the institutional structure of cohesion policy implementation remained exactly the same (which it rarely did), but rather to see if a certain ministry was generally involved in implementation, either as an MA or an intermediate body. Overall, continuity in implementing bodies was widespread. When it comes to the Lithuanian OPs Economic Growth and Promotion of Cohesion, the MA and almost all IBs (this being seven out of eight and seven out of nine) were already involved in cohesion policy implementation in the earlier financing period (LT 2004: 299, 301, 2007a: 123, 2007b: 137). Also, both Estonian OPs (Economic Environment, Living Environment) were stable both at the level of MA (again the Ministry of Finance) and IBs, where all involved ministries had previous experience in cohesion policy implementation (EE 2003: 301–302, 2007a: 140–142, 2007b: 157). The same is true for all ministries involved in the implementation of Latvian OP Infrastructure and Services (LV 2003: 305–308, 2007: 267). The Slovak Ministry of Environment, the MA of the country's OP Environment, was responsible for environmental infrastructure in 2004–2006 (SK 2007a: 46).

The same is true for the Ministry of Transport, Post and Communication (MA of OP Transport), both yielding experience from the earlier period (SK 2003: 150). The Czech Ministries of Environment and Transport, both MAs in the 2007–2013 financing period (CZ 2007a: 162, 2007b: 126), were both responsible for the implementation of the earlier OP Infrastructure (CZ 2004; Baun and Marek 2008: 171).

The Polish government changed the MA and centralized its functions (for all OPs at the central level) to the Ministry for Regional Development (PL 2007: 184). Still, both the main IBs in the programme, the Ministry of Environment and Ministry of Transport (back then Ministry of Infrastructure) were already involved in the 2004–2006 financing period (PL 2003a: 149, 2003b: 51). Similarly, Hungary established its National Development Agency (NDA) as the single MA for all OPs in 2006. Still, there is evidence that some bodies are still included from the earlier financing period (OP Environment and Energy features the Ministry of Environment and Water and the Energy Centre Public Benefit Company as IBs, both of which were involved in the earlier financing period) and that capacity was otherwise transformed into the new structures (HU 2003: 89). When it comes to transport infrastructure, the Hungarian Ministry of Economy and Transport was the MA of earlier OP Environmental Protection and Infrastructure (HU 2003: 89), but it is unclear if capacity was in this case also transferred to the NDA.

The only OP lacking bodies with previous experience from the earlier period, despite participation, is the Slovenian OP Environmental and Transport Infrastructure Development. The NSRF lists the Government Office for Local Self Government and Regional Policy as the MA (Kavas 2010: 10), and the Ministry of Infrastructure and Spacial Planning as well as the Ministry of Environment are mentioned as IBs on the former ministry's homepage (SI 2007). Still, none of these bodies is mentioned as part of the implementation procedure of the earlier financing period (SI 2003: 220). Still, Slovenia could nevertheless gain some experience with the implementation process, and it is possible that some of the capacities from other bodies were included into the new implementation system. In contrast, OPs Environment and Transport in both Bulgaria and Romania could not benefit from such experience in any previous financing period due to their later accession to the EU. These cases are therefore unlikely to feature 'islands of excellence'.

Calibration for different set memberships in the set 'islands of excellence' was modelled on the scale provided by Bachtler and colleagues. While both A (Consolidated/Strong) and B (Developing) should be seen as high quality capacity for the absorption of EU funds, both Basic (C) and Absent/Rudimentary (D) capacity will be limited in overcoming generally low administrative capacity (Bachtler et al. 2014: 741, 751). Accordingly, all cases with A are full members of the set 'islands of excellence'. While B still yields partial membership (0.67), everything below means partial- (in the case of C, 0.33) or full-non-membership (in the case of D, 0). Those cases with mixed scores were assigned here to the respective higher score, as overall absorption performance in this period seems to support treating them as cases with higher capacities.

4.4.3 *The Condition 'Centralized Management'*

Centralized management bodies are horizontal implementation structures with a genuine, non-sectoral interest in the implementation of cohesion policy. Section 2.1 offers an overview of the implementation structure necessary for the absorption of EU funds. At the centre of this structure is the MA, which is responsible for the proper administration of an OP as well as for the necessary reporting and communication with the EC. An interesting observation on the management and control systems in CEE countries in the 2007–2013 financing period is that they either rely on sectoral MAs which are each responsible for only a single OP, or one horizontal MA administering all (central) OPs simultaneously and thereby limiting the role of the sectoral ministries to that of intermediary bodies.

The latter cases give the central MA a much stronger role *vis-à-vis* the sectoral ministries than a mere coordination body (which is present in most member states) would have. First, the sectoral ministries regularly report to the MA as it chairs the sessions of the monitoring committees and writes the annual implementation reports (AIRs) for the EC. Thus, it has direct access to information on what is going on in the OPs, and can offer useful advice to the other ministries involved in implementation, also against the backdrop of its lessons learned from implementation processes in the other programmes that it manages. Second, the status of MA gives the central coordinating ministry the institutional powers to reign over sectoral ministries' implementation procedures. It acts as a gatekeeper between sectoral ministries and the EC, and must agree with every change enacted at the level of the programming documents (e.g. reallocations). Finally, its access to many OPs should also make decommitments less likely, as the reallocation of funds from underperforming OPs to better performing ones will be hindered less by 'turf wars' between single ministries.

In sum, single MA structures resemble very much the advantages of centralized management bodies for EU implementation processes stressed in the literature. The MA can offer technical assistance, monitor performance of the other ministries involved, and facilitate their communication with the EC (Dimitrova and Toshkov 2009: 3). At the same time, its institutional position equips it with enough powers to overcome sectoral interests and, for example, establish selective incentives for IBs to perform well in absorption (e.g. by threatening an automatic reallocation of endangered funds to better performing programmes) (similar Zubek 2005: 611–613). As these MAs are usually Ministries of Finance or Ministries of Regional Development, they do not have specific sectoral interests that might involve them in 'turf wars', but can be seen as equipped with a genuine stake in successful absorption. In contrast, sectoral ministries are more likely to focus on their own goals, and might rather lose funds before deciding to transfer them to another OP administered by a different ministry (let alone a competing party).

Accordingly, calibration asks for the structure of the management and control system in the set 'centralized management': OPs that are part of a single-MA management and control system, with sectoral ministries only in the position of IBs, are full members of this set (1). In contrast, OPs that are managed by sectoral ministries as MAs are accordingly full non-members of the set (0). An overview of the different management structures of the OPs is displayed in Table 4.3 in column four.

4.4.4 The Condition 'Frequent Party Alternation'

Alternating parties in the post-communist context are likely to politicize the ministerial bureaucracy. The relevant political alternations for OPs take place at the level of ministers, as ministries are in charge of OP implementation (either as MA or IB). Politicization often means the replacement of core staff involved in the implementation process of a certain OP. Changes can then also result in a shift of programme priorities and project preferences. Thus, OPs face a potential interruption and weakening of administrative capacity upon the advent of a new party in office. An alternation of party in control of a ministry charged with the implementation of a certain OP is thus likely to cause a huge interruption of the implementation process, resulting in delays of absorption.

Still, a single alternation between parties during the financing period should be quite manageable, as a period of seven years offers still enough time to recover or to have achieved earlier a reasonable volume of implementation. Therefore, it is expected that only frequent party alternations will make absorption more difficult as several such interruptions of the implementation process will be much more difficult to manage.

But where do frequent changes start? Even though the region has a history of unstable governments and frequent changes in office, this does not limit the effect of these changes. The fact that cabinets and government are often unstable in CEE has thus no influence on the calibration decision. Rather, a hint is taken from the duration of regular electoral terms. The seven-year period under investigation could possibly involve two elections, assuming that an electoral term lasts four years. If at both occasions the government is at least partially replaced, this could mean two changes during the whole period. On the one hand, this would hardly be unexpected, as only very few governments have been reelected so far in CEE (Meyer-Sahling and Veen 2012). On the other hand, it would still mean a rather high degree of political instability, as the OP would have to deal two times with fundamental changes. Thus, instances of two changes are coded as partial members of the set 'frequent party alternation' (0.67). Still, as even more turmoil was possible, full membership was awarded to those cases where more than two alternations were experienced (1.00). In contrast, cases with 1.00–1.99 changes are assigned partial non-membership (0.33) in the set 'frequent party alternation'. Uneven numbers of changes are possible because some OPs have many ministries involved in the implementation process, and the number of changes is accordingly only counted as a share of the total. While numbers with decimals can evolve for these OPs, others with a sectoral MA naturally only vary on integers. Finally, OPs with less than one alternation in office at the level of minister (again possibly higher than zero due to the involvement of many ministries) were counted as full non-members (0) of the set 'frequent party alternation'.

Establishing the number of changes of parties' controlling ministries involved in OP implementation is more complicated than measuring centralization or capacity based on existing indices. No readily available calculation of such changes is available for CEE countries during the financing period. Thus, the following paragraphs discuss the development of party alternation at the level of ministries involved in the implementation of the OPs in all ten CEE new member states in the period 2007–2013. The development in every case is shortly put into the context of the general evolution of party competition in the respective country. Then, the changes at the level of relevant ministries are described and counted. Counting includes all changes in all ministries involved in OP implementation, both as MAs and IBs. 'Party alternation' is only counted if there is a change of party. This means that independent candidates in office were not considered. A change from a party affiliated minister to an independent was not counted (why should the independent candidate politicize the bureaucracy?), but counting was relevant again for changes from an independent to a party affiliated candidate (who was then likely interested in getting rid of the staff of her predecessor). Table 4.4 provides an overview of party alternations that took

Table 4.4 Party alternation in the management and control systems (2007–2013)

Case	*2007*	*2008*	*2009*	*2010*	*2011*	*2012*	*2013*	*Party alternation*
ESTEE	4/4		1/4					**1.25**
LTC		7/7				7/7		**2**
ESTLE	6/6		2/6					**1.3**
LTEG		4/4				4/4		**2**
CZT				1		1		**2**
LVIS			3/9	4/8	6/8			**1.58**
PLIE	4/7				1/7			**0.71**
BGT			1					**1**
HUT				1				**1**
SKE			1	1		1		**3**
SKT				1		1		**2**
ROT	1	1				1		**3**
CZE	1			1				**2**
SIET		3/3			1/3	3/3	3/3	**3.3**
HUEE				1				**1**
ROE	1	1	1			1		**4**
BGE			1				1	**2**

Source The author's compilation. For the data base and all references see Appendix I, for a detailed discussion see the following paragraphs place during the financing period. The changes can also be seen in detail with information on the cabinet, election date, and names and party affiliations of the respective ministers in Appendix I. The development was traced on the basis of the *European Journal for Political Research (EJPR)* country reports and the party politics literature available for the selected countries. The information was triangulated using the Parlgov database (Döring and Manow 2014) and where necessary, information from ministries' homepages.

4.4.4.1 Bulgaria

During the 1990s, Bulgaria experienced a regular alternation of former communist Bulgarian Socialist Party (BSP) and anti-communist opposition (SDS) in office (Autengruber 2008: 136). In 2001 however, the party system imploded when a new party, the NDSV (National Movement Simeon II) emerged and replaced the SDS on the centre-right. The new party was founded by the former Bulgarian Tsar Simeon Sakskoburggotski, and managed to reach 42.7% in its first electoral contestation (Autengruber 2008: 136). The former tsar became prime minister in 2001, but the NDSV failed to fulfil its promises of cleaner politics and soon disintegrated. Already after the 2005 elections it was forced to join a grand coalition with the left 'Coalition for Bulgaria' (KzB, mainly consisting of the BSP) and the DPS (a Turkish minority party) (Spirova 2007: 906), and failed to achieve parliamentary representation in 2009 (Spirova and Kolarova 2010: 914).

The development is interesting as some experts had suggested that the political watershed of 2001 was a one-off event and that the party system was rather stable due to high public party finance and party membership (Spirova 2005: 608; Kostadinova 2007: 825). However, this analysis proved to be valid only for the centre-left. The fact that the communist successor BSP could draw on the largest membership (half of all party members were members of the BSP in 2003) and widespread party organization might explain its resilience as the major centre-left force even in times of crisis (Spirova 2005: 606). While the BSP has remained the centre of gravity on the centre-left, other stable parliamentary parties are only the Turkish minority 'Movement for Rights and Freedoms' (DPS) and the extreme-right Ataka party.

In 2009, the NDSV was replaced by a new centrist-populist party, the 'Citizens for a European Development of Bulgaria' (GERB). GERB won in a landslide just like the NDSV earlier, and was only four seats short of an absolute majority (Spirova and Kolarova 2010: 911). It is not a direct successor of the NDSV, though, and only one of its 117 MPs had previous parliamentary experience (Spirova and Kolarova 2010: 913). As the champion of the elections, GERB formed a single party government, counting on support from other centre-right or right parties in parliament for policy making (the 'Blue Coalition', containing the formerly central 'Union of Democratic Forces' (SDS), the Newcomer 'Order, Law, and Justice' (RZS), and Ataka) (Spirova and Kolarova 2010: 914). While GERB has dominated Bulgarian politics since 2009, it nevertheless lost power to the centre-left for one year in 2013, after a short stint of a cabinet of independents in office before elections (Kolarova and Spirova 2014: 48–51).

The Bulgarian implementation system for cohesion policy is organized at the sectoral level, making single ministries MAs for the different OPs. There are thus no ministries involved as IBs in programme implementation. This makes it easy to count relevant changes at the level of the ministries involved in implementation (Spirova and Kolarova 2010: 912; Kolarova and Spirova 2014: 52). On the one hand, the Ministry of Environment and Water was in charge as MA for OP Environment (BG 2007a: 78). Control of the ministry changed twice during the financing period, from the minority party DPS to GERB in 2009, and later back to the DPS in 2013. These two changes make OP Environment a partial member of the set 'frequent party alternation' (0.67). On the other hand, the situation was similar in OP Transport. Here, the Ministry of Transport was assigned the role of the MA (BG 2007b: 145). Still, control of this ministry shifted from BSP to GERB in 2009, but then only to an independent candidate in 2013. Therefore, the Bulgarian OP Transport is only a partial non-member of 'frequent party alternation' (0.33).

4.4.4.2 Czech Republic

The party system of the Czech Republic has one of the clearest regime divides in the region. Unlike in almost all other CEE countries, the former ruling party KSČM (Communist Party of Bohemia and Moravia) failed to reform itself and rather remained as an anti-system party in parliament after democratization (Grzymala-Busse 2006: 430). Despite the exclusion of this communist successor party from coalition formation, competition developed early along a socio-economic divide (Kopecký 2006: 128). This divide was formed around the conservative Civic Democratic Party (ODS) as the main centre-right party, and the Czech Social Democratic Party (ČSSD) as the force covering the centre-left

(Hloušek and Šedo 2008: 96). After the Czech party system had become ever more stable in the course of the first two decades of its existence (Kopecký 2006: 131; Deegan-Krause and Haugton 2010: 228), the recent development is a decline of this relative stability (after 2010 elections 32.5% of parliamentary seats went to entirely new parties, in 2013 again 30.5%) (Linek 2011: 948, 2014: 97).

The Czech NSRF established an equally simple implementation structure for the OPs Environment and Transport as in the Bulgarian case. OP Environment was managed at the sectoral level by the Ministry of Environment (CZ 2007a: 162), while the Ministry of Transport was the MA for OP Transport (CZ 2007b: 126). Overall, the Czech Republic appeared rather stable during the 2007–2013 period regarding the governmental level. The ODS ruled through the whole period and was also the party of the Prime Minister, with the brief exception of the Fischer caretaker government that was supported by both camps in 2009 (Linek and Lacina 2010: 939). However, the ODS relied on changing coalition partners.

Starting with a minority cabinet in 2006 (only ODS), Prime Minister Topolanek brokered a cooperation with the Christian-democrat KDU-ČSL and the newly established green party (SZ) in 2007 (Linek 2008: 949). After a series of scandals, Topolanek did not run for re-election and was replaced by Petr Nečas (also ODS), who was successful in the 2010 vote (Linek 2011: 953). These elections, however, also meant huge changes for the party system. First, both coalition partners of ODS, the KDU-ČSL and the SZ failed to achieve parliamentary representation (Linek 2011: 948). They were replaced, second, by two newcomer parties, the liberal TOP 09 (Tradition, Responsibility, Prosperity) and the populist VV (Public Affairs). These parties managed to win a combined 27.6% of the vote, and subsequently joined the cabinet as the ODS' new coalition partners (Linek 2011: 953). The VV, however, proved very unstable and quickly dissolved in the face of corruption scandals involving its party leader Vít Bárta (Linek 2012: 77). When the VV threatened to withdraw from the cabinet unless its position was enhanced, the party's cabinet members refused to resign and rather chose to form a new party, LIDEM (liberal democrats), which split from VV and replaced it in government (Linek 2013: 53). The VV was thus excluded from government, but its former ministers kept their offices. The government survived until the elections in October 2013, which were won by the ČSSD who subsequently formed a new centre-left government. This government, however, was inaugurated only after the end of the period under investigation (in January 2014) and is therefore of no concern for this study.

Overall, the instability of coalitions in the Czech Republic also translated into instability of parties in control of ministries. The Ministry of Transport was initially controlled by the ODS and only shifted to the populist newcomer VV in 2010 (Linek 2011: 950), until it went shortly back to the ODS in 2012 (Linek 2013: 51) until the advent of the expert Rusnok cabinet in 2013 (Linek 2014: 100). Still, this means overall two changes of party in charge of the ministry during the financing period. On the other hand, the Ministry of Environment changed as early as 2007 from the conservative ODS to the newcomer-green SZ (Linek 2008: 948), only to be returned to the ODS in 2010 (Linek 2011: 950). Thus, OP Environment experienced also two changes at the level of its MA, and is therefore a partial member of the set 'frequent party alternation', just as OP Transport (0.67).

4.4.4.3 Estonia

Estonia has seen a clear dominance of centre-right governments since independence from the Soviet Union (Mikkel 2006: 32). Still, this dominance was, for a long period, not linked to any specific party, as the party system remained in flux and newcomers managed to win a large proportion of the vote in 1995 and 2003. The attractiveness of the Russophone vote for the mainstream parties has reportedly had a detrimental effect both on the success of ethnic Russian parties as well as on that of nationalist Estonian parties (Mikkel 2006: 25). The emergence of the Res Publica party in 2003 was the last fundamental blow to the party system. Afterwards, competition stabilized around the Estonian Reform Party (RE) under the leadership of Prime Minister Ansip.

Both the Estonian implementation system and its party system are much more complicated than the two examples already discussed. This results from the fact that the implementation system is centralized with only a single MA (the Ministry of Finance) for all OPs, turning the other ministries into IBs. Thus, changes for every Estonian OP have to be followed at the level of several ministries in parallel.

On the one hand, besides the Ministry of Finance, the OP Economic Environment[7] included three other ministries in its implementation

[7]The official titles of the OPs are Operational Programme for the Development of Economic Environment (EE 2007a: 1) and Operational Programme for the Development of the Living Environment (EE 2007b: 1).

structure: the Ministry of Economic Affairs and Communications, the Ministry of Environment, and the Ministry of Education and Research (EE 2007a: 140–142). On the other hand, besides the MA, OP Living Environment had even five ministries in the role of IBs: the Ministry of Environment, the Ministry of Internal Affairs, the Ministry of Education and Research, the Ministry of Social Affairs, and the Ministry of Economic Affairs and Communications (EE 2007b: 157). Thus, all but the additional two ministries (Internal Affairs, Social Affairs) are shared by both OPs.

The most important parties during the period under investigation were the liberal RE and the conservative 'Pro Patria and Res Publica Union' (IRL) on the centre-right as well as the Social Democratic Party of Estonia (SDE) and the Centre Party (KeE) on the centre-left. The divide between these parties is socio-economic (the SDE left a government for neo-liberal anti-crisis measures it did not want to support) (Pettai 2010: 957), as well as cultural (the RE was firm on removing a Soviet era war memorial, while the KeE voiced the interests of war veterans and the Russophone population) (Pettai 2008: 965). The development relevant for the period under investigation starts in 2002.

In this year, Res Publica emerged as a challenger to the other parties on the centre-right, the RE and the IRL (Pettai 2004: 993). Res Publica was subsequently the major winner of the elections in 2003 and its leader Juhan Parts even called to form a cabinet (Pettai 2004: 993), resulting in a coalition between Res Publica, the RE, and the People's Union (Pettai 2004: 995). Still, already in 2004, the government faced severe headwind when three ministers resigned as a result of either incompetence or even misconduct (Pettai 2005: 1004–1005). The development finally culminated in the resignation of the whole government against the backdrop of Res Publica's falling popularity ratings and a failed merger with the Reform Party (Pettai 2006: 1094). This resulted into the formation of the first Ansip cabinet, in which the RE was joined by the centre-left KeE and again the People's Union (Pettai 2006: 1094). Ansip had only recently moved up into the cabinet in 2004, after the early resignation of the Minister of Economics and Communication (Pettai 2005: 1005). Nevertheless, he remained prime minister from 2005 until joining the EC in 2014. The following years were thus a period of political stability and consolidation in Estonia.

The victory of Ansip's RE in the 2007 elections allowed the prime minister to stay in power and to form a centrist government with the

IRL (a 2006 merger of Pro Patria and Res Publica) and the SDE (Pettai 2008: 962). This new government resulted in the highest number of party alternations during the whole financing period in Estonia, as control of all Ministries involved in implementation shifted to a different party (see Appendix I for a detailed overview). Thus, both OPs experienced one full alternation with the incoming second Ansip cabinet.

Still, the cabinet lasted only until the crisis hit the country and the coalition disagreed on how to deal with it. The SDE was not willing to support "a series of budgetary cuts and changes in labour laws" (Pettai 2010: 957), and was ultimately dismissed from government in 2009. The ministries controlled by the SDE went to the RE (Ministry of Finance) and the IRL (Ministry of Internal Affairs) (Pettai 2010: 955–956). At the OP level, this means that OP Economic Environment experienced an alternation of one out of four ministries (i.e. 1/4 or 0.25), and OP Living Environment changes in two out of six of its ministries (i.e. 2/6 or 0.33). Ansip continued with a minority government until the following elections in 2011.

He was then again reelected as prime minister, and received his own parliamentary majority for the earlier existing RE-IRL minority government (Sikk 2012: 91). Thus, the original coalition continued in office and no further party alternation resulted at the level of ministries. This means that the changes experienced by OP Economic Environment (a total of 1.25) and OP Living Environment (a total of 1.33) were very limited despite several changes at the level of government. Both Estonian OPs are therefore partial non-members of the set 'frequent party alternation' (0.33).

4.4.4.4 Hungary

In Hungary, the regime divide faltered early when the formerly oppositional and left-liberal Alliance of Free Democrats (SZDSZ) entered into a coalition with the former Communist Party MSZP in 1994 (Kiszelly 2008: 126). Still, competition remained strong along a cultural divide. Right and centre-right parties stand for "Christian-nationalist, morally conservative and anti-communist orientation, while 'left' is associated with communist legacy and with a libertarian-cosmopolitan orientation" (Enyedi 2006: 181). The cultural divide has remained the most important one, even as the Fidesz party (Hungarian Civic Alliance), founded originally as a left-liberal party, successfully managed to claim the position of the dominant power on the centre-right. Since the 1990s, the party system has mainly gone through an extensive process of concentration (Kiszelly 2008: 130), which has recently culminated in the dominance of Fidesz in the last two elections (52.7% in 2010 and 44.9% in 2014) (Varnagy 2011: 991, 2015: 134), fundamentally changing the arithmetic of Hungarian party competition away from the bipartisan pattern.

The Hungarian implementation system for cohesion policy is a special case as no ministry is in charge of a single OP as a responsible MA. In contrast, for this purpose the socialist government created the NDA as the centralized MA with departments for every OP (HU 2007: 99–100). In the earlier financing period, the Ministry of Economy and Transport had been charged with the role of MA for cohesion policy implementation, and the implementation structure was therefore similar to that of other CEE countries (HU 2003: 89). However, during the financing period, the implementation structure became ever more opaque. During the early years, it was at least clear, for example, that the Ministry of Environment and Water (Development Directorate) (HU 2007: 105) was involved as an IB in OP Environment and Energy. In 2010, however, the elections resulted in a landslide victory for Victor Orbán and the alliance of Fidesz and KDNP (a smaller Catholic party) (Varnagy 2011: 991; Kiszelly 2008: 125). The newly elected government did not only exchange all ministers, but also adjusted the institutional roles within the management and control system (Balas and Kiss 2011: 4). It was even able to pass constitutional reforms on the basis of its broad majority in parliament (Varnagy 2012: 129). This means that with regard to the implementation system of the OPs, it was unclear which ministry was then involved in the process, even though the NDA remained the central MA.

Nevertheless, this is not necessarily a problem for calibrating the Hungarian OPs. Despite its often antagonizing style, the Orban government was widely appreciated by many Hungarians, and even managed to be re-elected in 2014 (Varnagy 2015: 138). This means that power changed hands only once in Hungary during the financing period, in 2010, and in this instance wholesale, meaning that no party continued in office. Thus, the Hungarian implementation system experienced one single party alternation in office.[8] Both the Hungarian OP Transport and

[8]This way of counting the changes is further supported by empirical evidence stressing that the advent of the Orban government meant changes at the level of strategic documents, institutions, and staff involved in cohesion policy implementation (Balas and Kiss 2011: 4).

OP Environment and Energy are thus partial non-members of the set 'frequent party alternation' (0.33).

4.4.4.5 Latvia

Latvia has probably the most complicated party system as well as implementation structure of all CEE member states for its OP Infrastructure and Services. The major political divides in the country are along socio-economic and ethnic lines. Still, the ethnic divide between Latvians and Russophones is mediated by high levels of non-citizenship of this group (Pabriks and Stokenberga 2006: 54). The dominant centre-right camp experienced some changes since independence. After the liberal Latvia's Way (LC) and the conservative For the Fatherland and Freedom (TB/LNNK) had been successful during the 1990s, only TB/LNNK survived in the 2002 elections, together with another conservative party TP (People's Party) created in 1998 (Pabriks and Stokenberga 2006: 57). On the centre-left, there is the For Human Rights in a United Latvia union (PCTVL), consisting of the People's Harmony Party (TSP), the Equal Rights Movement (L), and the Communist Party (Pabriks and Stokenberga 2006: 57). A typical feature of Latvian politics are its short-lived, populist parties focussing mainly on the popularity of their leaders (Pabriks and Stokenberga 2006: 60). Such parties have become the strongest force in elections in 1995, 1998, and 2002.

Since 2004, the situation can be described as follows: the centre-right saw a (somewhat cannibalizing) competition between the New Era (JL) and Civic Union (PS) on the one side, and the TP and Latvia's First Party/Latvian Way (LPP/LC) on the other. The conservative TB/LNNK and the agrarian 'Union of Greens and Farmers' (ZZS) were also part of the centre-right, but not aligned with either of these camps. On the other hand, the centre-left consisted of the Harmony Centre and the PCTVL, of which the latter lost strongly to the benefit of the Harmony Centre during the period under investigation (Ikstens 2007: 1017). The centre-left and 'pro-Russian' Harmony Center subsequently became the strongest contender of centre-right dominance, emerging as the second strongest (2010) and the strongest (2011) single party in the most recent elections (Ikstens 2011: 1035, 2012: 175).

The implementation system of OP Infrastructure and Services includes no less than nine different ministries. Similar to the Estonian (and the Lithuanian) system, the Ministry of Finance is the responsible MA (LV 2007: 267). Then, the Ministry of Economics, the Ministry of Education and Science, the Ministry of Culture, the Ministry of Welfare, the Ministry of Regional Development and Local Government, the Ministry of Transport, the Ministry of Health, and the Ministry of Environment are involved as IBs in implementation (LV 2007: 267). These ministries experienced a series of changes during the financing period, however, probably fewer than the total of four different cabinets in 2007, 2009, 2010, and 2011 would suggest.

Latvia has seen a succession of right-wing governments in office since 2006. After the elections in 2006, Prime Minister Kalvītis formed a centre-right coalition consisting of the TP, the LPP/LC, the ZZS, and TB/LNNK (Ikstens 2007: 1015). The Kalvītis government suffered from scandals surrounding its ministers and their subsequent dismissals, but also the prime minister's own position was weakened after a failed attempt to remove the head of the anti-corruption bureau KNAB from office (Ikstens 2008: 1042). When Kalvītis stepped down at the end of 2007, Godmanis from the LPP/LC took over. The composition of the cabinet nevertheless remained unchanged when it comes to parties in charge of ministries (Ikstens 2008: 1042). The Godmanis government itself then collapsed in March 2009 against the backdrop of the looming economic crisis and the cabinet's apparent inability to take necessary measures (Ikstens 2010: 1055).

The new cabinet formed by Dombrovskis returned the JL to the executive, where it formed a government with its main rival TP as well as the PS (a splinter from TB/LNNK), the ZZS, and TB/LNNK (Ikstens 2010: 1051). Thus, the LPP/LC left the government (Ikstens 2010: 1052). As a result, three ministries changed hands, the Ministry of Finance (from TP to JL), the Ministry of Economics (from TB/LNNK to JL) and the Ministry of Transport (from LPP/LC to TB/LNNK) in 2009 (3/9) (Ikstens 2010: 1051). The new government united two strong rivals, New Era and the People's Party (Ikstens 2010: 1052).

Still, this inherent conflict was solved after elections in 2010, which voted Dombrovskis and the New Era into office. As his new vehicle V (Unity), a merger of JL with the PS and the Society for Different Politics (SCP) won enough votes to govern alone with the ZZS, the prime minister was able to exclude the People's Party (who had already left the coalition before the elections) from the new government (Ikstens 2011: 1038). The implementation structure was also altered during that year as the Ministries for Regional Development and Municipal Affairs and that of Environment were merged to a new Ministry of

Environmental Protection and Regional Development (Ikstens 2011: 1036). This means that from 2010 onwards 'only' eight ministries were left in OP implementation. Four of these ministries experienced an alternation of party in 2010 (4/8) (Ikstens 2011: 1036). The new government survived for less than a year, when again new elections were called, this time against the backdrop of a successful referendum on the dissolution of the parliament.

The elections saw the rise of a newly emerging centre-right force, Zatler's Reform Party (ZRP), which managed to become the strongest force within the camp and the second strongest party overall, trumped only by the winning centre-left 'Harmony' party (Ikstens 2012: 175). The Harmony Party had already shown a strong result in the 2010 elections, scoring second only behind 'Unity' (V) (Ikstens 2011: 1042). While the result of the election meant that all signs pointed towards political change, Dombrovskis still managed to remain in office. He benefited from a split within the ZRP shortly after the elections, impeding a coalition between the two winners of the election ZRP and Harmony Centre (Ikstens 2012: 178). The cabinet was then formed by the ZRP, Unity, the NA (former TB/LNNK) and a group of independents splitting away from the ZRP (Ikstens 2012: 178). The Harmony Centre, despite being the strongest party in parliament at the time, was again excluded from power. Once again, the new government resulted in six of the total of eight ministries changing hands between parties (6/8) (see Appendix I).

Overall, the changes in 2009 (3/9, or 0.33), 2010 (4/8, or 0.5), and 2011 (6/8, or 0.75) resulted in a total of 1.58 party alternations for OP Environment and Services. This is a rather low number considering the political turmoil experienced by the country. Nevertheless, it adequately reflects the situation in the implementation structure of the OP considering a careful counting of party alternations, weighed by the total number of ministries involved. The Latvian OP is therefore a partial non-member of the set 'frequent party alternation' (0.33).

4.4.4.6 Lithuania

Lithuania takes a somewhat middle ground between its Baltic neighbours Estonia and Latvia when it comes to the implementation structure as well as patterns of party competition. In Lithuania, the regime divide separated the reformed former communist party, the 'Lithuanian Democratic Labour Party' (LDDP) and Sąjūdis (later 'Homeland

Union'), the party of the anti-communist opposition, who alternated in power during the 1990s (Ramonaite 2006: 70–71). The party system changed fundamentally after the elections of 2000, when the new Liberal Union of Lithuania (LLiS) and the New Union (Social Liberals) (NS), won almost half of all seats in parliament (Ramonaite 2006: 71). The party system has changed in almost every election after the first post-communist decade and experienced the emergence of new parties in 2000 (LLiS, NS), in 2004 (Labour Party (DP), For Order and Justice (TT)), in 2008 (National Resurrection Party (TPP)), and in 2012 (Way of Courage). Still, while new parties had earlier won with 36.9% (2000) and 46.1% (2004) of the vote (Krupavicius 2005: 1094), the newcomers in 2008 and 2012 were far from winning the elections, ranking in the lower double or even single digits (Krupavicius 2013: 145). In contrast, the 'traditional parties' from the 1990s never vanished completely. They merged successfully with their close allies, i.e. the LDDP and the Social Democrats merged as the Lithuanian Social Democratic Party (LSDP) in 2001 (Ramonaite 2006: 73), while the Homeland Union and the Christian Democrats united as the 'Homeland Union – Lithuanian Christian Democrats' (TS-LKD) in 2008 (Krupavicius 2009: 1029). Even despite the electoral success of newcomer parties since 2000, the old parties formed along the regime divide during the 1990s still remain the centre of gravity in their respective camps, ceding at no point the post of prime minister to any other party (Ramonaite 2006: 77; Krupavicius 2009: 1023, 2013: 141).

The country's implementation system for cohesion policy is again centralized, with the MA for all OPs located in the Ministry of Finance, and other ministries involved as IBs. The OP Economic Growth is implemented by the Ministry of Economy, Ministry of Education and Science, and the Ministry of Transport and Communications (LT 2007a: 123). The OP Promotion of Cohesion involves six ministries besides the MA: the Ministry of Environment, the Ministry of Social Security and Labour, the Ministry of Health, the Ministry of Education and Science, the Ministry of Transport, and the Ministry of Interior (LT 2007b: 137). Thus, similar to Estonia and Latvia, alternation of parties must be followed simultaneously at the level of several different ministries.

The most recent elections before the financing period took place in 2004. The strong result of the newcomer Labour Party in these elections was already hinted at by the results of the preceding elections to the European Parliament, where it became the strongest force

(Krupavicius 2005: 1088). TS (Homeland Union) and LiCS (Liberal and Centre Union) were the main centre-right parties in Lithuania in 2004. However, they could not reach an agreement for collaboration for any of the elections taking place that year (European, presidential, parliamentary) (Krupavicius 2005: 1094). In contrast, the centre-left parties LSDP and NS signed agreements for both European and parliamentary elections (running as the 'Working for Lithuania' alliance) (Krupavicius 2005: 1093–1094).

The election result was then a blow to the formerly rather stable party system: parliament saw the entry of two protest parties, the Labour Party and the TT (Krupavicius 2005: 1094). The biggest losers of this development were the centre-left 'Working for Lithuania' coalition, which saw its seat-share halved, as well as the similarly affected liberal LiCS (Krupavicius 2005: 1089, 1095). Even though the centre-left camp suffered from losses, the former coalition of LSDP and the NS formed a government with the Labour Party and the LVLS (Lithuanian Peasant Popular Union), resulting in a complete reshuffle of the cabinet (Krupavicius 2005: 1096). The government experienced a major crisis in 2006, when the NS left the coalition because its MP and chairman of parliament was removed from his post by a vote of no-confidence (Krupavicius 2007: 1021). The move resulted from the attempt of a hostile takeover of the coalition by the Labour Party, who was not leading the coalition despite being its strongest force (Krupavicius 2007: 1022). This attempt to increase its influence proved futile for the Labour Party, which later also suffered the loss of nine of its MPs. These MPs formed a new party, Civic Democracy Party (PDP), which remained within the government (Krupavicius 2007: 1023). The Labour Party was further involved in a party finance scandal in the same year, as a result of which its leader Uspaskich left temporarily for Russia to escape prosecution (Krupavicius 2007: 1023). When the Labour Party had to withdraw its ministers from the government, Brazauskas also resigned as prime minister and a new government had to be formed (Krupavicius 2007: 1024). Initial talks on a grand coalition between LSDP and HU failed, and finally LSDP Defence Minister Kirkilas received majority support from the LSDP, the LiCS, the LVLS, the NS, the PDP, and the Labour Party (Krupavicius 2007: 1025). Still, the subsequent cabinet only included ministers form the LSDP, LVLS, LiCS, and PDP (Krupavicius 2007: 1025). This government was later joined by the NS, yielding its own parliamentary majority for the government (Krupavicius 2009: 1024) and the first relevant two alternations in the Ministry of Environment and Ministry of Education and Science in 2008 from the LSDP to the NS (Krupavicius 2009: 1024).

Still, this new coalition did not survive for long as the government was defeated in the following parliamentary elections in 2008. The newly incoming centre-right government consisted of the TS-LKD, the newcomer TPP, the Liberal Movement (LRLS, a split from LiCS) and the LiCS (Krupavicius 2009: 1027). Krupavicius calls the newcomer TPP an "openly non-ideological and non-programmatic party" (Krupavicius 2009: 1028), which subsequently proved to be a source of trouble for the coalition (Krupavicius 2011: 1050). At the same time, the government was very unpopular due to the implementation of austerity measures. Further problems of the coalition were related to the instability of some of the coalition's parties and the creation of a new 'Christian Party' in parliament (taking members of the TPP) (Krupavicius 2011: 1051). At the level of ministries, the almost wholesale alternation of government naturally meant shifts in almost all ministries (only the LiCS remained in charge of the Ministry of Interior, while an independent candidate was appointed Minister of Finance). Thus, OP Promotion of Cohesion experienced party alternation in five of its seven ministries, and OP Economic growth in three of its four ministries (see Appendix I for details) in 2008. The centre-right government was then reasonably successful and managed to fulfill its entire electoral term.

Then, however, the parliamentary elections in 2012 returned the LSDP to power in a centre-left alliance with the Labour Party, TT, and the Polish-minority party LLRA, after an election campaign which had focused heavily on the implemented austerity measures (Krupavicius 2013: 141). The 2012 elections also brought more stability than the previous ones, as the newcomer of these elections 'Way of Courage' had an even weaker presence than the TPP had previously in 2008 (Krupavicius 2013: 145). Even despite the defeat of the ruling centre-right alliance, President Grybauskaitė tried to keep the government in power and to prevent the Labour Party from participating in any new government (Krupavicius 2013: 145).[9] In the end, however, she had to give in and the three centre-left parties formed a coalition.

[9]The President even personally conducted 'tests' of candidates for ministerial office in order to keep the Labour Party out of government, besides others assessing their proficiency in at least one of the EU working languages (English, French, German) (Krupavicius 2013: 146).

This resulted in the second wholesale alternation of government, and this time all parties in charge of relevant ministries changed (seven out of seven, four out of four, see Appendix I for details). In sum, both Lithuanian OPs experienced 2 alternations at the level of ministries involved in implementation. This means partial membership in the set 'frequent party alternation' (0.67) for both OPs.

4.4.5 Poland

During the 1990s, Poland experienced strong competition along the regime-divide, mainly as a historical–cultural division based on attitudes towards the past and the role of the Catholic church in society, while economic divides played only a secondary role (Szczerbiak 2006: 101). This pattern of competition changed fundamentally when electoral support for the communist successor Democratic Left Alliance (SLD) collapsed in the aftermath of a corruption scandal during its 2001–2005 term in government (Bingen 2008: 81). Political competition subsequently overcame the post-communist—post-Solidarność divide and found a new equilibrium along a right—centre-right divide between two descendents of the Solidarność Movement, the Civic Platform (PO) and the Law and Justice Party (PiS) (Gwiazda 2009: 364–365). The new divide is still based on cultural values such as the role of the Catholic church in society, but also the liberal economics of the PO versus more statist ideas of the PiS (often framed as 'solidary Poland' vs. 'liberal Poland') (Bingen 2008: 83; Szczerbiak 2008: 422–423).

While party competition was clearly laid out in comparison to many other countries in the region, the implementation structure of OP Infrastructure and Environment was less simple. The management of all national-level OPs was centralized in the Ministry of Regional Development as the single MA (PL 2007: 184). Then however, six other ministries were involved in the implementation of OP Infrastructure and Environment, namely the Ministry of Environment, the Ministry of Transport, the Ministry of Economy, the Ministry of Culture and National Heritage, the Ministry of Health, and the Ministry of Science and Higher Education (PL 2007: 186–187). All of these ministries involved in implementation experienced hardly any party alternations during the financing period.

The elections of 2005 had resulted in a realignment of Polish politics that was markedly different from previous realignments (Jasiewicz and Jasiewicz-Betkiewicz 2006: 1231) and remained stable until the end of the period under investigation. Volatility had long been a problem of the Polish party system and was mainly the result of unstable parties on the centre-right (Szczerbiak 2006: 106). This time, however, it was for the first time caused by a large swing of voters from the left to the right (Jasiewicz and Jasiewicz-Betkiewicz 2006: 1231). The two most recent descendents from the Solidarność Movement, the PiS (conservatives) and the PO (liberals) emerged as the two strongest parties from the elections, while the centre-left communist-successor SLD lost three-quarters of its support (Jasiewicz and Jasiewicz-Betkiewicz 2006: 1235). Even though PiS and PO initially tried to form a coalition, interparty struggles with regard to the successive presidential elections and rising hostility prevented such an outcome (Jasiewicz and Jasiewicz-Betkiewicz 2006: 1243).

The first PiS government was then formed by Kazimierz Marcinkiewicz, but its minority situation soon proved untenable. In July 2006, Jarosław Kaczyński therefore formed a new coalition government with Self-Defence (SRP), the League of Polish Families (LPR) and independents, to counter the threat of new elections (Jasiewicz and Jasiewicz-Betkiewicz 2007: 1065). The PiS thereby broke a political taboo, entering a coalition with two extreme partners from outside its cultural-historical political camp (Jasiewicz and Jasiewicz-Betkiewicz 2007: 1068). The coalition, however, turned out to be fragile and was preoccupied with infighting (Jasiewicz and Jasiewicz-Betkiewicz 2008: 1096). New elections were already called in October 2007, and the PO defeated the PiS by a margin of almost 10-percentage-points, subsequently forming a coalition with the Polish Peasant Party (PSL) (Szczerbiak 2008: 424). This coalition was equally a new development, as the PSL had been until that time as a successor bloc party firmly entrenched with the SLD. The elections thus also meant the end of the predominance of the regime divide in Poland and the beginning of a new central division of the country in the camps of 'liberal Poland' (post-Solidarność liberals), mostly represented by the PO, and 'Poland of social solidarity' (post-Solidarność conservatives/nationalists) represented by PiS (Szczerbiak 2006: 106; Jasiewicz and Jasiewicz-Betkiewicz 2008: 1105).

The switch from the PiS-led to the new PO-PSL coalition resulted in a limited number of changes. Control of the MA shifted from one independent candidate to another, and is therefore not counted as a proper party alternation. In contrast, three ministries shifted from PiS and an independent candidate to the PO (Ministry of Infrastructure, Ministry of Science and Higher Education, Ministry of Culture and National Heritage), while one ministry went to the PSL (Ministry of Economy) (Jasiewicz and Jasiewicz-Betkiewicz 2008: 1102). Therefore, even despite the wholesale alternation of government, only four out of seven ministries (0.57) experienced party alternation, due to the Prime Minister's strong reliance on independent candidates (see Appendix I). The following years were then surprisingly stable.

The first Tusk government of PO and PSL managed to serve its full legislative period, and was in 2011 even the first Polish government confirmed in office (Jasiewicz and Jasiewicz-Betkiewicz 2012: 244). Overall, the Polish case is the most stable in the region during this period. The high stability is underlined by the constancy of Elżbieta Bieńkowska as the head of the Ministry for Regional Development since 2007. This means that the top-job at the MA in Poland was stable virtually throughout the whole financing period. There was only one minor change to be counted in 2011 from an independent to a PO candidate (1/7, or 0.14) (Jasiewicz and Jasiewicz-Betkiewicz 2012: 248). Adding this alternation to the already reported changes, the Polish OP Infrastructure and Environment experienced a total of only 0.71 party alternations throughout the whole financing period. It is therefore the only full non-member of the set 'frequent party alternation' (0).

4.4.6 Romania

The development of Romania somewhat resembles that of Bulgaria. During the 1990s, party competition was dominated by the regime divide and various successors of the former communist party (National Salvation Front (FSN), Party of Social Democracy in Romania (PDSR)) alternating in office with the anti-communist opposition in 1996 (Olteanu 2008: 152). Since 2000 however, the former anti-communist and historical parties, mainly the Christian Democratic National Peasants' Party (PNŢ-CD), have become irrelevant. During the 2000s, the party system was dominated by two former factions of the successor of the former communist party, the Social Democratic Party (PSD) and the Democratic Liberal Party (PD-L) (Pop-Eleches 2008: 466). The originally social democratic PD-L took advantage of the ideological vacuum that had emerged on the centre-right after the defeat of the

PNȚ-CD and rebranded itself as a conservative party in 2005 (switching also at the EU level from the European Socialists to the European People's Party) (Olteanu 2008: 151). Between these two poles, the National Liberal Party (PNL) and the UDMR, the party of the Hungarian minority, are stable features of Romanian party competition. It is less surprising that party competition is now taking place between the two successors of the former communist party, taking into account that even the anti-communist government marking the 'second regime change' in 1996 mainly consisted of former members of the communist party (Olteanu 2008: 155). The most relevant political divides between the two major parties are thus also not rooted in clear programmatic differences (Olteanu 2008: 156). Volatility is not only strong among voters, but also among politicians who often change their party affiliations both at the national and the local level (Olteanu 2008: 160–161).

The Romanian cohesion policy implementation system was organized at the sectoral level, with the Ministry of Transport in charge of OP Transport (RO 2007b: 88) and the Ministry of Environment as the responsible MA for OP Environment (RO 2007a: 104). Both programmes were heavily affected by the alternation of both ministers and parties during the financing period.

Romanian cabinets and coalitions are notoriously unstable. The country experienced a total of nine different cabinets in office with four different prime ministers between 2007 and 2013. Starting in 2004, the liberal Călin Popescu-Tăriceanu (PNL) headed different governments, consisting of his PNL, the UDMR, and initially also the Democratic Party (PD) and the PUR (Humanist Party) (Stan and Zaharia 2007: 1086). The break with the PD in 2007 meant changes for both the Ministries of Environment (from PD to UDMR) and Transport (from PD to PNL) (Stan and Zaharia 2008: 1118). The remaining PNL-UDMR government ultimately lost the election in 2008.

It was replaced by a grand coalition between PD-L (a merger of PD and the Democrat Liberal Party (PLD) [Stan and Zaharia 2008: 1122]) and the PSD and PC (Conservative Party) alliance (Stan and Zaharia 2009: 1090). This meant again two alternations of parties in 2008 as the Ministry of Transport went back to control of the PD-L (now renamed), and the PSD appointed the Minister of Environment (Stan and Zaharia 2009: 1090). This first cabinet of Emil Boc, however, collapsed already in the following year when the PSD left the coalition. The prime minister tried to save his post, first in an alliance with independents, and later also including the UDMR (Stan and Zaharia 2010: 1141). Both of these changes affected the Ministry of Environment, which in 2009 went after the break from the PSD to the new coalition partner UDMR (Stan and Zaharia 2010: 1140–1141). Stan and Zaharia suggest that the break-up of the coalition by the PSD was done on purpose, as the party aimed at blaming the effects of the emerging economic crisis on the PD-L in order to benefit politically (Stan and Zaharia 2010: 1149). Nevertheless, Boc managed to receive support from the National Union for Romania's Progress (UNPR), a group of former social democrats dissatisfied with their positions (Stan and Zaharia 2011: 1113), and thereby formed Boc IV in 2010 (Stan and Zaharia 2011: 1108). Boc IV survived only until the end of 2011.

Then, street protests erupted in the country, criticizing anti-crisis measures and stressing that the PD-L personnel focused much more on its own advantage than on the grievances of their country which was suffering under austerity measures (Stan 2013: 197–202). In a desperate attempt to save the coalition, former head of security services Mihai Răzvan Ungureanu (Ind.) replaced Boc as Prime Minister in early 2012. However, after defections from the coalition, a no-confidence motion in Ungureanu passed and Victor Ponta (PSD) formed a new centre-left cabinet with the support of the PNL and the PC (Stan 2013: 199). As a result, the PNL could regain control over the Ministry of Transport, and the PSD returned to the Ministry of Environment. This government was subsequently confirmed in the 2012 elections in a landslide victory, then also including the UNPR (Ponta II) (Stan 2013: 201).

Overall, both OPs Environment and Transport experienced an excessive alternation of both ministers (seven, eight) and parties (four, three, respectively). This clearly makes both Romanian cases full members of the set 'frequent party alternation' (1.00).

4.4.6.1 Slovakia

Slovakia experienced, like Poland and Hungary, regular wholesale alternations in government on the basis of its relatively clear competitive divides. During the 1990s, the country was dominated by the Movement for a Democratic Slovakia (HZDS) under Vladimír Mečiar and its allies who governed with a mixture of nationalism and anti-liberalism until 1998 (Rybar 2006: 153–154). The government was ultimately defeated by a rather heterogeneous alliance of oppositional liberal- and pro-EU forces managing to form a coalition led by Mikuláš Dzurinda of the Christian Democratic Party (SDKH) (Rybar 2006: 160). Their years in government saw the collapse of the centre-left Party of the Democratic Left (SDL) and the subsequent unification of centre-left forces in the new Smer-SD party ('Direction – Social Democracy'), founded by Robert Fico (Rybar 2008: 108; Rybář and Deegan-Krause 2008). This and the neo-liberal reforms of the 2002–2006 centre-right government created the conditions for the subsequent primacy of a socio-economic divide in Slovak politics (Rybar 2008: 109). The main contender of the Smer-SD is the centre-right SDKU-DS (Slovak Democratic and Christian Union—Democratic Party), together with KDH (Christian Democratic Movement) and recently SaS (Freedom and Solidarity). After the nationalist camp of the LS-HZDS (formerly HZDS) and SNS (Slovak National Party) had failed to rebrand themselves as centre-right parties, they allied with Smer-SD and ultimately formed a government in 2006 (Rybar 2008: 109).

The centre-left/far-right government formed in 2006 under Prime Minister Fico fulfilled its full parliamentary term until 2010. This government was also responsible for the creation of the management and control system. It placed control over the OPs Transport and Environment at the sectoral level to the Ministry of Transport (SK 2007b: 91) and the Ministry of Environment (SK 2007a: 136). The Smer-SD then became again the strongest party in the 2010 elections, succeeding now not only with its strong support for high social spending, but also with nationalist appeals, mainly against perceived threats from Hungarian citizenship policies, enabling it to take votes from its nationalist allies (as a result, LS-HZDS was even unable to re-enter parliament) (Malová and Učeň 2011: 1124). Despite this success, however, the elections were won by the centre-right.

Iveta Radičová formed a new coalition consisting of the SDKU-DS, the SaS (liberal, anti-establishment), the KDH, and the Hungarian Party Most–Híd (Malová and Učeň 2011: 1121). This wholesale alternation in government resulted in a change of Minister of Environment from the Smer-SD to Most–Híd, and of the Ministry of Transport from Smer-SD to the KDH (Malová and Učeň 2011: 1121). Radičová's government survived, however, only until 2011, when it collapsed as a result of a coalition crisis about Slovakia's position towards the European Financial Stability Facility (EFSF) (Malová and Učeň 2013: 208). Deprived of its parliamentary majority, the centre-right government stayed in power only as a caretaker until snap elections in March 2012.

Then, Smer-SD managed to win the parliamentary elections for the third time in a row, this time even with an absolute majority of seats (Malová and Učeň 2013: 208). Both ministerial portfolios thus returned to the Smer-SD (Malová and Učeň 2013: 211).

Overall, both ministries experienced two wholesale alternations of governments and therefore also of parties in office. Still, the Ministry of Environment had an additional alternation, when the ministry changed between the SNS and Smer-SD in 2009 (Malová and Učeň 2010: 1156). OP Environment is thus a full member (1.00) of 'frequent party alternation' with three party alternations, while OP Transport is only a partial member (0.67).

4.4.6.2 Slovenia

Slovenia is in many ways an outlier from both its former-Yugoslav as well as its CEE peers. The country's strongest political parties developed on the basis of socio-political organizations which had already existed during the communist period (Fink-Hafner 2006: 205). The most important of these was the Liberal Democracy of Slovenia (LDS), which evolved from communist youth organizations and dominated governments for most of the time until 2004 (Jou 2011: 33). The regime divide split two basically social democratic parties, the LDS and the SDS (Social Democratic Party of Slovenia). A consensual style of politics that sometimes also included oversized majorities was characteristic for Slovenia until 2004, when a shift of support to new parties led to a clearer division between centre-left and centre-right forces (Fink-Hafner 2006: 211). This was the year when the centre-right camp for the first time formed a coalition excluding the LDS under the leadership of the renamed and rebranded SDS (now 'Slovenian Democratic Party') (Fink-Hafner 2005: 1183). The subsequent elections saw both alternations between centre-right and centre-left governments (Fink-Hafner 2009: 1112, 2013: 218), as well as the rise of new parties such as Zares (For New Politics) in 2007 and Zoran Jankovic's List—Positive Slovenia (LZJ-PS) in 2011 (Fink-Hafner 2009: 1112). Currently, the Slovenian party system is among the more fragmented and the more unstable in the region.

The first centre-right Janša government in 2004 consisted of the SDS (centre-right), the New Slovenia/Christian People's Party (N.Si), Slovenian People's Party (SLS, also Christian Democratic), and the Democratic Party of Pensioner's in Slovenia (DeSUS) (Fink-Hafner 2005: 1181). Except for the DeSUS, the government was only comprised of centre-right parties (Fink-Hafner 2005: 1184). The elections had brought a fundamental change, as the formerly dominant LDS had lost the elections (Fink-Hafner 2005: 1183). The centre-right SDS was the clear winner of the elections, after the LDS had shifted to the left under former prime minister Rop (Fink-Hafner 2005: 1183). The country's first centre-right government was also responsible for creating its cohesion policy implementation system. Similar to the Baltic states, Slovenia established a centralized system, albeit with the Government Office for Local Self Government and Regional Policy as the MA (Kavas 2010: 10). Two further ministries were appointed as IBs, the Ministry of Infrastructure and Spacial Planning and the Ministry of Environment (SI 2016).

The Janša-government remained stable until the elections in 2008, when it was replaced by a centre-left government consisting of the Social Democrats (SD), the LDS, Zares (centre-left, a splinter of centre-left LDS), and DeSUS (Fink-Hafner 2009: 1112). The new government meant that all ministries involved in the implementation of OP Environment and Transport Infrastructure Development experienced a party alternation (3/3) (Fink-Hafner 2009: 1108). The government came under pressure when the financial and economic crisis hit the country, and finally collapsed over a no-confidence vote in 2011 (Fink-Hafner 2012: 293).

The early elections in the same year brought again a change of government with the second centre-right Janša cabinet, which was formed after long negotiations in February 2012. It included the SDS, the newly established Citizen's List of Gregor Virant (DIGV), the DeSUS, the SLS, and the N.Si (Fink-Hafner 2013: 218). Fink-Hafner stresses that the camps were deeply divided over the issue of how to tackle the crisis and how to proceed with the Slovenian welfare state (Fink-Hafner 2013: 219). The second Janša cabinet was overall a replication of the first one, except for the inclusion of the newcomer party DIGV. It furthermore changed both ministers and roles of ministries involved in OP implementation. The Ministry of Transport became the Ministry of Infrastructure and Spacial Planning and changed from the SD to the SDS (Fink-Hafner 2013: 218). The Ministry of Environment and Spatial Planning became the Ministry of Agriculture and Environment and changed from DeSUS to SLS (Fink-Hafner 2013: 218). Janša also abolished the existing MA, and shifted the role to the Ministry of Economic Development and Technology (Kavas 2013: 4). This means that three out of three relevant ministries had an alternation of party in office (3/3).

Still, the government changed again on 20 March 2013, when the prime minister lost a vote of confidence due to corruption allegations (Fink-Hafner and Krasovec 2014: 281). Alenka Bratušek (LZJ-PS) then formed a new centre-left government, consisting of her party LZJ-PS as well as DeSUS, Civic List (formerly DIGV), and the SD (Fink-Hafner and Krasovec 2014: 284). The new government resulted again, for the third time, in an alternation of parties at the level of all three ministries responsible for the Slovenian OP (3/3). Together with one smaller change in 2011 (the MA changed from DeSUS shortly to the SD) (Fink-Hafner 2012: 289), this makes a total of 3.3 changes. Thus, the Slovenian OP Environment and Transport Infrastructure Development is a full member of the set 'frequent party alternation' (1.00).

4.4.7 The Condition 'Severe Crisis'

All countries in the region had experienced high growth rates and easy access to external credit from 2000 to 2007 (Bideleux 2011: 340). While the exposure to lax international lending conditions and high domestic demand for investment were similar for all of the countries, the effect of the crisis was still differential. Taking into account growth rates in the region, an indicator which is often used to measure the extent of the crisis, it becomes clear that there are wide intraregional discrepancies. While the Baltic states suffered from extreme economic contraction and double-digit negative growth, Poland did not even fall into recession in 2009 and weathered the crisis without serious problems (see column two in Table 4.5). Some studies on absorption adhere to GDP growth figures to account for the effect of the crisis on financial absorption capacity (Tosun 2014: 378). Still, the full impact of member state's ability to access loans is only inadequately covered by this measure, as the way the contraction played out was strongly dependent on other relevant factors as, for example, Eurozone membership, the level of debt, and the countries' dependence on exports (Åslund 2010: 16, 43, 53–59).

Detailed studies on the economics of the region's crisis present a deeper insight into how new member states were affected. Overall, these studies agree that the largest suffering took place in the Baltic states as well as Hungary and Romania, while Poland, Czech Republic, Slovakia, and Slovenia fared best, and also Bulgaria largely escaped the crisis (Bideleux 2011: 355–356; Connolly 2012: 44–45; Åslund 2010: 31–51). These studies generally approve Bohle's idea (see Sect. 3.3) that the extent of the crisis depended strongly on the level of financialized and consumption based growth in every country shortly before and after accession to the EU (Connolly 2012: 35–36, 61; Myant and Drahokoupil 2012: 25). Still, in contrast to Bohle's pessimistic outlook, these studies paint a more differentiated picture of the region.

On the one hand, not all CEE countries were affected by the inflow of cheap credit for consumption in the same way. Column three in Table 4.5 shows that the extent of current account deficits, which is the mismatch between in- and outflows of goods and finance in the region, was very different between the two already identified clusters of countries. While the countries that fared best had current account deficits around 4%, the main crisis countries featured double-digit rates in this respect.

On the other hand, large current account deficits were only a problem if they were not matched simultaneously by large inflows of foreign direct investment (FDI). Credits fueling only consumption or the creation of real estate bubbles will at some point emerge as a problem for an economy, but FDI is more likely to have a beneficial effect. FDI is different as it is "less likely to be pulled out quickly, does not reach a maturity date after which it needs refinancing and, in addition, may contribute to export potential" (Myant and Drahokoupil 2012: 9). The question was therefore also whether or not the current account deficits were somehow balanced by FDI inflows which had come to stay. Overall, the first question for countries' vulnerability to the crisis was their extent of pre-crisis financialized (i.e. external-credit fueled [Myant and Drahokoupil 2012: 2]) growth and their dependence on cheap external credit to refinance short-term loans. In addition, also high overall levels of public debt could be a problem in this respect. In contrast, if countries had both healthy public finances as well as low levels of financialized growth during the last few years, they would mostly suffer because of a contraction of demand in their export markets. However, these countries' public finances were in good shape upon the advent of the crisis, so they could much more easily engage in anti-crisis measures (Connolly 2010: 259–260). The following paragraphs discuss how the literature on the region's economics perceived the extent of the crisis in the new member states.

When it comes to the first group, the Baltic states had been the countries with the best economic development prior to the crisis (Connolly 2012: 37), but were subsequently those with the biggest slump of all (Connolly 2010: 264). Their fiscal policy had been rather prudent, but the private sector had accumulated large stores of foreign currency denominated debt. EU membership made it impossible for these countries to shield themselves from these large capital inflows and growing imbalances, as capital controls are not allowed inside the common market (Åslund 2010: 59). The constant inflow of money led to an explosion of current account deficits as a percentage of GDP in Lithuania (−14.6%), Estonia (−18%), and especially in Latvia (−22.5%) (Åslund 2010: 5). Another indicator of the foreign financial dependence of the Baltic states is the credit/deposit ratio (Table 4.5, column 4), which was extremely distorted especially in Estonia and Latvia in favor of the credit (i.e. the credit had no equivalent in domestic savings) (Myant and Drahokoupil 2012: 12).

The reaction of all three governments to the crisis was to maintain their fixed exchange rates and rather conduct internal devaluation, which means "carrying out draconian state-imposed across-the-board cuts in incomes, transfer payments and public expenditure" (Bideleux 2011: 355). This decision established one of the fiercest austerity regimes in the Baltic states in the aftermath of the crisis. In a similar manner, Romania also had a distorted current account balance and much foreign denominated credit, however, all to a lesser extent than in the Baltic states. Most importantly, it had accumulated a much lower amount of debt, but needed early refinancing (Åslund 2010: 28). Even though it did not seem necessary from the outset as in Hungary and Latvia, the Romanian government finally received EUR 20 billion of assistance in the realm of an IMF agreement in 2009. This agreement subsequently bound its hands when it came to measures such as counter-cyclical spending to support the economy (Connolly 2010: 263), a measure that is also likely to have affected the use of money for structural funds absorption.

The situation of Hungary is substantially different from the other countries of this group. While the crisis in the other four countries was mainly the result of the quick accumulation of short-term debt, which was still comparatively low in total (Table 4.5, column 5), Hungary had been the basket case of CEE finance during the whole prior decade. It had a considerably higher level of public debt (66.1% of GDP) than all other CEE countries and was therefore strongly dependent on external finance (Myant and Drahokoupil 2012: 12). The unsustainability of the Hungarian financial situation was also acknowledged by Prime Minister Gyurcsány after his re-election in 2006, prior to the crisis, when he stated that only "divine providence, the abundance of cash in the world

Table 4.5 The global financial and economic crisis in CEE

	GDP growth 2009[a]	*Current account deficit 2007 (% of GDP)*[b]	*FDI in relation to current account deficit*[c]	*State debt/GDP 2007*[d]	*Credit/deposit ratio 2007*[e]	*Loans in foreign currencies/total loans 2008*[f]	*Exchange rate policy*[g]	*IMF standby programme*[h]
Poland	1.6	−4.0	Balanced	45.0	112.6	32.6	Floating rate	–
Czech Republic	−4.5	−3.1	Balanced	28.9	83.0	13.6	Floating rate	–
Slovakia	−4.9	−4.8	Balanced	29.6	101.8	23.6 (2007)	Euro	–
Slovenia	−8.0	−4.2	Balanced	23.4	155.3	9.6 (2007)	Euro	–
Bulgaria	−5.5	−25.4	Balanced	19.8	95.3	66.9	Currency board	–
Estonia	−14.1	−18.0	Not fully financed	3.7	203.7	85.3	Currency board	–
Lithuania	−14.7	−14.6	Not fully financed	16.9	163.6	64.0	Currency board	–
Romania	−6.6	−14.4	Not fully financed	12.6	114.2	55.5	Floating rate	March 2009
Latvia	−18	−22.5	Not fully financed	9.0	241.3	88.4	Currency board	December 2008
Hungary	−6.8	−6.4	Not fully financed	66.1	161.5	65.7	Floating rate	October 2008

Source The author's compilation, based on [a]World Bank Data (World Bank 2015); [b,c,g,h]from Åslund (2010: 4, 5, 16); [d–f]from Myant and Drahokoupil (2012: 12, 14). Spaces coloured grey were stressed in the literature as major influences on the way the crisis affected a respective country (as discussed in detail in the text) economy, and hundreds of tricks" (*The Independent* 2006) had made re-election of his government possible. Still, the worst was yet to come when the financial crisis put a stop to this 'abundance' and did not allow Hungary to refinance its large debt pile. The government thus had to turn to the IMF and accept strict budget cuts (Bartha et al. 2010: 5).

In contrast, the second group which was least affected by the financial crisis comprised the Czech Republic, Poland, Slovakia, Slovenia, and also Bulgaria (Connolly 2012: 44; Åslund 2010: 42). The boom of external credit for private consumption had been more moderate in the Central European countries Poland, Czech Republic, and Slovakia. On the one hand, interest rates in the Czech Republic were lower in Czech Crowns than in Euro or Swiss Francs, making borrowing in foreign currencies unattractive (Åslund 2010: 18). On the other hand, Poland and Slovakia had stricter regulation alongside floating exchange rates, posing a more visible danger for borrowers who might suffer from exchange rate fluctuations (Åslund 2010: 18). As a result, the buildup of foreign (currency denominated) debt worked much slower in these countries (see Table 4.5, column 7).

Poland was eventually the least affected of all countries during the crisis, as it could rely on a healthy domestic market (Connolly 2010: 257). Its low level of debt and its rather closed economy made it the best performer in the region, as it was the only country experiencing positive growth even in 2009 (Connolly 2010: 264; Vazac 2011: 132). The development was not as good but similar in the Czech Republic, which also entered the crisis with healthy public finances (Vazac 2011: 128) and a low current account deficit. The country also had a strong domestic deposit base, making it more independent from external finance and therefore less vulnerable to global crises (Connolly 2010: 259). The fact that both countries had floating currencies allowed Poland and the Czech Republic to let their currencies depreciate during the crisis, and thereby take pressure from their economies (Bideleux 2011: 355). The Eurozone members Slovakia and Slovenia were more strongly affected by the crisis, but they had access to ECB liquidity and were therefore not subject to the credit crunch, despite their poorer economic situation (especially in Slovenia) (Åslund 2010: 43). Overall, all four countries could engage in countercyclical spending upon the advent of the crisis, in contrast to the drastic cuts which had to be implemented in the other countries (Åslund 2010: 28, 43). This was mainly possible because these countries had entered the crisis without excessive levels of public debt (in contrast to

Hungary) (Connolly 2010: 259–260; Bideleux 2011: 356) and depended less on external financial resources. "Central Europe, the subregion most integrated with the European Union, largely escaped the financial crisis (apart from fiscally irresponsible Hungary)" (Åslund 2010: 24).

Bulgaria is an interesting case as it did not feature the low current account deficits of the other countries of this second group. Its crisis is also related to its dependence on external capital, leading to a collapse of investment by one fifth (21.1%) in 2009 (Connolly 2010: 262). Still, its current account deficit was just as in the other non-crisis countries matched by unusually high levels of FDI (Åslund 2010: 16). It entered the crisis with "the shield of stable financial conditions and confidence in the financial market" (Karatchomakov 2011: 82). As a result, Bulgaria was mentioned as having experienced little suffering after 2008 (Åslund 2010: 42).

As already stressed above, there is much consensus in the literature on the financial crisis in the region that the Baltic states, Hungary, and Romania were hit hardest by the crisis countries. All five countries are therefore members of the set 'severe crisis'. Nevertheless, it still makes sense to differentiate within the group as only three of them had to seek an IMF programme, a fact that is likely to have further affected their ability for public spending. Accordingly, also Åslund emphasized Latvia, Hungary, and Romania as the main crisis countries (Åslund 2010: 7). They are therefore full members of the set 'severe crisis' (1.00). On the other hand, Estonia and Lithuania experienced a massive contraction of their economies. Nevertheless, they managed to cut their way out of the crisis on their own and did not depend on external assistance. These two countries are therefore only partial members of the set (0.67).

In contrast, the second group fared much better than the first. The fact that Poland, the Czech Republic, Slovakia, and Slovenia all could access finance in one way or the other and could even engage in counter-cyclical policies, makes drastic effects of the crisis unlikely on the financial capacities to finance cohesion policy implementation. Therefore, all four countries are full non-members of the set 'severe crisis' (0). Bulgaria also weathered the crisis reasonably well, however, it suffered more against the backdrop of its higher current account deficit and the government rather had to get the budget deficit under control than to allow higher spending (Åslund 2010: 42). Bulgaria is therefore only a partial non-member of the set 'severe crisis' (0.33).

Table 4.6 Data matrix with calibrations[a] outcome

Case	*Rate (%)*	*'Absorption problems'*	*Party alter-nations*	*'Frequent party alter-nation' (FPA)*	*Executive capacity score*	*'Low exec-utive capac-ity' (LEC)*	*2004–2006 capac-ity rating*	*'Islands of excel-lence' (IoE)*	*MA*	*'Centralized manage-ment' (CM)*	*Financial and economic crisis*	*'Severe crisis' (SC)*
ESTEE	77.90	0	1.25	0.33	6.4	0.33	B	0.67	Central	1	Severe	0.67
LTC	69.35	0	2	0.67	7.1	0	B	0.67	Central	1	Severe	0.67
ESTLE	68.50	0	1.33	0.33	6.4	0.33	B	0.67	Central	1	Severe	0.67
LTEG	67.50	0	2	0.67	7.1	0	B	0.67	Central	1	Severe	0.67
CZT	54.61	0.33	2	0.67	5.1	0.67	B/C	0.67	Sectoral	0	No Crisis	0
LVIS	53.49	0.33	1.58	0.33	7.4	0	B/C	0.67	Central	1	Severe/ IMF	1
PLIE	53.20	0.33	0.71	0	7.2	0	B/C	0.67	Central	1	No Crisis	0
BGT	50.83	0.33	1	0.33	4.8	1	NA	0	Sectoral	0	Limited	0.33
HUT	42.82	0.67	1	0.33	5.2	0.67	B/C	0.67	Central	1	Severe/ IMF	1
SKE	41.85	0.67	3	1	5.4	0.67	B/C	0.67	Sectoral	0	No Crisis	0
SKT	37.04	0.67	2	0.67	5.4	0.67	B/C	0.67	Sectoral	0	No Crisis	0
ROT	32.24	1	3	1	4.4	1	NA	0	Sectoral	0	Severe/ IMF	1
CZE	32.90	1	2	0.67	5.1	0.67	B/C	0.67	Sectoral	0	No Crisis	0
SIET	30.51	1	3.3	1	4.4	1	C	0.33	Central	1	No Crisis	0
HUEE	29.83	1	1	0.33	5.2	0.67	B/C	0.67	Central	1	Debt/ IMF	1
ROE	26.69	1	4	1	4.4	1	NA	0	Sectoral	0	Severe/ IMF	1
BGE	14.05	1	2	0.67	4.8	1	NA	0	Sectoral	0	Limited	0.33

[a]Cells coloured grey display a value conducive for the outcome 'absorption problems'

4.5 Analysis of Necessity and Sufficiency

The calibrated data matrix (Table 4.6) is now the basis for the fsQCA. In a first step, the available data is tested for necessary conditions. Necessary conditions are important as well as rare, because they have to be consistently linked to the presence of the outcome. It is possible to have a case with the presence of a necessary condition without the occurrence of the outcome, however, never the other way around. The search for necessary conditions is especially relevant when it comes to absorption research, as many studies stress the importance of a single variable (administrative capacity) which could well surmount to a necessary condition. In a second step, the data is used for the analysis of sufficiency. Sufficiency tackles the central question of this study, thus the combination of conditions which are consistently linked to the outcome. While robustness is discussed in every analytical step (see the respective footnotes), an overview of different models and tests can be found in the online Appendix IV. All analyses were conducted using the R-packages 'QCA' (Dusa 2007) and 'Set-Methods' (Medzihorsky et al. 2017).[10]

4.5.1 Analysis of Necessity

Necessity implies that a condition is always present when the outcome is present. Table 4.7 reports the result of the test for necessity of all conditions and their negations (their so-called 'complements') included in this analysis, both for the outcome and its absence. The crucial column is here 'consistency' which provides a numerical measure for the question whether or not the outcome is always in a subset-relation to the respective condition. Ideally, a necessary condition's consistency value should be close to 1.00, as this would mean a perfect subset relationship of the outcome to the necessary condition. Unfortunately, the empirical world does rarely offer such clear-cut relationships. Still, it is generally agreed that no condition below a consistency level of 0.9 should be regarded as necessary for an outcome. When it comes to the actual values of the conditions under scrutiny, only 'low executive capacity' (0.859) comes close to reaching the 0.9 threshold. The analysis is thus somewhat in line with the expectation that capacity problems have the highest consistency

[10] Parts of this fsQCA were already published in the *Journal of European Public Policy* (Hagemann 2017).

Table 4.7 Test for necessary conditions: presence and absence of all conditions are tested for their necessity for the outcome and its complement

	'Absorption problems'					
	Presence of condition			*Absence of condition*		
	Con.	*Cov.*	*RoN*	*Con.*	*Cov.*	*RoN*
Frequent party alternation	0.786	0.733	0.724	0.391	0.521	0.749
Low executive capacity	0.859	0.827	0.814	0.283	0.361	0.674
Severe crisis	0.499	0.559	0.702	0.536	0.577	0.695
Islands of excellence	0.501	0.558	0.700	0.712	0.769	0.808
Centralized management	0.357	0.370	0.585	0.643	0.750	0.818
	~'Absorption problems'					
	Presence of condition			*Absence of condition*		
	Con.	*Cov.*	*RoN*	*Con.*	*Cov.*	*RoN*
Frequent party alternation	0.563	0.432	0.552	0.652	0.714	0.833
Low executive capacity	0.390	0.309	0.522	0.782	0.820	0.880
Severe crisis	0.523	0.481	0.667	0.520	0.461	0.641
Islands of excellence	0.741	0.679	0.762	0.518	0.460	0.642
Centralized management	0.739	0.630	0.706	0.261	0.250	0.600

for necessity for absorption problems, but still not enough to speak of a proper necessary condition. Why is consistency lowered?

To explore the cases causing a reduction of consistency, it is possible to take a look at an *x/y*-plot. If the outcome is consistently a subset of the (potential) necessary condition, the membership values of all cases in the outcome must be lower or equal to that of the necessary condition. Figure 4.1 displays a plot for the set-relationship between 'absorption problems' and 'low executive capacity'.[11]

[11] In order to make otherwise overlapping cases visible, cases' exact positions in the plot were minimally altered (jittered).

At first glance, most cases conform to the relationship of necessity and can be found below the diagonal in the *x/y*-plot. Cases on the lower right side do not contradict the relationship of necessity because they are not members in the outcome. As shown in the plot, a total of four cases increases inconsistency: The Czech OP Environment and the Hungarian OP Environment and Energy have a higher membership in the outcome than in the condition (frankly said, it means that while their capacities are bad, their absorption performance is even worse). In contrast, the Latvian OP Infrastructure and Services and the Polish OP Infrastructure and Environment have no absorption problems, however, they have even better capacities than their good absorption performance would suggest (at least in set-theoretic terms when it comes to their fuzzy-memberships).

There are several interesting points to note here. First, there is no fundamental contradiction in the cases producing the inconsistency. Even though four cases are inconsistent, this is rather a difference in degree than in kind. Both 'groups' of cases producing the inconsistency nicely conform to the expected direction of the effect of the condition: The Latvian and Polish OPs are non-members of the outcome as well as of the condition, while the Czech and Hungarian OPs are members of both outcome and condition (see Fig. 4.1)—this means that there is simply no case featuring the outcome without the condition LEC. The inconsistency is only uncovered here by the use of fuzzy-sets in contrast to crisp-sets. Thus, the fact that LEC drops below 0.9 consistency is rather owed to the fact that there is a sum of smaller inconsistencies, in contrast to one fundamental and thus also theoretically much more meaningful inconsistency.

In a similar vein, Ragin stresses that it is possible to distinguish between the importance of cases producing an inconsistency. Those cases with high membership scores in the outcome and the condition under scrutiny should be treated as more important in the analysis, because their influence is more important to the set-theoretic argument (Ragin 2006: 295). To remember: The argument is that the outcome is always present when the necessary condition is present. It makes sense that it is more important to have a case where the outcome is present but the necessary condition is only partially present, in contrast to a case were neither is present, be it partially or not. Still, the formula for consistency does not differentiate between these two scenarios and treats every kind of inconsistency alike.

This means in our case that the two cases which are both members of the outcome and of the necessary condition producing inconsistency

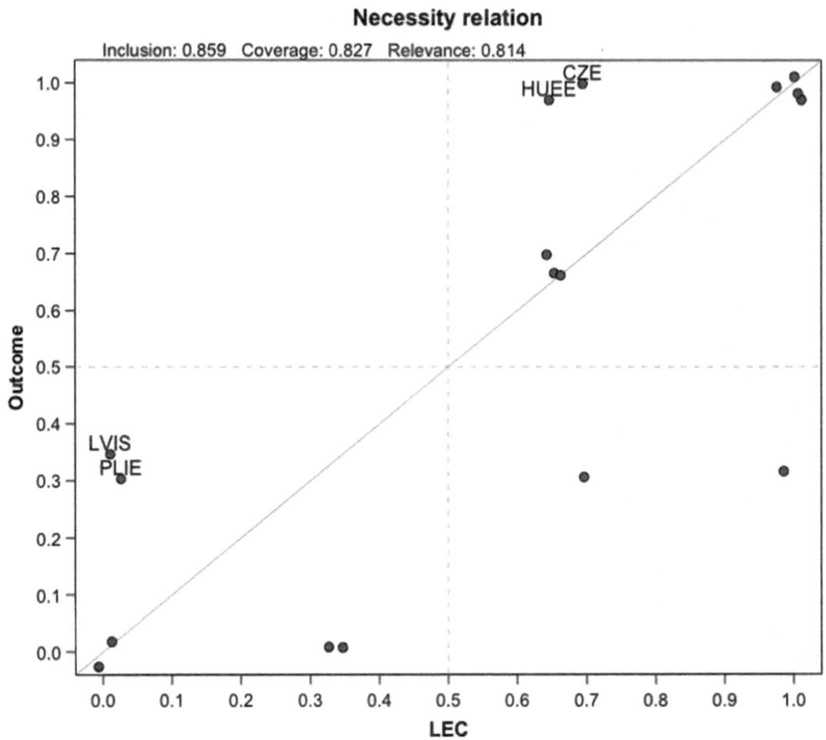

Fig. 4.1 Necessity of 'low executive capacity'

(Czech OP Environment, Hungarian OP Energy and Environment) are more important than the two other cases which are non-members of the outcome. The inclusion of such a more 'qualitative' reasoning seems well placed here as it goes beyond the mere mathematically produced consistency result and engages more closely with the set-theoretic logic of fsQCA. It can thus be stressed that LEC is, just as argued in the literature, very close to a necessary condition for absorption problems with only limited contradictions lowering consistency, even if this status has to be eventually denied if one is to take the use of fuzzy sets seriously.

The relevance of LEC is further underlined by its coverage values, presented in the third column of Table 4.7. Coverage measures the empirical importance of a necessary condition. For example, a condition might be perfectly consistent with the statement of necessity, but when the condition is found in the majority of other cases as well, the necessary condition detected is rather trivial. Take, for example, the condition 'EU membership' for 'absorption problems'. It is obviously a necessary condition as non-EU members do not even have access to the funds. Still, it is a trivial necessary condition as not only the low performers are members of the EU (and of the set 'EU membership'), but also all other cases. It thereby comes close to the importance of many other very general factors which are necessary but not very unique to the outcome. Therefore, the more equal the relationship of cases with the necessary condition which are at the same time also members of the outcome in relation to the general occurrence of the necessary condition, the more important the necessary condition.

The values in column two in Table 4.7 reveal a fairly high coverage (0.827) for LEC. This results from the fact that low executive capacities are almost only present when we also see the outcome. A glance back at the data matrix presented in Table 4.6 reveals that only the Czech OP Transport and the Bulgarian OP Transport are members in LEC while they are not members in the outcome. All other cases featuring low capacities are members of the outcome. This means that the presence of 'low executive capacity' is always found when there are 'absorption problems', but also and most importantly only found rarely when there are no 'absorption problems'.

In sum, 'low executive capacity' comes very close to being a necessary condition for the outcome 'absorption problems', even though failing the generally applied consistency threshold of 0.9. This result thereby adds to the importance of the condition stressed in the literature.

4.5.2 Analysis of Sufficiency

The analysis of sufficiency is at the heart of every QCA. In order to detect sufficient conditions or combinations of conditions for the outcome, it is necessary to turn the calibrated data matrix into a truth table. The truth table is different from the calibrated data matrix in a very central respect: While the size of the data matrix (the number of rows) depends on the number of cases involved in the analysis, the size of the truth table is independent from the number of cases. Rather, it is directly linked to the number of conditions considered in the analysis. The more conditions are included, the more logically possible combinations of conditions (and thus rows) in the truth table. The maximum of five conditions included in this study yields 32 possible combinations, or rows of the truth table (calculated as rows $= 2^k$, when k is the number of conditions). QCA depends thus not necessarily on the number of cases available, but rather on their configurations of set membership. Still, with more cases included the number of configurations covered by these cases usually also increases. A high number of conditions is a problem for a QCA as many rows will remain empty. In this analysis, the total of 17 cases will even in the best possible situation not cover all 32 rows of the truth table of five conditions. Rather, it is likely that some cases will be in the same row, so that not even 17 of the logically possible combinations will be covered, while the rest will remain logical remainders.

In order to make the best use of the data at hand, I calculated two models. Model 1 considers the conditions from the absorption literature 'low executive capacities' and 'severe crisis', alongside the condition 'frequent party alternation'. The model therefore tests politics' relevance for absorption in the form of changing party control over OPs together with the conditions mentioned most prominently in the literature. It is therefore an effort to test the most interesting factor for this study in the context of existing theory, relying as much as possible on the data at hand and less on the rows with logical remainders and assumptions.

Model 2 then takes the opposite approach: In addition to the three conditions in model one, it further tests the influence of 'centralized management' and 'islands of excellence'.[12] While these conditions are less prominently mentioned in the literature, especially when it comes to absorption research, they are still potentially interesting context conditions that could shed light on further specific aspects of absorption problems. Including more conditions and allowing for further differentiation between the cases, the model might also serve to include more cases which are potentially excluded for consistency reasons in model 1. This approach focusses accordingly on testing all potentially interesting conditions.[13]

[12]A further model controlling for policy sector was also run and is reported in the Appendix IV. Testing also for the relevance of 'environmental OP' resulted in paths which are subsets of the results found in model 1, but with a severely lowered coverage. It was thus concluded that controlling for policy does, as already argued above, not yield further relevant results.

[13]Adding a further condition to further differentiate between cases is a recommended strategy from the literature to resolve contraditions and thereby increase consistency (Rihoux and De Meur 2009: 48–49; Schneider and Wagemann 2012: 120–121).

Table 4.8 Truth table for the outcome 'absorption problems' (model 1)

FPA	*LEC*	*SC*	*OUT*	*N*	*Consistency*	*PRI*	*Cases*
1	1	1	1	2	0.83	0.80	**ROT, ROE**
1	1	0	1	6	0.81	0.75	CZT, **SKE, SKT, CZE, SIET, BGE**
0	1	1	1	2	0.75	0.67	**HUT, HUEE**
0	1	0	0	1	0.62	0.40	BGT
0	0	0	0	1	0.40	0.12	PLIE
1	0	1	0	2	0.31	0.12	LTC, LTEG
0	0	1	0	3	0.30	0.14	ESTEE, ESTLE, LVIS
1	0	0	–	0	–	–	–

Note Cases in bold type are members of the outcome

Consistency plays a central role also for the analysis of sufficiency. Consistency in the case of sufficiency refers to the question whether or not there are contradictory truth table rows. Such contradictory rows feature both cases which are members of the outcome and non-members at the same time. In fsQCA, apart from these so-called true logical contradictions, consistency is further reduced when cases simply have a higher membership in a combination of conditions than they have in the outcome.

The analysis of sufficiency starts with the three conditions considered in model 1. Table 4.8 presents the truth table for the analysis. The threshold for rows to be included into minimization was set at the usually advised minimum level of 0.75[14] (Ragin 2006: 293). This threshold works very well here, as it serves to include all members of the outcome 'absorption problems' (cases in bold type), while it also uses a relevant gap to the next non-member of the outcome BGT (0.623). Unfortunately, with the Czech transport programme there is also a case covered which is not a member of the outcome (thus a true logical contradiction), but still the concerned row has a high consistency (0.81) and includes five other cases which are members of the outcome. We can thus be reasonably confident to nevertheless include it into the minimization process.

[14]To test for robustness, the analysis was also run with an increased level of consistency (0.8). The result remained stable, albeit excluding the Hungarian cases (presence of the outcome) and the Bulgarian transport programme (complement), thereby reducing the number of paths detected (see the online Appendix IV for more detailed information).

Table 4.9 Sufficient combinations of conditions for absorption problems and its complement (model 1; complex solution) (0.75)

	'Absorption problems'		*~'Absorption problems'*	
	Path 1	*Path 2*	*Path 1*	*Path 2*
Frequent party alternation	●			⊗
Low executive capacity	●	●	⊗	
Severe crisis		●	●	⊗
Consistency	0.875	0.858	0.848	0.77
PRI	0.843	0.835	0.821	0.669
Raw coverage	0.750	0.429	0.480	0.433
Unique coverage	0.394	0.073	0.308	0.261
Cases	**SKE**	**HUT**	**ESTEE**	**BGT**
	SKT	**HUEE**	**ESTEE**	**PLIE**
	CZE	ROT	**LVIS**	
	CZT	ROE	**LTC**	
	SIET		**LTEG**	
	BGE			
	ROT			
	ROE			
Consistency total	0.885		0.775	
PRI total	0.858		0.692	
Coverage total	0.823		0.741	

Note Uniquely covered cases are in bold type

The three truth table rows with high consistency can now be used for minimization. The results of this analysis are displayed in Table 4.9 in the notation introduced by Ragin and Fiss (Ragin and Fiss 2008; Fiss 2011) which uses a black dot for the presence of a condition, a crossed dot for its absence, and a blank space for a redundant condition. The fact that all rows of the truth table but one are covered with cases leads to a situation in which all three possible solutions (complex, intermediate, and most parsimonious) for the presence of the outcome are identical.[15] The analysis yields two equifinal paths to the outcome 'absorption problems'.

The first sufficient combination of conditions for 'absorption problems' (path 1) consists of 'low executive capacity' and 'frequent party alternation'. This combination is highly consistent (0.875) and covers

[15] Only the analysis of the complement changes, as 'severe crisis' drops from path 1 in the intermediate and parsimonious solution.

the Slovak cases, the Romanian cases, the Bulgarian and Czech environmental programmes, and the Slovenian case, thus accounting for the absorption problems of all but the Hungarian OPs (77.78%). Also, the PRI values (proportional reduction in inconsistency) are high and very close to the consistency values, indicating that the combination is not at the same time also sufficient for the absence of the outcome (Schneider and Wagemann 2012: 241–244). The result is very much in line with the theoretical expectations for the relevance of politics: Incoming parties suddenly in control of an OP are expected to spare no efforts to implement their spending preferences, often to the disadvantage of existing priorities and staff.[16] Account evidence from evaluation reports suggests that capacities are not simply overcharged by frequent changes of political control and thereby preferences, but that also changes of staff play an important role here. For example, a report on absorption in Slovakia on the year of government change stressed 'high fluctuations of administrative capacities' (Frank 2012: 12) managing EU funds as one of the main reasons behind absorption delay. In the Czech Republic, the results of the 2010 parliamentary elections led in the country's management and control system to a 'dramatic scale of fluctuation even of professional staff' (Blažek 2011: 4). An evaluation study of absorption in Romania criticized that changes of government tended to interrupt implementation as the administration expected shifts in EU funds' priorities (RO 2010: 64). Specifically in the Romanian transport sector, many high level positions were found to be filled as a result of 'political patronage' (World Bank 2010: 52), and to improve performance it was necessary to 'limit the sanction of replacement of the [beneficiary] companies' management staff to failure to comply with performance obligations only' (RO 2011: 11). The combination seems thus plausible and as further evidence for the relevance of politics for absorption problems.

The plot in Fig. 4.2 (left side) presents the solution term from model 1 again in a different format. It shows that all cases but one (the Czech OP Transport) conform to the statement of sufficiency and are thus above

[16]Robustness was tested by changing the set membership of the Latvian case in FPA (from partial non- to partial membership) and the membership of SKT in the outcome (to full membership). The results remained very stable with only slight changes of the parameters of fit (see the online Appendix IV for more detailed information).

the diagonal.[17] This distribution is not perfect, but still a reasonably clear result, as even the inclusion of the contradictory Czech case leaves consistency at a very high level (0.89).

The second sufficient combination (path 2) combines 'low executive capacity' with 'severe crisis'. It consistently (0.858) accounts for the two Hungarian cases, but also covers the two Romanian ones. Again, crisis seems to be a problem only in contexts of low capacities, as successful absorbers like Estonia, Latvia, and Lithuania also experienced double-digit negative growth in 2009 (Connolly 2010: 245). In contrast, Hungary was hit very hard by the crisis as it featured an unusually high level of public debt for the region and depended on external finance (Myant and Drahokoupil 2012: 12). The Hungarian government was thus the first to turn to the IMF for help and to accept strict budget cuts in return (Bartha et al. 2010: 5). Overall, the influence of financial and economic crisis accounts uniquely in combination with low capacities only for absorption problems in Hungary. This weak result for 'severe crisis' echoes other studies (Tosun 2014: 383), and makes sense as EU funds were often not a burden to crisis torn countries, but rather the last funds available for countercyclical spending (Frank 2013: 9).

The table also displays the analysis of the complement, that is the absence of the outcome (~'absorption problems'). The analysis is based on the truth table in Table 4.10, using a 0.75 consistency threshold that serves again for a very clear distinction between members- and

[17] It is difficult to tell why the Czech OP Transport is here a deviant case for consistency. The Nečas government came into office in mid-2010 and control of the Ministry of Transport changed from ODS to VV. Officials working at the ministry at that time confirm that the shift disturbed the implementation process: "[...] [S]ome ministers wanted to carry out quiet radical changes in the financing, and we had to prepare some changes in the OP that would shift money from rail to road projects. That was not implemented in the end, but it took time, and the EC really didn't like it. And after this there was a new minster that in fact stopped it. But no doubt, the changes of the managing are influencing the work of the managing authority. From the point of view of implementation of the projects, there was a problem in 2010 as a railway project was stopped for 5 months which still influences the state of drawing of the railway priority axis because of these changes. It was in 2010, under the Nečas government with minister Bartha. We didn't exactly know what he was trying to achieve, but such things happened" (CZ3 2014). The fact that the change of party affected the OP as expected but did not lead to low absorption shifts attention to the progress of implementation. The fact that commitments in OP Transport were already at the end of 2010 at 96.8% (Blažek 2011: 10) suggests that the programme had successfully prepared a high number of projects before the change. Thus, its effect was possibly cushioned.

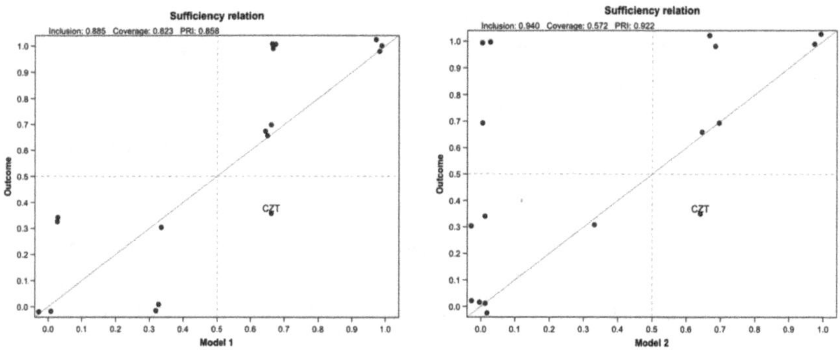

Fig. 4.2 Plots for sufficiency (model 1, model 2)

Table 4.10 Truth table for the complement~'absorption problems' (model 1)

FPA	*LEC*	*SC*	*OUT*	*n*	*Consistency*	*PRI*	*Cases*
0	0	1	1	3	0.90	0.88	**ESTEE, ESTLE, LVIS**
1	0	1	1	2	0.89	0.86	**LTC, LTEG**
0	0	0	1	1	0.80	0.72	**PLIE**
0	1	0	1	1	0.75	0.60	**BGT**
0	1	1	0	2	0.50	0.33	HUT, HUEE
1	1	0	0	6	0.43	0.25	**CZT**, SKE, SKT, CZE, SIET, BGE
1	1	1	0	2	0.33	0.20	ROT, ROE
1	0	0	–	0	–	–	–

Note Cases in bold type are members of the outcome

non-members of the outcome. The analysis of the complement yields two paths which cover only members of the outcome (but fail to include CZT). The first sufficient combination of conditions (path 1) consists of~'low executive capacity' and 'severe crisis'. This combination is highly consistent (0.848) and covers the bulk of non-members of the outcome (the Estonian and Lithuanian cases, as well as the Latvian OP). The result is very much in line with the theoretical expectations and underlines the importance of the absence of capacity problems for the absence of absorption problems, or in other words and less formally correct: the relevance of functioning capacities for successful use of EU funds. This result is very much in line with the existing literature on absorption. The fact that also 'severe crisis' is part of the combination should be seen of limited relevance: as there is hardly a reason why 'severe crisis' should help to use EU funds, it seems rather that limited empirical diversity and the resulting lack of a row for minimization causes the presence of the condition.[18]

The second path is empirically less relevant and less consistent (0.77), covering only the Polish OP and the Bulgarian transport programme, but still theoretically more interesting. It combines the absence of 'frequent party alternation' with the absence of 'severe crisis'. It thereby hints at the existence of a possible second path beyond highly developed capacity towards absorption success: In cases where party alternation is limited and which are spared from crisis, absorption can still be successful. Unfortunately, this applies only to BGT, as the Polish case features high capacities and thus only serves here to turn LEC redundant.

The next step is the inclusion of further conditions and thus the analysis of model 2. Based on the five conditions considered in model 2, the truth table in Table 4.11 contains 32 possible combinations of conditions,[19] only nine of which are covered with empirical cases. Despite of this limited number of cases, QCA offers the possibility to include also logical remainder rows into minimization. This inclusion works via the use of counterfactual assumptions, which can be based on theory (so-called 'easy counterfactuals') or only aim at the highest level of minimization (so-called 'difficult counterfactuals', usually computer-generated) (Ragin 2008: 160–163). While the original three conditions considered in model 1 are all expected to lead in their presence to the outcome, the opposite is true for the further conditions 'centralized management' and 'islands of excellence'. These expectations are now considered in the analysis to produce the intermediate solution, while computer generated assumptions are used for the parsimonious one. The inclusion of both types of counterfactuals to produce the intermediate and most parsimonious solution is usually referred to as the 'standard analysis' in QCA (Ragin 2008: 174). The results in Table 4.12 again display the results in the notation of Ragin and Fiss, but now also include a further aspect of this notation: the dots pointing at the presence or absence of the condition are now displayed in different sizes. A large dot means that a condition is present in all three solutions, while a small dot means that a condition is only present in the complex and intermediate solution (Fiss 2011: 407).

[18] The condition also vanishes in the intermediate solution, leaving only LEC as sufficient.

[19] Due to limited space, the table only displays the rows covered with cases.

Table 4.11 Truth table for the outcome 'absorption problems' in model 2

FPA	*LEC*	*SC*	*CENTRAL*	*ISLAND*	*OUT*	*N*	*incl*	*PRI*	*Cases*
1	1	0	0	0	1	1	1	1	**BGE**
1	1	1	0	0	1	2	1	1	**ROT, ROE**
1	1	0	0	1	1	4	0.87	0.80	CZT, **SKE, SKT, CZE**
0	1	0	0	0	1	1	0.83	0.66	BGT
0	1	1	1	1	0	2	0.67	0.60	**HUT, HUEE**
1	1	0	1	0	0	1	0.50	0.50	**SIET**
1	0	1	1	1	0	2	0.33	0.14	LTC, LTEG
0	0	1	1	1	0	3	0.30	0.12	ESTEE, ESTLE, LVIS
0	0	0	1	1	0	1	0.17	0.00	PLIE

Note Cases in bold type are members of the outcome. The truth table displays only the rows containing cases

Table 4.12 Sufficient combinations of conditions for absorption problems and its complement (model 2; intermediate solution)

	'Absorption problems' (0.85)	*~'Absorption problems' (0.66)*	
	Path 1	*Path 1*	*Path 2*
Frequent party alternation	●		⊗
Low executive capacity	•	⊗	
Severe crisis			⊗
Islands of excellence		•	
Centralized management	⊗	•	
Consistency	0.940	0.929	0.770
PRI	0.922	0.911	0.669
Raw coverage	0.572	0.567	0.433
Unique coverage	–	0.308	0.173
Cases	**SKE**	**ESTEE**	**BGT**
	SKT	**ESTEE**	PLIE
	CZE	**LVIS**	
	CZT	**LTC**	
	BGE	**LTEG**	
	ROT	PLIE	
	ROE		
Consistency total	0.940	0.811	
PRI total	0.922	0.737	
Coverage total	0.572	0.741	

Note Uniquely covered cases are in bold type

The threshold for inclusion of conditions into minimization is set at 0.85 (the dashed line) (Ragin 2006: 293). This higher level than in model 1 is based on the high level of consistency of the non-member row including only BGT (0.83). As considering this row for minimization would not make sense, the consistency level is increased. When it comes to coverage, CZT is again the only non-member covered (the right plot in Fig. 4.2), while now even three members of the outcome are not included in consistent paths (HUEE, HUT, SIET), resulting in a much-reduced coverage in contrast to model 1 (0.572 vs. 0.823). In contrast, the higher applied threshold and exclusion of low consistency cases increases consistency of the solution term (0.94).[20]

Minimization of the consistent rows of model 2 results in a single path to the outcome (intermediate solution) which is at the same time a subset of path 1 in model 1. It combines frequent party alternation with low capacities and now also the absence of centralized management in a highly consistent (0.94) combination covering six members of the outcome. Despite of the addition of two further conditions, the result is thus only minimally altered and in line with the findings from model 1. Furthermore, the added conditions work into the expected direction, with the absence of centralized management as an INUS condition for the outcome. The analysis thus yields further support to the findings from model 1, as well as the expected further specification of another context conditions. Still, it seems questionable whether the analysis sheds more light on 'absorption problems' than model 1 as the differentiation leads not as hoped to the inclusion of more, but fewer cases into the analysis.

When it comes to the complement, consistency was set at the unusually low level of 0.66. This decision is justified by the theoretical relevance of the case BGT, which remains in this way included without adding further non-members of the outcome to the solution term.[21] In path 1, the absence of 'low executive capacity' found in model 1 is complemented by the presence of 'islands' as well as 'centralized management'. This is again

[20]As in model 1, robustness was tested in model 2 by changing the set membership of the Latvian case in FPA (from partial non- to partial membership) and the membership of SKT in the outcome (to full membership). The results remained also here stable with only slight changes of the parameters of fit (see the online Appendix IV for more detailed information) and the occasional loss of path two in the analysis of the complement.

[21]To test for robustness, the model was also run again at a consistency level of 0.75. With this higher threshold BGT naturally drops out and thus also path 2, while path 1 remains the same. The result is thus stable for different levels of consistency (see the online Appendix IV for more detailed information).

Table 4.13 Truth table for the complement ~'absorption problems' in model 2

FPA	*LEC*	*SC*	*CENTRAL*	*ISLAND*	*OUT*	*n*	*incl*	*PRI*	*Cases*
0	0	0	1	1	1	1	1	1	**PLIE**
0	0	1	1	1	1	3	0.90	0.88	**ESTEE, ESTLE, LVIS**
1	0	1	1	1	1	2	0.89	0.86	**LTC, LTEG**
0	1	0	0	0	1	1	0.67	0.34	**BGT**
1	1	0	0	0	0	1	0.57	0.00	BGE
1	1	0	0	1	0	4	0.50	0.20	**CZT**, SKE, SKT, CZE
1	1	0	1	0	0	1	0.50	0.50	SIET
0	1	1	1	1	0	2	0.50	0.40	HUT, HUEE
1	1	1	0	0	0	2	0.12	0.00	ROT, ROE

Note Cases in bold type are members of the outcome. The truth table displays only the rows containing cases

a subset of the result of the intermediate solution from model 1, with conditions working into the expected direction. In addition, path 2 even stays completely unaltered despite of the further conditions and inclusion of counterfactuals (Table 4.13).

4.6 Discussion of Results: A Conjunction of Party Alternation and Low Capacity

The fsQCA of 17 OPs in Central and Eastern Europe has produced interesting results contributing to our understanding of the absorption process. There are several distinct contributions.

The first important aspect is the analysis of necessity. 'Low executive capacity' (LEC) is with a consistency below 0.9 for necessity not a necessary condition, but there are still several arguments supporting its relevance. Crucially, there is always low executive capacity when there are absorption problems, while it is otherwise rarely found. This is strongly in line with the general emphasis in the literature on the importance of administrative and government capacity to account for countries' absorption performance (Milio 2007; Bachtler et al. 2014; Tosun 2014). The result of this analysis thus partly confirms the literature's claim that administrative and government capacity is of great importance for a country's absorption performance, albeit not on its own.

When it comes to sufficiency, the fuzzy-set QCA in model 1 shows that the combination of 'frequent party alternation' and 'low executive capacity' covers seven out of nine cases with a low level of EU fund absorption. This combination is highly consistent (0.875) and based on the original data and calibration, and thus does not depend on easy or difficult counterfactual assumptions (model 1). It remains stable also after testing further for the relevance of earlier developed 'islands of excellence' and the creation of a centralized management and control system for EU fund management (model 2). In this constellation, party alternation and low capacities are further complemented by the absence of 'centralized management', a solution with higher consistency but lower coverage than in model 1.

Besides party alternation, also 'severe crisis' matters for absorption problems. Still, it does so only in model 1 and uniquely accounts for absorption problems only in the two Hungarian cases. While it is theoretically a relevant second path, it was apparently empirically not that important for absorption whether or not a country was deeply affected by or spared from the global financial and economic crisis. It was thus mostly not an external shock applied to the implementation process leading to the low performance, but rather domestic conditions causing absorption problems. This result also makes intuitively sense when looking at the data. It is intriguing that especially the highly successful absorbers in the Baltic states suffered most from the crisis when it comes to negative growth (cf. Sect. 3.3). It could thus well be that EU funds rather played a role as a source of counter-cyclical spending when all other sources dried up, in contrast to the argument of EU funds as a further burden on the budget in need of co-financing, as the original reasoning would go. The result thus echos the weak impact of the crisis on absorption found in other studies (Tosun 2014: 383), and is in line with earlier hints from case studies that changes of political control or politicization hamper absorption (Milio 2008; Buzogány and Korkut 2013; Surubaru 2017b). The most interesting and also empirically most relevant finding to account for absorption problems is thus the interplay of party alternation and capacities in the member states.

Overall, the analysis yields three interesting insights on the role of party alternation for absorption: First, it plays a crucial role for absorption problems in contexts of low capacities. Most cases have suffered from absorption problems when they had both frequent changes of parties in control of EU funds and generally low capacities for their management. This hints at a more dynamic role of capacities in the absorption process. Instead of assuming a stable level of capacities without any development, the detected conjunction leads to the possible conclusion that it takes more than low capacities to cause absorption problems, as most ministries will try to improve capacities if the conditions are conducive for this. In struggling programmes, however, it could be the case that while absorption is initially hampered by capacity problems, this situation is perpetuated as frequent changes of party control lead both to a politicization of spending priorities and crucially a change of staff. Also, it could be that 'islands of excellence' built during a previous, more stable period to manage EU funds are terminated by politicization from another political party. This would explain why capacities seemingly often do not improve over time, even though interest in using EU money is high, as well as why funds are managed worse after a more successful preceding period. This finding is also supported by the analysis of the complement.

Second, in path 2 of the complement the Bulgarian transport programme manages to use its EU funds reasonably well despite of its generally 'low executive capacities'. Here, the absence of 'severe crisis' and also the absence of 'frequent party alternation' is systematically linked to the absence of absorption problems. This finding mirrors the argument from the analysis of the outcome: Capacities might thus develop in the absence of frequent alternation of political control, and potentially work as an 'islands of excellence' in an otherwise low capacity contexts to make absorption work. This means that successful absorption is possible also despite of generally low capacities, even if it might still be very vulnerable to external influence when power shifts to another party. This finding is, however, somewhat weaker than the finding for the outcome as it has lower consistency, is based only on a single case, and rather vulnerable to robustness test as the Bulgarian case easily drops out (for example, when setting a higher consistency threshold). Still, it receives support from another qualitative analysis comparing the Romanian and Bulgarian implementation experience.

Surubaru finds in the Bulgarian case much better sectoral administrative capacities than in Romania, "characterized by more balanced institutional design, simpler procedures and stronger human resources capabilities" (Surubaru 2017a: 846). He links this difference and the following much better absorption performance to governmental stability under the Borisov government that offered political support and focussed on improving the absorption process (Surubaru 2017a: 850). Still, also in Bulgaria there were differences: the strongest political emphasis lay apparently on implementing the large-scale transport infrastructure projects (Surubaru 2017a: 851). This is in line with the detected much better performance in OPT than in OPE. When it comes to the latter, Surubaru highlights that in Bulgaria especially the environmental OP suffered from political infighting for and a "politicised distribution of large tender contracts" (Surubaru 2017b: 114–116), which he links to the OP's limited performance. This evidence is in line with the finding from the QCA that the Bulgarian OPT performed better than its environmental counterpart as it was less subject to politicization. It also underlines how during a period of stability capacities for management of the Bulgarian transport programme could improve.

Finally, the analysis of the complement further underlines that party alternation and the associated politicization of the absorption process seem to matter much less in contexts with high capacities. The two Lithuanian cases display clear non-membership in the outcome, despite of two full alternations even between different political camps and not only parties. Nevertheless, their high levels of capacities seem to have spared them from absorption problems, even in the additional face of severe economic crisis.

It can thus be concluded that politics does matter for EU funds' absorption problems, but only in low capacity contexts. Just as expected in the literature, well-developed capacities led in any case to successful absorption (analyses of the complement). In contrast, in low capacity contexts sectoral EU fund management systems were less resilient and apparently more vulnerable in case of frequent alternation of political control of programmes. Still, the fsQCA underlines that also cases with low capacities can use their EU funds well when their implementation efforts are not disturbed by such political interference. Due to the empirical importance of the conjunction of generally low capacities and frequent party alternation, the mechanism behind it leading to absorption problems will be further explored in the process tracing analysis.

References

Allen, D. (2008). Cohesion Policy Pre- and Post-enlargement. In M. Baun & D. Marek (Eds.), *EU Cohesion Policy After Enlargement* (pp. 15–33). Basingstoke: Palgrave.

Åslund, A. (2010). *The Last Shall Be the First: The East European Financial Crisis.* Washington, DC: Peterson Institute for International Economics.

Autengruber, C. (2008). Bulgarien: Zwischen anfänglichen Konsolidierungstendenzen und aktuellen Umbrüchen. In E. Bos & D. Segert (Eds.), *Osteuropäische Demokratien als Trendsetter? Parteien und Parteiensysteme nach dem Ende des Übergangsjahrzehnts* (pp. 133–146). Opladen and Farmington Hills: Verlag Barbara Budrich.

Bachtler, J., Downes, R., & Gorzelak, G. (2000). Transition, Cohesion and Regional Policy in Central and Eastern Europe: Conclusions. In J. Bachtler, R. Downes, & G. Gorzelak (Eds.), *Transition Cohesion and Regional Policy in Central and Eastern Europe* (pp. 355–378). Aldershot et al.: Ashgate.

Bachtler, J., Mendez, C., & Oraže, H. (2014). From Conditionality to Europeanization in Central and Eastern Europe: Administrative Performance and Capacity in Cohesion Policy. *European Planning Studies, 22*(4), 735–757.

Bailey, D., & De Propris, L. (2002). EU Structural Funds, Regional Capabilities and Enlargement: Towards Multi-level Governance? *Journal of European Integration, 24*(4), 303–324.

Bailey, D., & De Propris, L. (2004). A Bridge Too Phare? EU Pre-accession Aid and Capacity-Building in the Candidate Countries. *JCMS: Journal of Common Market Studies, 42*(1), 77–98.

Balas, G., & Kiss, G. (2011). Hungary. *Expert Evaluation Network.* Budapest: HEFTA Centre for Analyses. Available at http://ec.europa.eu/regional_policy/index.cfm/en/policy/evaluations/ec/2007-2013/#1. Accessed 29 May 2017.

Balas, G., Borbas, G., & Herczeg, B. (2012). Hungary. *Expert Evaluation Network.* Budapest: HEFTA Centre for Analyses. Available at http://ec.europa.eu/regional_policy/sources/docgener/evaluation/pdf/eval2007/expert_innovation/2012_synt_rep_hu.pdf. Accessed 29 May 2017.

Balas, G., Kiss, G., & Borbas, G. (2013). Hungary. *Expert Evaluation Network.* Budapest: HEFTA Centre for Analyses. Available at http://ec.europa.eu/regional_policy/sources/docgener/evaluation/pdf/eval2007/2013_een_task2_hu.pdf. Accessed 29 May 2017.

Bartha, A., Nagy, K., Gyukics, R., & Kopint, T. (2010). Hungary. *Expert Evaluation Network.* Brussels: European Commission, Directorate-General Regional Policy. Available at http://ec.europa.eu/regional_policy/sources/docgener/evaluation/pdf/eval2007/country_reports/hungary.pdf. Accessed 29 May 2017.

Baun, M. J., & Marek, D. (2008). The Czech Republic. In D. Marek & M. J. Baun (Eds.), *EU Cohesion Policy After Enlargement* (pp. 165–186). Basingstoke: Palgrave Macmillan.

Berglund, S., Gange, I., & Van Waarden, F. (2006). Mass Production of Law. Routinization in the Transposition of European Directives: A Sociological-Institutionalist Account. *Journal of European Public Policy, 13*(5), 692–716.

BG. (2007a). OP Environment Bulgaria 2007–2013. *National Strategic Reference Framework*. Sofia: Ministry of Environment, Bulgaria. Available at archive.eufunds.bg/document/463. Accessed 12 Feb 2016.

BG. (2007b). OP Transport Bulgaria 2007–2013. *National Strategic Reference Framework*. Sofia: Ministry of Transport, Bulgaria. Available at http://www.optransport.bg/upload/docs/2_SOPT_FINAL.pdf. Accessed 12 Feb 2016.

Bideleux, R. (2011). Contrasting Responses to the International Economic Crisis of 2008–10 in the 11 CIS Countries and in the 10 Post-communist EU Member Countries. *Journal of Communist Studies and Transition Politics, 27*(3–4), 338–363.

Bingen, D. (2008). Polen: Wie ein labiles Parteiensystem zu einer Stabilisierung der Demokratie beiträgt. In E. Bos & D. Segert (Eds.), *Osteuropäische Demokratien als Trendsetter? Parteien und Parteiensysteme nach dem Ende des Übergangsjahrzehnts* (pp. 77–90). Opladen and Farmington Hills: Verlag Barbara Budrich.

Blažek, J. (2011). Czech Republic. *Expert Evaluation Network*. Prague: Charles University. Available at http://ec.europa.eu/regional_policy/index.cfm/en/policy/evaluations/ec/2007-2013/#1. Accessed 29 May 2017.

Blažek, J. (2012). Czech Republic. *Expert Evaluation Network*. Prague: Charles University. Available at http://ec.europa.eu/regional_policy/sources/docgener/evaluation/pdf/eval2007/expert_innovation/2012_een_task2_cz.pdf. Accessed 12 Feb 2016.

Blažek, J. (2013). Czech Republic. *Expert Evaluation Network*. Prague: Charles University. Available athttp://ec.europa.eu/regional_policy/sources/docgener/evaluation/pdf/eval2007/2013_een_task2_cz.pdf. Accessed 12 Feb 2016.

Börzel, T. A., Hofmann, T., Panke, D., & Sprungk, C. (2010). Obstinate and Inefficient: Why Member States Do Not Comply with European Law. *Comparative Political Studies, 43*(11), 1363–1390.

Bubbico, R. L., & De Michelis, N. (2011). *The Financial Execution of Structural Funds* (Regional Focus No. 3/2011). Brussels: European Commission, Directorate-General for Regional Policy. Available at http://ec.europa.eu/regional_policy/sources/docgener/focus/2011_03_financial.pdf. Accessed 12 Feb 2016.

Buzogány, A., & Korkut, U. (2013). Administrative Reform and Regional Development Discourses in Hungary: Europeanisation Going NUTS? *Europe–Asia Studies, 65*(8), 1555–1577.

Connolly, R. (2010). The EU Economy: Member States Outside the Euro Area in 2009. *JCMS: Journal of Common Market Studies, 48*(Annual Review), 243–266.

Connolly, R. (2012). The Determinants of the Economic Crisis in Post-socialist Europe. *Europe–Asia Studies, 64*(1), 35–67.

CZ. (2004). OP Infrastructure 2004–2006. *National Strategic Reference Framework.* Prague: Ministry of Regional Development, Czech Republic. Available at http://www.strukturalni-fondy.cz/en/Fondy-EU/Programy-2004-2006/Operacni-programy/OP-INFRASTRUKTURA. Accessed 12 Feb 2016.

CZ. (2007a). OP Environment 2007–2013. *National Strategic Reference Framework.* Prague: Ministry of Environment, Czech Republic. Available at http://en.opzp2007-2013.cz/ke-stazeni/515/5060/detail/the-operational-programme-environment---for-the-period-2007-2013/. Accessed 12 Feb 2016.

CZ. (2007b). OP Transport 2007–2013. *National Strategic Reference Framework.* Prague: Ministry of Transport, Czech Republic. Available at http://www.opd.cz/Providers/Document.ashx?id=48. Accessed 12 Feb 2016.

CZ3. (2014). *Interview in Prague with Czech Official on 06 June 2014.*

CZ6. (2015). *Interview in Prague with Czech Official on 14 May 2015.*

Deegan-Krause, K., & Haugton, T. (2010). A Fragile Stability. The Institutional Roots of Low Party System Volatility in the Czech Republic, 1990–2009. *Czech Journal of Political Science (Politologický časopis), 17*(3), 227–241.

Dimitrova, A., & Toshkov, D. (2009). Post-accession Compliance Between Administrative Co-ordination and Political Bargaining. *European Integration Online Papers, 13*, Article 19. http://eiop.or.at/eiop/texte/2009-019a.htm. Accessed Jan 2016.

Döring, H., & Manow, P. (2014). *Parliament and Government Composition Database (ParlGov): An Infrastructure for Empirical Information on Parties, Elections and Governments in Modern Democracies.* Version 14/12–29 December 2014. Available at http://parlgov.org/. Accessed 27 Jan 2015.

Dusa, A. (2007). User Manual for the QCA (GUI) Package in R. *Journal of Business Research, 60*(5), 576–586.

EE. (2003). Single Programming Document 2004–2006. *National Strategic Reference Framework.* Tallinn: Government of Estonia. Available at www.digar.ee/arhiiv/en/download/22611. Accessed 12 Feb 2016.

EE. (2007a). OP Economic Environment 2007–2013. *National Strategic Reference Framework.* Tallinn: Ministry of Finance, Estonia. Available at http://www.struktuurifondid.ee/public/inglisekeelsed_dokumendid/Modified_Economic_Environment_OP_070311.pdf. Accessed 12 Feb 2016.

EE. (2007b). OP Living Environment 2007–2013. *National Strategic Reference Framework.* Tallinn: Ministry of Finance, Estonia. Available at http://www.struktuurifondid.ee/public/inglisekeelsed_dokumendid/Modified_Living_Environment_OP_070311.pdf. Accessed 12 Feb 2016.

Emmenegger, P. (2011). Job Security Regulations in Western Democracies: A Fuzzy Set Analysis. *European Journal of Political Research, 50*(3), 336–364.

Enyedi, Z. (2006). The Survival of the Fittest: Party System Concentration in Hungary. In S. Jungerstam-Mulders (Ed.), *Post-communist EU Member States: Parties and Party Systems* (pp. 177–202). Farnham and Burlington, VT: Ashgate.

European Commission. (2013a). *Analysis of the Budgetary Implementation of the Structural and Cohesion Funds in 2013* (Commission Staff Working Paper). Brussels: European Commission, Directorate-General Budget. Available at http://ec.europa.eu/budget/library/biblio/documents/2013/sf_implem_rep_2013_en.pdf. Accessed 12 Feb 2016.

European Commission. (2013b, April 18). Cohesion Policy: Strategic Report 2013. *COM(2013) 210 final*. Brussels: European Commission. Available at http://ec.europa.eu/regional_policy/how/policy/doc/strategic_report/2013/strat_report_2013_en.pdf. Accessed 15 Mar 2017.

European Commission. (2014). *Analysis of the Budgetary Implementation of the Structural and Cohesion Funds in 2014* (Commission Staff Working Paper). Brussels: European Commission, Directorate-General Budget. Available at http://ec.europa.eu/budget/biblio/publications/publications_en.cfm#anastrucofunds_2014. Accessed 29 May 2017.

Falkner, G., Hartlapp, M., Leiber, S., & Treib, O. (2004). Non-compliance with EU Directives in the Member States: Opposition Through the Backdoor? *West European Politics, 27*(3), 452–473.

Fink-Hafner, D. (2005). Slovenia. *European Journal of Political Research, 44*(7–8), 1179–1187.

Fink-Hafner, D. (2006). Slovenia: Between Bipolarity and Broad Coalition-Building. In S. Jungerstam-Mulders (Ed.), *Post-communist EU Member States: Parties and Party Systems* (pp. 203–231). Farnham and Burlington, VT: Ashgate.

Fink-Hafner, D. (2009). Slovenia. *European Journal of Political Research, 48*(7–8), 1106–1113.

Fink-Hafner, D. (2012). Slovenia. *European Journal of Political Research Political Data Yearbook, 51*(1), 288–296.

Fink-Hafner, D. (2013). Slovenia. *European Journal of Political Research Political Data Yearbook, 52*(1), 217–222.

Fink-Hafner, D., & Krasovec, A. (2014). Slovenia. *European Journal of Political Research Political Data Yearbook, 53*(1), 281–286.

Fiss, P. C. (2011). Building Better Causal Theories: A Fuzzy Set Approach to Typologies in Organization Research. *Academy of Management Journal, 54*(2), 393–420.

Frank, K. (2012). Slovakia. *Expert Evaluation Network*. Bratislava: Slovak Academy of Sciences. Available at http://ec.europa.eu/regional_policy/sources/docgener/evaluation/pdf/eval2007/expert_innovation/2012_een_task2_sk.pdf. Accessed 29 May 2017.

Frank, K. (2013). Slovakia. *Expert Evaluation Network*. Bratislava: Slovak Academy of Sciences. Available at http://ec.europa.eu/regional_policy/sources/docgener/evaluation/pdf/eval2007/2013_een_task2_sk.pdf. Accessed 29 May 2017.

Gorzelak, G., & Kozak, M. W. (2013). Poland. *Expert Evaluation Network*. Warsaw: EUROREG. Available at http://ec.europa.eu/regional_policy/

sources/docgener/evaluation/pdf/eval2007/2013_een_task2_pl.pdf. Accessed 12 Feb 2016.
Grzymala-Busse, A. (2006). Authoritarian Determinants of Democratic Party Competition: The Communist Successor Parties in East Central Europe. *Party Politics, 12*(3), 415–437.
Gwiazda, A. (2009). Poland's Quasi-institutionalized Party System: The Importance of Elites and Institutions. *Perspectives on European Politics and Society, 10*(3), 350–376.
Hagemann, C. (2017). How Politics Matters for EU Funds' Absorption Problems—A Fuzzy-Set Analysis. *Journal of European Public Policy*, 1–19. Available at https://doi.org/10.1080/13501763.2017.1398774
Haverland, M., & Romeijn, M. (2007). Do Member States Make European Policies Work? Analysing the EU Transposition Deficit. *Public Administration, 85*(3), 757–778.
Hloušek, V., & Šedo, J. (2008). Tschechien: Konsolidierung des Parteiensystems bei anhaltenden Problemen der Mehrheitsbildung. In E. Bos & D. Segert (Eds.), *Osteuropäische Demokratien als Trendsetter? Parteien und Parteiensysteme nach dem Ende des Übergangsjahrzehnts* (pp. 91–103). Opladen and Farmington Hills: Verlag Barbara Budrich.
Horvat, A. (2005). *Why Does Nobody Care About the Absorption? Some Aspects Regarding Administrative Absorption Capacity for the EU Structural Funds in the Czech Republic, Estonia, Hungary, Slovakia and Slovenia Before Accession* (WIFO Working Papers). Wien: Österreichisches Institut für Wirtschaftsforschung. Available at http://www.wifo.ac.at/jart/prj3/wifo/resources/person_dokument/person_dokument.jart?publikationsid=25750&mime_type=application/pdf. Accessed 29 May 2017.
HU. (2003). OP Environmental Protection and Infrastructure 2004–2006. *National Strategic Reference Framework*. Budapest: Ministry of Economy and Transport, Hungary. Available at http://www.inforse.org/europe/Structuralfunds/SF_docs/HU_SF_KIOP_en.pdf. Accessed 12 Feb 2016.
HU. (2007). OP Environment and Energy 2007–2013. *National Strategic Reference Framework*. Budapest: Government of the Republic of Hungary. Available at http://www.inforse.org/europe/Structuralfunds/SF_docs/SF_KEOP_07_13.pdf. Accessed 12 Feb 2016.
HU. (2013). OP Transport Hungary 2007-2013. *National Strategic Reference Framework*. Budapest: Government of Hungary. Available at https://www.google.de/url?sa=t&rct=j&q=&esrc=s&source=web&cd=2&cad=rja&uact=8&ved=0ahUKEwjA3OusjKzLAhXLiywKHYgtCkQFggpMAE&url=https%3A%2F%2Fwww.palyazat.gov.hu%2Fdownload.php%3FobjectId%3D1787&usg=AFQjCNHjB-JZPXEmt_eFxVhA3RmYF9Fjug. Accessed 12 Feb 2016.

Huszák, L. (2010). *Der Wettbewerb der Regionen: regionale Unterschiede in der Absorption der EU-Fördermittel: Eine empirische Analyse*. Frankfurt: Peter Lang.
Ikstens, J. (2007). Latvia. *European Journal of Political Research, 46*(7–8), 1012–1018.
Ikstens, J. (2008). Latvia. *European Journal of Political Research, 47*(7–8), 1039–1047.
Ikstens, J. (2010). Latvia. *European Journal of Political Research, 49*(7–8), 1049–1057.
Ikstens, J. (2011). Latvia. *European Journal of Political Research, 50*(7–8), 1035–1044.
Ikstens, J. (2012). Latvia. *European Journal of Political Research Political Data Yearbook, 51*(1), 175–186.
Jasiewicz, K., & Jasiewicz-Betkiewicz, A. (2006). Poland. *European Journal of Political Research, 45*(7–8), 1231–1246.
Jasiewicz, K., & Jasiewicz-Betkiewicz, A. (2007). Poland. *European Journal of Political Research, 46*(7–8), 1063–1074.
Jasiewicz, K., & Jasiewicz-Betkiewicz, A. (2008). Poland. *European Journal of Political Research, 47*(7–8), 1096–1107.
Jasiewicz, K., & Jasiewicz-Betkiewicz, A. (2012). Poland. *European Journal of Political Research Political Data Yearbook, 51*(1), 243–256.
Jou, W. (2011). Left-Right Orientations and Ideological Voting in New Democracies: A Case Study of Slovenia. *Europe–Asia Studies, 63*(1), 27–47.
Kaeding, M. (2006). Determinants of Transposition Delay in the European Union. *Journal of Public Policy, 26*(3), 229–253.
Kalvet, T. (2011). Estonia. *Expert Evaluation Network*. Tallinn: Ragnar Nurkse School of Innovation and Governance. Available at http://ec.europa.eu/regional_policy/en/policy/evaluations/ec/2007-2013/#1. Accessed 12 Feb 2016.
Kalvet, T. (2012). Estonia. *Expert Evaluation Network*. Tallinn: Ragnar Nurkse School of Innovation and Governance. Available at http://ec.europa.eu/regional_policy/sources/docgener/evaluation/pdf/eval2007/expert_innovation/2012_een_task2_ee.pdf. Accessed 12 Feb 2016.
Kalvet, T. (2013). Estonia. *Expert Evaluation Network*. Tallinn: Ragnar Nurkse School of Innovation and Governance. Available at http://ec.europa.eu/regional_policy/sources/docgener/evaluation/pdf/eval2007/2013_een_task2_ee.pdf. Accessed 12 Feb 2016.
Karatchomakov, M. (2011). Bulgaria: The Deferred Crisis. In J. Jungmann & B. Sagemann (Eds.), *Financial Crisis in Eastern Europe: Road to Recovery* (pp. 64–107). Wiesbaden: Gabler Verlag.
Kavas, D. (2010). Slovenia. *Expert Evaluation Network*. Ljubljana: Institute for Economic Research. Available at http://ec.europa.eu/regional_policy/

sources/docgener/evaluation/pdf/eval2007/country_reports/slovenia.pdf. Accessed 12 Feb 2016.

Kavas, D. (2012). Slovenia. *Expert Evaluation Network*. Ljubljana: Institute for Economic Research. Available at http://ec.europa.eu/regional_policy/sources/docgener/evaluation/pdf/eval2007/expert_innovation/2012_een_task2_sl.pdf. Accessed 12 Feb 2016.

Kavas, D. (2013). Slovenia. *Expert Evaluation Network*. Ljubljana: Institute for Economic Research. Available at http://ec.europa.eu/regional_policy/sources/docgener/evaluation/pdf/eval2007/2013_een_task2_si.pdf. Accessed 12 Feb 2016.

Kiszelly, Z. (2008). Ungarn: Auf dem Weg zum Kartellparteiensystem. In E. Bos & D. Segert (Eds.), *Osteuropäische Demokratien als Trendsetter? Parteien und Parteiensysteme nach dem Ende des Übergangsjahrzehnts* (pp. 121–132). Opladen and Farmington Hills: Verlag Barbara Budrich.

Kolarova, R., & Spirova, M. (2014). Bulgaria. *European Journal of Political Research Political Data Yearbook, 53*(1), 45–56.

Kopecký, P. (2006). The Rise of the Power Monopoly: Political Parties in the Czech Republic. In S. Jungerstam-Mulders (Ed.), *Post-communist EU Member States: Parties and Party Systems* (pp. 125–146). Farnham and Burlington, VT: Ashgate.

Kostadinova, T. (2007). The Impact of Finance Regulations on Political Parties: The Case of Bulgaria. *Europe–Asia Studies, 59*(5), 807–827.

Krupavicius, A. (2005). Lithuania. *European Journal of Political Research, 44*(7–8), 1086–1101.

Krupavicius, A. (2007). Lithuania. *European Journal of Political Research, 46*(7–8), 1019–1031.

Krupavicius, A. (2009). Lithuania. *European Journal of Political Research Political Data Yearbook, 48*(7–8), 1022–1036.

Krupavicius, A. (2011). Lithuania. *European Journal of Political Research, 50*(7–8), 1045–1057.

Krupavicius, A. (2013). Lithuania. *European Journal of Political Research Political Data Yearbook, 52*(1), 140–151.

Lackowska-Madurowicz, M., & Swianiewicz, P. (2013). Structures, Procedures and Social Capital: The Implementation of EU Cohesion Policies by Subnational Governments in Poland. *International Journal of Urban and Regional Research, 37*(4), 1396–1418.

Linek, L. (2008). Czech Republic. *European Journal of Political Research, 47*(7–8), 947–951.

Linek, L. (2011). Czech Republic. *European Journal of Political Research, 50*(7–8), 948–954.

Linek, L. (2012). Czech Republic. *European Journal of Political Research Political Data Yearbook, 51*(1), 76–81.

Linek, L. (2013). Czech Republic. *European Journal of Political Research Political Data Yearbook, 52*(1), 50–55.

Linek, L. (2014). Czech Republic. *European Journal of Political Research Political Data Yearbook, 53*(1), 92–103.

Linek, L., & Lacina, T. (2010). Czech Republic. *European Journal of Political Research, 49*(7–8), 939–946.

Linos, K. (2007). How Can International Organizations Shape National Welfare States? Evidence from Compliance with European Union Directives. *Comparative Political Studies, 40*(5), 547–570.

LT. (2004). *Single Programming Document for 2004–2006*. Vilnius: Government of Lithuania. Available at http://www.transp.lt/en/eu_support/stuctural_funds/single_programming_document. Accessed 12 Feb 2016.

LT. (2007a). OP Economic Growth 2007–2013. *National Strategic Reference Framework*. Vilnius: Government of Lithuania. Available at https://www.google.de/url?sa=t&rct=j&q=&esrc=s&source=web&cd=5&ved=2ahUKEwjFovdouPeAhVqB8AKHbSlDvQQFjAEegQIBRAC&url=http%3A%2F%2Fwww.esparama.lt%2Fdocuments%2F42901%2F0%2FOperational%2Bprogramme%2Bfor%2Bthe%2BEconomical%2BGrowth%2Bfor%2B2007%25E2%2580%25932013%2F579dfea9-95a9-4feb-a151-1913e29c0121&usg=AOvVaw0rZZr5nO4s6qZZcctqEZ86. Accessed 5 Nov 2018.

LT. (2007b). OP Promotion of Cohesion 2007–2013. *National Strategic Reference Framework*. Vilnius: Government of Lithuania. Available at https://www.google.de/url?sa=t&rct=j&q=&esrc=s&source=web&cd=2&cad=rja&uact=8&ved=0ahUKEwjJzJPOj6zLAhUL1SwKHXMFD9EQFgglMAE&url=http%3A%2F%2Fwww.esparama.lt%2Fdocuments%2F42901%2F0%2FOperational%2BProgramme%2Bfor%2BPromotion%2Bof%2BCohesion%2Bfor%2B2007%25E2%2580%25932013%2Fdd445cb5-b9be-4fbe-ada5-13bbe530a42c&usg=AFQjCNFmnHuKBauyvV0Zv7ZAIs8aQqKsRQ. Accessed 12 Feb 2016.

Lucaciu, L. O. (2012). Romania. *Expert Evaluation Network*. Bucharest: LIDEEA. Available at http://ec.europa.eu/regional_policy/sources/docgener/evaluation/pdf/eval2007/expert_innovation/2012_een_task2_ro.pdf. Accessed 12 Feb 2016.

LV. (2003). Single Programming Document 2004–2008. *National Strategic Reference Framework*. Riga: Government of Latvia. Available at http://www.esfondi.lv/upload/05-saistosie_dokumenti/spd_en_09112006.pdf. Accessed 12 Feb 2016.

LV. (2007). OP Infrastructure and Services 2007–2013. *National Strategic Reference Framework*. Riga: Ministry of Finance, Latvia. Available at http://www.esfondi.lv/upload/04-kohezijas_politikas_nakotne/op/3_op_2009-07-09_ENG.pdf. Accessed 12 Feb 2016.

Malová, D., & Učeň, P. (2010). Slovakia. *European Journal of Political Research, 49*(7–8), 1154–1162.

Malová, D., & Učeň, P. (2011). Slovakia. *European Journal of Political Research, 50*(7–8), 1118–1129.

Malová, D., & Učeň, P. (2013). Slovakia. *European Journal of Political Research Political Data Yearbook, 52*(1), 208–216.

Maniokas, K., & Miseliuniene, A. (2012). Lithuania. *Expert Evaluation Network*. Vilnius: ESTEP. Available at http://ec.europa.eu/regional_policy/sources/docgener/evaluation/pdf/eval2007/expert_innovation/2012_een_task2_lt.pdf. Accessed 12 Feb 2016.

Maniokas, K., & Miseliuniene, A. (2013). Lithuania. *Expert Evaluation Network*. Vilnius: ESTEP. Available at http://ec.europa.eu/regional_policy/sources/docgener/evaluation/pdf/eval2007/2013_een_task2_lt.pdf. Accessed 12 Feb 2016.

Markovic Hribernik, T., Kirbiš, M., & Vek, U. (2008). Institutional Regulation and the Effectiveness of Absorbing EU Funds: The Experiences of Ireland, Estonia and Slovenia. *Društvena istraživanja, 17*(6), 1219–1239.

Mbaye, H. A. D. (2001). Why National States Comply with Supranational Law: Explaining Implementation Infringements in the European Union, 1972–1993. *European Union Politics, 2*(3), 259–281.

Medzihorsky, J., Oana, I.-E., Quaranta, M., & Schneider, C. Q. (2017). *Setmethods: Functions for Set-Theoretic Multi-method Research and Advances QCA. R Package Version 2.1.* https://CRAN.R-project.org/package=SetMethods.

Meyer-Sahling, J.-H. (2009). *Sustainability of Civil Service Reforms in Central and Eastern Europe Five Years After EU Accession* (Sigma Paper No. 44). Paris: OECD. Available at http://www.oecd-ilibrary.org/governance/sustainability-of-civil-service-reforms-in-central-and-eastern-europe-five-years-after-eu-accession_5kml60pvjmbq-en. Accessed 12 Feb 2016.

Meyer-Sahling, J.-H., & Veen, T. (2012). Governing the Post-communist State: Government Alternation and Senior Civil Service Politicisation in Central and Eastern Europe. *East European Politics, 28*(1), 4–22.

Mikkel, E. (2006). Patterns of Party Formation in Estonia: Consolidation Unaccomplished. In S. Jungerstam-Mulders (Ed.), *Post-communist EU Member States: Parties and Party Systems* (pp. 23–47). Farnham and Burlington, VT: Ashgate.

Milio, S. (2007). Can Administrative Capacity Explain Differences in Regional Performances? Evidence from Structural Funds Implementation in Southern Italy. *Regional Studies, 41*(4), 429–442.

Milio, S. (2008). How Political Stability Shapes Administrative Performance: The Italian Case. *West European Politics, 31*(5), 915–936.

Milio, S. (2010a). Multi-level Governance and Implementation Performance: Lessons from Italy. In S. Milio (Ed.), *From Policy to Implementation in the*

European Union: The Challenge of a Multi-level Governance System (pp. 59–122). London and New York: IB Tauris.
Milio, S. (2010b). The Struggle to Implement European Union Policies: Political and Administrative Factors in the Member States. In S. Milio (Ed.), *From Policy to Implementation in the European Union: The Challenge of a Multi-level Governance System* (pp. 1–57). London and New York: IB Tauris.
Minena, D., Karaboev, S., & Stefanov, R. (2012). Bulgaria. *Expert Evaluation Network*. Sofia: Centre for the Study of Democracy. Available at http://ec.europa.eu/regional_policy/sources/docgener/evaluation/pdf/eval2007/expert_innovation/2012_een_task2_bg.pdf. Accessed 12 Feb 2016.
Myant, M., & Drahokoupil, J. (2012). International Integration, Varieties of Capitalism and Resilience to Crisis in Transition Economies. *Europe–Asia Studies, 64*(1), 1–33.
Noetzel, R., & Stumm, T. (1997). *Factors Influencing the Spending of Structural Money: A Discussion at the European and Member State Level, with Special Regard to the European Regional Policy*. Regional Policy Series. Luxembourg. Available at http://bookshop.europa.eu/en/factors-influencing-the-spending-of-structural-funds-money-pbQAREGIW24/. Accessed 9 Feb 2016.
Noutcheva, G., & Bechev, D. (2008). The Successful Laggards: Bulgaria and Romania's Accession to the EU. *East European Politics & Societies, 22*(1), 114–144.
Olteanu, T. (2008). Rumänien: Vom Einparteiensystem zum Einheitsbrei. In E. Bos & D. Segert (Eds.), *Osteuropäische Demokratien als Trendsetter? Parteien und Parteiensysteme nach dem Ende des Übergangsjahrzehnts* (pp. 147–166). Oplanden and Farmington Hills: Verlag Barbara Budrich.
Pabriks, A., & Stokenberga, A. (2006). Political Parties and the Party System in Latvia. In S. Jungerstam-Mulders (Ed.), *Post-communist EU Member States: Parties and Party Systems* (pp. 51–67). Farnham and Burlington, VT: Ashgate.
Perkins, R., & Neumayer, E. (2007). Do Membership Benefits Buy Regulatory Compliance? An Empirical Analysis of EU Directives 1978–99. *European Union Politics, 8*(2), 180–206.
Pettai, V. (2004). Estonia. *European Journal of Political Research, 43*, 993–999.
Pettai, V. (2005). Estonia. *European Journal of Political Research, 44*(7–8), 1002–1007.
Pettai, V. (2006). Estonia. *European Journal of Political Research, 45*(7–8), 1094–1100.
Pettai, V. (2008). Estonia. *European Journal of Political Research, 47*(7–8), 962–968.
Pettai, V. (2010). Estonia. *European Journal of Political Research, 49*(7–8), 955–963.
PL. (2003a). *National Development Plan 2004–2006*. Warsaw: Government of Poland. Available at http://www.funduszestrukturalne.gov.pl/English/National+Development+Plan/. Accessed 12 Feb 2016.

PL. (2003b). OP Transport 2004–2006. *National Strategic Reference Framework*. Warsaw: Ministry of Infrastructure, Poland. Available at http://www.funduszestrukturalne.gov.pl/NR/rdonlyres/951EFC81-C785-461C-B4E9-28289B71DFA3/0/sop_transport_english.pdf. Accessed 12 Feb 2016.

PL. (2007). OP Infrastructure and Environment 2007–2013. *National Strategic Reference Framework*. Warsaw: Ministry of Regional Development, Poland. Available at http://www.pois.2007-2013.gov.pl/English/Documents_POIS/Documents/7122008_POIiS_ENG.pdf. Accessed 11 Mar 2016.

Pop-Eleches, G. (2008). A Party for All Seasons: Electoral Adaptation of Romanian Communist Successor Parties. *Communist and Post-communist Studies, 41*(4), 465–479.

PRSG. (2001). *Political Risks Services Group. The International Country Risk Guide: Methodology*. Available at http://www.prsgroup.com/wp-content/uploads/2014/08/icrgmethodology.pdf. Accessed 20 Nov 2015.

Ragin, C. C. (2006). Set Relations in Social Research: Evaluating Their Consistency and Coverage. *Political Analysis, 14*(3), 291–310.

Ragin, C. C. (2008). *Redesigning Social Inquiry: Set Relations in Social Research*. Chicago: University of Chicago Press.

Ragin, C. C., & Fiss, P. C. (2008). Net Effects Versus Configuration: An Empirical Demonstration. In C. C. Ragin (Ed.), *Redesigning Social Inquiry: Fuzzy Sets and Beyond* (pp. 190–212). Chicago: University of Chicago Press.

Ragin, C. C., & Rihoux, B. (2008). *Configurational Comparative Methods: Qualitative Comparative Analysis (QCA) and Related Techniques*. London et al.: Sage.

Ramonaite, A. (2006). The Development of the Lithuanian Party System: From Stability to Perturbation. In S. Jungerstam-Mulders (Ed.), *Post-communist EU Member States: Parties and Party Systems* (pp. 69–90). Farnham and Burlington, VT: Ashgate.

Rihoux, B., & De Meur, G. (2009). Crisp-Set Qualitative Comparative Analysis (csQCA). In B. Rihoux & C. C. Ragin (Eds.), *Configurational Comparative Methods: Qualitative Comparative Analysis (QCA) and Related Techniques* (pp. 33–68). London et al.: Sage.

RO. (2007a). OP Environment 2007–2013. *National Strategic Reference Framework*. Bucharest: Ministry of Environment, Romania. Available at www.posmediu.ro/ShowDocument.aspx?path=NFw1XDQucGRm. Accessed 12 Feb 2016.

RO. (2007b). OP Transport 2007–2013. *National Strategic Reference Framework*. Bucharest: Ministry of Transport, Romania. Available at http://old.fonduri-ue.ro/res/filepicker_users/cd25a597fd-62/Doc_prog/prog_op/5_POST/2_POST_Eng.pdf. Accessed 12 Feb 2016.

RO. (2010). A Formative Evaluation of Structural Instruments in Romania: Final Report. *Conducting Evaluations for the Period 2009–10*. Bucharest:

Ministry of Public Finance, Romania. Available at http://ec.europa.eu/regional_policy/sources/docgener/evaluation/library/romania/1010_formative_nsrf_eval_en.pdf. Accessed 29 May 2017.

RO. (2011). Second Ad Hoc Evaluation: Review of Investment in Transport and Environment Infrastructure: Final Report. *Conducting Evaluations for the Period 2009–10*. Bucharest: Ministry of Public Finance, Romania. Available at http://www.evaluare-structurale.ro/ro/list-viewreports-menu/details/8/31/rapoarte-evaluare-second-ad-hoc-evaluation-review-of-investment-in-transport-and-environment-infrastructure. Accessed 29 May 2017.

RO. (2014). Raportul Anual de Implementare 2013. *Annual Implementation Report*. Bucharest: Ministry of Transport, Romania.

Rybar, M. (2006). Old Parties and New: Changing Patterns of Party Politics in Slovakia. In S. Jungerstam-Mulders (Ed.), *Post-communist EU Member States: Parties and Party Systems* (pp. 147–176). Farnham and Burlington, VT: Ashgate.

Rybar, M. (2008). Slowakei: Vom Regimekonflikt zur Dominanz der sozioökonomischen Konfliktlinie. In E. Bos & D. Segert (Eds.), *Osteuropäische Demokratien als Trendsetter? Parteien und Parteiensysteme nach dem Ende des Übergangsjahrzehnts* (pp. 105–120). Opladen and Farmington Hills: Verlag Barbara Budrich.

Rybář, M., & Deegan-Krause, K. (2008). Slovakia's Communist Successor Parties in Comparative Perspective. *Communist and Post-communist Studies, 41*(4), 497–519.

Schneider, C. Q., & Wagemann, C. (2007). *Qualitative Comparative Analysis (QCA) und Fuzzy Sets: Ein Lehrbuch für Anwender und jene, die es werden wollen*. Opladen and Farmington Hills: Verlag Barbara Budrich.

Schneider, C. Q., & Wagemann, C. (2012). *Set-Theoretic Methods for the Social Sciences: A Guide to Qualitative Comparative Analysis*. Cambridge: Cambridge University Press.

SGI. (2014a). Policy Performance and Governance Capacities in the OECD and EU. *Sustainable Governance Indicators*. Gütersloh: Bertelsmann Stiftung. Available at https://www.bertelsmann-stiftung.de/fileadmin/files/BSt/Publikationen/GrauePublikationen/Policy_Performance_and_Governance_Capacities_SGI2014_Overview.pdf. Accessed 29 May 2017.

SGI. (2014b). *Sustainable Governance Indicators 2014 Codebook*. Available at http://www.bertelsmann-stiftung.de/bst/en/media/xcms_bst_dms_37442__2.pdf. Accessed 24 Sept 2014.

Shalov, P., & Stefanov, R. (2013). Bulgaria. *Expert Evaluation Network*. Sofia: Centre for the Study of Democracy. Available at http://ec.europa.eu/regional_policy/sources/docgener/evaluation/pdf/eval2007/2013_een_task2_bg.pdf. Accessed 12 Feb 2016.

SI. (2003). *Single Programming Document 2004–2006*. Ljubljana: Government of Slovenia. Available at http://www.eu-skladi.si/other/programski-dokumenti/epd. Accessed 12 Feb 2016.
SI. (2007). OP Environmental and Transport Infrastructure Development for the Period 2007–2013. *National Strategic Reference Framework*. Ljubljana: Ministry of Infrastructure, Slovenia. Available at http://www.mzip.gov.si/en/areas_of_work/investment_monitoring_and_finance_division/program_period_2007_2013/. Accessed 12 Feb 2016.
SI. (2016). *OP Environmental and Transport Infrastructure Development 2007–2013*. Ljubljana: Ministry of Infrastructure, Slovenia. Available at http://www.mzi.gov.si/en/areas_of_work/investment_monitoring_and_finance_division/program_period_2007_2013/. Accessed 12 Feb 2016.
Siegel, S.N. (2006). *Law and Order in the European Union: Explaining Variations in Compliance with the European Community Treaty* (Discussion Paper SP IV 2006-303). Berlin: Wissenschaftszentrum Berlin für Sozialforschung. Available at http://www.ssoar.info/ssoar/bitstream/handle/document/11351/ssoar-2006-siegel-law_and_order_in_the.pdf?sequence=1. Accessed 12 Feb 2016.
Sikk, A. (2012). Estonia. *European Journal of Political Research Political Data Yearbook, 51*(1), 90–95.
SK. (2003). OP Basic Infrastructure 2004–2006. *National Strategic Reference Framework*. Bratislava: Ministry of Construction and Regional Development, Slovakia. Available at https://www.nsrr.sk/download.php?FNAME=1216974413.upl&ANAME=OP_ZI_2004-2006_06042004.pdf. Accessed 5 Nov 2018.
SK. (2007a). OP Environment 2007–2013. *National Strategic Reference Framework*. Bratislava: Ministry of Environment, Slovakia. Available at http://www.nsrr.sk/en/operational-programmes/environment/. Accessed 12 Feb 2016.
SK. (2007b). OP Transport 2007–2013. *National Strategic Reference Framework*. Bratislava: Ministry of Transport, Slovakia. Available at http://www.nsrr.sk/en/operational-programmes/transportation/. Accessed 12 Feb 2016.
Spendzharova, A., & Versluis, E. (2013). Issue Salience in the European Policy Process: What Impact on Transposition? *Journal of European Public Policy, 20*(10), 1499–1516.
Spirova, M. (2005). Political Parties in Bulgaria: Organizational Trends in Comparative Perspective. *Party Politics, 11*(5), 601–622.
Spirova, M. (2007). Bulgaria. *European Journal of Political Research, 46*(7–8), 901–908.
Spirova, M., & Kolarova, R. (2010). Bulgaria. *European Journal of Political Research, 49*(7–8), 909–918.
Stan, L. (2013). Romania. *European Journal of Political Research Political Data Yearbook, 52*(1), 196–207.

Stan, L., & Zaharia, R. (2007). Romania. *European Journal of Political Research, 46*(7–8), 1082–1095.
Stan, L., & Zaharia, R. (2008). Romania. *European Journal of Political Research, 47*(7–8), 1115–1126.
Stan, L., & Zaharia, R. (2009). Romania. *European Journal of Political Research, 48*(7–8), 1087–1099.
Stan, L., & Zaharia, R. (2010). Romania. *European Journal of Political Research, 49*(7–8), 1139–1153.
Stan, L., & Zaharia, R. (2011). Romania. *European Journal of Political Research, 50*(7–8), 1108–1117.
Steunenberg, B., & Toshkov, D. (2009). Comparing Transposition in the 27 Member States of the EU: The Impact of Discretion and Legal Fit. *Journal of European Public Policy, 16*(7), 951–970.
Surubaru, N.-C. (2017a). Administrative Capacity or Quality of Political Governance? EU Cohesion Policy in the New Europe, 2007–13. *Regional Studies, 51*(6), 844–856.
Surubaru, N.-C. (2017b). Revisiting the Role of Domestic Politics: Politicisation and European Cohesion Policy Performance in Central and Eastern Europe. *East European Politics, 33*(1), 106–125.
Szczerbiak, A. (2006). Power Without Love? Patterns of Party Politics in Post-1989 Poland. In S. Jungerstam-Mulders (Ed.), *Post-communist EU Member States: Parties and Party Systems* (pp. 91–124). Farnham and Burlington, VT: Ashgate.
Szczerbiak, A. (2008). The Birth of a Bipolar Party System or a Referendum on a Polarizing Government? The October 2007 Polish Parliamentary Election. *Journal of Communist Studies and Transition Politics, 24*(3), 415–443.
The Independent. (2006, September 19). *Budapest Rioters Storm TV Station in 'Lying PM' Protest*. Available at http://www.independent.co.uk/news/world/europe/budapest-rioters-storm-tv-station-in-lying-pm-protest-416640.html. Accessed 27 Oct 2015.
Thomson, R. (2007). Time to Comply: National Responses to Six EU Labour Market Directives Revisited. *West European Politics, 30*(5), 987–1008.
Thomson, R. (2009). Same Effects in Different Worlds: The Transposition of EU Directives. *Journal of European Public Policy, 16*(1), 1–18.
Toshkov, D. (2007). Transposition of EU Social Policy in the New Member States. *Journal of European Social Policy, 17*(4), 335–348.
Tosun, J. (2014). Absorption of Regional Funds: A Comparative Analysis. *JCMS: Journal of Common Market Studies, 52*(2), 371–387.
Vanags, A., & Skruzkalne, K. (2012). Latvia. *Expert Evaluation Network*. Riga: Baltic International Centre for Economic Policy Studies. Available at http://ec.europa.eu/regional_policy/sources/docgener/evaluation/pdf/eval2007/expert_innovation/2012_een_task2_lv.pdf. Accessed 12 Feb 2016.

Varnagy, R. (2011). Hungary. *European Journal of Political Research, 50*(7–8), 991–998.

Varnagy, R. (2012). Hungary. *European Journal of Political Research Political Data Yearbook, 51*(1), 129–135.

Varnagy, R. (2015). Hungary. *European Journal of Political Research Political Data Yearbook, 54*(1), 133–140.

Vazac, R. (2011). Czech Republic: Crisis Postponed—Navigation to Recovery. In J. Jungmann & B. Sagemann (Eds.), *Financial Crisis in Eastern Europe: Road to Recovery* (pp. 109–175). Wiesbaden: Gabler Verlag.

World Bank. (2010). Romania: Transport Sector: Final Report. *Functional Review*. Washington, DC: World Bank. Available at http://documents.worldbank.org/curated/en/2010/10/17055950/romania-functional-review-transport-sector. Accessed 29 May 2017.

World Bank. (2015). *World Bank Governance Indicators: Government Effectiveness*. Available at http://info.worldbank.org/governance/wgi/pdf/ge.pdf. Accessed 20 Dec 2015.

Zubek, R. (2005). Complying with Transposition Commitments in Poland: Collective Dilemmas, Core Executive and Legislative Outcomes. *West European Politics, 28*(3), 592–619.

CHAPTER 5

A Causal Mechanism for Absorption Problems

5.1 Overview: A Causal Mechanism for Absorption Problems

Process tracing has recently evolved as one of the most prominent case-study methods (Beach and Pedersen 2013; Bennett and Checkel 2015). Combining the method with QCA in this study means that the causal mechanism to be tested has to be formulated on the basis of the detected sufficient combination of conditions of 'frequent party alternation', 'low executive capacity', and absence of 'centralized management' (model 2). It is argued that frequent party alternation encountering a context of low capacity leads to the outcome of absorption problems. However, this mechanism works likely only with the scope condition absence of 'centralized management'.

The chapter proceeds as follows. The causal mechanism is first formulated on the basis of the fsQCA results in combination with the theoretical literature. Then, the mechanism is operationalized. In process tracing, operationalization is the formulation of empirical manifestations, which should be found to be confident that a certain part of the mechanism was actually present. Evidence for the mechanism can be diverse and come from different sources in the form of 'causal process observations' (Collier et al. 2004: 252).[1] The evidence for the

[1] In contrast to the data set observations which were needed for the QCA.

C. Hagemann, *EU Funds in the New Member States*, Palgrave Studies in European Union Politics,
https://doi.org/10.1007/978-3-030-02092-7_5

case studies is collected from the programme's annual implementation reports, expert reports, minutes from meetings of the monitoring committees (MCs), and evaluation studies. This general knowledge is then supplemented with insider statements from the member states. In 2014–2015, I conducted several semi-structured interviews with ministerial bureaucrats, local experts, and NGO representatives during five field trips to the Czech Republic, Lithuania, and Romania. The information gathered in these interviews offers further first-hand experience from implementation processes during the financing period. Interviewees were selected from those people actively involved in the implementation of OPs (often for several years or even the entire financing period, and often on high positions), experts charged with evaluations, and representatives from NGOs interested in the use of EU funds. In order to guarantee the confidentiality of their statements, neither insiders' names nor their exact positions are disclosed. Still, to make it easier to evaluate their statements, a list linking statements (country code + number, e.g. CZ1) to interviewees' positions (official, expert, NGO representative) is provided in Appendix II.

Before the mechanism can be tested however, it is necessary to select cases for analysis. It is generally highlighted that testing two cases is preferable to only a single case study (Schneider and Rohlfing 2013: 566; Beach and Rohlfing 2018: 17), not least because it helps to distinguish between general and idiosyncratic, case specific aspects of a mechanism. Thus, the Czech OP Environment (OPE) and the Romanian OP Transport (OPT) are studied. These cases are the most diverse 'typical cases' covered by the sufficient combination of conditions (see Sect. 5.2).

Overall, the analysis provides plausible evidence for the presence of the same causal mechanism in both cases. Still, while the general mechanism is the same, it plays out differently in the two OPs. In the Czech Republic, politicization is, as expected, conducted by parties alternating in office. The change of staff results in a serious interruption of the implementation process from which the programme recovers only slowly. In contrast, in Romania ministers exert most discretion regarding staff appointments, resulting in very frequent changes, especially at the level of the beneficiary companies. This did not only lead to an interruption of the implementation process, but also to a constant impediment of adaptation measures (see Sect. 5.6 for a detailed discussion).

5.2 Case Selection: Typical Cases for the Solution Term

The Romanian OPT and the Czech OPE are selected as 'typical cases' for the sufficient combination of conditions detected in the QCA (see Chapter 4). They are also the typical cases most different from one another, following a selection strategy of maximum difference. Testing a causal mechanism in two very dissimilar typical cases is supposed to increase confidence that the causal mechanism is also present in other typical cases.

The general idea of conducting a process tracing analysis after a QCA is "to increase our confidence that there is a link between the term and the outcome and to enhance knowledge of how the underlying causal mechanism works" (Schneider and Rohlfing 2013: 575). Process tracing thus provides further qualitative evidence for the plausibility of QCA results (triangulation), which is generally assumed to be a good standard of QCA research (Schneider and Wagemann 2010: 400). In addition, the process tracing case studies provide inferential knowledge which is distinct from that produced in the QCA. Testing a causal mechanism based on the QCA solution term shows how the conditions are actually connected to the outcome, thus information which is not possible to be obtained in a QCA. The case studies are therefore not merely a supplement to the broader analysis, but they offer their very own inferences the QCA could not produce on its own.

In order to learn more about the relationship between the combination of conditions and the outcome, typical cases have to be selected for the process tracing analysis. Typical cases are cases where "the probability of a case's representativeness is high, relative to other cases" (Gerring 2008: 650). If a causal mechanism exists based on the detected combination of conditions, it should be found in these cases. The identification of typical cases can follow different practices. For example, their representativeness can be decided in an inductive way considering certain predefined criteria. In regression analysis, typical cases can be found close to the regression line (Gerring 2008: 649). Still, there are distinct procedures to identify typical cases after a QCA. Schneider and Rohlfing pioneered the combination of QCA and process tracing methods or what they call set-theoretic multi-method research (Schneider and Rohlfing 2013, 2016). They stress that in a QCA, typical cases for sufficiency can be found in the upper right corner of the *x/y*-plot of the sufficient combination of conditions and the outcome (Schneider and Rohlfing 2013: 585; 2016: 549, similar Beach and Pedersen 2018: 849). Thus, typical cases are all cases covered by the sufficient combination of conditions and also featuring the outcome.

This first path from the intermediate solution of model 2 is used as the backdrop for process tracing, as it is empirically highly relevant (covering six members of the outcome); as it contains more theoretically interesting context conditions than model 1; and as the result is still a subset of findings from model 1, and might thus also well tell something about the empirically most relevant path 1 from model 1.

The plot shows that there are six typical cases for the sufficient combination: The Romanian OPs, the Slovak OPs, as well as the Czech and Bulgarian Environmental programmes, all of which are unique members in the (single) path connected to the outcome. In order to learn more about the link between a sufficient combination of conditions and the outcome, several typical cases should be selected for the analysis (Schneider and Rohlfing 2013: 575). Schneider and Rohlfing recommend a strategy of maximum difference for selecting cases for the process tracing case studies (Schneider and Rohlfing 2013: 587). This follows the assumption that if the same causal mechanism can be found in two very dissimilar cases, our confidence in its importance for the cases between these polar cases will be increased (Schneider and Wagemann 2012: 309). In order to make a meaningful choice, it is important to distinguish between the typical cases. Generally, in order to explain how a combination of conditions produces the outcome, "there is no better empirical instance than the one in the upper right corner of the plot" (Schneider and Rohlfing 2016: 548). The plot in Fig. 5.1 shows that only the Romanian OPs are located in this corner, meaning that they are the 'ideal typical cases'. What is then the most different case to be selected alongside one of the Romanian OPs?

From a purely set-theoretic perspective, the strategy of maximum difference of cases is only linked to the different membership scores of cases in both the outcome and the solution term (Schneider and Rohlfing 2013: 587). In this regard, one of the Slovak cases would be most different from the Romanian OPs, as they have only partial membership in both the outcome and the solution term.

Still, numerical measures for case selection are ideally combined with qualitative case knowledge in order to guarantee a proper selection of cases (Gerring 2008: 650). Considering such qualitative background

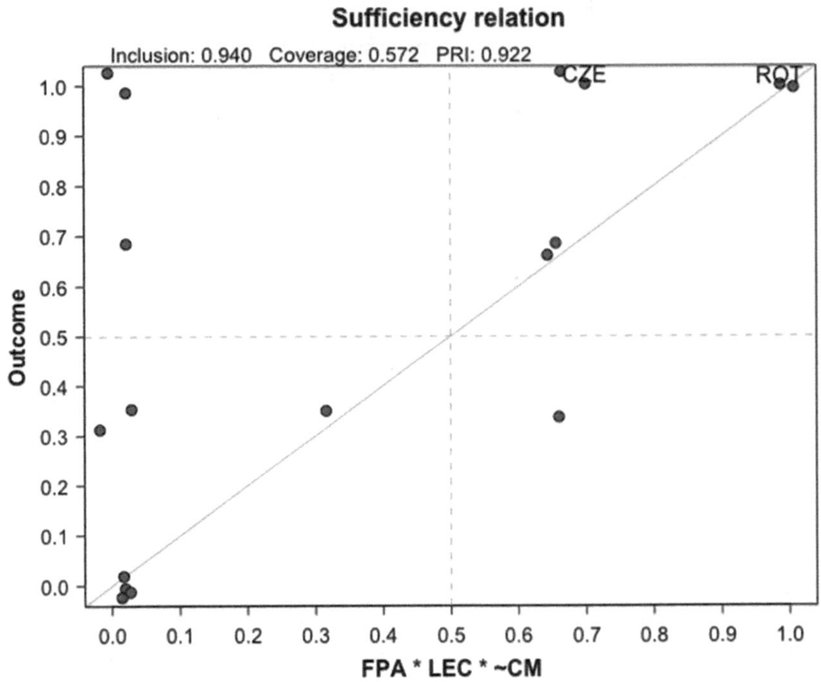

Fig. 5.1 Selection of typical cases for path 1 from model 2

knowledge, the case from the Czech Republic should be maximally different from the Romanian cases. On the one hand, the Czech Republic is usually seen as a champion of post-communist reform. It has a comparatively stable political environment, its democracy was never in doubt after transition, and its high level of pre-communist industrialization and bureaucratic professionalization makes it an outstanding case in the region (Kitschelt 2001: 308; Motyl 2004: 54). In contrast, both Bulgaria and Slovakia were often seen as close to Romania as descendants of a patrimonial type of communist rule (Kitschelt 2001: 308). All three countries had doubtful democratic trajectories during the 1990s, poor levels of economic reform, a high level of corruption and rent-seeking, and joined only later the group of candidate countries for EU accession (Beichelt 2004: 45; Motyl 2004: 54–55; Vachudova 2005: 20). Also, selecting the Czech OPE only partially violates the demand of maximum difference in set membership, as it only differs in its membership in the outcome from the Slovak cases. Therefore, the generally greater difference makes the Czech case the most adequate and relevant choice for a process tracing case study.

The Romanian OPT is selected among the two Romanian OPs as it offers further variation on the type of OP and thus the projects realized in contrast to the Romanian OPE. In sum, the Czech OPE and the Romanian OPT are the most dissimilar typical cases available, varying on crucial background variables such as OP content, accession rounds (2004 and 2007), pre-communist legacies, and post-communist reform trajectories. Finding the same mechanism working in both cases will therefore strongly boost our confidence that it is actually relevant for the outcome and could also be present in the other typical cases (Schneider and Rohlfing 2013: 566; Beach and Pedersen 2013: 153).

5.3 A Mechanism for Absorption Problems: Low Capacity and Politicization Working Together

5.3.1 *Formulating a Mechanism for Absorption Problems*

The fsQCA produced the following solution term which will be used as the starting point of the theory-testing process tracing analysis:

$$FPA^* \sim CM^*LEC \rightarrow \text{Absorption problems}$$

It means that the combination of frequent party alternation (FPA), the absence of centralized management structures (~CM), and low executive capacity (LEC) leads to the outcome of absorption problems. The causal mechanism between the conditions and the outcome, however, is not the result of the fsQCA, but must be spelled out in detail (Schneider and Wagemann 2010: 412). The task of this chapter is therefore just that: to spell out the causal mechanism leading to the outcome, based on the solution formula resulting from the fsQCA.

The first question now is the differentiation between causal factors and scope conditions in the causal mechanism. Beach distinguishes between causes and scope conditions when turning fsQCA results into a mechanism: While causes are active parts of a mechanism, scope conditions are less active and have just to be present to make other causes relevant (Beach 2018). Thinking about the possible role of the conditions in theoretical terms as discussed in Chapter 3, it is difficult to imagine what the absence of centralized management structures might actually do in order to bring about the outcome. It seems rather a context condition which is important to be present so that other conditions (e.g. FPA) can fully unfold their influence. However, it does not actively do something. Therefore, the absence of centralized management structures is treated as a scope condition in the analysis.

There are then two more conditions left to formulate what I refer to as the 'politicization mechanism'. The mechanism expects frequent party alternation to offer multiple occasions for changing ministers to politicize both the administrative structures dealing with the implementation of cohesion policy as well as the programming and planning of an OP. These applied changes happen in a low capacity context already suffering from implementation problems. As a result of politicization, implementation is interrupted, capacity is weakened, and adaptation of administrative structures becomes more difficult. In addition, time is lost due to changes in programming and planning. All of these influences add up to long delays in the implementation process, ultimately resulting in absorption problems.

The process is expected to work in a mechanism consisting of two distinct steps: In the first step, a new minister comes into office and implements changes to the management and control system and the programming documents of the OP. It was assumed in the QCA that such changes are most likely if this person belongs to a different party than the predecessor. Incoming ministers from a different party will lack trust in the present administrative staff, because this staff has a history of working with a different party, and its reliability in properly implementing new ministers' policy priorities is doubtful (Meyer-Sahling 2004: 77). In order to ensure control of policy implementation, ministers will be motivated to replace existing staff with their own candidates. Such changes at the management level will have an even stronger effect if lower levels of bureaucrats are exchanged as well.

Naturally, the establishment of control over the ministry follows a distinct purpose. This purpose is most likely the implementation of own policy preferences in the realm of the programme, or even the use of EU funds as a political resources as found in earlier studies (Bloom and Petrova 2013: 1613). The higher level of control over the bureaucracy is therefore likely to be used to change the priorities or projects of the OP in order to channel funds into a direction more aligned with ministers' or parties' own preferences. This means that while changes of staff happen to establish control, this control itself is most likely only a means to the end of assuring the implementation of policy priorities.

In the second step, the effect of the changes hits the implementation process. The most immediate result of this is likely to be an interruption of the process, leading to delays. The process is halted for some time for the very least, or seriously interrupted if core staff is exchanged and the new managers have to learn their job from scratch. The politicization of the process thus means at the same time a direct lowering of administrative capacity.

Furthermore, the cases under investigation already suffer from generally low administrative capacity at the national level. Administrative capacity is still defined following Bachtler et al. (2014), focussing on three different dimensions. First, the organizational structures created to implement cohesion policy. This aspect comprises the functioning of the management and control systems, the necessary institutions in place, the adherence to EU financing rules, and the effectiveness and stability of the coordination mechanism (Bachtler et al. 2014: 748). Second, the "adequacy and quality of human resources" (Bachtler et al. 2014: 748), thus whether or not enough staff with relevant training is available to implement the programme. And, finally, the capacity of the administration to adapt to new challenges and to conduct institutional learning (Bachtler et al. 2014: 748). Overall, a lack of human resources and malfunctioning structures are most likely to already impact the implementation process.

Politicized changes are in such an environment likely to weaken human resources, but in addition also the third dimension of adaptation, thus the very ability to overcome the deficiencies of the first two dimensions. The politicization of structures in a low capacity context hits a very damageable environment, which can be impacted in two ways: If an 'islands' exists that has facilitated implementation up to this point, politicization does harm to these structures which is difficult to repair. The implementation process will thus be interrupted and it will be difficult to get it going again or respond adequately to the continuously appearing challenges in the implementation of a highly demanding OP. In contrast, when capacity in the EU funds management structures is as low as in the general public administration, politicization will impede its improvement as only stability would facilitate long-term learning processes helping to improve absorption. In contrast, changes make adaptation more difficult, as the lessons-learned during implementation which have not yet been incorporated into the process (i.e. institutionalized) will leave together with the outgoing staff. Thus, procedures remain slow or deficient, and even a suspension of certification (the ability to claim funds from the EC) becomes more likely if compliance with EU rules is in doubt. Overall, frequent changes make it therefore much more difficult to improve the administrative capacity of the management and control system.

In addition, changes of programming documents or projects should equally cause delays. The development of infrastructure projects usually takes a lot of time. The interruption of projects could thus mean that a lot of time is lost on projects only half prepared and then entirely stopped or at least postponed. The complete termination of a project seems unlikely in the context of EU funds as preparation is also scrutinized by the EC in the annual implementation reports. Still, also a reorientation of resources to another project without the entire termination of the one developed earlier means that preparation is both less efficient and effective. The project might be realized later, but starting the procedure anew after some time will take much longer than finishing one project at a time (especially if staff has changed). A shifting focus in programme priorities and the loss of experienced staff mean therefore an accumulation of delays that will be difficult to overcome within the initially planned schedule. However, this very schedule is usually of prime importance in order to avoid decommitments and to implement the strategic objectives of an OP.

Low capacity and politicization of the bureaucracy thus work in the second step together. Crucially, an incoming minister applying changes to staff and programme priorities first has to trigger the mechanism. In contrast, without politicization by incoming ministers, even a struggling bureaucracy might be able to adapt over time and acquire the necessary skills during the process. It is therefore the combination of both changes and low capacities making implementation impossible within the originally planned schedule.

5.3.2 *How to Test the Politicization Mechanism*

How can these steps be identified in the case studies? What tells us that the mechanism is actually relevant? The presence of the mechanism's steps is followed on the basis of distinct empirical manifestations.

These manifestations are the very evidence that has to be found in order to be convinced that a certain part of the mechanism was in place. After its specification, it is thus possible to look for this evidence in the case studies, and to determine if the proposed causal mechanism makes sense. In order to evaluate the evidence, the idea of Van Evera is used who proposes to check for its uniqueness for a certain hypothesis and the certainty of obtaining it. In his four tests, evidence can thus either be not unique and not certain ('straw-in-the-wind test'), relatively certain and unique (depending on the size of the 'hoop' in the 'hoop test'), certain and unique for both the argument and its opposite ('doubly-decisive-test'), and highly unique but very uncertain to be obtained (the 'smoking gun test') (Van Evera 1997: 32). Evidence should pass ideally at least a rather narrow 'hoop-test' to be convincing for a hypothesis.

This logic can be transferred to the politicization mechanism. In the first step, evidence should be found for changes of staff and/or of programme priorities. The occurrence of party politicization is most often traced on the basis of interviews in which experts or insiders inform on the percentage of staff usually exchanged after an election (Kopecký et al. 2012; Meyer-Sahling and Veen 2012). This practice offers a good overview of the general extent of politicization, however, it is of limited use to determine how much staff was actually exchanged after a specific change of minister or party in office. In addition, it is possible that politicization varies among administrative bodies, and that for example those units which are part of the core executive or dealing with international institutions are spared from changes (Kopecký and Spirova 2011: 910). The general level of politicization might thus be less informative for the concrete occurrence of changes in a specific department or organization at a specific point in time. Therefore, it would be much better to have a direct look at organizational charts of the bodies which are part of the management and control system in order to determine whether or not changes occurred and when. Still, this data is difficult to obtain as usually hardly the present staffing of the ministerial bureaucracy is publicly available, let alone the staffing during a seven-year-period.

Changes to projects and priorities are unlikely to be found in the annual implementation reports that offer a regular overview of the implementation performance of an OP. This is related to the fact that changes are overall rather difficult. Contracted projects cannot be erased from the programme's list, and even the shift of funds between the different priority axes (PAs) of an OP has to be approved by the EC and needs therefore a strong, practical argument why it was necessary. It is thus unlikely that politicians will tackle existing priorities (which are difficult to change) or ongoing projects (which are impossible to terminate) in order to implement their preferences. Rather, changes are likely to take place during the preparation stage of (calls for) projects, which are initiated, but then terminated as priorities change. These kinds of changes are the most likely ones to result in delays of the implementation process. Unfortunately, they take place at a rather unobservable level, as the planning of projects and calls is a measure which is usually not mentioned in the regular reports or programming documents because it concerns the preparatory stage before implementation. Evidence for such changes can therefore only come from insiders or evaluation reports stressing that they actually took place. Changes during the very implementation of the OPs are therefore even more difficult to prove than changes of staff.

In the second step, it has to be plausibly shown that these changes put a further strain on the implementation of the OP, ultimately resulting in absorption problems. For example, a stop of absorption after politicized changes to the administration and the implementation process could signal that there was an effect. Still, cohesion policy implementation is a long term process and the occurrence of absorption often influenced by further factors such as the certification of funds by the CA, the speed of the EC in reimbursing funds, and other cyclical factors unrelated to the day-to-day business (Bubbico/De Michelis 2011: 2–3). It is rather difficult to link concrete absorption developments directly to an interruption of the implementation process. Therefore, it would be again much better to have direct evidence from insiders to the process or evaluation reports informing on the actual effect of the staff and programme changes detected in the first step.

Then, it is especially important that the politicized changes unfolded their effect as expected in the context of a generally low level of capacity, meaning that existing well-functioning EU fund management capacities ('islands') cannot react resiliently to the sudden impact, or that poor capacities will not adapt over time as witnessed in other cases (e.g. Slovakia in the 2004–2006 financing period; the Bulgarian OPE in the 2007–2013 period). Information on the quality of capacity is most likely found in the annual implementation reports. These reports have an obligatory section on core challenges faced by the OP during a given year. Capacity problems will manifest themselves as a lack of staff, inadequate rules and procedures, and a malfunctioning of the management and control system as a whole. The expected impact of politicized changes is then a sudden occurrence of these deficiencies (if an 'island' existed before; especially in the realm of human resources) or a lack of adaptation and thus stagnation at a very low level. As a result of politicization, problems should thus suddenly surface and impact absorption (hitting an 'island of excellence'), or be mentioned continuously (in a low capacity context without an 'island'), instead of structures improving after a certain problem was detected and mentioned in the reports. Suspensions should occur if the EC perceives deficiencies at the level of the management and control system to be grave and in non-compliance with EU regulations (see Sect. 2.1 for details). In the most extreme scenario, the very same set of capacity problems should haunt the OP throughout the whole period under investigation because of the inability to adapt. While the continuation of the very same problems would be good evidence for the influence of changes on adaptation (i.e. a congruence), a mentioning of the connection between changes and capacity problems (e.g. in evaluation reports or by insiders) would be even better, providing more unique evidence for the link. Equally, the mentioning of sudden problems in a low capacity context could hint that the 'island' responsible for the earlier successful implementation was seriously hit by politicization and can thus no longer guarantee progress.

On the other hand, the effect of changes on programme or project priorities is almost as difficult to establish as their occurrence. The effect of these changes, that of a slow implementation process, is hardly distinguishable from the effect of the ongoing lack of capacity. It is also unlikely to be found in the implementation reports, as ministers will hardly use them as a tool for self-accusation in front of the EC. The influence of changes of programme or project priorities can therefore only be found on the basis of insider information, either provided in external evaluation reports or in direct discussions with staff involved in the implementation process. This evidence is very difficult to obtain, but it would then also be very unique to prove the effect of changes on the low performance of EU fund absorption.

Finally, the outcome of absorption problems is established as a low absorption rate, as well as the occurrence of decommitments, and (the attempt of) reallocations pursued in order to save funds from

Table 5.1 A politicization mechanism for absorption problems

			Step 1		*Step 2*		*Outcome*
Causal Mechanism	*Frequent Party Alternation (FPA)*	→	*Newly incoming ministers exchange staff and/or OP priorities and (calls for) projects*	→	*Changes disturb or even interrupt the implementation process and/or harm the adaptation of rules and procedures in a low capacity context (LEC)*	→	*Absorption Problems*
Empirical Manifestations			Patterns of change of administrative staff follow alternation of incumbents in office. Projects or programme priorities are also affected		Functioning administrative capacity is weakened ('island of excellence') or poor capacity is not able to adapt, the implementation process is interrupted and delayed		
Types of Expected Evidence			<u>Account Evidence</u>: Changes of programme priorities could be mentioned by insiders or in evaluation reports <u>Pattern Evidence</u>: Pattern of staff changes is displayed on organizational charts and related to alternation of ministers		<u>Sequence Evidence</u>: After change problems start or even get worse and it gets more difficult to resolve them <u>Account Evidence</u>: Insiders and/or evaluation reports directly link changes to implementation problems		
Scope Condition	~CM		The existing central coordination body is institutionally weak and has no decisive influence on the implementation process. Its role is enhanced in the following 2014–2020 financing period				

decommitment. Evidence for the outcome is thus rather naturally the same as in the QCA.

The influence of the scope condition~CM is not directly part of the mechanism and it would also be highly speculative how the absence of a certain structure was important. Still, there are two possibilities to get closer to the relevance of~CM as a scope condition. First, every OP has some sort of centralized management or coordination structure. It is therefore interesting to see how this structure acted in the context of OP implementation, whether it was the weak actor assumed in the fsQCA, and if its influence could have potentially been beneficial if it had had more authority. This is, of course, in part rather difficult counterfactual argumentation, but the best one can get. The evidence can be further substantiated by, second, taking into account changes to the organization of the management and control system in the 2014–2020 financing period. The very fact that the system has been much more centralized in the subsequent financing period would strongly underline that also the Czech and Romanian governments and most probably the EC perceived the lack of a strong central actor as a distinct disadvantage during the earlier financing period (Table 5.1).

5.4 OP Environment in the Czech Republic: Interruption with Severe Consequences

OP Environment is one of the two biggest programmes implemented in the Czech Republic in the 2007–2013 financing period.[2] It aims mainly at the renewal and building of water management infrastructure, the reduction of air pollution, the sustainable use of energy sources, and the improvement of waste management. Projects within OPE are implemented along eight distinct PAs (CZ 2007a: 88):

- PA1: Improvement of Water Management Infrastructure and Reduction of Floods Risks
- PA2: Improvement of Air Quality and Reduction of Emissions
- PA3: Sustainable Use of Energy Sources

[2]The only bigger programme in the Czech Republic is OP Transport with a total allocation of EUR 5774 million (CZ 2007b: 158).

- PA4: Improvement of Waste Management and Rehabilitation of Old Ecological Burdens
- PA5: Limitation of Industrial Pollution and Environmental Risks
- PA6: Improvement of State of Nature and Landscape
- PA7: Development of Infrastructure for Environmental Education, Consultance and Awareness Raising
- PA8: Technical Assistance

OPE was allocated a total of EUR 4917 million for the implementation of projects in these areas during the 2007–2013 period (CZ 2007a: 88). Almost half of these funds were to be spent in PA1. The money is often, but not only spend by public beneficiaries (CZ 2007a: 98). The Ministry of Environment is at the centre of the OP's management and control system. Within the ministry, the EU Funds Department was assigned the role of the MA (CZ 2007a: 162). The EU Funds Department was therefore responsible for implementation, however, did not manage the whole process on its own. The more practical aspects of implementation such as the assessment of applications for funding, the review of claims for reimbursement, and further more technical tasks were assigned to the State Environmental Fund (SEF) (CZ 2007a: 164–165), thus acting in the position of an intermediary body for OPE. The role of both audit and certifying authority (AA, CA) was taken up by the Ministry of Finance (CZ 2007a: 170, 176).

The following chapter tests the politicization mechanism for absorption problems in the case of OPE. It is supposed to illuminate why at the end of the financing period in 2013 only around a third of the funds allocated to the OP had been spent, and a substantial amount had already been lost due to decommitments and corrections. The following paragraphs provide evidence for every step of the causal mechanism, the results are summarized in Table 5.2.

5.4.1 Test of the Causal Mechanism

5.4.1.1 Frequent Party Alternation in the Ministry of Environment

High levels of political instability marked the 2007–2013 financing period in the Czech Republic. Governments as well as Ministers of Environment rarely fulfilled their terms in office and changed on a regular basis.

Table 5.2 Testing the causal mechanism in the Czech OP Environment

			Step 1		*Step 2*		*Outcome*
Causal Mechanism	*Frequent Party Alternation (FPA)*	→	*Newly incoming ministers exchange staff and/or OP priorities and (calls for) projects*	→	*Changes disturb or even interrupt the implementation process and/or harm the adaptation of rules and procedures in a low capacity context (LEC)*	→	*Absorption Problems*
Empirical Manifestations	Two alternations among parties, seven alternations between ministers		Important administrative staff is exchanged, the patterns follow clearly shifts of parties in charge of the ministry. Also, evidence for different project preferences		The changes result in a loss of institutional knowledge, interrupt implementation, make the solution of the suspension-crisis more difficult, as well as that of earlier problems of the implementation process (e.g. contracting)		Only a third of available funds have been used at the end of the financing period, resulting in a decommitment of funds in 2013
Types of Evidence			Account Evidence: Insiders link staff changes to politicization Pattern Evidence: Pattern of staff changes in organizational chart supports claim of party politicization		Sequence Evidence: After change the process is interrupted and it gets more difficult to resolve implementation problems Account Evidence: Insiders link changes directly to interruption of implementation		

(continued)

Table 5.2 (continued)

			Step 1		Step 2		Outcome
Causal Mechanism	*Frequent Party Alternation (FPA)*	→	*Newly incoming ministers exchange staff and/or OP priorities and (calls for) projects*	→	*Changes disturb or even interrupt the implementation process and/or harm the adaptation of rules and procedures in a low capacity context (LEC)*	→	*Absorption Problems*
Test Strength			(Narrow) Hoop Test: There is no convincing alternative argument to account for changes, there is interview evidence making this connection (increasing the uniqueness of the evidence)		Narrow Hoop Test or Smoking-Gun Test: The changes are directly linked by interview partners to the predicted effect (highly unique evidence, certainty to find it was low)		
Scope Condition	~CM	Central coordination body is institutionally weak and has no decisive influence on the implementation process, even though its role was enhanced after some time. Its role was institutionally strengthened in the 2014–2020 financing period					

The first Topolanek (Civic Democratic Party, ODS) government came into office as a minority cabinet in 2006 (Linek 2007: 932). The prime minister managed to receive a majority only in 2007, when he formed a coalition with the newcomer Green Party (SZ) and the Christian and Democratic Union—Czechoslovak People's Party (KDU-ČSL). In this new cabinet, Martin Bursík (SZ) took over the Ministry of Environment from Petr Kalaš (independent, ODS) (Linek 2008: 948). Still, the coalition between the unequal partners lasted only for two years, because Topolanek lost a no-confidence motion in parliament on 24 March 2009 (Linek and Lacina 2010: 939). The fall of the government was especially surprising against the backdrop of the fact that not only the two ČSSD (Czech Social Democratic Party) dissidents who had supported the coalition had voted against the government, but also two members from both the conservative ODS and the SZ (Linek and Lacina 2010: 939). The two major parties ODS and ČSSD subsequently refused to form a grand coalition, but agreed to put a caretaker cabinet into power (starting its term on 7 May) until new elections in October. Still, the constitutional court refused to agree to this early date, and the caretaker government under Prime Minister Fischer remained in office until elections took finally place in May 2010.

This development meant several changes in the Ministry of Environment: Martin Bursík (SZ) had lost his office after the fall of the government on 7 May 2009, but two further SZ appointed candidates shortly held the position (Ladislav Miko, 8 May–30 November 2009, later replaced by Jan Dusík 1 December 2009–19 March 2010). The office shifted even a third time under the caretaker government to the former deputy minister Rut Bízková, who was originally appointed by the ODS.

The elections in 2010 produced then a narrow victory for the ODS, and Topolanek's successor Petr Nečas formed a government consisting of his ODS and two newcomer parties, TOP 09 (a liberal party) and VV (a centrist-populist party) (Haughton et al. 2011: 399; Linek 2011: 951–952). The ODS controlled the Ministry of Environment again, and interim Minister Bízková was replaced by Pavel Drobil (ODS). However, this did not result in more stability for the ministry, as the unfortunate Minister Drobil had to resign already five months later and Tomáš Chalupa, also from the ODS, became the new minister (Linek 2011: 950). The Nečas government ultimately collapsed over a security scandal in mid-2013 (Linek 2014: 92). It was followed by an interim government proposed by President Miloš Zeman (ČSSD). However, this cabinet failed to achieve a parliamentary majority, especially as many of the ministerial candidates had a history of working with centre-left governments and Zeman had failed to consult with parliament before proposing the new cabinet (Linek 2014: 99). Nevertheless, the president's cabinet remained in office until the formation of a new government resulted in a majority for a new cabinet in January 2014 (Linek 2014: 99). This means that this caretaker government under Prime Minister Jiří Rusnok was the last change during the period under investigation, and Tomáš Podivínský (independent, KDU-ČSL)[3] the last acting Minister of Environment until the end of 2013 (Linek 2014: 100).

Overall, the Ministry of Environment experienced seven different ministers during the 2007–2013 period. Two of these changes were alternations between parties: First, the ministry changed from an independent candidate appointed by the conservative ODS to the green SZ in 2007. Then, the change was reversed in 2010 when the ODS regained control over the Ministry of Environment.

5.4.1.2 First Step: New Party, New Staff

The shifts at the political level subsequently affected the administrative and management positions further below. There are three administrative levels of interest for the OP within the Ministry of Environment. Directly below the minister, there is a Deputy Minister who heads the Section 300. This section includes the EU Funds Department (330). Within this department 330, different units are in charge of different tasks of the MA (see Table 5.3 for an overview). Finally, there is also the SEF as the intermediary body of OPE, responsible for practical implementation and project management (see Table 5.4).

The management of OPE changed several times, but in a different manner at different levels. At the highest level, the Deputy Minister in charge since 2006 had originally been appointed by the ODS, but remained in office after the SZ took over the ministry in 2007. She only briefly left her post in 2010 to become interim minister. This means that this position remained surprisingly stable, even though it is the most likely candidate for party politicization.

[3]Tomáš Podivínský remained during his short stint as minister member of the KDU-ČSL, but his position was "expert rather than party member" (Linek 2014: 100), thus turning him not only into an interim, but also independent candidate who is not counted.

Table 5.3 Staff changes in the Czech Ministry of Environment 2007–2013

	2006	*2007*	*2008*	*2009*	*2010*	*2011*	*2012*	*2013*	*2014*
Government	**Topolanek I** *4 September 2006 ODS min.*	**Topolanek II** *9 January 2007 ODS, SZ, KDU-ČSL*		**Fischer I** *8 May 2009 Caretaker supported by ODS, ČSSD, SZ*	**Nečas I** *13 July 2010 ODS, TOP09, VV (later LIDEM)*			**Rusnok I** *10 July 2013 Caretaker appointed by President,* ***but not confirmed***	**Subotka I** *29 January 2014 ČSSD, ANO 2011, KDU-ČSL*
Minister of Environment	Petr Kalaš (Ind., ODS)	**Martin Bursík (SZ)** 9 January 2007–7 May 2009		Ladislav Miko, 8 May–30 November 2009 later repl. by Jan Dusík 1 December 2009–19 March 2010 (both ind., SZ)	Jan Dusík, Interim by Minister of Agriculture, later Rut Bízková (Ind., ODS) 15 April–12 July 2010 **Pavel Drobil (ODS) 13 July 2010–21 December 2010**	**Tomáš Chalupa (ODS)** 17 January 2011–10 July 2013		Tomáš Podivínský 11 July 2013–29 January 2014 (Ind., KDU-ČSL)	**Richard Brabec (ANO 2011)** 29 January 2014-ongoing
Deputy Minister, Head of Section 300 Economics and Env. Policy	Newly Appointed 18 June 2006–14 April 2010	–	–	–	Newly Appointed 16 April–13 July 2010 Newly Appointed 14 July 2010–6 April 2011	interim 7 April 2011–20 September 2011, Newly Appointed 21 September 2011–26 August 2012	Newly Appointed 1 September 2012–2 October 2012 Newly Appointed 3 October 2012–30 September 2013	Newly Appointed 1 October 2013–31 January 2014	Newly Appointed 3 February 2014-ongoing
Head of EU Funds Department 330 (MA)	Newly Appointed 18 September 2006–8 July 2007	Newly Appointed 9 July 2007–30 July 2010	–	–	Newly Appointed 1 October 2010–31 May 2011	Newly Appointed 1 June 2011–23 October 2011 Newly Appointed 24 October 2011–30 September 2013	–	Since March 2013 new acting Director of EU funds as new structure over both departments Since November 2013 until Feb. 2014 again new acting director of EU funds	Newly Appointed 1 March 2014-ongoing

(continued)

Table 5.3 (continued)

	2006	*2007*	*2008*	*2009*	*2010*	*2011*	*2012*	*2013*	*2014*
Government	**Topolanek I** *4 September 2006 ODS min.*	**Topolanek II** *9 January 2007 ODS, SZ, KDU-Č SL*		**Fischer I** *8 May 2009 Caretaker supported by ODS, Č SSD, SZ*	**Nečas I** *13 July 2010 ODS, TOP09, VV (later LIDEM)*			**Rusnok I** *10 July 2013 Caretaker appointed by President, **but not confirmed***	**Subotka I** *29 January 2014 Č SSD, ANO 2011, KDU-Č SL*
Head of Department 340[a]	X	X	X	X	X	X	X	Newly Appointed (March 2013–February 2014)	– (the department is discontinued in March 2014)
Head of Unit of Methodologies and Monitoring	–	Newly Appointed	–	–	–	Newly Appointed	–	–	–
Head of Financing Unit	–	Newly Appointed	–	Newly Appointed	Newly Appointed	–	–	Newly Appointed	–
Head of Unit of Controls and Audits	X	X	X	X	X	X	Newly Appointed	–	–
Head of Unit of Projects, PA1	–	Newly Appointed	–	–	–	–	Newly Appointed	Newly Appointed	–
Head of Unit of Projects, PA2–7								Newly Appointed	–
Head of Unit Technical Ass.	X	Newly Appointed	Newly Appointed (2)	–	Newly Appointed (2)	Newly Appointed	Newly Appointed	Newly Appointed	Newly Appointed
Head of Unit Prep. New Prog. Period	–	–	–	–	–	–	–	Newly appointed	–

Source The author's compilation, information provided by the Czech Ministry of Environment. Ministers in bold type are party affiliated, cells coloured grey show the expected pattern of party politicization. Information provided every time a new candidate is appointed to a position in the organizational chart

[a]In March 2013, the Department of EU funds was split and 340 added as a second department. Both departments acted as equals, and were subject to an acting director who was either head of one of the departments or, for most of 2013, an extra appointed person

Table 5.4 Staff changes at the State Environmental Fund (IB)

	2006	*2007*	*2008*	*2009*	*2010*	*2011*	*2012*	*2013*
Director	–	Newly Appointed	–	–	Newly Appointed (05.08.2010) Newly Appointed	–	–	Newly Appointed (9/2013) Newly Appointed (12/2013)
Deputy, OPE Management Department/Director of Project Management	–	Newly Appointed	–	–	Newly Appointed	Newly Appointed	Newly Appointed	–
Deputy, Department 'Other Programmes Management'	–	–	–	Newly Appointed	Newly Appointed	Newly Appointed	Newly Appointed	–
Deputy, Economic Department	–	–	–	–	Newly Appointed	Newly Appointed	–	Newly Appointed
Director of Project Preparation and Audit	–	Newly Appointed	–	–	Newly Appointed	–	–	–

Source The author's compilation, information provided by the SEF. Changes are indicated where applicable

In contrast, the level below her position, the Head of the EU Funds Department (i.e. head of MA), was subject to stronger politicization. First, in parallel with the newly incoming Green Party minister in 2007, the head of department left his post and a new person was appointed director. This person remained on this post until September 2010, thus leaving shortly after Minister Drobil from the ODS came into office. Drobil then appointed a new head of the EU Funds Department. Still, changes after this alternation of party went even further down to subunits of the department. Also, the Head of the Financing Unit and the Head of the Technical Assistance Unit changed. These changes can be followed in detail in Table 5.3.

Overall, the data displayed in Table 5.3 shows the expected pattern of party politicization. The patterns of changes of the most important positions follow the change of parties in charge of the ministry and not that of ministers. A change of the Director of the EU funds Department happened both when the SZ took over the ministry in 2007, and when it went to the ODS in 2010. In contrast, no changes took place during the time in office of the interim ministers. It could be argued that they have no real stake in re-staffing the ministry because of their short period in office. Thus, the crucial test for the party politicization hypothesis is the change from Minister Drobil to his early successor, Chalupa, both being fully appointed ministers from the same party.

At first glance, it seems that this change is about the same as between SZ and ODS and therefore disproves the argument: The post of director of the EU Funds Department switches again, and also a new Deputy Minister is appointed. Still, in order to understand these changes, the reason for the resignation of the minister and the events connected to his resignation are important: Minister Drobil had to leave office against the backdrop of a scandal related to the attempted misuse of EU funds for party purposes. The scandal involved the Director of the SEF, who was reportedly approached from inside the ministry with the intention of rigging a tender procedure in favour of a certain law firm (Česká Pozice 2011b). After the SEF's director made this attempt public, also incriminating the minister, he was dismissed from his position (Linek 2011: 954). Only later, against the backdrop of the emerging scandal and public pressure, also Minister Drobil had to resign, even though he had the initial backing of Prime Minister Nečas, and later received a high post in the party bureaucracy (Linek 2011: 954).

The scandal and its consequences thus explain the further changes at the staff level between Chalupa and Drobil: Minister Drobil had fired the head of the Intermediate Body (SEF) before he left office early in December 2010, so the just appointed head of the EU Funds Department simply went to take the position as Director at the SEF, thereby leaving her post as director of the MA. The Deputy Minister concerned is said to have left herself. As these changes are rather collateral damage, it is more important that the post of Director of EU funds then stabilized with the next Director appointed in 2011 in office for almost the next two years. The ongoing changes at the level of deputy minister were by insiders explained as resulting from the problem of finding a proper candidate (CZ6 2015). The clearest pattern emerging from the changes of staff is thus that of changes of parties in control of the ministry.

This argument is further supported by the development in 2014 (the period not covered in this study, but also displayed in Table 5.3), when a centre-left coalition won the elections and the newcomer party ANO (Action of Dissatisfied Citizens) appointed Richard Brabec as Minister of Environment. As a result, the person originally Heading EU Funds Department 330 in 2007 could return to the Ministry of Environment and even received the post of Deputy Minister. The post of the head of the MA also shifted on 1 March 2014. This means that again after a change of party in office the two core positions were changed in a short period of time after the political shift.

The same pattern observed at the ministry can be seen in a similar manner at the SEF, the OP's intermediate body. The director of the SEF changed also every time the party in control of the Ministry of Environment changed (2007, 2010, 2013), however, not more often (see Table 5.4). This is a further strong argument for the pattern of party politicization of the management and control system of OPE.

In sum, the fact that important staff shifts took place in parallel with different parties in charge of the ministry is pattern evidence for the hypothesis that the origin of these changes is party politicization. In addition, one could also argue that some of the evidence presented in the following step can count as account evidence for the political motivation of changes (with some insiders stressing that some people 'had to leave', for example). There is also no other argument that would make the same predictions and be equally plausible: It is, for example, difficult to see how the financial and economic crisis should have affected staff shifts apart from massive layoffs. In addition, if crisis was the reason for shifts, it would not be able to account for the changes of the head of the MA in 2007 when the SZ came into power, as the financial crisis only affected the region in 2009. There is thus reasonable evidence in the sense of a very narrow 'hoop test' that the staff changes are a result of party politicization.

5.4.1.3 Second Step: The Changes Interrupt the Implementation Process

The changes at the level of administrative staff interrupted the implementation process of OPE and caused long delays. The most crucial alternation in this regard was the change from SZ to ODS in 2010. First, it happened during a phase when implementation was hindered by eligibility questions in the important PA1 and when many projects selected were not yet contracted due to a special contracting procedure. Second, problems of the management and control system would let the EC soon suspend the certification of funds. This suspension resulted in a more than a year-long period of difficult negotiations, audits, and double work for the weakened bureaucracy, resulting in further delays. The subsequent low rate of absorption and the decommitment of funds in 2013 were thus the result of vulnerable administrative capacity hit by politicization.

The implementation system of OPE worked rather well at the beginning of the financing period, even though it faced some problems right from the start. In line with the observation of Bachtler and colleagues (2014) that the Czech Republic had developed rather well functioning EU fund management bodies right after accession, many crucial aspects of the management and control system were already in place when OPE started. For example, the level of human resources was a problem only briefly at the beginning of the financing period when the extent of administrative staff available did not meet the demand from potential beneficiaries. Even though there was experience from the earlier financing period, the amount of funds was substantially higher and thus also the number of projects to be handled. The number of staff was accordingly increased both at the MA and the SEF, which was even relocated during this process to accommodate the new staff (CZ 2009a: 27–28). While it took some time to find people and train them, the increase of staff at the SEF was still accomplished in a reasonable timeframe of about a year (CZ8 2015). Problems with human resources resurfaced at a later stage of the implementation period (e.g. CZ 2012: 48), but the initial problems were rather quickly resolved during these first years.

In contrast to this swift resolution of staff problems, other problems connected to both EU and national rules proved much more difficult to handle. On the one hand, there were specific problems on PA1 concerning the ineligibility of Czech water management infrastructure for EU funds. This matter was one of the core obstacles to programme implementation (CZ1 2014), as a substantial share of funds (about 40%) was designated to be used in this area, and projects in PA1 covered the largest share of those approved until the end of 2009 (CZ 2010a: 16). The problem of ineligibility was related to the privatization of the water management infrastructure during the 1990s. The EC was unwilling to tolerate contracts which had been closed between municipalities and private operators for decades to come without a tender procedure, and that would allow these operators to benefit from EU funds without the obligation of investing in the maintenance of this infrastructure in the future (CZ6 2015; CZ7 2015). The obligation was therefore that contracts would need to be changed before the facilities could benefit from OPE (CZ7 2015). Changing these contracts, however, was far from easy due to multiple ownership structures of the infrastructure, many different types of contracts, and also sometimes multiple parties to these contracts (CZ7 2015). Still, as long as the contracts were not changed and the problems no resolved, the EC would not start financing the planned interventions.

On the other hand, there were also problems connected to the rules of the implementation system itself. Difficult public procurement procedures led to a constant gap between the amount of funds covered by approved projects and those already contracted. Even though procurement is the most difficult aspect of the programming cycle in virtually all programmes and member states, in OPE the difference between the two steps was also the result of specific procedures of the programme. The MA of OPE would issue the Grant Award Decision (GAD), which is the declaration that a project will receive financial support, only after procurement procedures had been finalized without procedural mistakes. Projects are thus only properly contracted after beneficiaries signed the contract with the winner of the procurement procedure (CZ8 2015).[4] Still, exactly this obligation to produce the documentation according

[4]For example, if a project aims at building something, it is not before the selection of the construction company that would execute the project that the beneficiary would receive the formal confirmation that the project can benefit from EU funds.

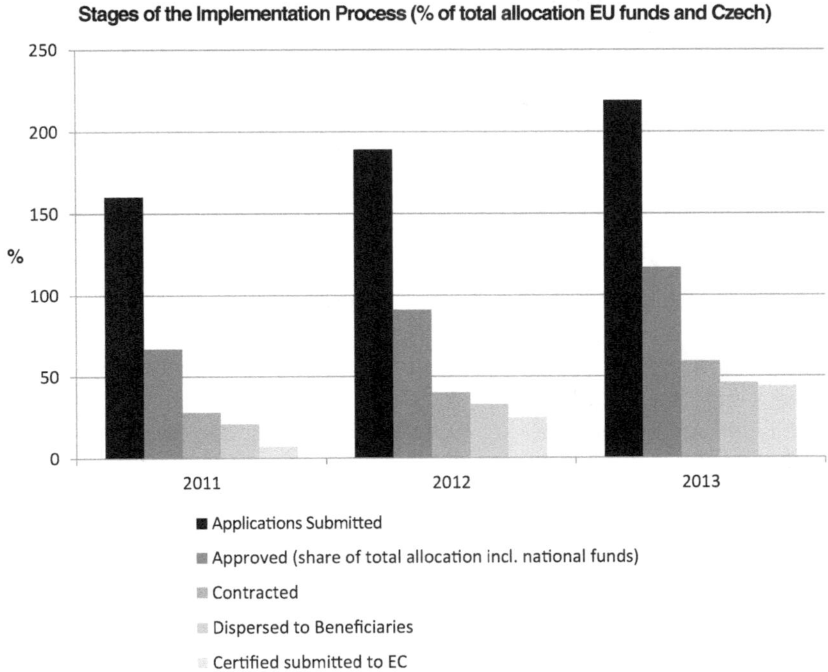

Fig. 5.2 Progress at different stages of the implementation process—Czech OP Environment (% of total EU and National Contribution) (*Source* The author's compilation based on annual implementation reports [see Appendix III for the data])

to all necessary rules proved very difficult for many applicants. The AIR 2008 already stressed that not financing and programming, but rather the documentation and correct application for a GAD was the biggest obstacle for absorption in the programming cycle (CZ 2009a: 14; 2010a: 14). The rules are generally described as very complicated and mistakes can make it necessary to relaunch the whole procedure, postponing again the actual start of project implementation (CZ7 2015).

Figure 5.2 visualizes the problem of contracting of projects, using the actual data of the different phases of the programming cycle from 2011–2013. It shows the progress reached in all of these phases for every year in the second half of the financing period, thus during those years when the implementation process normally accelerates. The most obvious observation is that the number of applications submitted (the black bar) exceeds strongly all other bars. This is quite natural as there have to be almost by definition more applications submitted than are to be accepted. At the same time, it shows that OPE was in a rather comfortable position when it comes to the submission of projects. A more striking observation is thus the second huge difference between bars: the difference between the approved projects (the second bar from the left) and all others. While the approval of projects progressed well and reached almost the full allocation in 2012, the actual contracting of projects, i.e. the phase that settles the realization of EU finance for these projects, lagged behind.

In sum, the problems of OPE during the early years of implementation mainly refer to the management and control system (procedures, organization, and planned interventions). Human resources were less of an issue before party alternation took place in 2010. Then, the problems already lining up would not be easily overcome anymore after the politicized changes and the subsequent weakening of staff in 2010 and therefore cause a major interruption of the implementation process, resulting subsequently in long delays.

Evidence for the effect of politicized changes on the implementation process is, for example, provided in the AIR: Shifts at the management level are mentioned in the AIR of 2011 as a significant problem for the implementation process, lowering administrative capacity (CZ 2012: 47–48). Talking to people involved in the implementation process at that time, most of them highlighted the strongly adverse effects of these changes on the implementation of OPE.[5] Problems are especially mentioned with regard to a loss of institutional knowledge and routine, causing a stop of the implementation process:

> But in the year 2010 the governmental change came, which kind of stopped the whole process because, if I simplify it, the person who knew how to do it was gone and the new people had no idea what to do [...]. It just caused some delays and these delays were actually until the end of 2012. Everything was slowed down and a lot of new problems arose. (CZ7 2015)

[5] Interviews were conducted with ministerial officials, NGO representatives, and policy experts in 2014 and 2015. In order to guarantee confidentiality, neither the names nor the exact functions of interviewees are disclosed. Still, in Appendix II a list is provided including all interview partners, dates of interviews, as well as their more general position (official, expert, civil society).

It is crucial to note that not only the general process of implementation was disrupted, but especially the sensitive step between project approval and the issuance of GAD, thus the final contracting of an intervention, was mentioned as directly affected by the changes:

> [Until 2010] we were able to make great progress in the field of registration form. I mean we were able to approve projects and to give them the registration form. After he [the Director] was stepped down or fired in 2010, there were big problems, because there was no pressure on beneficiaries to continue in implementation. I mean public procurement and give us papers for grant decision etc. There was a big pause. (CZ6 2015)

The loss of management staff meant that there was no more pressure on the beneficiaries to hand in the necessary documentation for the crucial contracting of projects. Without this contracting, however, financing and thus absorption could not start. The detected gap between approval and contracting, which was earlier rather natural due to the specific nature of the rules, was now prolonged and became a problem due to the interruption of the process (CZ7 2015). The statement above also matches very well with the reported situation in the AIR for the following year, when the contracting of funds did not proceed as it was hoped. Even though administrative adaptations were taken during 2012, it was not possible to shorten the decisive period between project approval and issuance of grant decision, which still stood at a very broad span of 12–25 months (CZ 2013: 36). The MA expected adaptations of procedures only to make a difference in 2013.

Furthermore, also the coherent planning of calls for project proposals suffered from the political shift. There was no clear schedule making calls more predictable for applicants, who could then prepare the projects more thoroughly (CZ6 2015). This led to a situation in which only a very low number of new calls could be launched and thereby new projects attracted (CZ6 2015). At the same time, there were seemingly also different preferences at work when it comes to the calls. While it is very difficult for an incoming government to discontinue projects once they have been approved, it is easier to focus on the future calls to realize changes (CZ1 2014). It was mentioned, for example, that calls for projects were developed, but then later rejected by the new government and subsequently not launched (CZ7 2015). While preferential shifts are notoriously difficult to follow as they leave hardly any traces in the official documentation, this could be a sign that also, if not the general policies of the programme, at least some priorities changed.

These reported implementation problems were not only the direct result of management changes, but also connected to more profound changes at the lower levels of the administrative hierarchy. Some of these shifts are related to direct politicized changes at the lower levels. Others, however, are also an indirect result of the changes at the management levels of the administration:

> The disruption is in a sense that they change the deputy minister and the top officials and they would also change the heads of departments and also below. So, the lowest level of officials would be frustrated and would leave to another position. I would not say voluntarily, but it's also change induced by the coming new boss. (CZ1 2014)

This general decrease of quantity and quality of human resources starting in 2010 is also mentioned in the regular reports. The AIR stressed that there was an urgent lack of staff due to people leaving the department. As a result, "necessary agendas where only achieved with maximum effort" (CZ 2012: 47). Certain departments were in an especially precarious situation, operating at only half of their capacity (e.g. the monitoring department between April and September 2011) (CZ 2012: 48). This pattern was described even more dramatically by insiders:

> It is important to say that when [the director] finished [...] here, it lead not only to his leaving, but also other people from his department went away, for example 40 or 45 people. One third of the people were away and it was a big impact on this department. So, there were new managers and I don't want to say that they were wrong. It's not like that. There was a big problem in the department itself, we weren't able to do our job, not because of our managers, but because also our colleagues were away and we had to prepare new colleagues for the process. (CZ6 2015)

Just as expected in the mechanism, the loss of staff resulting from politicization could not be overcome easily. The result of the politicized changes of staff was thus both directly and indirectly a lowering of administrative capacity in the management of OPE in the earlier rather unproblematic dimension of human resources. This loss of capacity in the human resource dimension then proved an even bigger problem, when issues in another capacity-related dimension (management and control system) caused a suspension of the programme by the EC.

The first suspension happened at the national level. It was initiated by the Czech Ministry of Finance and was the result of the already mentioned Drobil-scandal. It comes with no surprise that just one day after the minister's resignation on 22 December 2010, the certification of funds for OPE was suspended. The move was justified with the "suspected intent to misuse European funds through the OPE at the SEF" (CZ 2012: 44). In order to overcome the suspension, an external team was hired to conduct audits at the SEF from January to March 2011 (CZ 2012: 44). The result of the audits were recommendations for improvements, which were included into an action plan that was sent both to the relevant Czech Ministries as well as the EC (CZ 2012: 44). The attempted misuse of funds by a party caused thus a first interruption, however, only because it was revealed.

While certification was subsequently relaunched at the national level, it was then the EC starting a suspension procedure on 15 June 2011 (CZ 2012: 45). The reason for this was not only the previous affair at the SEF, but also the result of audit reports from both the EC and the audit authority (CZ 2012: 45). It is clear that general capacity problems in the form of deficiencies of the management and control system had their fair share in the suspension of funds. The suspension of funds was justified with questions regarding the independence of the PAS (audit bodies), the activities of the audit authority, and the capacities for management and control (CZ 2013: 47). At the same time, experts continue to stress the low level of trust of the EC towards the Czech Republic, both against the backdrop of many scandals as well as the negative evaluation of the earlier financing period (Česká Pozice 2011a). The suspension from the EC further prolonged the period of audits, which would then last well into the second half of 2012.

Discussions between the EC and the MA to overcome apparent deficiencies in the management and control system continued until the end of 2011. In order to restore the credibility of the Ministry of Environment and the SEF, the EC demanded a re-inspection of 92 statistically selected projects that had been executed in the realm of OPE until June 2012 (CZ 2012: 46). The audit of the 92 projects was not only conducted by internal ministerial auditors, but also external auditors and former controllers from the Czech supreme audit office participated

(CZ 2013: 46). The Ministry of Finance finally sent the overall audit report to the EC on 20 June 2012, with a detected error rate in the samples of 3.14% (CZ 2013: 46). In the course of July, the EC continued with its own investigation, checking again ten projects from the original sample of 92 (CZ 2013: 46).

The EC initially proposed a flat-rate correction of 13.32% on all certified expenditure against the backdrop of the detected error rate. The Czech Republic, however, refused to accept such a high amount and an agreement was finally found at a rate of 5% (CZ 2013: 46). Thus, the Czech Republic did not receive reimbursement from the EC in the value of 5% of all expenditures paid until 31 August 2012. As its absorption rate was at this point very low, this meant only an overall sum of EUR 65.77 million (CZ 2014: 38). Upon acceptance of the correction, certification was ultimately re-opened on 25 October 2012.

What was the effect of the suspension on the absorption performance? The most obvious result is the loss of funds due to the correction payment. However, another much more crucial effect was avoided, that is the loss of funds due to the *N*+2/*N*+3 decommitment rules.[6] Substantial amounts of funds could have been lost if certification had not been re-opened before the end of 2012 (CZ 2013: 36). Beyond that, however, the impact of the suspension might be more indirect than could be expected. Overall, the suspension of certification of funds to the EC does not mean that the programme is completely halted. Rather, implementation can progress as usual, as long as both beneficiaries and the respective ministry do not crucially depend on the immediate reimbursement of funds (CZ6 2015). That this was not the case can be derived from the AIR 2011, reporting that funds for certification where presented to the CA at the end of 2011 (CZ 2012: 25), even though no claims for reimbursement were sent to the EC. Another clear sign for on-going implementation is the comparatively high amount of funds claimed by the Czech Republic for OPE at the end of 2012 after the suspension was lifted (making the absorption rate rise from 7.2 to 25% in 2012) (CZ 2012: 24; 2013: 27–28). If the programme had been halted during the suspension, there would have been no progress and thus also no claims to file.

[6] The *N*+rules specify that funds provided by the EU will be lost if not used latest two (*N*+2) or three (*N*+3) years after the year they were allocated (see Sect. 2.1 for further information).

Therefore, the effect of the suspension on the implementation process (apart from the direct loss of funds via corrections) is rather found in the additional workload created by the extensive audits during the suspension period. These were of no help to the implementation process, as they only served to restore credibility in the management and control system. The audits were not only extra work in addition to the general implementation process, but did also take place in the context of the political shift in the ministry, which had caused the loss of crucial human resources and institutional memory. It has to be seen against the backdrop of this context that the implementation of OPE became even more difficult during this period. The distractive influence of the suspension procedure was also stressed by insiders as the main effect on the implementation process:

> [A] part of our personal capacity had to be excluded for issues we didn't have to do before. That was the problem for us. [...] In fact, it was not a big problem in the field of money, but it was a problem that, as I said, we had to discuss with national authorities, with European Commission, and devote our time to something else than the implementation process itself. That was the main problem. (CZ6 2015)

Interestingly, this statement does not only stress the strongly distractive effect of the suspension, but also dismisses a lack of funds in the aftermath of the financial crisis as an argument for a slow implementation process. This also matches well with other accounts stressing that the Czech Republic was only weakly affected by the crisis, and that it could engage in counter-cyclical spending to avoid recession in contrast to the fierce austerity measures adopted in other countries (Åslund 2010: 28). Money was obviously not the problem for implementation, but it was rather the lack of competent staff that would deal with both the suspension procedure and implementation, resulting from the shift in political control of the ministry.

In sum, the politicization of staff by the incoming ODS minister in 2010 caused a major loss of human resources and managerial experience buildt up in previous years. This loss meant that problems related to complicated procedures (GAD) would result in a delay of implementation, because beneficiaries struggled to reach the step of contracting for their already selected projects. The subsequent suspension of the certification process was then the result of a capacity problem, namely deficiencies in the institutional set-up of the management and control system and in the application of EU rules. Still, it would be incomplete and incorrect to argue that these kinds of capacity problems were the main reason for the low absorption performance. It is correct that the suspension was in fact a result of capacity problems in the form of deficiencies of the management and control system present during the first years of the financing period. However, the suspension had a serious effect on the implementation process only against the backdrop of the politically induced weakening of human resources, which had happened with the incoming ODS ministers. It meant that a lower number of also less experienced staff had to deal with double-work, thus both auditing already finished as well as administering new projects. This would obviously result in delays of the implementation process.

There is further evidence supporting the argument that staff changes lowering capacities were a huge problem for implementation and that these changes resulted from party politicization. On the one hand, many interviewees stressed that they expected the upcoming civil service legislation to be very beneficial for implementation in the future (CZ7 2015; CZ1 2015). The Czech Republic was the only country entering the EU in 2004 without such legislation to limit staff changes after elections in place. While other countries have already shown that such a law is not necessarily a remedy against politicization (many of the rules were simply repealed, or civil servant status extends overall only to few people in the administration) (Goetz 2001: 1045; Meyer-Sahling 2009: 7, 20), it is still important to note these comments as they stress the awareness that politicization of staff is in fact an important problem for implementation and a threat to absorption. One interviewee even reported the example of an EC official stating that frequent staff changes were the core problem in the Czech Republic:

> I was once in Brussels and one of the EU officials told me: Do you know what is the most frustrating thing concerning cohesion policy in the Czech Republic? We are going there or they are coming here, we say, 'Okay, here is the problem'. We agree on a solution, we will come three months later or six months later to see whether it was implemented or not, and completely new people are there. Completely new people. We are starting again from scratch. (CZ1 2015)

On the other hand, also other OPs were affected by similar changes. Blažek reports, for example, that the OP Research and Development was disrupted after the elections by a "dramatic scale of fluctuation even of professional staff" (Blažek 2011: 4). This means that staff changes did not only complicate the implementation of OPE, but were a more general pattern resulting in an overall rather low absorption performance of the whole country at that time.

5.4.1.4 Outcome: The Result Is Absorption Problems

Absorption naturally stagnated between 2010 and 2012 as a result of the inability of the MA to send claims for reimbursements to the EC. It then made a jump in October 2012 to 25.02% of the total allocation when all the claims accumulated during the suspension period were handed in at once. Still, this rate was overall much lower than what had been planned. With an eye on the different commitment rates among all Czech OPs, Blažek stressed that OPE was "in sharp contrast" (Blažek 2012: 8) to the rest. While 13 out of 18 OPs had committed already three-quarters of their available funds, OPE was due to all the mentioned problems still stuck at only 30% (Blažek 2012: 8).

The years 2012 and 2013 thus required a substantial effort to increase absorption. After suspension was over, all actors involved invested a lot in improving the implementation record of the programme. However, at the end of 2013 the effect of these efforts was still limited and the loss of EUR 274 million from the programme allocation could not be avoided (CZ6 2015). The main reasons for this were the problems of the preceding years and the inability of the MA to make up for the accumulated delays in a very short period of time. The problem was most strongly felt in the central PA1 due to the ineligible projects and the late resolution of this question:

> [W]ithin the first half of implementation of the operational programme there was a big delay, and we can see now these problems because we have to find the solution now what to do with the money and there is really small time for making a decision now. It would be easier if the money was given to projects and these projects were implemented, let's say in 2010/2011, and we had the time to make a decision in 2012/2013 what to do with the money. In fact we had to do this decision in 2014 and the result is we lost some money in 2013 and now we are not sure that we will be able to spend all the money […]. (CZ6 2015)

The year 2013 was also more difficult than the previous ones due to the overlapping of *N*+2 and *N*+3 financing rules (CZ 2013: 28).

Thus, a substantially higher amount of funds had to be absorbed to avoid decommitments. In order to reach the spending targets, the MA both tried to improve procedures as well as engage in reallocations. In order to save money from decommitment, the ministry developed a plan for the acceleration of absorption (CZ 2013: 50–51) and created a special department for capital intensive projects at the SEF, focussing mainly on the shortening of the period between approval and contracting (CZ 2013: 51). Coordination between the Ministry of Environment and the SEF became in general much closer, peaking in weekly meetings of their senior management (CZ 2013: 53). This cooperation was also stressed in the 2013 report, when both MA and IB worked together to reduce the expected “loss at a maximum” (CZ 2014: 27).

At the same time, the MA shifted funds to better performing areas of the programme in order to accelerate spending (CZ6 2015). Money was reallocated if PAs were clearly underperforming, and if they included large projects that would take too long to implement before the end of the absorption period (CZ7 2015). Financial shifts took place within PA1 (EUR 150 million) and within PA3 (EUR 111 million, and again EUR 104 million from renewable energy sources support to energy saving). These changes were decided by the MC in June 2011, and they were accepted by the EC on 20 February 2012 (AIR 2012, 54). Further changes were discussed and decided in the MC meeting on 29 November 2012 (AIR 2012, 56) (see Table 5.5). Overall, a total of EUR 786.4 million was shifted within the OP among Areas of Intervention (AoI) within the PAs, which is almost a fifth of the total allocation.

Most importantly, however, one shift of funds failed to receive the EC’s approval. The MC decided during its meeting on 19 June 2013 that a total of EUR 147.18 million (or CZK 3.7 Billion) should be transferred from PA 4 and PA 8 to the better performing OPT (CZ 2014: 13). The shift was motivated by the desire to save the funds, as it had become clear that absorption would not reach the necessary level by the end of the year and that funds could only be saved if shifted to another programme. Still, the EC rejected this proposal for reallocation and the money was ultimately lost (CZ 2014: 58).

All of these measures undertaken at the end of the financing period were not unnecessary or failed their purpose. However, they were ultimately not enough and came too late to achieve the aspired target. The main problem for absorption was still the prolonged and difficult phase between approval and contracting of projects. For most of the

Table 5.5 Reallocations on the PAs of Czech OP Environment 2007–2013

Priority axis	*Decided MC/ Accept. EC*	*Changes*	*Sum reallocations (million EUR)*
PA1	06-2011/02-2012	Transfer of EUR 150 million from AoI 1.2 (Drinking Water Quality) to 1.3 (Reduction of Flood risks)	310
	11-2012/12-2013	Transfer of EUR 160 million from AoI 1.3 to AoI 1.1	
PA2		New Activities included in AoI 2.1: Improving Air Quality	201.1
	11-2012/12-2013	New Supported Activity: Alternative forms of public transport	
		Transfer of EUR 201.1 million from AoI 2.1 to AoI 2.2	
PA3	06-2011/02-2012	Ca. EUR 111 million from AoI 3.1 Renewable Energy Sources to 3.2 Energy Saving and Waste Heat Recovery	275.3
		Ca. EUR 104 million from 3.1 Renewable Energy Sources to 3.2	
	11-2012/12-2013	Transfer of EUR 60.3 million from AoI 3.1 to AoI 3.2	
PA4	06-2013/rejected	Transfer proposed to OP Transport	
PA5		No changes	
PA6		Inclusion of new supported activities (animal passage through fragmented landscape) in AoI 6.2 Support for Biodiversity	
		Developing Forest Management: New Activity in AoI 6.3	
		New Supported Activity: Prevention of Landslides, AoI 6.6	
PA7		No changes	
PA8	06-2013/rejected	Transfer proposed to OP Transport	
Sum			**786.4**

Source The author's compilation, based on Annual Implementation Reports (CZ 2012: 50; 2014: 58) time, the MA was unable to overcome this problem in the programming cycle. Even in the 2012 progress report it is still mentioned, just as in the beginning of the period, that the problem with procurement compliance "disproportionately increases the time taken to move to the implementation phase of the project and thereby to the drawdown of funds" (CZ 2013: 21). Interestingly, the 2012 report does no longer only blame the applicants starting the implementation before they were issued a GAD for this problem. Rather, it is stressed that the delay is caused by a lack of project managers at the level of the SEF (CZ 2013: 21). The problem is thus also rooted in a lack of human resources to conduct this crucial task properly. There was also again a tender to recruit new staff in 2013, and it was stressed that human resources at the IB should be increased for the next financing period (CZ 2014: 54). The on-going problems are caused by difficulties with administrative capacities as well as the aftermath of the political changes in 2010. The AIR links these ongoing problems in the programming cycle directly to the decommitment of funds in 2013:

> For this reason [i.e. the ongoing GAD problem], the situation occurred that in 2013, N+2 rule for 2011 allocation and N+3 rule for 2010 allocation were not met, leading to an automatic cancellation of part of the obligation in the amount of between CZK 6-10 billion [EUR 220-370 million]. (CZ 2014: 27)

It took until 2013, the last year in the financing period (though not the last year for absorption), to make substantial progress. Only then, "[a]fter several months of decline and stagnation, OPE started to show significant progress at the end of the year" (CZ 2014: 51). The crucial duration between approval and GAD had finally been reduced from 12–25 months to an average duration of less than twelve months (CZ 2014: 39). Even though this progress is important, its effect on the performance in 2013 was obviously limited. Even at the end of the year, only projects worth 55% of the whole allocation had received a GAD and could therefore be financed. In contrast, and as already mentioned above, 13 OPs in the country had arrived at a rate of 75% already in 2012 (Blažek 2012: 8). Thus, it is hardly surprising that even despite this progress the AIR 2013 still warned that a higher loss of funds might follow in the remaining years 2014 and 2015 of the absorption period (CZ 2014: 33, 56).

5.4.2 The Importance of the Scope Condition ~CM

The causal mechanism presented above works when politicization hits a low capacity context that cannot easily make up for substantial changes or losses of staff, even if the system used to work rather well before. Still, the lack of a centralized management structure was also a crucial contextual feature for the mechanism to produce the outcome absorption problems. The Czech Republic decided for a sectoral management structure with MAs at the level of ministries for every OP. Still, the Ministry of Regional Development was assigned the role of National Coordination Authority (NCA) and was thereby responsible for the central coordination of cohesion policy implementation in the country (CZ 2007a: 165–166). There are two aspects with regard to centralized management offering potentially interesting information on the influence of the scope condition for the mechanism to work: On the one hand, it is interesting to ask for the actual involvement of the NCA in the adaptation of OPE, especially during the later years of the programme. On the other hand, it also makes sense to take a look at the role given to the NCA in the following financing period 2014–2020. It is likely that lessons-learned from the period under scrutiny in this analysis might reveal perceived deficits of the institutional system by the very decision-makers who were responsible for the implementation of the programme.

First, the NCA supported the MA in the process of adaptation of the operational programme throughout the financing period. However, the role of the NCA was institutionally weak and did not comprise strong formal powers. The fact that it was not the single MA for all central programmes meant that it had no control over the processes taking place, let alone a veto power to block changes. Rather, it could attend meetings of the MC, collect data, offer methodological advice, and provide regular reports on the progress of absorption in the different programmes. While it was in a position to offer advice on implementation, it was not able to make the other ministries do something they would not want to do. Its role was thus mostly that of a monitoring or consultative body, rather than a hierarchical superior agent that could enforce its decisions directly at the level of the OPs.

At the beginning of the financing period, the NCA was mostly mentioned as a supervisory body, working on the different monitoring indicators to follow the progress of OPE and ensuring their comparability with other programmes (Blažek 2011: 15; CZ 2012: 20). Its role was enhanced, however, as soon as the crises of the OP started. During the suspension of OPE in 2011, the NCA was ordered to apply so-called 'strengthened management' over OPE (Blažek 2012: 10). Thus, the government was apparently of the opinion that in times of crisis a central actor could deliver a contribution to its solution. The NCA created an action plan to overcome suspension and to implement the demanded changes to the programme and the implementation structure (CZ 2013: 47). It further monitored the highly important capital intensive projects of OPE as a result of the inclusion of the programme into the 'strengthened management' group of risky OPs (CZ 2013: 53). When the MA worked on measures to avoid a loss of funds in 2012 and 2013, the NCA offered its expertise for the adaptation of the programme's methodology when it comes to the presentation of reimbursement claims to the EC (CZ 2014: 55). The proposal to save funds through a shift from OPE to OPT was also apparently based on a proposal of the NCA (CZ6 2015).

Overall, it seems that the NCA was involved during critical periods and in difficult questions of OPE implementation. In fact, it was appreciated by the other institutions in its role as a consultant and sometimes an arbiter between the MA and the EC:

> I think they tried to help us, because they organised a meeting and asked us whether they should discuss something with the Commission which can help us. (CZ6 2015)

At the same time, also the provision of general support and lessons from other OPs were mentioned as helpful:

> I would say they created some platforms where it was possible to discuss some issues which [...] a lot of operational programs [have] in common, e.g. if it's related with the necessity of legal changes of some legal act, then there is a platform, when people from all the programmes are coming and they are saying 'Ok we have this issue with this process on this legal act

> and we would prefer some change', and there is some kind of discussion. For this kind of creating space to discuss problems across the operational programs, there is their role and they definitely are doing it. It's cool that they are doing it. (CZ7 2015)

However, even though the role of the NCA was generally evaluated positively, it was still done so explicitly with a focus on the NCA as an actor with limited formal powers. The NCA received a stronger role in the face of the OP's problems, but it was still clear that even "Enhanced Risk Management" (CZ 2014: 57) towards an OP did not equip the NCA with more than monitoring powers. The whole mechanism would mean rather that the NCA and the MA would attend

> [...] once a month to a meeting for discussions on where the problem is, what can be done, whether it was already done something, and so on. So, it was just regular meetings with the representative of the managing authorities, just how to push them to do something. So this is no, I would say, martial law in public administration, but just kind of more frequent meetings [...] Strengthened management is just some kind of, I would say, fancy and good-sounding title or vehicle for trying to push the managing authority, to find some way how to intervene if you can't intervene. (CZ1 2015)

Thus, the MA appreciated NCA's advice, but it was still seen as an actor external to the implementation process whose direct (formal) influence was rejected. This can also be concluded from the fact that the NCA's enhanced role in the next financing period was seen very sceptical from the part of the MA (CZ6 2015; CZ7 2015). In addition, the NCA seemed also often rather side-lined in the meetings of the MC. Especially during the first years, the NCA appears often as an actor who needs to fight for its involvement in the process, stressing on several occasions, for example, that it had not been informed about a change when the MA would have been formally obliged to (CZ 2009b: 4; 2010c: 4; 2010b: 3). Overall, the NCA was constantly involved into the process of adaptation of the programme, but its influence over the MA was weak, as it did not have any formal powers to intervene into the implementation process. Still, it is an open question whether or not the NCA could have made a change if it had had stronger formal powers. An obvious change which is easier for an external body would have been an earlier reallocation of funds to another OP. While strong sector interests suggest that a ministry will be very reluctant to transfer funds to another OP earlier than in the very last moment, it could have been that some of the lost funds might have been saved through an earlier intervention by a stronger central body.

It is further interesting to note that the role of the NCA was clearly enhanced in the 2014–2020 financing period. On the one hand, it proved politically completely unacceptable to remove the responsibility for OPs from the sectoral ministries (CZ1 2015). It was thus not possible to create a single-MA structure like in many other countries. On the other hand, the NCA was still given more powers. This is especially interesting in the area of methodology. The NCA stresses explicitly on its homepage that its role was adapted against the backdrop of the experience of the earlier financing period and as a measure to avoid a loss of funds in the future:

> Central management and coordination in the programming period 2014–2020 is being strengthened based on experience from the programming period 2007–2013 and performed evaluations in the area of efficiency of the management system [...] which include elements requiring far stronger management and coordination at the central level in order to achieve the objectives and priorities of the Partnership Agreement. The aim of the set-up of the system and activities of the NCA is mainly to ensure the ability of the CR to efficiently exhaust the entire allocation assigned from the EU Funds. (CZ 2015)

In sum, the NCA was in a rather weak position during the 2007–2013 financing period and its ability to influence OPE's management was restricted to a role of consultation and monitoring. In the face of traditionally strong sectoral interests in the Czech Republic, the strengthening of its role in the 2014–2020 financing period has to be seen as an important step. Especially the focus on unified methodology hints at perceived problems during the earlier period, for example the special procedure in OPE to reach GADs accumulating a high level of risk. The combination of weak influence and an enhanced position has thus to be seen as a clear sign that the role of the NCA was perceived as too weak in the period under scrutiny, and that the strengthening of central management is seen as a step towards a better absorption performance in the new financing period.

5.5 OP Transport in Romania: Initial Neglect and Constant Meddling

The Romanian OPT focused on the creation and rehabilitation of railway and road infrastructure in the country. Years of neglect and a lack of funds have left 60% of the national roads "in need of repair or rehabilitation" (RO 2007: 16). The NSRF summarizes the vital importance of investments in the Romanian transport sector as follows:

> The poor quality of transport infrastructure and services is a major obstacle to social cohesion and the economic development; e.g. it impedes competitiveness, movement of goods and labour, business settlements, investment, etc. The upgrading of the transport system is urgent and requires huge investments, but financial constraints require prioritization based on the earlier sound diagnosis of the transport sector, clear objectives and an integrated strategy to achieve them. (RO 2007: 56)

In line with the size of the task, roughly one quarter (EUR 4565 million) of all funds allocated to Romania were concentrated in OPT in the 2007–2013 financing period (RO 2007). The funds are spend in four PAs (RO 2007: 59):

- PA1: Modernization and Development of TEN-T[7]
- PA2: Modernization and Development of National Transport Infrastructure Outside TEN-T
- PA3: Modernization of Transport Sector Aiming at Higher Degree of Environmental Protection, Human Health, and Passenger Safety
- PA4: Technical Assistance

[7]The Trans-European Transport Network (TEN-T) is an EC programme for the creation of transport infrastructure with the "overreaching goal of European competitiveness, job creation and cohesion" (European Commission 2016).

The Ministry of Transport was at the centre of the management and control system. The task of the MA was assigned to the ministry's General Directorate for Foreign Financial Affairs (RO 2007: 88). Furthermore, the Ministry of Economy and Finance was in charge as the CA, while the Romanian Court of Accounts was in the position of the AA (RO 2007: 88–89).

It is a distinct feature of transport programmes that they have mostly public beneficiaries. In the Romanian case, two public companies receive almost all funds allocated to the programme. These companies are the National Company for Motorways and National Roads (CNADNR) and the National Company for Railways (CFR) (RO 2007: 89). The concentration of funds on these two companies means that the main actors in OP implementation are the MA, CNADNR, and CFR.[8]

Overall, the implementation of OPT was stressed as crucial for the Romanian economy and probably one of the major benefits of EU accession. Still, at the end of 2013, only a third of funds had been spent and the prospect of their future use was uncertain. The following chapter provides the second test of the politicization mechanism for absorption problems, and the results are again summarized in Table 5.6.[9]

5.5.1 *Test of the Causal Mechanism*

5.5.1.1 Frequent Party Alternation: Switching Between PD-L and PNL

Romanian governments as well as Ministers of Transport changed several times during the period under investigation. The financing period had initially been prepared by and started under the government of Prime Minister Popescu-Tăriceanu (National Liberal Party, PNL) who was governing in a coalition together with the Democratic Party (PD). The PD, however, left the government after constant quarrels between the two parties' leaders, Popescu-Tăriceanu and the then President of Romania Traian Băsescu. The PNL thus continued with the Hungarian

[8] All three are even located in the same building in Bucharest.

[9] The case study is based in parts on interviews with insiders to the implementation process in Romania. Interviews were conducted with ministerial officials, NGO representatives, and policy experts in 2014 and 2015. In order to guarantee confidentiality, neither the names nor the exact functions of interviewees are disclosed. Still, in Appendix II a list is provided including all interview partners, dates of interviews, as well as their more general position (official, expert, civil society).

Table 5.6 Testing the politicization mechanism in the Romanian OP Transport

			Step 1		*Step 2*		*Outcome*
Causal Mechanism	*Frequent Party Alternation (FPA)*	→	*Newly incoming ministers exchange staff and/or OP priorities and (calls for) projects*	→	*Changes disturb or even interrupt the implementation process, and harm the adaptation of rules and procedures in a low capacity context (LEC)*	→	*Absorption Problems*
Empirical Manifestations	Three alternations among parties, eight changes of minister		Important management staff is exchanged by almost every newly incoming minister. Ministers also influence project planning		Changes result in a loss of time due to the shift of attention to new projects, a poor quality of preparation, and a lack of adaptation of the management and control system		Only a third of available funds have been used at the end of the financing period, resulting in a decommitment of funds in 2013
Types of Evidence			Account Evidence: Insiders and evaluation reports stress that priorities and staff change due to politicization Pattern Evidence: Ministers immediately exchange core management staff upon their appointment, especially at the beneficiary companies		Pattern Evidence: Most problems of the implementation process remain the same throughout the period, changes are taking place all the time while the absorption rate remains low Account Evidence: Insiders and evaluations link the late start of the implementation process, the high number of mistakes in project preparation, and delays to changes of priorities and politicization		
Test Strength			(Narrow) Hoop Test: There is no convincing alternative argument to account for changes, there is interview evidence making this connection (further increasing the uniqueness of the evidence)		Narrow Hoop Test or Smoking-Gun Test: The changes are directly linked by interview partners and evaluation reports to the predicted effect (highly unique evidence, certainty to find it was low)		
Scope Condition	~CM		Creation of a (weak) central management body helps to adapt procedures; the system is strongly centralized at the level of the Ministry of EU Funds in the following financing period				

minority party UDMR as a minority cabinet in office, and the Ministry of Transport changed hands from the PD to the PNL. The minority government ultimately lost power after regular elections in November 2008.

After these elections, a coalition was formed between the Democratic-Liberal Party (PD-L, a merger of the PD with a smaller liberal party) and a left-wing alliance (Socialist Party (PSD) with the Conservative Party (PC)) (Stan and Zaharia 2009: 1089). The formation of a grand coalition between the major competitors PD-L and PSD came as a surprise, even as the elections had not resulted in a clear majority for one of the camps (Stan and Zaharia 2009: 1091). The coalition also resulted in a change of party in control of the Ministry of Transport. In 2007, the breakdown of the earlier PNL-PD government had led to a switch from PD to PNL. Now, it was the other way round: Prime Minister Emil Boc appointed Radu Mircea Berceanu (PD-L) as Minister of Transport, following Ludovic Orban (PNL) in office. Still, the coalition of the two major Romanian parties proved very unstable and the PSD left the government only one year later in October 2009 (Stan and Zaharia 2010: 1139–1140). The position of Minister of Transport, however, changed hands again only in 2010, when Anca Boagiu (also PD-L) was appointed minister in what was already the fourth cabinet under Premier Boc (Stan and Zaharia 2011: 1108).

Boc ultimately lost his position in 2012 against the backdrop of general popular dissatisfaction with the PD-L. When Mihai Răzvan Ungureanu (independent, PD-L) all of a sudden took over the premiership, it was a desperate attempt to save PD-L's control over the government. In Ungureanu's new cabinet, Alexandru Nazare (PD-L) received the post of Minister of Transport. However, the cabinet survived only 68 days in office, and fell over a vote of no confidence on 18 April 2012. The result was the second wholesale alternation in government after 2008, and Victor Ponta (PSD) formed a coalition with the PNL, replacing the ruling PD-L in power (Stan 2013: 197–202). As a result, the PNL regained control of the Ministry of Transport and appointed subsequently three different ministers in the course of the following 22 months: First Ovidiu Silaghi, then Relu Fenechiu, and finally Ramona Mănescu, the latter of these remaining in office until early 2014.

In sum, the ministry experienced seven changes on its highest position during the 2007–2013 financing period. These changes were often the result of cabinet reshuffles, but also three changes between parties took place. First in 2007, when the PNL took over the ministry from the PD.

Table 5.7 Changes at the executive level of the MA and the beneficiary companies

Minister	*MA Director*	*CFR Director*	*CNADNR Director*
Berceanu (PD) (13 June 2006–4 April 2007)	Newly Appointed (2007–2009)	**Newly Appointed** (28 August 2006–1 May 2007)	
Orban (PNL) (5 April 2007–21 December 2008)	–	**Newly Appointed** (2 May 2007–23 December 2008)	Newly Appointed
Berceanu (PD-L) (22 December 2008–2 September 2010)	Newly Appointed (2010–2012)	**Newly Appointed (interim)** (24 December 2008–29 June 2009) **Newly Appointed** (30 June 2009–8 October 2009) Newly Appointed (interim) (9 October 2009–31 January 2010) Newly Appointed (1 February 2010–26 August 2010) Newly Appointed (interim) (27 August 2010–1 September 2010)	Newly Appointed (2 May 2009)
Boagiu (PD-L) (3 September 2010–8 February 2012)	–	**Newly Appointed** (2 September 2010–15 December 2010) Newly Appointed (16 December 2010–15 May 2012)	Newly Appointed (23 November 2010) Newly Appointed (25 July 2011)
Nazare (PD-L) (9 February 2012–6 May 2012)	–	–	–

(continued)

Table 5.7 (continued)

Minister	*MA Director*	*CFR Director*	*CNADNR Director*
Silaghi (PNL) (7 May 2012–20 December 2012)	Newly Appointed (2012)	**NA (position vacant)** (16 May 2012–11 December 2012) Newly Appointed (12 May 2012–19 December 2012)	Newly Appointed (interim) (27 May 2012) Newly Appointed (interim) (24 July 2012)
Fenechiu (PNL) (21 December 2012–11 July 2013) (Prime Minister Ponta interim: 12 July 2013–25 August 2013)	**Newly Appointed** (2013)	**Newly Appointed** (20 December 2012–15 April 2013) Newly Appointed (16 April 2013–16 January 2014)	
Mănescu (PNL) (26 August 2013–4 March 2014)	–	–	Newly Appointed (28 August 2013)

Note Those candidates clearly appointed as director of CFR in a temporal conjunction with an incoming new minister are in bold type. The alternation of candidates on the other executive positions could not as easily be linked to changes of minister due to a lower quality of the data (provided only as names of directors in charge during a certain year, and not the exact appointment and dismissal dates). Nevertheless, the pattern seems to be similar in all three bodies, especially at the level of the beneficiary companies

Source Own compilation, based on EJPR annual reports (ministers, see Appendix I for detailed sources), the CNADNR homepage (CNADNR Directors), and information provided by the Ministry of Transport (MA Director) and CFR (CFR Director)

Then in 2008, when this change happened in reverse. Third in 2012, when the ministry switched again from the PD-L to the PNL. An overview of these changes is presented in the first column of Table 5.7.

5.5.1.2 First Step: The Ministers Politicize, Not the Parties

The overview of both party alternations and changes of ministers presented above underlines that the Ministry of Transport was in great turmoil during the financing period. The changes had serious repercussions for the implementation system of OPT, as well as the programme's strategy and project selection. On the one hand, it was rather the appointment of a new minister, and not the change of party in office leading to politicized changes. Ministers tended to exchange important management staff upon their appointment in office, leading to constant reshuffles on core positions. On the other hand, they also tried to adapt transport strategies and project selection according to their own preferences, resulting in changes at the level of project planning for OPT.

When it comes to staff changes, the alternation at the political level went hand in hand with changes on important management positions. Table 5.7 shows the changes of management staff in the three most important bodies involved in the implementation of the programme: the Directorate-General Management of External Funds (the MA), and CFR and CNADNR as the two biggest beneficiaries of the programme. The most stable position was that of the Director of the MA, despite of three changes taking place. Starting with the candidate appointed by Minister Berceanu, her successor followed only in 2010, then the next in 2012, and finally in 2013. The total of four directors of the MA is a rather high number, just about the same as in the equally weakly performing Czech OPE. Nevertheless, the numbers are modest in comparison to what happened at the level of the beneficiary companies.

CFR had not less than nine directors between 2007–2013, and that is not even counting interim takeovers in-between alternations of fully appointed directors. CNADNR had at least seven directors during the same period. Unfortunately, the data available for the two beneficiary companies differs: While CFR provided the full information readily with appointment dates, the data for CNADNR had to be collected from the company's homepage. Overall, while there is much information on the different directors, it is not possible to claim that all CNADNR directors are presented in Table 5.7. However, it is still clear that the tendency is exactly the same as in CFR.

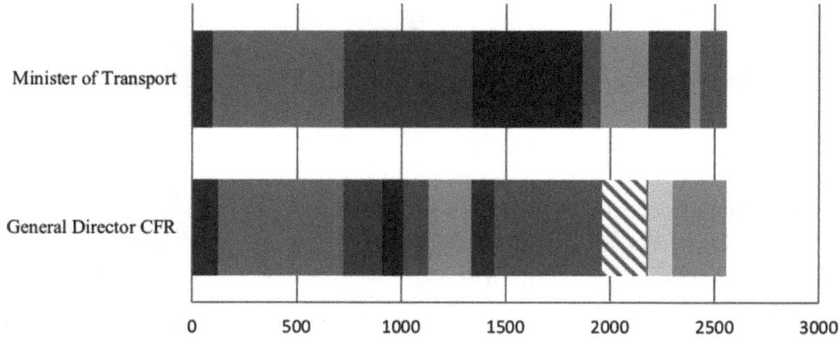

Fig. 5.3 Duration in office in days of Romanian Ministers of Transport and General Directors at CFR (*Source* The author's compilation based on EJPR reports and information provided by CFR [see Appendix III for a detailed calculation of days in office, and Table 5.7 for the dates])

It is now interesting to compare the alternation of the management staff with that of ministers. CFR is the best example in this regard, because it offers the highest quality appointment data. Table 5.7 shows that almost every newly incoming minister appointed an own candidate for the post of director of CFR. In fact, only two out of eight ministers, Nazare and Mănescu, have not appointed a new director during their (also very short) time in office, and Minister Silaghi immediately dismissed the incumbent director without a direct replacement. All others appointed at least one new director, usually directly after their own appointment as Minister of Transport.

Figure 5.3 presents this information in a different visualization. The days in office of both ministers and CFR directors are presented in an additive bar-chart. It is easy to see that every time a new minister comes into office, shortly afterwards also a new bar for a CFR director begins. Rather surprisingly, two directors started their terms one day earlier than their respective ministers, what might be linked to technicalities of the appointment process. Overall, the pattern of changes is clear: The director of the beneficiary company CFR generally changes with the Minister of Transport, independently of the minister's party affiliation. Thus, in the Romanian case also changes between ministers from the same party are relevant for staff-politicization.

As already stated above, the pattern is a bit more difficult to interpret for CNADNR due to data limitations. The dates in brackets behind the directors of CNADNR are not the appointment dates of these directors as in the CFR column (because they are unknown), but rather the points in time when they could be verified as directors on the CNADNR homepage.[10] Interestingly, also in this case new directors were generally found on the company's homepage after the appointment of a new minister. The dates are thus not as closely linkable to the appointment of ministers, but the pattern is the same as for CFR: A new minister of transport appoints a new director, independently from the minister's party affiliation.

In contrast, changes at the level of the MA are less frequent. The first director served both under PD and PNL control of the ministry as head of the MA. The following served under the PD-L (the successor party of the PD), and left office in 2012. Here, it is unclear whether he was dismissed under the last (and very short PD-L) government of newly appointed minister Ungureanu, or already under PNL rule (what seems more likely). What is clear, though, is that the next director had only a very short stint in office, and that the next one followed when the PNL was again in charge of the ministry after the elections. Therefore, if any, the pattern of party changes is closest to the pattern of changes in the office of director of the MA, even though it directly accounts only for one out of three crucial changes of party in control of the Ministry of Transport. The data might therefore rather point into the direction of the general finding that even in highly politicized contexts, those bodies dealing directly with international institutions are often spared from frequent changes to guarantee a more stable interaction (Kopecký and Spirova 2011: 910). While the MA is interacting directly with the EC in contrast to the beneficiary companies, this could well be the motivation.

Besides the observation of pattern evidence for politicized staff changes, the issue was also highlighted in different evaluation reports. One review stressed that the financial statements issued by CFR and CNADNR reveal different signatures of general managers almost

[10]It seems that not even official evaluators had for their work on the Romanian transport sector all of this information available, as a report stresses the alternation of directors on the basis of director's changing signatures on official documents at different points in time (RO 2011b: 52).

every year, while there is no explanation for why they were removed or appointed (RO 2011b: 52). It closes with the demand to "limit the sanction of replacement of the companies' management staff to failure to comply with performance obligations only" (RO 2011b: 11). Also, the World Bank highlights the fact that a high number of positions in the Romanian transport sector were filled as a result of "political patronage" (World Bank 2010: 52). There is therefore robust evidence that staff politicization is a ubiquitous issue in the management structures of the Romanian transport sector and as a result also in the management system of structural funds.

Overall, there is a clear pattern that the beneficiary companies experienced more frequent changes than the MA. In order to understand these appointments, it is interesting to take a look at institutional relationships within the Romanian transport sector. CFR and CNADNR were originally founded as public companies in order to assure their independence from short-term politicized planning (World Bank 2010: vi). A public company is not run by the ministry, but rather independently by a board of directors that is regularly appointed by the company's assembly of shareholders. In the case of the two public infrastructure companies, however, the Ministry of Transport is their de facto shareholder and thus controls also the appointment of the management. This has direct repercussions for their independence from political influence:

> [I]nevitably they [the officials] will on the whole be motivated more by the political interests of their Minister, and/or the bureaucratic interests of their Ministry, than by the long-term interests of the companies to whose Boards they are appointed. (World Bank 2010: 14)

The appointment of management staff gives ministers indirect control over the companies. This control is interesting, as it offers access to project planning and decisions over priorities of transport policy. In order to understand how this affects the transport sector, one can simply take a look at the development of transport strategies. In general, Romania has a long tradition of ever-changing transport strategies during the last two decades. The abandoned strategies comprise, besides others, a transport master plan that was immediately dropped after its adoption in 1998 and the 2003 transport strategy (RO 2011b: 30). Even though there is a 'Sustainable Transport Strategy for 2007–2013, 2020, 2030' (adopted 2008) and an 'Integrated Strategic Plan for the Transport Sector' (adopted 2009), these documents do not actually inform transport sector strategy (World Bank 2010: 25).

The lack of strategic planning is directly linked to the politicization of planning. Administrative units of the Ministry of Transport focus only on the legal requirements of transport planning, but the decision-making on actual projects is strongly influenced by the political actors involved (World Bank 2010: 30). Together with ever-changing Ministers of Transport this led to the constant adoption of new projects without taking into account their effect on the budget (World Bank 2010: 30). As a result, the transport sector was overwhelmed with projects without proper funding, leading to a situation in which the "annual capital expenditure for all modes of transport in 2010 was more than six times the MOT's [Ministry of Transport] total annual budget" (World Bank 2010: x) (according to another, later evaluation even nine times [RO 2011b: 18]). The evaluation stresses that every newly incoming minister is simply adding new projects to the general agenda without taking into account the existing obligations of already ongoing projects. This resulted in a "ballooning capital investment program overloaded with unfunded or inadequately funded projects, causing inevitable postponement and delays in implementation" (RO 2011b: 30).

In sum, priorities of transport sector planning are the result of (tactical) political decision-making and not of strategic and long-term planning (World Bank 2010: 30). Romania's practice is thereby in sharp contrast to the procedure in the EU 15 countries, where medium term (3–5 years) programmes and budgets prevail, a necessary condition to achieve proper progress in the transport sector (RO 2011b: 68).

But are these changes also possible in OPT, a programme that is subject to strong external control? While the general strategies are described as fluid, OPT is seen as one of the only constant programmes pursued over a couple of years in the sector in Romania. "Strategies except the projects 'fixed' in the SOP T [OPT] are as volatile as the leadership" (RO 2011b: 18). In addition, insiders agreed that projects in OPT would not be changed by newly incoming ministers as soon as they had reached the implementation phase (RO1 2015). This makes sense as it would be hard to justify to the EC why, for example, the construction of a certain piece of infrastructure would no longer be pursued. Such a late intervention is much more difficult than the early interruption of planning procedures for certain projects and the change of course on the preparation stage.

Tracking changing preferences is thus extremely difficult, as they leave their fingerprints below the radar of project lists and fixed priorities. Still, their effect is the same, namely that time and efforts are wasted on projects that are not implemented in the end. Even though it is difficult to find, there is still some evidence for an impact of political interests on programme priorities. At a general level, evaluations criticized that political changes had a disturbing impact on programme priorities:

> The frequent changes of government contribute to a situation in which priority setting for SI [Structural Instruments] is inconstant and inconsistent. This weakens the motivation to plan SI interventions with the least delay, because changes of government usually incur a measure of hesitancy at both the management and operational levels within the administration. (RO 2010a: 64)

This is complemented by evidence for shifts in certain priority areas. One evaluation reported that changes take place in areas where projects are not fixed:

> The fact that some projects under PA2 (the priority status of which is not well documented) have changed since the preparation of the SOP T [OPT], could indicate that these are nevertheless high on the political agenda. Thus, the Annex 3 of SOP T contains as likely projects the rehabilitation of several national roads, although the focus has shifted to bypasses. (RO 2011b: 45)

It makes sense that these changes are taking place in PA2, which is focussing on the creation of national roads apart from the TEN-T network. Changes in PAs related to this network would be hardly possible, as they are part of a wider European transport strategy and thus fixed in the programming documents.

In line with the quoted evaluation reports, also insiders highlighted that new people coming to office would bring with them new ideas for projects. As already mentioned, incoming ministers would not stop projects with signed contracts and implementation of ongoing measures would usually proceed (RO1 2015). Still, the situation is different for the general strategy of the programme, the importance of certain projects, and thus the time invested in different interventions:

> A new manager came with a new idea, with a new deadline, with a new, I don't know, idea of who should lead the tendering team [...]. All these changes affected of course the initial schedule. (RO2 2015)

> [I]t's a matter of strategy what can we do in the next 5 years. I can go in the next two years with this project, after two months come other people and say just go the other direction. This is the main effect of these political and high administrative changes. (RO1 2015)

This stresses the fact that not only staff, but also the general agenda of project planning and the prioritization of certain projects were the object of interest of incoming new ministers. It seems plausible that they would exchange the most important management staff in order to control transport strategies. This would go along with a change of priorities at the level of transport projects. The politicization of the transport sector thus clearly affected both levels of staff as well as projects.

5.5.1.3 Second Step: These Changes Subsequently Cause Implementation Problems

The politicization of staff as well as project priorities had serious effects on the implementation process. First, frequent changes meant that a great deal of time was lost during the preparation process. Ministers focused on the spending of less-controlled national funds as long as possible (i.e. until the crisis), neglecting EU funds during the first years of the financing period. When the crisis hit the country and EU funds were the only money left, politicians increased the pressure on the MA and the beneficiary companies to achieve progress. This pressure, however, resulted in a hastened preparation process prone to mistakes and thereby further delays. Second, the strong sector politicization led also to the neglect of important tasks, such as the adaptation of the implementation process and the management and control system. Staff possessed often only short experience on the job, and learning was not institutionalized, for example in a functioning risk management system. As a result, well-known and persistent problems of the implementation process were not systematically tackled and could hinder absorption throughout the financing period.

OPT started late into the financing period and registered during the first years barely any progress. The rate of approved and contracted projects increased only very slowly until the end of 2010. Projects

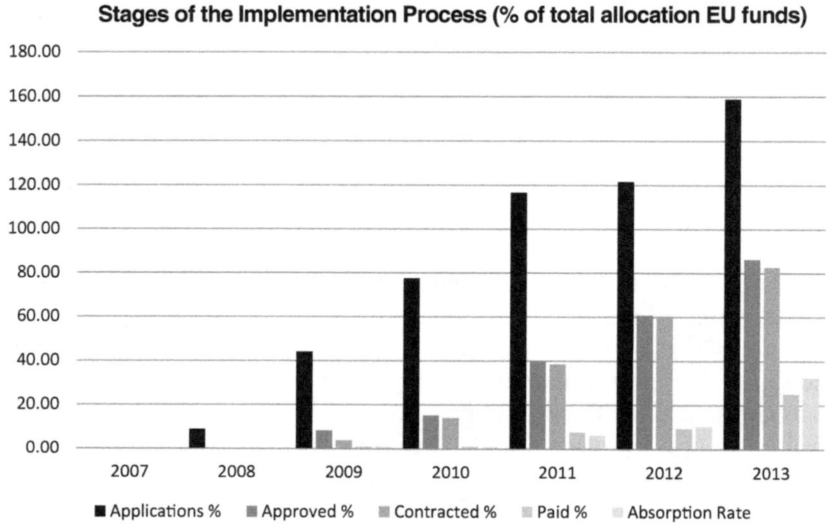

Fig. 5.4 Progress at different stages of the implementation process—Romanian OP Transport (% of total allocation of EU funds) (*Source* The author's compilation based on annual implementation reports [see Appendix III for detailed information])

approved/contracted developed from 0.16%/0.01% in 2008 towards 8.25%/3.62% in 2009, and 15.08%/13.84% in 2010. At the same time, actual absorption of EU money was virtually non-existent and below one percent of the total allocation (0.9% in 2010) (see Fig. 5.4 for an overview over the development). Already in 2009, EUR 1 billion had been spent less than originally planned (World Bank 2010: 24). One of the main reasons for this slow progress was that the programme started in 2007 from an "unprepared level" (RO1 2015). The lack of preparation was subsequently crucial for the development of the financing period:

> Another issue at the very beginning of the programming was, this was actually the main reason why the programme didn't perform quite well, we weren't really prepared of starting the implementation. (RO2 2015)

Evaluation reports link the poor level of preparation of OPT during the first years to a lack of political support for the absorption of EU funds that was for implementation "a distinct disadvantage"

(RO 2010a: 64). This comes as a surprise: Why would a country with access to billions of EU funds neglect programme planning and therefore absorption? When it comes to the transport sector, the low level of preparedness is not only linked to poor capacities or the complexity of projects, but also to the very dominance of political interests in transport sector planning. Especially the availability of domestic funds that could be applied with much more discretion made the EU funds an unattractive alternative during these years:

> Romania was having quite high economic growth rates, I think 8%, something like that, per year. The state budget was, let's say, pretty rich. There were also these IFI [International Financial Institutions] loans and they have enough to focus on, so 'let's forget about this free money that we get'. So they didn't pay that much attention, I mean this was a little bit encouraged by the political, let's say, leaders of that time. They were more interested in doing quick things and these quick things were done quicker obviously if you were following the Romanian legislation or the IFI rules, because they were much simpler. (RO2 2015)

Thus, the neglect of EU funds is best understood against the backdrop of the logic of transport sector politicization by ministers. The use of domestic resources meant a burden for the budget, but projects were easier to implement using less strict domestic rules. Therefore, projects funded from domestic sources of IFIs took precedence in contrast to projects within OPT. However, the situation changed dramatically upon the advent of the crisis. Romania's economy shrank by 6.6% in 2009 and the country had to seek a standby programme from the IMF in order to avoid defaulting on its debt. The sudden lack of domestic funds available for transport projects suddenly made the EU funds much more attractive.

> Of course, when the crisis hit, this political view on things changed dramatically, because suddenly the budget shrank, there was no longer easy money to get from elsewhere and these European funds were the only source of funding. (RO2 2015)

The loss of alternative opportunities for financing as a result of the crisis could thus well have been a positive influence on the implementation process. It was now inevitable to deal with EU funds as more attractive funds were no longer available. Still, the stronger political focus on EU funds proved to be a double-edged sword when politician's pushing for progress in project preparation met a context of low capacity.

The low level of capacity was an issue for OPT throughout the financing period, both with regard to the implementation system as well as human resources. During the initial years, there was clearly a lack of rules and procedures in place to assure the smooth functioning of the management and control system. The system was put to its first test only in 2007, as Romania had before not been a member of the EU. Especially rules for public procurement and a very complicated set of rules governing applications for funds proved during these years a problem for the public beneficiary companies (RO 2010a: 123–124).

The process of public procurement is the most difficult phase of implementation in all member states and many mistakes happening here slowing down absorption. Romania had suffered from problems with its procurement legislation already during the pre-accession phase. Its NSRF stated that these lessons learned had been included into a new public procurement law as well as knowledge on the necessary maturity of projects (RO 2007: 51). Still, this experience did apparently not help very much to improve procedures. Procurement decisions were especially during the first years frequently contested in courts, postponing the start of practical implementation as a result and making absorption more difficult. Procurement procedures were subsequently a core issue for implementation, resulting in "delays, high frequency of errors and the resulting financial sanctions" (Lucaciu 2012: 15). One reason for this was the complexity of the rules, which were prone to different interpretations, and with regard to control procedures even stricter than demanded by the EU's financial regulations (so-called 'gold-plating') (RO 2010a: 15). The problem was long neglected and authorities failed to adapt procurement procedures according to the experience of their limited usefulness (RO 2010a: 72). Only a change of legislation in 2010 (RO 2011b: 41), together with the necessary standardization of documents and a strengthening of procurement departments finally made a difference (Lucaciu 2012: 15). Still, these changes also came at the price of even longer evaluation procedures, and an almost exclusive focus on quantitative (mostly the price) despite qualitative project selection criteria (Lucaciu 2012: 15).

Beyond procurement procedures, the legal framework for implementation was often still inconsistent and had to be adapted well into the financing period (RO 2010a: 69). This adaptation, however, also proved difficult for the implementation process. If regulations were changed during the process of project submission, it was a burden for the beneficiaries to follow all updates of guidelines and to accommodate to new requirements in the course of the process (RO 2010a: 70–71) At the same time, regulations could also be changed, for example with regard to eligibility, resulting in the sudden ineligibility of formerly eligible expenditure (RO 2010a: 69). Finally, some important procedures were also simply not yet developed in the first years of the financing period, such as the adequate methodology to conduct cost-benefit analysis, or efficient procedures regarding the crucial process of land expropriation (RO 2009: 19). Still, also as late as 2013 Lucaciu reports that the key problem of implementation was still the "limited reliability of the management and control system" (Lucaciu 2013: 15).

Second, a lack of human resources was also frequently reported to slow down implementation. Romania has a history of low administrative capacity and lack of (qualified) human resources in the transport sector. At a general level, the EC stressed already in 2005 that capacities relating to financial management and control and the institutional structures have to be strengthened (RO 2007: 49). Also the Romanian government was aware of the fact that human resource limitations would have a prohibitive effect on the use of structural funds in the financing period. The Ministry of Transport itself stated in the NSRF, the main planning document for the financing period:

> In the pre-accession period there was a high level of fluctuation of the personnel involved in the management of EU funds, caused mainly by low salaries within the MT. This aspect had repercussions on the management and the implementation of the projects, mainly because of the delays in accomplishing the tasks of the projects, caused by the difficulties to recruit qualified people, the time needed and the associated costs like training new personnel, etc. In order to strengthen the institutional capacity for managing Community funds, the Romanian Government had undertaken a corrective measure in order to increase the financial motivation of the personnel involved in the management of these funds (Law 490/2004). (RO 2007: 50)

The lack of staff and its effect were thus well known. Nevertheless, the lack of human resources in both the necessary quantity and quality to ensure efficient implementation of the programme was mentioned as a constant problem throughout the financing period that was not easily overcome (RO 2010b: 21–22; 2011a: 22; Lucaciu 2012: 15; RO 2013: 28). In 2007, for example, 30 new people could be hired, but at the same time 19 others quit their service at the ministry (RO 2009: 19). The level of staff turnover constantly increased over the first years and rose from only 3% in 2006, to 12% in 2007, to even 20% in 2008 (RO 2009: 19). Thus, every fifth employee of the MA switched the position in 2008, causing loss of institutional memory, expertise, and routines. At the same time, also the occupation rate for positions in the MA stood only at 86% (with 15 positions still vacant and ten with suspended activities) (RO 2009: 19). Problems resulted also from the fact that some positions were filled, but not actively occupied. Staff that left temporarily for maternity leave or other reasons, but was not replaced by a substitute, made up ten percent of all positions in all MAs in Romania at the end of 2009, a high rate considering the fact that also only nine out of ten posts were filled at this time (87%) (RO 2010a: 124).

Staff figures involved in OPT are also low compared at the national level: OPE, the programme closest in size to OPT, has a total number of 73 project related staff, while OPT has with 34 barely half of this number (RO 2010a: 126). This is also reflected in the ratio of allocated grant to project related staff, which is twice the amount per person in OPT in comparison to OPE (RO 2010a: 126). The general observation of a lack of human resources was also stressed during the interviews: "Well, the bottom line was that we never had the people we wanted. We wanted a lot more people than this" (RO2 2015).

Both weak human resources and weak implementation structures became an even bigger problem in the context of strong sector politicization. First, the urge to finalize 'their own' projects led ministers to put pressure on the administration. This pressure then obviously not resulted in faster procedures, but rather more mistakes and thus delays. Second, the frequent changes also weakened capacity, especially at the executive level. This weak and unstable executive capacity then impeded the adaptation of general administrative capacity, as knowledge was frequently lost and not institutionalized. Rather than an event, the interaction of politicization and low capacity was thus more of a pattern in OPT.

When political interest shifted towards EU funds, there was high pressure from the political level put on the MA as well as beneficiary companies to get projects ready that could be financed from the OP's budget (RO2 2015). Ministers did not only want their preferred projects to be developed, they also wanted them fast against the backdrop of the usually short time in office. Still, rushing the projects meant that "the quality of the preparation was hurt, because of course, you cannot do in four months what you have to do in twelve months" (RO2 2015).

As a result, the implementation process was not accelerated, because poorly prepared projects as well as calls for proposals caused many problems during all stages of the implementation process. Especially contestations of tender procedures in court, i.e. the decision on who would execute a project and therefore benefit from it, were much easier on the basis of poorly prepared documents:

> Again the quality of the documentation was poor and this was felt in the tendering process. Because this was the next big problem after preparation, tendering. Tendering took a long, long time. […] So there were these contestations […] in a lot of tenders. In reality, a lot of this came from bad preparation. Obviously if you are going to tender poor documentation […] the competitors can find lots of flaws in the documentation and contest them or appeal on them. (RO2 2015)

The slow pace of the implementation process was thus a result of poor preparation, which was itself the result of the initial neglect of EU funds, and the subsequent necessity "to finish the preparation quickly" (RO2 2015). Procurement decisions on who would execute a project were then frequently contested in courts, which would further delay the start of the implementation of a project (RO 2011a: 21).

The 'discovery' of EU funds by transport ministers came at another price. The fact that ministers would now hasten project development only to result in poor project quality meant that ministers had shifted their attention from domestic to EU funds in order to implement their preferred projects. Still, the fact that ministers changed frequently in office, and with them their staff, meant that this hastened planning and execution of projects would happen repeatedly under different ministers, with different management staff in charge of ever-changing project priorities. One insider described the effect of these frequent changes of strategy, which are linked to the changes of ministers and central management staff, in a rather drastic way:

> The head of the ministry, a politician, the minister, came with other political ideas. For him another project was the most important, not one which the previous minister considered to be the important one. So, all efforts on the

> project were stopped and 'let's focus on the new project and forget about the last'. This changing in priorities was often with the change of ministers. Unfortunately, this strand continued. [...] I've been quite long in the ministry and on average I had one minister per year. That is unacceptable. (RO2 2015)

Political changes are thus blamed for a loss of time in the preparation process of projects that would be started, but then dropped again. This pattern did not so much affect ongoing projects which had reached the phase of practical implementation, but rather the crucial phase of strategy and preparation. These are exactly the stages which would mean most of the work of the MA and the beneficiary companies. While these changes go rather unnoticed in the official documentation, they are of great importance as time and capacity is wasted for projects that never reach the phase of practical implementation.

> You never get to finish what you started if you keep changing priorities. Because they would fall on the second or the third place in your concerns. Even if they would happen, they would happen much slower than previously planned. (RO2 2015)

> Not necessarily everybody would go and work on that, but the focus of the management would be that. I mean, a few would come to work and instead of discussing what was your priority until then, you discuss new priority every day. How to do that? Of course, you forget about the other one or at least it comes second or third in your timeline. (RO2 2015)

It comes with no surprise that these changes went hand in hand with slow progress of programme implementation. Those projects that finally reached the implementation stage and managed to overcome the mentioned procurement contestations subsequently met the reality of a difficult and until then untested practical implementation process. This process again suffered from the poor quality of project preparation (RO 2012b: 26). Problems were related to the improper execution of the procurement processes, leading to corrections; expropriations by CFR; the proper supervision of contracts by the beneficiaries; problems with feasibility studies and technical documentation; and the slow progress reached by the contractors executing the projects (RO 2012b: 26; 2013: 28). These risks to the implementation process were not managed properly and, as a consequence, the implementation of contracts suffered: the

Table 5.8 Problems Encountered During the Implementation of OP Transport

	2008	2009	2010	2011	2012	2013[a]
Human Resources	X	X	X	-	X	-
Rules	X	-	-	-	X	-
Quality of Projects	X	X	X	X	X	-
Tender (Selection and Contestation)	-	-	X	X	X	X
Local Authorities[b]	-	X	-	X	-	-
Lack of Funds	-	X	X	-	X	-
Lack of Overall Strategy	-	X	X	-	-	-
Lack of Information System	-	-	X	-	-	-
Low Quality Consultants	-	-	X	-	-	-
Contract Supervison	-	-	-	X	X	-
Slow Contractors	-	-	-	X	X	-

Sources The author's compilation, based on Annual Implementation Reports (cells marked with x mean the mentioning of a problem in this area in the AIR covering the respective year) (RO 2009: 18–20; 2010b: 20–23; 2011a: 21–22; 2012b: 26; 2013: 28–29; 2014: 34)

[a] The section of major problems encountered during the year is rather short in the 2013 report and mainly focusing on the issue of possible decommitment of funds and the phasing of projects which cannot be finished until the end of the financing period (RO 2014: 34)

[b] Cooperation with local authorities is necessary to facilitate expropriations and relocations, issue construction permits, environmental consultation, and other tasks (RO 2010b: 23)

process was delayed, mistakes detected too late and certification interrupted (June 2012 until 2013) and even pre-suspended (2012), causing financial problems, a loss of time, and a lower rate of absorption (Lucaciu 2013: 14; Pop et al. 2013: 102; RO 2013: 29; RO2 2015). The interruption of certification even resulted in a correction of 20% of all procurement decision in OPT made until October 2011, which could still be used but implied that the reduction had first to be borne by the domestic budget (only the acceptance of the correction helped that the OP was not suspended) (RO 2012a).

Table 5.8 summarizes the central challenges met by OPT as mentioned in the AIRs during the financing period. The most important result is that all problems mentioned seem to be valid for almost all of the time under investigation. The fact that some problems surface only later is most likely linked to the fact that they concern a later phase of the implementation cycle that was only then reached (e.g. 'contract supervision' or 'slow contractors'). This means that OPT could not escape most of its problems until the very end of the financing period.

Why could these practical problems not be overcome? The answer to this question is linked to the second influence of transport sector politicization on the implementation of OPT: the neglect of constant and systematic adaptation of the implementation process. In the face of frequent changes of core management staff, it proved very difficult to establish a systematic follow-up on adaptation. As it was the country's first encounter with cohesion policy implementation, it would have been useful to establish a process of institutionalized learning in the OP, like a functioning risk management system, in order to receive early warnings and avoid recurring mistakes. A risk management system could have detected dangers to OP implementation earlier and thereby facilitated a more strategic approach to implementation (RO 2011b: 45).

However, evaluations stress that the bodies involved lacked "the necessary institutional memory, capacity to exert leadership and ability to manage risk" (RO 2011b: 45). The problem of adaptation is thus linked directly to the frequent occurrence of shifts at the management level that produce delays "even in the absence of policy shifts" (RO 2010a: 62). For example, the biggest beneficiary CNADNR has no institutionalized system or procedure to deal with risks, even though most of them are well known and considered major problems with regard to delays (RO 2011b: 47). The absence of proper risk management means that there is little to no exchange of knowledge between the MA, CFR, and CNADNR on important topics such as the design of road projects or land expropriation, a new topic for CFR, but not for CNADNR (RO 2011b: 46). While problem-solving and learning could have been institutionalized, it rather remained highly informal (RO 2011b: 46), and institutional knowledge easily fell prey to staff changes. The ministry and beneficiary companies thus remained reactive in their approach and short-term tactical solutions were given way to long term strategic ones. Accordingly, an evaluation report directly demanded that politicized changes of the leadership of the beneficiary companies should be stopped and replacements limited to merit-based criteria, in order to ensure a coherent management and strategy for the beneficiaries (RO 2011b: 52, 57).

Apart from the implementation structure and procedures, the lack of adaptation concerned also the level of human resources. The issue of human resources was mostly ignored by ministers and as a result even investments in staff qualification from the pre-accession period were lost over time.

> No genuine human resources policy for administrative entities seems to have been designed and implemented, in spite of the fact that several training programmes – also targeting the MAs and national IBs – having been implemented over the past decade. Decisions related to staff numbers and the hiring and firing of staff appear not based on a clear assessment of the mandate and workload of the different departments in the administration. (RO 2010a: 15)

This is especially surprising against the backdrop of the fact that the reports on 2009 and 2010 link virtually all problems of the implementation process (e.g. poor preparation of projects, feasibility and technical studies, slow pace of contracting and procurement, and prolonged periods for the reimbursement claims to be handed in) to both a lack of quality and quantity in staff available for implementation (RO 2010b: 21–22; 2011a: 22).

An obvious measure to retain qualified staff would have been to offer competitive salaries and attractive career paths. However, rather the opposite was the case: Low salaries are often mentioned as the reason for staff shortages at the MAs (RO 2010a: 64). In the face of high demands against low benefits, even changes within the public administration system (not only to the private sector) are an attractive option (RO 2011b: 39). The existing staff is also not actively encouraged to improve its skills. For example, CNADNR offers extra training, but the participation is unrelated to payment and promotion. "The key issues of low salaries and promotions are not based on competency and performance but on longevity of service" (World Bank 2010: 26).

Attempts to improve absorption ultimately failed often until the very end of the financing period because of "unresolved core problems (such as poor functioning of systems and inter-institutional cooperation, instability of structures and managers, limited effectiveness of human resources and management function, etc.)" (Lucaciu 2013: 5). The consequences of high sector politicization and continuing low administrative capacity are nicely summarized by the World Bank:

> There may be temporary fixes to enhance the administrative mechanism for the use of such funds, but as long as the fundamental issues covered by the review are not addressed, the chances of using even a fraction of these funds within the current deadlines will remain limited. (World Bank 2010: 29)

In sum, the poor performance of OPT can be strongly linked to the high level of transport sector politicization by ever-changing ministers. Only after domestic sources had dried up, ministers started to focus on EU funds. Unfortunately, the goal was quick-spending and the hastened process of project preparation resulted in many mistakes, slowing down practical implementation in the end. Weak human resources meant that a high workload lasted only on few shoulders, increasing the pressure further and making mistakes and delays more likely (RO 2010b: 22; 2011b: 9). Ever-changing ministers changed project priorities and management staff, confusing the implementation process further. While many different problems haunted implementation, they could have been managed more thoroughly, as risks were often well-known and recurring. However, systematic learning and adaptation of structures and human resources was impeded by frequent changes of management staff leading to a loss of institutional knowledge and a lack of institutionalized risk management.

What about alternative arguments for the low performance? One could be that the financial crisis struck the implementation process hard and made therefore implementation more difficult. The changes of project priorities and management staff are sustained by clear evidence, but the crisis could at least be an additional factor making implementation more difficult. This argument makes intuitively sense, but most actors involved in the process denied an important impact of the crisis (RO1 2015). Romania received a EUR 20 billion bailout from the IMF (RO 2011b: 43) and also just like Lithuania a co-financing facility of EUR 1 billion from the European Investment Bank (EIB) for co-financing of OPT and OPE (RO 2010a: 68). This means that generally money for co-financing was available. Also, the EC supported crisis-torn countries in their efforts to use EU funds, and allowed Slovakia and Romania an exemption from the *N*+2 rule to give them more time to use their funds (Frank 2013: 9; RO 2014: 35). In contrast to representing a burden, the funds available in the transport sector could also have been used as a crucial source of investment in a period where other sources dried up (World Bank 2010: 29). This means that in contrast to the idea that the economic crisis was an impediment to fund implementation, it could have helped to cushion its effects.

However, the government rather made implementation more difficult by ordering both wage cuts and a hiring-stop that would not spare the areas of the public administration which are part of the cohesion policy implementation system (RO2 2015). These cuts were obviously linked to demands from the IMF. Still, they could have been applied more wisely if the attainment of EU funds had been the most important objective (which it probably should have been at this point). The cuts have also to be seen against the backdrop of general criticism of the government's austerity programme that "stemmed mostly from Boc's fund misallocation to unnecessary projects at a time when his cabinet closed down hospitals and schools" (Stan 2013: 204). It was perceived as largely unfair and "shouldered disproportionately by ordinary Romanian citizens, and not the political elite and its many clients" (Stan and Zaharia 2011: 1111). If the crisis had an effect, it was thus also made worse by the political decision-makers at that time.

5.5.1.4 The Result Is Absorption Problems

The programme started to see some more substantial progress in 2011, when the rate of contracted projects reached 38.46% of the total allocation, and the volume of applications exceeded for the first time the total allocation (116.58%). Still, the gap between contracted projects and reimbursements remained and the absorption rate developed much slower than the contracting rate (10.24%/60.35% in 2012, and finally 32.24%/82.64% in 2013). Thus, barely a third of all funds were absorbed at the end of the financing period in 2013. The large difference between contracting and absorption is also linked to the overall character of the projects implemented within the programme. OPT implements almost exclusively big infrastructure interventions taking a long time for both preparation and execution, and progress is thus more likely to happen slowly but surely as big projects start to get finished. Nevertheless, it was clear at a very early point in time that the programme was seriously delayed and that the government's initial hesitance to engage more forcefully in the absorption of funds meant that it would be soon too late to avoid decommitments (RO 2010a: 150). The slow start of the financing period and the difficulties experienced on each step of the implementation process met the reality of slow implementation by contractors and practical problems (archaeological discoveries, difficult weather conditions) that added to the slow performance. The EC's expert report stressed in 2013 that "it is evident that the delays experienced up until 2011 cannot be recovered even by a markedly improved level of expenditure" (Lucaciu 2013: 11).

In order to save the money from decommitment, the Romanian government both negotiated with the EC and engaged in reallocations within the programme. First, the government managed to receive an exemption from the *N*+2 rule for 2011 and 2012, i.e. a postponement of decommitments (RO2 2015). Second, money within the programme was shifted away from the generally delayed railway projects to more mature road projects. These reallocations concentrated funds further, shifting them away from the areas of rail transport and 'other transport interventions' to roads (Lucaciu 2013: 9). Other aspects of OPT were also simply cancelled, such as the naval infrastructure project with Bulgaria, the acquisition of rail equipment, and the roads safety project, while the allocation for technical assistance was further reduced (Lucaciu 2013: 9–10). Reallocations in favor of road projects amounted to a total sum of EUR 425.9 million (Lucaciu 2013: 10). Still, despite these measures it was too late to make up for the accumulated delays. Therefore, a total sum of EUR 137 million was lost in 2013 and despite of the exemptions from the *N*+2 rule.

5.5.2 *The Importance of the Scope Condition ~CM*

Had implementation been different with a centralized management system? The management of cohesion policy in Romania happened mostly at the sectoral level. Ministries were responsible for single programmes, while there was no overarching structure envisaged with a role beyond mere coordination. The NSRF mentions only briefly a National Coordination Committee for Structural Instruments (NCCSI) that was apparently already established in 2004 (RO 2007: 88). Significantly, it is the only body mentioned in the chapter describing the implementation structure that does not receive a further introduction or specification of its institutional locus and tasks. The body is also never mentioned in any of the AIRs and seems therefore negligible.

In contrast, the situation changed in 2011, when the Ministry of European Affairs under Leonard Orban was created (Stan 2013: 198), quickly to be rebranded under the new Ponta government as the Ministry of European Funds (Stan 2013: 201). The new ministry was supposed to collect data and to help MAs overcome their problems, for example related to public procurement procedures (RO 2015b). It was thus an attempt to implement stronger central management and oversight of structural funds absorption, however, without the possibility to equip the new ministry with strong institutional powers towards any of the independently operating MAs. While its competences were limited, however, the influence of the ministry was still seen in general as positive:

> The creation of the Ministry of European Affairs did not produce a surprising improvement, however its contribution to the horizontal measures undertaken i.e., public procurement, pre-financing changes, simplification of the procedures, unblocking of the vacant positions and new positions approved could not be contested. (Lucaciu 2012: 15).

Interestingly, the benefits mentioned in this statement strongly overlap with those expected theoretically from a strong centralized structure, such as support for the adaptation of procedures. The statement is even more interesting against the backdrop of the fact that adaptation in general suffered strongly from politicized changes of management and the resulting loss of knowledge. This situation could apparently be attenuated by the addition of an external actor that would support the Ministry of Transport in this regard. It is thus plausible that the very lack of such an actor offered a context for the politicization mechanism to have a much stronger effect on absorption, as central management staff did not focus on constant adaptation until very late in the financing period.

The creation of the Ministry of European Funds was generally evaluated positively, even though it was not an immediate game changer. This was, however, also very unlikely from the start as the overall institutional structure did not change and sectoral ministries remained as MAs at the heart of 'their' OP's implementation processes. The new ministry had thus no important role to play in decisions on, for example, reallocations and would remain a rather consultative body. In addition, it is also hard to tell if a different status could have been a decisive move after OPT had initially lacked crucial political support and so much time had already been lost.

Nevertheless, it seems that there was a strong impression at either the level of the Romanian government or of the EC that the lack of a centralized management structure was a distinct disadvantage in the 2007–2013 period. This is stressed by the fact that the Ministry of EU Funds was promoted to the role of the most important MA for the following financing period. It became in 2014 the MA for the new Operational Programme Large Infrastructure, combining the formerly separate environment and transport programmes and covering with almost EUR 9.5 billion almost half of the total allocation to Romania for the new financing period (European Commission 2015). This new structure could provide at least two advantages. First, lessons from the creation of infrastructure in one sphere can be transferred to the other, for example when it comes to the development of projects and their management. Second, funds can also be shifted more easily from underperforming areas, as they are then only taking place between PAs and no longer between different OPs. The change of the institutional structure means thus a strong shift towards centralization into the direction of a body only charged with the implementation of the EU's cohesion policy.

Overall, this is strong evidence for the assumption that the lack of a central management body in the 2007–2013 period was seen by implementing actors as a deficit. Shifts towards a stronger centralization during the financing period as well as the assignment of the role of the MA to the Ministry of EU Funds clearly point into this direction. Therefore, also this factor was plausibly important to offer a context in which the politicization mechanism could play out its influence on absorption.

5.6 Discussion of Results: Politicization's Impact on Implemenation and Capacities

5.6.1 Convincing Evidence for the Causal Mechanism in Both Cases

This chapter tests a causal mechanism for absorption problems of EU funds in the cases of the Czech Operational Programme Environment and the Romanian Operational Programme Transport. Both programmes had used only about a third of their funds at the end of the financing period in December 2013, and also suffered from decommitments due to their belated spending. The cases are selected as typical cases, thus members of the sufficient solution term for absorption problems found earlier in the fsQCA (see Chapter 4).

Both cases provide convincing evidence for the politicization mechanism. When it comes to the Czech OPE, newly incoming ministers from a different political party than their predecessor regularly exchanged important management staff. There were also smaller hints for changes in project planning, and a general interest of parties in using EU funds for their own purposes (like the Drobil-affair). Still, the main and also best-documented result of party alternation was the change of staff. This change of staff then weakened human resources in an OP that was until then generally functioning, but already suffering from problems with implementing rules and its management and control system. Deficiencies of the management and control system even led the EC to suspend certification of funds for the OP. This decision produced extra work in the form of audits to lift the suspension, all in a situation when human resources were weakened as a result of politicized changes and new executive staff not yet fully accustomed to the job. As a result, implementation was seriously interrupted and delays could not be made up for until the end of 2013.

On the other hand, the Romanian OPT also experienced the regular politicization of staff. This politicization however, was rather connected to the alternation of ministers and thus produced even more frequent changes during the financing period. In addition to changes of staff, changing project preferences also seem to have been at work. They produced delays and duplication of work every time an incoming minister introduced a new strategic focus (which is problematic when ministers change seven times during a seven-year period). Just as in the Czech case, the changes affected the human resources available for programme implementation, also through absence of strategic planning in this area. Still, the 2007–2013 financing period was Romania's first exercise of cohesion policy implementation, and OPT had much lower administrative capacity to begin with. The frequent alternation on important executive positions at the beneficiary companies meant that the bodies involved in implementation could hardly ever benefit from learning processes in the form of the adaptation of the programme against the backdrop of experience (and were thus incapable of building an 'island of excellence' for EU fund management in the ministry). Capacity therefore remained low and virtually the same problems of the implementation process were reported throughout the financing period.

Overall, the effect of politicization in the transport sector in Romania was more of a recurring pattern, resulting in constantly low administrative capacity and delays as a result of shifting strategic foci. In contrast, the effect of politicization in the Czech OPE was more of an event. Capacity, especially when it comes to human resources, was severely lowered the very moment politicized changes took place, but it seems plausible that existing staff had otherwise been able to adapt the implementation structures and to cope with the upcoming challenges (which is also underlined by the improving performance of the OP after 2013 [CZ6 2015]). Thus, even though the same mechanism was in place in both cases, it played out differently, mostly because the level of politicization of the state bureaucracy and the OP differed between the two cases, as well as the prior experience in cohesion policy implemenation.

Interestingly, the pattern of politicization practices matches expected differences between countries with 'patrimonial' and 'bureaucratic-authoritarian' communist legacies. In descendents from 'patrimonial communism', patronage is expected to be a practice for rewarding loyal supporters, and mostly linked to individual politicians rather than parties (Kopecký and Spirova 2011: 902–903). In contrast, in countries with 'bureaucratic-authoritarian' legacies the appointment of staff is guided by a desire to control the state rather than reward supporters, and parties play the major role in controlling patronage appointments (Kopecký and Spirova 2011: 903). In this sense, the different structural conditions in the two countries seem to make a difference also for EU fund management. Still, this difference only results in a difference in degree but not in kind between the cases, as both suffer from absorption problems after politicization. There is another interesting point detected only in the case studies: politicized changes did not always play out in the same way. In the Czech case, the change from SZ to ODS in 2010 shortly before the suspension of the OP caused much more trouble than the earlier alternation. It is thus also reasonable to expect a varying impact of politicization on implementation depending on the state and phase of the implementation process.

The evidence found for each part of the mechanism is highly unique and was mostly very uncertain to be found. First, the changes implemented to the state bureaucracy clearly match the pattern of changes of party (in the Czech case) or of minister (in the Romanian case) in office. This means that even though the subject of politicization apparently differs between the cases, the process is the same, as the change of staff is a political decision and not one based, for example, on merit. This pattern is unique for the expectation that incoming ministers will exchange staff, as there is no competing hypothesis, which could account equally well for this pattern. Why should there be changes on a regular basis if, for example, the crisis was the reason for layoffs, which also struck the region only in 2009?

Furthermore, the evidence presented, based on actual information of staff alternation, was very uncertain to be found as research on politicization is most often based on rather general interview data. Thus, the very fact that this data was obtained for both cases and then supported the pattern clearly strengthens the argument. Also, in both cases the pattern is supported by other evidence (an evaluation report in the Romanian case, insider statements in the Czech case), stressing that the changes are about politicization. The fact that insiders as well as evaluation reports stressed the importance of differing preferences of ministers in the Romanian OP was also uncertain to be found. In the absence of traceable changes in the programming documents (as changes happened at the level of planning), this is most probably the best evidence one can obtain for these processes.

This all surmounts at least to a very narrow 'hoop test' for this first part of the mechanism. Still, this also only considers that a 'smoking gun test' would have been a written document by a minister ordering staff and project changes for political reasons, or a list with changes of projects that could be related to different ministers. Here, the patterns of changes match the theoretical expectations, and changes and the expected trigger are linked by insiders and evaluation reports. Without settling the question of whether or not different evidence would even be realistic to obtain, it is possible to conclude that the test strength of the first step of the mechanism is very high in both cases.

Second, it then became clear that the changes further weakened the capacity and produced delays. In the Czech case, insiders directly stated that especially the alternation from SZ to ODS in 2010 resulted in a major interruption of the implementation process, causing problems due to both the inexperience of newly incoming staff as well as the lack of staff. It thus makes sense that the suspension by the EC and the procedure to lift it was then a huge strain on the implementation process, producing duplication of work for fewer and less experienced staff. Thus, politicization and capacity problems clearly worked together to produce the delay. In Romania, the lack of adaptation (reported as the reoccurrence of the very same implementation problems in almost every annual report, as well as being mentioned in the evaluations) and the frequent changes at the management level were more of a recurring pattern than a single event. Still, while insiders stressed the significance of shifting preferences in creating delays, an evaluation report directly linked the lack of administrative adaptation to the frequent changes of directors of beneficiary companies.

In both cases, insider statements and/or evaluation reports stress a link between applied changes and resulting implementation problems, providing highly unique evidence that also the second step of the mechanism is in place as expected. Again, it was not very certain to find such a clear connection, because links between politicization and implementation problems are usually not stated in the general implementation reports written by the ministries. It is thus even more convincing that absorption problems were caused by a combination of politicization and low capacity, and that both apparently interacted to produce delays of implementation.

Apart from the mechanism, the scope condition ~CM did not actively contribute to the outcome, but evidence was found for the claim that it had to be in place for the mechanism to work properly. It is obviously difficult to argue why something not in place was actually important. Still, it is interesting to note that both countries decided for a much more centralized management and control system in the following financing period. In Romania, authorities even tried to lay down all projects for the 2014–2020 period in a 'Transport Masterplan', which can then no longer be altered and was apparently set as a condition for access to infrastructure support in the 2014–2020 period by the EC (RO 2015a). In addition, it became clear that the existing weak central bodies did contribute to implementation, however remained rather consultative as they lacked formal powers to influence the ministries. This evidence is again unique as it is not easy to find a different argument for stronger centralization apart from bad experience in the earlier financing period. It was also not very certain to be found, as bodies of limited importance do not feature very prominently in regular reports or evaluations. Test strength is thus also reasonably high in this case to stress that ~CM was a scope condition for the politicization mechanism to work.

Overall, there is convincing evidence that the proposed politicization mechanism was in place in both cases. What does that tell us about generalization? Accounts on set-theoretic multi-method research underline that the "more supportive evidence we find in an increasing number of typical cases, the stronger our confidence that the finding we made holds for other unstudied typical cases as well" (Beach and Rohlfing 2018: 17, see also Schneider and Rohlfing 2013: 566). Thus, evidence for the same mechanism in the two cases analyzed above suggests that the causal mechanism was likely also present in the two Slovak cases as well as the Romanian and Bulgarian OPs Environment, which are all members of the solution term. This generalization makes sense against the backdrop of careful case selection and the fact that if it would be necessary to study all cases before generalization is possible, we would "no longer have to generalize" (Schneider and Rohlfing 2016: 556) after such an endeavor. In contrast, the mechanism cannot be generalized to the Hungarian cases not covered by the solution term (Schneider and Rohlfing 2013: 566), and one should als be careful with the Slovenian case which was only covered in model 1. Especially the Hungarian cases most probably feature a different mechanism as they are members of a different, equifinal combination of conditions leading to absorption problems.

References

Åslund, A. (2010). *The Last Shall Be the First: The East European Financial Crisis.* Washington, DC: Peterson Institute for International Economics.

Bachtler, J., Mendez, C., & Oraže, H. (2014). From Conditionality to Europeanization in Central and Eastern Europe: Administrative Performance and Capacity in Cohesion Policy. *European Planning Studies, 22*(4), 735–757.

Beach, D. (2018). Achieving Methodological Alignment When Combining QCA and PT in Practice. *Sociological Methods & Research, 47*(1), 64–99.

Beach, D., & Pedersen, R. B. (2013). *Process-Tracing Methods: Foundations and Guidelines.* Ann Arbor: University of Michigan Press.

Beach, D., & Pedersen, R. B. (2018). Selecting Appropriate Cases When Tracing Causal Mechanisms. *Sociological Methods & Research, 47*(4), 837–871.

Beach, D., & Rohlfing, I. (2018). Integrating Cross-Case Analyses and Process Tracing in Set-Theoretic Research Strategies and Parameters of Debate. *Sociological Methods & Research, 47*(1), 3–36.

Beichelt, T. (2004). *Die Europäische Union nach der Osterweiterung*. Wiesbaden: VS Verlag.

Bennett, A., & Checkel, J. T. (Eds.). (2015). *Process Tracing: From Metaphor to Analytic Tool*. Cambridge: Cambridge University Press.

Blažek, J. (2011). Czech Republic. *Expert Evaluation Network*. Prague: Charles University. Available at http://ec.europa.eu/regional_policy/index.cfm/en/policy/evaluations/ec/2007-2013/#1. Accessed 29 May 2017.

Blažek, J. (2012). Czech Republic. *Expert Evaluation Network*. Prague: Charles University. Available at http://ec.europa.eu/regional_policy/sources/docgener/evaluation/pdf/eval2007/expert_innovation/2012_een_task2_cz.pdf. Accessed 12 Feb 2016.

Bloom, S., & Petrova, V. (2013). National Subversion of Supranational Goals: 'Pork-Barrel' Politics and EU Regional Aid. *Europe-Asia Studies, 65*(8), 1599–1620.

Bubbico, R. L., & De Michelis, N. (2011) *The Financial Execution of Structural Funds* (Regional Focus No. 3/2011). Brussels: European Commission, Directorate-General for Regional Policy. Available at http://ec.europa.eu/regional_policy/sources/docgener/focus/2011_03_financial.pdf. Accessed 12 Feb 2016.

Česká Pozice. (2011a). *Finance Ministry Suspends EU Fund License (Published 15 April 2011)*. Available at http://ceskapozice.lidovky.cz/finance-ministry-suspends-eu-fund-license-fil-/tema.aspx?c=A110415_163858_pozice_11946. Accessed 11 July 2015.

Česká Pozice. (2011b). *SFŽP Whistle-Blower Given Kč 500,000 Reward (Published 23 March 2011)*. Available at http://ceskapozice.lidovky.cz/sfzp-whistle-blower-given-kc-500-000-reward-fct-/tema.aspx?c=A110323_172658_pozice_9493. Accessed 22 Dec 2015.

Collier, D., Brady, H. E., & Seawright, J. (2004). Sources of Leverage in Causal Inference: Toward an Alternative View of Methodology. In H. E. Brady & D. Collier (Eds.), *Rethinking Social Inquiry: Diverse Tools, Shared Standards* (pp. 229–266). Lanham et al.: Rowman & Littlefield.

CZ. (2007a). OP Environment 2007–2013. *National Strategic Reference Framework*. Prague: Ministry of Environment, Czech Republic. Available at http://en.opzp2007-2013.cz/ke-stazeni/515/5060/detail/the-operational-programme-environment—for-the-period-2007-2013/. Accessed 12 Feb 2016.

CZ. (2007b). OP Transport 2007–2013. *National Strategic Reference Framework*. Prague: Ministry of Transport, Czech Republic. Available at http://www.opd.cz/Providers/Document.ashx?id=48. Accessed 12 Feb 2016.

CZ. (2009a). Annual Report for 2008. *Annual Implementation Report*. Prague: Ministry of Environment, Czech Republic. Available at http://en.opzp2007-2013.cz/ke-stazeni/515/5061/detail/annual-report-op-environment-2008/. Accessed 12 Feb 2016.

CZ. (2009b). *Meeting of the Monitoring Committee of Czech OP Enviroment on 3 December 2009.* Prague: Ministry of Environment, Czech Republic. Available at www.opzp2007-2013.cz/soubor-ke-stazeni/22/6873-minutes_6th_mc_ope_12_03_2009_final.pdf. Accessed 3 June 2015.

CZ. (2010a). Annual Report for 2009. *Annual Implementation Report.* Prague: Ministry of Environment, Czech Republic, Available at http://en.opzp2007-2013.cz/ke-stazeni/515/14284/detail/annual-report-ope-2009/. Accessed 12 Feb 2016.

CZ. (2010b). *Meeting of the Monitoring Committee of Czech OP Enviroment on 2 December 2010.* Prague: Ministry of Environment, Czech Republic. Available at https://www.sfzp.cz/soubor-ke-stazeni/40/12032-Minutes_8th_MC%20OPE_02_12_2010.pdf. Accessed 3 June 2015.

CZ. (2010c). *Meeting of the Monitoring Committee of Czech OP Enviroment on 3 June 2010.* Prague: Ministry of Environment, Czech Republic. Available at https://www.sfzp.cz/soubor-ke-stazeni/36/11082-Minutes_7th_MC_OPE_06_03_2010.pdf. Accessed 3 June 2015.

CZ. (2012). Annual Report for 2011. *Annual Implementation Report.* Prague: Ministry of Environment, Czech Republic. Available at http://en.opzp2007-2013.cz/ke-stazeni/515/14283/detail/annual-report-op-environment-2011-incl-annexes/. Accessed 12 Feb 2016.

CZ. (2013). Annual Report for 2012. *Annual Implementation Report.* Prague: Ministry of Environment, Czech Republic. Available at http://en.opzp2007-2013.cz/ke-stazeni/515/15626/detail/annual-report-ope-for-2012-incl-appendices/. Accessed 12 Feb 2016.

CZ. (2014). Annual Report for 2013. *Annual Implementation Report.* Prague: Ministry of Environment, Czech Republic. Available at http://en.opzp2007-2013.cz/ke-stazeni/515/15731/detail/annual-report-op-environment-for-2013-incl-annexes/. Accessed 12 Feb 2016.

CZ. (2015). *Ministry of Regional Development, Czech Republic: National Coordination Authority.* Available at http://62.109.144.163/en/Fondy-EU/Narodni-organ-pro-koordinaci. Accessed 11 July 2015.

CZ1. (2014). *Interview in Prague with Policy Expert on 3 June 2014.*

CZ1. (2015). *Interview in Prague with Policy Expert on 14 May 2015.*

CZ6. (2015). *Interview in Prague with Czech Official on 14 May 2015.*

CZ7. (2015). *Interview in Prague with Czech Official on 14 May 2015.*

CZ8. (2015). *Interview in Prague with Czech Official on 15 May 2015.*

European Commission (2015) *EU Will Invest Nearly €9.5 Billion in Romania for Transport, Environment and Energy.* Brussels: European Commission. Available at http://ec.europa.eu/regional_policy/how/policy/strategic_report_en.cfm. Accessed 12 Feb 2016.

European Commission. (2016). *Innovation and Networks Executive Agency: TEN-T Programme 2007–2013.* Available at https://ec.europa.eu/inea/en/ten-t. Accessed 18 Feb 2016.

Frank, K. (2013). Slovakia. *Expert Evaluation Network*. Bratislava: Slovak Academy of Sciences. Available at http://ec.europa.eu/regional_policy/sources/docgener/evaluation/pdf/eval2007/2013_een_task2_sk.pdf. Accessed 29 May 2017.

Gerring, J. (2008). Case Selection for Case-Study Analysis: Qualitative and Quantitative Techniques. In J. M. Box-Steffensmeier, H. E. Brady, & D. Collier (Eds.), *The Oxford Handbook of Political Methodology* (pp. 645–684). Oxford: Oxford University Press.

Goetz, K. H. (2001). Making Sense of Post-communist Central Administration: Modernization, Europeanization or Latinization? *Journal of European Public Policy, 8*(6), 1032–1051.

Haughton, T., Novotná, T., & Deegan-Krause, K. (2011). The 2010 Czech and Slovak Parliamentary Elections: Red Cards to the 'Winners'. *West European Politics, 34*(2), 394–402.

Kitschelt, H. (2001). Divergent Paths of Postcommunist Democracies. In L. Diamond & R. Gunther (Eds.), *Political Parties and Democracy* (pp. 299–323). Baltimore and London: Johns Hopkins University Press.

Kopecký, P., Mair, P., & Spirova, M. (2012). *Party Patronage and Party Government in European Democracies*. Oxford: Oxford University Press.

Kopecký, P., & Spirova, M. (2011). 'Jobs for the Boys'? Patterns of Party Patronage in Post-communist Europe. *West European Politics, 34*(5), 897–921.

Linek, L. (2007). Czech Republic. *European Journal of Political Research, 46*(7–8), 929–937.

Linek, L. (2008). Czech Republic. *European Journal of Political Research, 47*(7–8), 947–951.

Linek, L. (2011). Czech Republic. *European Journal of Political Research, 50*(7–8), 948–954.

Linek, L. (2014). Czech Republic. *European Journal of Political Research Political Data Yearbook, 53*(1), 92–103.

Linek, L., & Lacina, T. (2010). Czech Republic. *European Journal of Political Research, 49*(7–8), 939–946.

Lucaciu, L. O. (2012). Romania. *Expert Evaluation Network*. Bucharest: LIDEEA. Available at http://ec.europa.eu/regional_policy/sources/docgener/evaluation/pdf/eval2007/expert_innovation/2012_een_task2_ro.pdf. Accessed 12 Feb 2016.

Lucaciu, L. O. (2013). Romania. *Expert Evaluation Network*. Bucharest: LIDEEA. Available at http://ec.europa.eu/regional_policy/sources/docgener/evaluation/pdf/eval2007/2013_een_task2_ro.pdf. Accessed 12 Feb 2016.

Meyer-Sahling, J.-H. (2004). Civil Service Reform in Post-communist Europe: The Bumpy Road to Depoliticisation. *West European Politics, 27*(1), 71–103.

Meyer-Sahling, J.-H. (2009). *Sustainability of Civil Service Reforms in Central and Eastern Europe Five Years After EU Accession* (Sigma Paper No. 44).

Paris: OECD Publishing. Available at http://www.oecd-ilibrary.org/governance/sustainability-of-civil-service-reforms-in-central-and-eastern-europe-five-years-after-eu-accession_5kml60pvjmbq-en. Accessed 12 Feb 2016.

Meyer-Sahling, J.-H., & Veen, T. (2012). Governing the Post-communist State: Government Alternation and Senior Civil Service Politicisation in Central and Eastern Europe. *East European Politics, 28*(1), 4–22.

Motyl, A. J. (2004). Communist Legacies and New Trajectories: Democracy and Dictatorship in the Former Soviet Union and East Central Europe. In Y. Brudny, J. Frankel, & S. Hoffman (Eds.), *Restructuring Post-communist Russia* (pp. 52–67). Cambridge: Cambridge University Press.

Pop, R., Doroftei, I. M., & Dimulescu, V. (2013). Risks of Corruption and the Management of EU Funds in Romania. *Romanian Journal of Political Sciences, 13*(1): 101–123.

RO. (2007). OP Transport 2007–2013. *National Strategic Reference Framework*. Bucharest: Ministry of Transport, Romania. Available at http://old.fonduri-ue.ro/res/filepicker_users/cd25a597fd-62/Doc_prog/prog_op/5_POST/2_POST_Eng.pdf. Accessed 12 Feb 2016.

RO. (2009). Raportul Anual de Implementare 2008. *Annual Implementation Report*. Bucharest: Ministry of Transport, Romania.

RO. (2010a). A Formative Evaluation of Structural Instruments in Romania: Final Report. *Conducting Evaluations for the Period 2009–10*. Bucharest: Ministry of Public Finance, Romania. Available at http://ec.europa.eu/regional_policy/sources/docgener/evaluation/library/romania/1010_formative_nsrf_eval_en.pdf. Accessed 29 May 2017.

RO. (2010b). Raportul Anual de Implementare 2009. *Annual Implementation Report*. Bucharest: Ministry of Transport, Romania.

RO. (2011a). Raportul Anual de Implementare 2010. *Annual Implementation Report*. Bucharest: Ministry of Transport, Romania.

RO. (2011b). Second Ad Hoc Evaluation: Review of Investment in Transport and Environment Infrastructure: Final Report. *Conducting Evaluations for the Period 2009–10*. Bucharest: Ministry of Public Finance, Romania. Available at http://www.evaluare-structurale.ro/ro/list-viewreports-menu/details/8/31/rapoarte-evaluare-second-ad-hoc-evaluation-review-of-investment-in-transport-and-environment-infrastructure. Accessed 29 May 2017.

RO. (2012a). Government of Romania: Nota de Fundamentare HG nr.1200/04.12.2012. Available at http://gov.ro/ro/guvernul/procesul-legislativ/note-de-fundamentare/nota-de-fundamentare-hg-nr-1200-04-12-2012&page=738. Accessed 20 Dec 2015.

RO. (2012b). Raportul Anual de Implementare 2011. *Annual Implementation Report*. Bucharest: Ministry of Transport, Romania.

RO. (2013). Raportul Anual de Implementare 2012. *Annual Implementation Report*. Bucharest: Ministry of Transport, Romania.

RO. (2014). Raportul Anual de Implementare 2013. *Annual Implementation Report*. Bucharest: Ministry of Transport, Romania.

RO. (2015a). *Government of Romania: General Transport Master Plan, Approved by the Government*. Available at http://gov.ro/en/government/cabinet-meeting/general-transport-master-plan-approved-by-the-government. Accessed 18 Feb 2016.

RO. (2015b). *Ministry of EU Funds*. Romania: Prezentare MFE. Available at http://www.fonduri-ue.ro/minister/prezentare. Accessed 18 Feb 2016.

RO1. (2015). *Interview in Bucharest with Romanian Official on 15 June 2015*.

RO2. (2015). *Interview in Bucharest with Romanian Official on 20 June 2015*.

Schneider, C. Q., & Rohlfing, I. (2013). Combining QCA and Process Tracing in Set-Theoretic Multi-method Research. *Sociological Methods & Research, 42*(4), 559–597.

Schneider, C. Q., & Rohlfing, I. (2016). Case Studies Nested in Fuzzy-Set QCA on Sufficiency. Formalizing Case Selection and Causal Inference. *Sociological Methods & Research, 45*(3), 526–568.

Schneider, C. Q., & Wagemann, C. (2010). Standards of Good Practice in Qualitative Comparative Analysis (QCA) and Fuzzy-Sets. *Comparative Sociology, 9*(3), 397–418.

Schneider, C. Q., & Wagemann, C. (2012). *Set-Theoretic Methods for the Social Sciences: A Guide to Qualitative Comparative Analysis*. Cambridge: Cambridge University Press.

Stan, L. (2013). Romania. *European Journal of Political Research Political Data Yearbook, 52*(1), 196–207.

Stan, L., & Zaharia, R. (2009). Romania. *European Journal of Political Research, 48*(7–8), 1087–1099.

Stan, L., & Zaharia, R. (2010). Romania. *European Journal of Political Research, 49*(7–8), 1139–1153.

Stan, L., & Zaharia, R. (2011). Romania. *European Journal of Political Research, 50*(7–8), 1108–1117.

Vachudova, M. A. (2005). *Europe Undivided: Democracy, Leverage, and Integration After Communism*. Oxford: Oxford University Press.

Van Evera, S. (1997). *Guide to Methods for Students of Political Science*. Ithaca, NY: Cornell University Press.

World Bank. (2010). Romania: Transport Sector: Final Report. *Functional Review*. Washington, DC: World Bank. Available at http://documents.worldbank.org/curated/en/2010/10/17055950/romania-functional-review-transport-sector. Accessed 29 May 2017.

CHAPTER 6

Conclusions and Implications for the Region and Beyond

6.1 Empirical Results

This study asks why some CEE member states struggle to use their EU funds. The answer to this question for absorption problems is strongly linked to the success of post-communist and pre-accession reforms and the prevaling practices of party politicization in the new member states. Only those countries with a successful trajectory of horizontal administrative capacity building could expect a largely successful use of EU funds, what is in line with existing knowledge. In contrast, those countries with only sectorally adapted capacities for EU fund management where more likely suffering from absorption problems, as the resilience of these units in the face of politicized changes by alternating political actors was low. Overall, the detailed analyses of implementation processes in the region shows that especially those countries with generally low levels of capacities and also frequently occurring changes of political control over programmes, resulting in politicized changes of the state bureaucracy, struggle to use their EU fund allocation in time, despite of meanwhile adapted sectoral capacities. This finding is supported by the results of two empirical analyses.

On the one hand, the fsQCA including all possible conditions resulted in the sufficient combination for absorption problems of 'frequent party alternation', 'low executive capacity', and the absence of 'centralized management'. This combination covers six cases, or two-thirds of the cases considered here facing absorption problems.

C. Hagemann, *EU Funds in the New Member States*, Palgrave Studies in European Union Politics,
https://doi.org/10.1007/978-3-030-02092-7_6

The result and especially the combination of low capacities and frequent party alternation is stable both for the exclusion and inclusion of further conditions like previously existing 'islands of excellence'. While there is also evidence for a role of the financial and economic crisis in absorption problems, mainly in the two Hungarian OPs studied, this is empirically much less relevant.

Furthermore, the combination is supported by the results of the process tracing analysis. A detailed analysis of two typical cases for the sufficient combination for absorption problems detected in model 2 shows that especially party changes at the level of ministries and low capacity in the management and control system work in conjunction to lead to absorption problems. There is strong support for a distinct politicization mechanism in the two cases which is triggered by the change of a minister in office, leading to changes of staff and programme priorities in a low capacity context, resulting in an interruption of the implementation process, a further weakening of capacity, and ultimately a strongly delayed absorption performance. Both the Czech OP Environment and the Romanian OP Transport provide convincing evidence for this mechanism, which is supported by the absence of a strong centralized management body controlling implementation, a factor detected in the course of the QCA and supported by evidence from the case studies.

6.2 Competing Explanations

The most likely competing explanation for absorption problems, that is a singular role for the lack of capacity, is flawed in two ways. On the one hand, there is no case which is only explained by static low administrative capacities resulting from the minimization procedure. On the other hand, there were also instances of programmes with low capacity that nevertheless featured a successful absorption performance. Thus, the sole focus on capacity does not suffice to account for absorption problems in the cases studied.

But what about the effect of the financial and economic crisis? Many evaluation reports stress the crisis as an important influence on the implementation process. The empirical analysis yields support for the relevance of the crisis only in a single model, which solely only accounts for the two Hungarian cases. There is thus support for the crisis as an explanation of absorption problems, but it is rather weak and empirically limited. In the other instances, 'severe crisis' was minimized from the solution term as its presence was redundant. In addition, many insiders from ministerial bureaucracies as well as country experts stressed that access to finance was usually not a crucial issue for absorption. This also seems plausible in the face of the well-performing Baltic states which were by many accounts the epicentre of the crisis in CEE.

Finally, there is a lot of evidence for actions taken both by the EC and the member states to increase absorption in the future, which are in line with the explanation offered by the politicization mechanism. First, the Romanian infrastructure programme for the 2014–2020 period is no longer controlled by the Ministry of Transport, but managed by a central Ministry for EU Funds. In addition, the EC made it conditional to adopt a 'Transport Masterplan' with fixed projects to access the funds in the new financing period (RO 2015). Both of these decisions are to be seen as clear countervailing measures against political interference with the implementation process as a result of changing ministers. Second, a similar albeit weaker process of centralization could also be observed in the new Czech implementation system, with the Ministry of Regional Development receiving a more important role. In addition, insiders stressed the importance of missing civil service legislation for EU fund absorption (CZ1 2015), thus underlining the threat posed by politicized staff changes for the implementation process during the 2007–2013 period. In sum, all of these observations strongly suggest that the processes leading to absorption problems discussed above were perceived in a similar manner by core actors involved in the implementation process and seen as a major cause of absorption problems in the 2007–2013 financing period.

Overall, the QCA and the process tracing analysis account for absorption problems in at least six of the nine relevant cases. The presence of (three) unexplained or poorly explained cases (model 2) highlights the presence of equifinality, thus other combinations of conditions also leading to absorption problems. This is in line with the general scope of set-theoretic methods which do not seek a single model with the best fit, but rather seek instances of potentially equifinal 'multiple conjunctural causation' (Berg-Schlosser et al. 2009: 8). Still, this does not preclude the generalization of the findings within the boundaries of the results. Overall, the results offer relevant insights for several different fields of study.

6.3 The Results in the Context of Europeanization Studies

The findings support absorption literature's stress of the importance of administrative and government capacity for the absorption of EU funds. The finding that 'low executive capacity' is closest to a necessary condition for 'absorption problems' is in line with probabilistic research stressing that capacity is an important variable (Tosun 2014: 379), and other case studies highlighting the centrality of administrative capacity (Milio 2007; Bachtler et al. 2014). Thus, the importance of capacity is also supported in this study, albeit only partly.

While high capacities account pretty well as expected for high absorption rates, the lack of capacity is not sufficient to find absorption problems. Rather, it needs one or two other INUS conditions to lead to the outcome, depending on the model tested. This finding is not merely a result of QCA's focus on conjunctural causation, but says much about the situation in the different cases. For example, two cases were found to have low capacities but still a reasonably high absorption performance at the end of 2013 (the Czech and the Bulgarian Transport OPs). In contrast to the general expectation, especially the Bulgarian OP apparently managed to develop a high ability to use EU funds in the absence of political perturbations, even despite of overall low capacity. The results of this study thus provide neither a contradiction nor a confirmation of the existing literature, but rather a more fine-grained specification of the explanation: A lack of capacity is important for absorption to suffer, however, not decisive, and ultimately the inability to adapt existing capacity (which is linked to other factors) and to develop an 'island of excellence' in the EU fund management system seems to be in a low capacity context more relevant than a country's initial capacity-endowment. This is also in line with the finding of the earlier, shortened financing period during which studies underlined well-developed EU fund management units even in countries with otherwise low capacities and also a successful absorption performance (Bachtler et al. 2014: 752; Tosun 2014: 382).

Also, the results de-emphasize the role of the financial and economic crisis for absorption problems as the condition was only relevant in a limited number of cases. This is in line with findings in other studies that the crisis did not have a crucial impact on absorption in CEE (Tosun 2014: 383). It also agrees with further evidence suggesting that several sources of external finance still remained accessible for CEE countries hit hard by the crisis (like EIB co-finance loans) and that some countries managed to use the funds as an instrument of counter-cyclical spending. Thus, it seems that the way the crisis played out in the member states and affected absorption was as much a question of political strategy as it was of the actual deterioration of economic fortunes (see Sect. 4.4).

The importance of politics in cohesion policy implementation is strongly underlined by the finding of conjunctural causation involving the alternation of parties at the level of ministries, and it is also supported by the case studies as evidence for a politicization of the implementation process. The results thus go beyond the often very technical focus on cohesion policy implementation, and are in line with the limited existing research stressing the importance of politics in the absorption process (Milio 2008; Surubaru 2017), but also when it comes to the allocation of funds in CEE countries (Bloom and Petrova 2013) and in the old member states (Bouvet and Dall'Erba 2010; Bodenstein and Kemmerling 2011: 17; Dellmuth and Stoffel 2012: 427; Chalmers 2013: 826; Schraff 2014: 286, but see Dellmuth 2011: 1029). This study takes these earlier findings of political actors using funds as a political resource and changing administrative staff to their liking one step further, and tests the importance of these practices for the actual absorption of funds in the entire region. The results underline that the factor of politics in EU fund absorption will lead to delays when politicians do not only use funds for their own benefits, but where they are also ready to risk the success of overall absorption only to implement changes matching their own (spending) preferences. Cohesion policy might thus fail its goals not only because regions which are relatively affluent receive the funds (as often suggested in the allocation literature), but also because funds remain unused and are finally decommitted or spend outside the lines of initial strategic planning.

There is no evidence for an overall similar pattern of cohesion policy implementation in the region. The CEE countries are not extraordinarily successful in using their EU funds, as some findings from the shortened 2004–2006 financing period would suggest (Tosun 2014), as well as earlier results on other fields of post-accession EU implementation (Sedelmeier 2008). In contrast, an evaluation of the 2007–2013 financing period even stresses that four out ouf a total of five 'very late absorbers' are from the region (Slovakia, Czech Republic, Bulgaria and Romania) (Ferry and Kah 2017: 29). Still, they neither fail as a group the test of cohesion policy implementation as the post-accession pessimists might have expected (Falkner and Treib 2008; Falkner et al. 2008). Thus, the results for the 2007–2013 period are in line with other findings stressing the heterogeneous performance of the region when it comes to post-accession implementation of EU policy. These studies stress that different outcomes are mainly linked to countries governments' different sector-specific preferences and actor constellations (Dimitrova and Toshkov 2009: 12; Maniokas 2009: 11; Sedelmeier 2012: 35). The results of this study supplement these findings with further evidence that heterogeneous results can also be linked to varying levels of capacity in the region, and different levels of stability at the level of governments. Thus, one of the main results of this analysis is that CEE countries differ among each other in many important respects, and that they are also far from representing an 'eastern problem' (Sedelmeier 2008) for the EU in cohesion policy implementation.

6.4 What Do We Learn for the Process of Post-communist Transformation and Pre-accession Reforms?

The results of this study support those stressing that post-communism is more than a mere reference to the past, and still has important repercussions for the present (e.g. Kitschelt et al. 1999; Ekiert and Hanson 2003; Stykow 2006; Segert 2007). Still, it is important to understand in how far the past matters for the present, as certain trajectories are continued but also new paths taken. Especially the process tracing case studies revealed that the communist practice of 'over-politicization' (Goetz and Wollmann 2001) of the state bureaucracy is still common in the region. Apart from the two countries under study in Chapter 5, also insiders from the MA in Lithuania stressed that politicized changes took place upon the alternation of power between centre-right and centre-left forces in the country (LT4 2014).[1] Thus, this communist legacy is important as a prevailing informal institution that still serves the goals of rational political actors. In this form, it has not only important repercussions for these countries, but it is also very likely to continue. Still, this should not overshadow the persisting as well as the developed heterogeneity of the region that we witness today.

[1] In Lithuania, ministers lost also their office in the course of scandals related to the misuse of EU funds, just like in the other cases (Krupavicius 2012: 191).

On the one hand, the *persisting* heterogeneity of the region is important in the form of different legacies of the past. Especially Kitschelt and colleagues (Kitschelt et al. 1999; Kitschelt 2001) stressed that there was not one, but rather three different types of communist rule as a result of different conditions in CEE countries during the interwar period. The results of the process tracing case studies stress that these different trajectories still carry weight today. For example, the practice of politicization in the formerly 'bureaucratic-authoritarian' Czech Republic is linked only to parties, while it is linked to changing ministers in Romania, a descendent of 'patrimonial communism'. These observations are in line with a more recent reformulation of Kitschelt's thesis for the politicization of bureaucracies in CEE (Kopecký and Spirova 2011), as well as other studies stressing the continued importance of these different types of communist rule for CEE countries' development (Jahn and Müller-Rommel 2010: 38).

Still, the different historical trajectories now mostly result in a difference in degree between the countries. Despite these very different legacies, both the Czech Republic and Romania experienced the same absorption problems as a result of the same mechanism. The distinct type of communist legacy only affected the way the mechanism played out in the country, but not the overall result nor its functioning.

On the other hand, the *developed* heterogeneity is mostly linked to the outcomes of reform processes in the region during the last two decades. The finding of differing levels of capacity in the region shows that the countries were unequally successful in reforming their state apparatuses, and it shows that the differences at the moment of transition between the countries were not directly reproduced. Now, especially the Baltic states and Poland feature very high capacities to implement policies, while earlier champions like Hungary and the Czech Republic have fallen behind. This finding, based on the 'executive capacity' indicator (SGI), is in line with other studies stressing a change in the pace of reform in some countries, while mainly Bulgaria and Romania take their expected places at the bottom-end of the group (Meyer-Sahling 2009: 516–517).

Thus, the differences between CEE countries are no longer only attributable to different legacies of the past, but are now mostly the result of different levels of success in reforms. Especially the QCA results stress that today there is a 'difference in kind' between the CEE countries. For example, politicization did not harm the absorption process in Lithuania as much as in the two case studies, because the country's high level of capacity made it more resilient in the face of staff changes (LT4 2014).

The finding of varying levels of capacity also stresses that the influence of the EU was not sufficient when it comes to capacity building in the region. While some studies underline that "the EU has made a systematic difference in good governance in those countries that it offered membership" (Börzel and Schimmelfennig 2017: 291), both the different starting points and paces of reform mean that this in general positive impact did not lead to a broad convergence of the region. Rather, drawing on the SGI scores presented above, it seems that the region's heterogeneity is now comparable to that among the old member states.

These results also add to the debate on the EU's external and internal integration capacity, that is its ability to prepare non-members for accession and to maintain their functioning as member states afterwards (Börzel et al. 2017: 161). When it comes to the 'external integration capacity', results hint at a rather limited performance. While 'islands' created for the transposition of the *acquis* are still working in new member states (Börzel and Sedelmeier 2017: 211), those created for the management of EU funds emerged more likely after accession and proved also less persistent. Overall, the EU has thus only a limited external integration capacity in the field of cohesion policy. In contrast, the situation looks better when it comes to the internal integration capacity. The findings of Bachtler and colleagues (Bachtler et al. 2014) of rather well-developed capacities after the first, shortened financing period as well as the rather successful Bulgarian Transport programme reported in this analysis underline that the strengthening of capacities was still possible after accession. Also, the EC's apparently highly successful intervention in very low absorbing countries, using its 'Task Force for Better Implementation' to increase spending (see Sect. 2.2), underlines that it has the ability to assure the functioning of crucial EU policies in difficult settings. This finding therefore supports the idea of a high internal integration capacity. Still, this comes with the caveat of the persisting influence of polticization.

The failure to de-politicize public administrations in the region proves to be a continued liability which is still very difficult to overcome. Just as the EU has to strengthen its political integration capacity to deal better with instances of democratic backsliding after accession (Börzel and Schimmelfennig 2017: 292), it has to improve its instruments to enforce de-politicization and stabilize public administrations before and especially after accession. While strengthening sectoral capacities in the form of 'islands of excellence' of EU fund management works apparently well, these capacities are too vulnerable to politically induced changes. There are two possible remedies to this problem: One would be to strengthen overall capacities, like in the Lithuanian case, to make EU funds management units also more resilient and make politicization matter less. However, this is a long-term process depending mainly on a strong domestic reform constituency. The second option is to combine the already existing successful experiences of sectoral capacity building in otherwhise weak capacity contexts with direct measures of stabilization. This process should be twofold: On the one hand, staff needs to be selected according to merit and should ideally lack links to any political camp, making it easier for politicians from all colours to work with officials. Dismissals should be limited to failing performance obligations only. On the other hand, especially in low capacity contexts the strategy of capacity building to manage EU funds should not only aim at attracting talent, but also to retain it. This means offering salaries matching the responsibility, expertise and workload, as well as attractive career options in the public service. Such a policy should especially aim at retaining staff that was earlier extensively trained and prepared for the job, in order to avoid regularly losing efforts invested in such capacity building measures.

6.5 What Do the 'New' Member States Tell Us About the 'Old' Ones?

To what extent can the argument developed in this study be applied to the old member states? Despite of the focus on the post-communist trajectory of the region, I argue that the study of the old member states nevertheless has much to learn from the CEE countries. Overall, the analysis contributes novel insights to the observation that what matters to a successful and effective cohesion policy is not only the right combination of different capital factors, but crucially also the quality of governance in a member state. In its most recent cohesion report, the EC prominently underlines that a low quality of governance negatively affects innovation potentials, environmental performance, and public investment decisions (European Commission 2017: 136). Whereas politicization and patronage are one factor lowering the quality of governance in a country, the new member states are far from the only countries with low levels of such quality in the EU (Charron et al. 2012: 8).

The post-communist context with a legacy of 'over-politicization' is but one possibility for why countries feature high levels of politicization and patronage. The post-communist context is, in a methodological sense, a scope condition for the combination of conditions as well as for the mechanism to work (Ragin 2000: 61). Thus, it is possible to re-formulate this context in more general terms as 'countries with a high level of politicization and patronage', independently of any communist experience. There are different circumstances highlighted under which parties tend to politicize their states' bureaucracies. The most prominent and general argument is made by Shefter, who stresses that party-building elites from within the state (organizing what he calls 'internally mobilized parties') will tend to use state resources as patronage to achieve their political goals, unless bureaucratic autonomy has become entrenched before the mobilization of masses into politics takes place (Shefter 1994: 31). This argument matches very well the point made in Sect. 3.1 on the persistence of over-politicization in CEE, but is also applicable well beyond this context. It is thus more a general question of the relative timing of the establishment of bureaucratic autonomy and political mobilization that is important for the prevalence of these practices, which is not necessarily linked to the post-communist context.

In the context of EU funds, Milio provides a possible example in Sicily, an Italian region, where clientelist practices of staff appointment and politics in general lead in combination with frequent changes of regional ministers to a failure to use EU funds (Milio 2008: 928–929). Thus, also another context with a constellation 'favourable' to politicization and patronage could suffice for the mechanism to work, as long as the other conditions of low capacity and a lack of centralized management are also in place. Against the backdrop of Milio's paper, it comes with now surprise that Italy is the only old member state which is part of the group of "very late absorbers" (Ferry and Kah 2017: 29) in the 2007–2013 financing period, while both Italy and Greece are mentioned in the cohesion report alongside Bulgaria and Romania as the member states with the least effective governments (European Commission 2017: 137). Thus, the argument is also a promising explanation for absorption problems and also the low quality of institutions in the old member states.

Against the backdrop of its relevance in new and old member states, there are several promising avenues for future research. First, future studies should aim at including also the old member states and especially those with traditions of politicization and patronage into analyses to test in how far the results are transferable. Second, detailed studies of the successful cases will also hold promising insights on how to overcome absorption problems. In this regard, a focus on the role and relevance of central management bodies for successful absorption in the Baltic states and Poland will be of high value. In addition, also exploring the Bulgarian OPT and its surprisingly successful trajectory in greater detail is of high relevance for the development of more concrete policy recommendations for struggling member states. Third, looking at the 2014–2020 financing period, a general evaluation of adaptations is important. Did the conduct of governments change against the backdrop of problems in the preceeding financing period? Are EU funds management units now less subject to politicization? Are there examples of institutional innovation making these units more resilient also in contexts of generally low capacities? Also, the successful cases are interesting: Did Poland again manage to use its funds successfully even after the change of government? Poland is a country with high capacities but a history of strong politicization. It will be thus interesting to see whether the argument of resilient capacities holds beyond the Baltic states.

Overall, it seems important to note that patronage practices are not only, but still very often associated with lower levels of economic development, thus especially likely to be present in the very contexts targeted by cohesion policy. The results of this study thus highlight a problem that could be a fundamental impediment to cohesion policy implementation in the EU as a whole.

References

Bachtler, J., Mendez, C., & Oraže, H. (2014). From Conditionality to Europeanization in Central and Eastern Europe: Administrative Performance and Capacity in Cohesion Policy. *European Planning Studies, 22*(4), 735–757.

Berg-Schlosser, D., De Meur, G., Rihoux, B., & Ragin, C. C. (2009). Qualitative Comparative Analysis (QCA) as an Approach. In B. Rihoux & C. C. Ragin (Eds.), *Configurational Comparative Methods: Qualitative Comparative Analysis (QCA) and Related Techniques* (pp. 1–18). London et al.: Sage.

Bloom, S., & Petrova, V. (2013). National Subversion of Supranational Goals: 'Pork-Barrel' Politics and EU Regional Aid. *Europe-Asia Studies, 65*(8), 1599–1620.

Bodenstein, T., & Kemmerling, A. (2011). Ripples in a Rising Tide: Why Some EU Regions Receive More Structural Funds Than Others. *European Integration Online Papers, 16*(1). http://eiop.or.at/eiop/texte/2012-001a.htm. Accessed Jan 2016.

Börzel, T. A., & Schimmelfennig, F. (2017). Coming Together or Drifting Apart? The EU's Political Integration Capacity in Eastern Europe. *Journal of European Public Policy, 24*(2), 278–296.

Börzel, T. A., & Sedelmeier, U. (2017). Larger and More Law Abiding? The Impact of Enlargement on Compliance in the European Union. *Journal of European Public Policy, 24*(2), 197–215.

Börzel, T. A., Dimitrova, A., & Schimmelfennig, F. (2017). European Union Enlargement and Integration Capacity: Concepts, Findings, and Policy Implications. *Journal of European Public Policy, 24*(2), 157–176.

Bouvet, F., & Dall'Erba, S. (2010). European Regional Structural Funds: How Large Is the Influence of Politics on the Allocation Process? *JCMS: Journal of Common Market Studies, 48*(3), 501–528.

Chalmers, A. W. (2013). Regional Authority, Transnational Lobbying and the Allocation of Structural Funds in the European Union. *JCMS: Journal of Common Market Studies, 51*(5), 815–831.

Charron, N., Lapuente, V., & Dijkstra, L. (2012). *Regional Governance Matters: A Study on Regional Variation in Quality of Government Within the EU.* Available at http://ec.europa.eu/regional_policy/sources/docgener/work/2012_02_governance.pdf. Accessed 10 Nov 2018.

CZ1. (2015). *Interview in Prague with Policy Expert on 14 May 2015.*

Dellmuth, L. M. (2011). The Cash Divide: The Allocation of European Union Regional Grants. *Journal of European Public Policy, 18*(7), 1016–1033.

Dellmuth, L. M., & Stoffel, M. F. (2012). Distributive Politics and Intergovernmental Transfers: The Local Allocation of European Union Structural Funds. *European Union Politics, 13*(3), 413–433.

Dimitrova, A., & Toshkov, D. (2009). Post-accession Compliance Between Administrative Co-ordination and Political Bargaining. *European Integration Online Papers, 13*, Article 19. http://eiop.or.at/eiop/texte/2009-019a.htm. Accessed Jan 2016.

Ekiert, G., & Hanson, S. E. (Eds.). (2003). *Capitalism and Democracy in Central and Eastern Europe: Assessing the Legacy of Communist Rule.* Cambridge: Cambridge University Press.

European Commission. (2017). *My Region, My Europe, Our Future. Seventh Report on Economic, Social and Territorial Cohesion.* Brussels: European Commission, Directorate-General Regional and Urban Policy. Available at http://ec.europa.eu/regional_policy/sources/docoffic/official/reports/cohesion7/short_7cr_en.pdf. Accessed 20 June 2018.

Falkner, G., & Treib, O. (2008). Three Worlds of Compliance or Four? The EU-15 Compared to New Member States. *JCMS: Journal of Common Market Studies, 46*(2), 293–313.

Falkner, G., Treib, O., & Holzleithner, E. (2008). *Compliance in the Enlarged European Union: Living Rights or Dead Letters?* Aldershot and Burlington, VT: Ashgate.

Ferry, M., & Kah, S. (2017). *Research for REGI-Lessons Learnt from the Closure of the 2007–13 Programming Period*. Brussels. http://doi.org/10.2861/25187.

Goetz, K. H., & Wollmann, H. (2001). Governmentalizing Central Executives in Post-communist Europe: A Four-Country Comparison. *Journal of European Public Policy, 8*(6), 864–887.

Jahn, D., & Müller-Rommel, F. (2010). Political Institutions and Policy Performance: A Comparative Analysis of Central and Eastern Europe. *Journal of Public Policy, 30*(1), 23–44.

Kitschelt, H. (2001). Divergent Paths of Postcommunist Democracies. In L. Diamond & R. Gunther (Eds.), *Political Parties and Democracy* (pp. 299–323). Baltimore and London: Johns Hopkins University Press.

Kitschelt, H., Mansfeldová, Z., Markovski, R., & Toka, G. (1999). *Post-communist Party Systems: Competition, Representation, and Inter-Party Cooperation*. Cambridge: Cambridge University Press.

Kopecký, P., & Spirova, M. (2011). 'Jobs for the Boys'? Patterns of Party Patronage in Post-communist Europe. *West European Politics, 34*(5), 897–921.

Krupavicius, A. (2012). Lithuania. *European Journal of Political Research Political Data Yearbook, 51*(1), 187–200.

LT4. (2014). *Interview in Vilnius with Lithuanian Official on 7 May 2014*.

Maniokas, K. (2009). Conditionality and Compliance in Lithuania: The Case of the Best Performer. *European Integration Online Papers, 13*, Article 20. http://eiop.or.at/eiop/pdf/2009-020.pdf. Accessed 5 Jan 2016.

Meyer-Sahling, J.-H. (2009). Varieties of Legacies: A Critical Review of Legacy Explanations of Public Administration Reform in East Central Europe. *International Review of Administrative Sciences, 75*(3), 509–528.

Milio, S. (2007). Can Administrative Capacity Explain Differences in Regional Performances? Evidence from Structural Funds Implementation in Southern Italy. *Regional Studies, 41*(4), 429–442.

Milio, S. (2008). How Political Stability Shapes Administrative Performance: The Italian Case. *West European Politics, 31*(5), 915–936.

Ragin, C. C. (2000). *Fuzzy-Set Social Science*. Chicago: University of Chicago Press.

RO. (2015). *Government of Romania: General Transport Master Plan, Approved by the Government.* Available at http://gov.ro/en/government/cabinet-meeting/general-transport-master-plan-approved-by-the-government. Accessed 18 Feb 2016.

Schraff, D. (2014). Buying Turnout or Rewarding Loyalists? Electoral Mobilization and EU Structural Funding in the German Länder. *European Union Politics, 15*(2), 277–288.

Sedelmeier, U. (2008). After Conditionality: Post-accession Compliance with EU Law in East Central Europe. *Journal of European Public Policy, 15*(6), 806–825.

Sedelmeier, U. (2012). Is Europeanisation Through Conditionality Sustainable? Lock-in of Institutional Change after EU Accession. *West European Politics, 35*(1), 20–38.

Segert, D. (2007). Postsozialismus–Spätsozialismus–Staatssozialismus. Grundlinien und Grundbegriffe einer politikwissenschaftlichen Postsozialismusforschung. In D. Segert (Ed.), *Postsozialismus: Hinterlassenschaften des Staatssozialismus und neue Kapitalismen in Europa* (pp. 1–23). Wien: Braumüller.

Shefter, M. (1994). *Political Parties and the State: The American Historical Experience.* Princeton: Princeton University Press.

Stykow, P. (2006). *Staat und Wirtschaft in Russland: Interessenvermittlung zwischen Korruption und Konzertierung.* Wiesbaden: VS Verlag.

Surubaru, N.-C. (2017). Revisiting the Role of Domestic Politics: Politicisation and European Cohesion Policy Performance in Central and Eastern Europe. *East European Politics, 33*(1), 106–125.

Tosun, J. (2014). Absorption of Regional Funds: A Comparative Analysis. *JCMS: Journal of Common Market Studies, 52*(2), 371–387.

Bibliography

Allen, D. (2008). Cohesion Policy Pre- and Post-enlargement. In M. Baun & D. Marek (Eds.), *EU Cohesion Policy After Enlargement* (pp. 15–33). Basingstoke: Palgrave.

Åslund, A. (2010). *The Last Shall Be the First: The East European Financial Crisis*. Washington, DC: Peterson Institute for International Economics.

Autengruber, C. (2008). Bulgarien: Zwischen anfänglichen Konsolidierungstendenzen und aktuellen Umbrüchen. In E. Bos & D. Segert (Eds.), *Osteuropäische Demokratien als Trendsetter? Parteien und Parteiensysteme nach dem Ende des Übergangsjahrzehnts* (pp. 133–146). Opladen and Farmington Hills: Verlag Barbara Budrich.

Bache, I. (2015). Cohesion Policy: A New Direction for New Times? In H. Wallace, M. Pollack, & A. R. Youn (Eds.), *Policy-Making in the European Union* (pp. 243–262). Oxford: Oxford University Press.

Bachtler, J., Downes, R., & Gorzelak, G. (2000). Transition, Cohesion and Regional Policy in Central and Eastern Europe: Conclusions. In J. Bachtler, R. Downes, & G. Gorzelak (Eds.), *Transition Cohesion and Regional Policy in Central and Eastern Europe* (pp. 355–378). Aldershot et al.: Ashgate.

Bachtler, J., & Gorzelak, G. (2007). Reforming EU Cohesion Policy: A Reappraisal of the Performance of the Structural Funds. *Policy Studies, 28*(4), 309–326.

Bachtler, J., & McMaster, I. (2008). EU Cohesion Policy and the Role of the Regions: Investigating the Influence of Structural Funds in the New Member States. *Environment and Planning C: Government and Policy, 26*(2), 398–427.

C. Hagemann, *EU Funds in the New Member States*, Palgrave Studies in European Union Politics,
https://doi.org/10.1007/978-3-030-02092-7

Bachtler, J., & Mendez, C. (2007). Who Governs EU Cohesion Policy? Deconstructing the Reforms of the Structural Funds. *JCMS: Journal of Common Market Studies, 45*(3), 535–564.

Bachtler, J., Mendez, C., & Oraže, H. (2014). From Conditionality to Europeanization in Central and Eastern Europe: Administrative Performance and Capacity in Cohesion Policy. *European Planning Studies, 22*(4), 735–757.

Bailey, D., & De Propris, L. (2002a). The 1988 Reform of the European Structural Funds: Entitlement or Empowerment? *Journal of European Public Policy, 9*(3), 408–428.

Bailey, D., & De Propris, L. (2002b). EU Structural Funds, Regional Capabilities and Enlargement: Towards Multi-level Governance? *Journal of European Integration, 24*(4), 303–324.

Bailey, D., & De Propris, L. (2004). A Bridge Too Phare? EU Pre-accession Aid and Capacity-Building in the Candidate Countries. *JCMS: Journal of Common Market Studies, 42*(1), 77–98.

Balas, G., & Kiss, G. (2011). Hungary. *Expert Evaluation Network.* Budapest: HEFTA Centre for Analyses. Available at http://ec.europa.eu/regional_policy/index.cfm/en/policy/evaluations/ec/2007-2013/#1. Accessed 29 May 2017.

Balas, G., Kiss, G., & Borbas, G. (2013). Hungary. *Expert Evaluation Network.* Budapest: HEFTA Centre for Analyses. Available at http://ec.europa.eu/regional_policy/sources/docgener/evaluation/pdf/eval2007/2013_een_task2_hu.pdf. Accessed 29 May 2017.

Banaszewska, M., & Bischoff, I. (2016). *The Political Economy of EU-Funds in Poland: Evidence for the Period 2007–2013* (Joint Discussion Paper Series in Economics). Available at http://www.uni-marburg.de/fb02/makro/forschung/magkspapers. Accessed May 2016.

Bartha, A., Nagy, K., Gyukics, R., & Kopint, T. (2010). Hungary. *Expert Evaluation Network.* Brussels: European Commission, Directorate-General Regional Policy. Available at http://ec.europa.eu/regional_policy/sources/docgener/evaluation/pdf/eval2007/country_reports/hungary.pdf. Accessed 29 May 2017.

Baun, M., & Marek, D. (2008a). EU Cohesion Policy and Sub-national Authorities in the New Member States. *Contemporary European Studies.* Olomouc: Palacký University. Available at http://www.4europartners.cz/prezentace/Baun_Marek_EU_Cohesion_Policy_and_Sub-National_Authorities_in_the_New_Member_States.pdf. Accessed 12 Feb 2016.

Baun, M. J., & Marek, D. (2008b). The Czech Republic. In D. Marek & M. J. Baun (Eds.), *EU Cohesion Policy After Enlargement* (pp. 165–186). Basingstoke: Palgrave Macmillan.

Beach, D. (2018). Achieving Methodological Alignment When Combining QCA and PT in Practice. *Sociological Methods & Research, 47*(1), 64–99.

Beach, D., & Pedersen, R. B. (2013). *Process-Tracing Methods: Foundations and Guidelines.* Ann Arbor: University of Michigan Press.

Beach, D., & Pedersen, R. B. (2016). Selecting Appropriate Cases When Tracing Causal Mechanisms. *Sociological Methods & Research, 47*(4), 837–871.

Beach, D., & Rohlfing, I. (2018). Integrating Cross-Case Analyses and Process Tracing in Set-Theoretic Research Strategies and Parameters of Debate. *Sociological Methods & Research, 47*(1), 3–36.

Beichelt, T. (2004). *Die Europäische Union nach der Osterweiterung*. Wiesbaden: VS Verlag.

Bennett, A., & Checkel, J. T. (Eds.). (2015). *Process Tracing: From Metaphor to Analytic Tool*. Cambridge: Cambridge University Press.

Berg-Schlosser, D., De Meur, G., Rihoux, B., & Ragin, C. C. (2009). Qualitative Comparative Analysis (QCA) as an Approach. In B. Rihoux & C. C. Ragin (Eds.), *Configurational Comparative Methods: Qualitative Comparative Analysis (QCA) and Related Techniques* (pp. 1–18). London et al.: Sage.

Berglund, S., Gange, I., & Van Waarden, F. (2006). Mass Production of Law. Routinization in the Transposition of European Directives: A Sociological-Institutionalist Account. *Journal of European Public Policy, 13*(5), 692–716.

Beugelsdijk, M., & Eijffinger, S. C. (2005). The Effectiveness of Structural Policy in the European Union: An Empirical Analysis for the EU-15 in 1995–2001. *JCMS: Journal of Common Market Studies, 43*(1), 37–51.

BG. (2007a). OP Environment Bulgaria 2007–2013. *National Strategic Reference Framework*. Sofia: Ministry of Environment, Bulgaria. Available at archive.eufunds.bg/document/463. Accessed 12 Feb 2016.

BG. (2007b). OP Transport Bulgaria 2007–2013. *National Strategic Reference Framework*. Sofia: Ministry of Transport, Bulgaria. Available at http://www.optransport.bg/upload/docs/2_SOPT_FINAL.pdf. Accessed 12 Feb 2016.

Bideleux, R. (2011). Contrasting Responses to the International Economic Crisis of 2008–10 in the 11 CIS Countries and in the 10 Post-communist EU Member Countries. *Journal of Communist Studies and Transition Politics, 27*(3–4), 338–363.

Bingen, D. (2008). Polen: Wie ein labiles Parteiensystem zu einer Stabilisierung der Demokratie beiträgt. In E. Bos & D. Segert (Eds.), *Osteuropäische Demokratien als Trendsetter? Parteien und Parteiensysteme nach dem Ende des Übergangsjahrzehnts* (pp. 77–90). Opladen and Farmington Hills: Verlag Barbara Budrich.

Blažek, J. (2011). Czech Republic. *Expert Evaluation Network*. Prague: Charles University. Available at http://ec.europa.eu/regional_policy/index.cfm/en/policy/evaluations/ec/2007-2013/#1. Accessed 29 May 2017.

Blažek, J. (2012). Czech Republic. *Expert Evaluation Network*. Prague: Charles University. Available at http://ec.europa.eu/regional_policy/sources/docgener/evaluation/pdf/eval2007/expert_innovation/2012_een_task2_cz.pdf. Accessed 12 Feb 2016.

Blom-Hansen, J. (2005). Principals, Agents, and the Implementation of EU Cohesion Policy. *Journal of European Public Policy, 12*(4), 624–648.

Bloom, S., & Petrova, V. (2013). National Subversion of Supranational Goals: 'Pork-Barrel' Politics and EU Regional Aid. *Europe–Asia Studies, 65*(8), 1599–1620.

Bodenstein, T., & Kemmerling, A. (2011). Ripples in a Rising Tide: Why Some EU Regions Receive More Structural Funds Than Others. *European Integration Online Papers, 16*(1). http://eiop.or.at/eiop/texte/2012-001a.htm. Accessed Jan 2016.

Boeckhout, S., Boot, L., Hollanders, M., Reincke, K.-J., & De Vet, J. M. (2002). *Key Indicators for Candidate Countries to Effectively Manage the Structural Funds* (Principal Report). Rotterdam: NEI Regional and Urban Development. Available at http://www.evaluace.cz/dokumenty/hodnot_zpr_eu/souhrnna_studie.pdf. Accessed 12 Feb 2016.

Bohle, D. (2011). East European Transformations and the Paradoxes of Transnationalization. In J. DeBardeleben & A. Hurrelmann (Eds.), *Transnational Europe: Promise, Paradox, Limits* (pp. 130–151). Basingstoke: Palgrave Macmillan.

Börzel, T. A. (2000). Why There Is No 'Southern Problem': On Environmental Leaders and Laggards in the European Union. *Journal of European Public Policy, 7*(1), 141–162.

Börzel, T. A., Dimitrova, A., & Schimmelfennig, F. (2017). European Union Enlargement and Integration Capacity: Concepts, Findings, and Policy Implications. *Journal of European Public Policy, 24*(2), 157–176.

Börzel, T. A., Hofmann, T., & Panke, D. (2012). Caving in or Sitting It Out? Longitudinal Patterns of Non-compliance in the European Union. *Journal of European Public Policy, 19*(4), 454–471.

Börzel, T. A., Hofmann, T., Panke, D., & Sprungk, C. (2010). Obstinate and Inefficient: Why Member States Do Not Comply with European Law. *Comparative Political Studies, 43*(11), 1363–1390.

Börzel, T. A., & Schimmelfennig, F. (2017). Coming Together or Drifting Apart? The EU's Political Integration Capacity in Eastern Europe. *Journal of European Public Policy, 24*(2), 278–296.

Börzel, T. A., & Sedelmeier, U. (2017). Larger and More Law Abiding? The Impact of Enlargement on Compliance in the European Union. *Journal of European Public Policy, 24*(2), 197–215.

Bos, E., & Segert, D. (2008). Osteuropa als Trendsetter? Parteiensysteme in repräsentativen Demokratien unter mehrfachem Druck. In E. Bos & D. Segert (Eds.), *Osteuropäische Demokratien als Trendsetter? Parteien und Parteiensysteme nach dem Ende des Übergangsjahrzehnts* (pp. 323–336). Opladen and Farmington Hills: Verlag Barbara Budrich.

Bouvet, F., & Dall'Erba, S. (2010). European Regional Structural Funds: How Large Is the Influence of Politics on the Allocation Process? *JCMS: Journal of Common Market Studies, 48*(3), 501–528.

Brosig, M. (2010). The Challenge of Implementing Minority Rights in Central Eastern Europe. *European Integration, 32*(4), 393–411.

Bubbico, R. L., & De Michelis, N. (2011). *The Financial Execution of Structural Funds* (Regional Focus No. 3/2011). Brussels: European Commission, Directorate-General for Regional Policy. Available at http://ec.europa.eu/regional_policy/sources/docgener/focus/2011_03_financial.pdf. Accessed 12 Feb 2016.

Buzogány, A. (2012). Accelerating or Back-Pedalling? *L'Europe en Formation.* Brussels: Centre International de Formation Européenne. Available at (accessed).

Buzogány, A., & Korkut, U. (2013). Administrative Reform and Regional Development Discourses in Hungary: Europeanisation Going NUTS? *Europe–Asia Studies, 65*(8), 1555–1577.

Buzogány, A., & Stuchlík, A. (2010). Wandlungen in Kafkas Schloß? Verwaltungsreform und -Modernisierung in Mittel- und Osteuropa. In H. Hill (Ed.), *Verwaltungsmodernisierung 2010* (pp. 255–281). Baden-Baden: Nomos.

Cace, C., Cace, S., & Nicolaescu, V. (2010). Management of the Structural Funds Within the Context of the Global Economic Crisis. *Review of International Comparative Management, 11*(1), 87–101.

Camyar, I. (2010). Europeanization, Domestic Legacies and Administrative Reforms in Central and Eastern Europe: A Comparative Analysis of Hungary and the Czech Republic. *Journal of European Integration, 32*(2), 137–155.

Česká, Pozice. (2011a). *Billions in EU Funds May Go Up Dobeš's Chimney (Published 5 April 2011).* Available at http://ceskapozice.lidovky.cz/billions-in-eu-funds-may-go-up-dobes-s-chimney-fn4-/tema.aspx-?c=A110404_121659_pozice_10614. Accessed 13 Feb 2016.

Česká Pozice. (2011b). *Finance Ministry Suspends EU Fund License (Published 15 April 2011).* Available at http://ceskapozice.lidovky.cz/finance-ministry-suspends-eu-fund-license-fil-/tema.aspx?c=A110415_163858_pozice_11946. Accessed 11 July 2015.

Česká Pozice. (2011c). *SFŽP Whistle-Blower Given Kč 500,000 Reward (Published 23 March 2011).* Available at http://ceskapozice.lidovky.cz/sfzp-whistle-blower-given-kc-500-000-reward-fct-/tema.aspx?c=A110323_172658_pozice_9493. Accessed 22 Dec 2015.

Chalmers, A. W. (2013). Regional Authority, Transnational Lobbying and the Allocation of Structural Funds in the European Union. *JCMS: Journal of Common Market Studies, 51*(5), 815–831.

Charron, N., Lapuente, V., & Dijkstra, L. (2012). *Regional Governance Matters: A Study on Regional Variation in Quality of Government Within the EU.* Available at http://ec.europa.eu/regional_policy/sources/docgener/work/2012_02_governance.pdf (accessed).

Chayes, A., Chayes, A. H., & Mitchell, R. B. (2000). Managing Compliance: A Comparative Perspective. In E. B. Weiss (Ed.), *Engaging Countries: Strengthening Compliance with International Environmental Accords* (pp. 39–62). Cambridge, MA: MIT Press.

Collier, D., Brady, H. E., & Seawright, J. (2004). Sources of Leverage in Causal Inference: Toward an Alternative View of Methodology. In H. E. Brady & D. Collier (Eds.), *Rethinking Social Inquiry: Diverse Tools, Shared Standards* (pp. 229–266). Lanham et al.: Rowman & Littlefield.

Connolly, R. (2010). The EU Economy: Member States Outside the Euro Area in 2009. *JCMS: Journal of Common Market Studies, 48*(Annual Review), 243–266.

Connolly, R. (2012). The Determinants of the Economic Crisis in Post-socialist Europe. *Europe–Asia Studies, 64*(1), 35–67.

Council of Ministers. (2006, July 11). *Laying Down General Provisions on the European Regional Development Fund, the European Social Fund and the Cohesion Fund and Repealing Regulation (EC) No. 1260/1999* (Council Regulation (EC) No. 1083/2006). Brussels: Council of the European Union. Available at http://eur-lex.europa.eu/legal-content/EN/ALL/?uri=CELEX%3A32006R1083. Accessed 17 Mar 2014.

Crawford, B. (1995). Post-communist Political Economy: A Framework for the Analysis of Reform. In B. Crawford (Ed.), *Markets, States, and Democracy: The Political Economy of Post-communist Transformation* (pp. 3–42). Boulder: Westview Press.

Crouch, C. (2008). What Will Follow the Demise of Privatised Keynesianism? *Political Quarterly, 79*(4), 476–487.

CZ. (2004). OP Infrastructure 2004–2006. *National Strategic Reference Framework.* Prague: Ministry of Regional Development, Czech Republic. Available at http://www.strukturalni-fondy.cz/en/Fondy-EU/Programy-2004-2006/Operacni-programy/OP-INFRASTRUKTURA. Accessed 12 Feb 2016.

CZ. (2007a). OP Environment 2007–2013. *National Strategic Reference Framework.* Prague: Ministry of Environment, Czech Republic. Available at http://en.opzp2007-2013.cz/ke-stazeni/515/5060/detail/the-operational-programme-environment---for-the-period-2007-2013/. Accessed 12 Feb 2016.

CZ. (2007b). OP Transport 2007–2013. *National Strategic Reference Framework.* Prague: Ministry of Transport, Czech Republic. Available at http://www.opd.cz/Providers/Document.ashx?id=48. Accessed 12 Feb 2016.

CZ. (2009a). Annual Report for 2008. *Annual Implementation Report.* Prague: Ministry of Environment, Czech Republic. Available at http://en.opzp2007-2013.cz/ke-stazeni/515/5061/detail/annual-report-op-environment-2008/. Accessed 12 Feb 2016.

CZ. (2009b). *Meeting of the Monitoring Committee of Czech OP Enviroment on 3 December 2009.* Prague: Ministry of Environment, Czech Republic. Available

at www.opzp2007-2013.cz/soubor-ke-stazeni/22/6873-minutes_6th_mc_ope_12_03_2009_final.pdf. Accessed 3 June 2015.
CZ. (2010a). Annual Report for 2009. *Annual Implementation Report.* Prague: Ministry of Environment, Czech Republic, Available at http://en.opzp2007-2013.cz/ke-stazeni/515/14284/detail/annual-report-ope-2009/. Accessed 12 Feb 2016.
CZ. (2010b). *Meeting of the Monitoring Committee of Czech OP Enviroment on 2 December 2010.* Prague: Ministry of Environment, Czech Republic. Available at https://www.sfzp.cz/soubor-ke-stazeni/40/12032-Minutes_8th_MC%20OPE_02_12_2010.pdf. Accessed 3 June 2015.
CZ. (2010c). *Meeting of the Monitoring Committee of Czech OP Enviroment on 3 June 2010.* Prague: Ministry of Environment, Czech Republic. Available at https://www.sfzp.cz/soubor-ke-stazeni/36/11082-Minutes_7th_MC_OPE_06_03_2010.pdf. Accessed 3 June 2015.
CZ. (2012). Annual Report for 2011. *Annual Implementation Report.* Prague: Ministry of Environment, Czech Republic. Available at http://en.opzp2007-2013.cz/ke-stazeni/515/14283/detail/annual-report-op-environment-2011-incl-annexes/. Accessed 12 Feb 2016.
CZ. (2013). Annual Report for 2012. *Annual Implementation Report.* Prague: Ministry of Environment, Czech Republic. Available at http://en.opzp2007-2013.cz/ke-stazeni/515/15626/detail/annual-report-ope-for-2012-incl-appendices/. Accessed 12 Feb 2016.
CZ. (2014). Annual Report for 2013. *Annual Implementation Report.* Prague: Ministry of Environment, Czech Republic. Available at http://en.opzp2007-2013.cz/ke-stazeni/515/15731/detail/annual-report-op-environment-for-2013-incl-annexes/. Accessed 12 Feb 2016.
CZ. (2015). *Ministry of Regional Development, Czech Republic: National Coordination Authority.* Available at http://62.109.144.163/en/Fondy-EU/Narodni-organ-pro-koordinaci. Accessed 11 July 2015.
CZ1. (2014). *Interview in Prague with Policy Expert on 3 June 2014.*
CZ1. (2015). *Interview in Prague with Policy Expert on 14 May 2015.*
CZ3. (2014). *Interview in Prague with Czech Official on 06 June 2014.*
CZ6. (2015). *Interview in Prague with Czech Official on 14 May 2015.*
CZ7. (2015). *Interview in Prague with Czech Official on 14 May 2015.*
CZ8. (2015). *Interview in Prague with Czech Official on 15 May 2015.*
Deegan-Krause, K., & Haugton, T. (2010). A Fragile Stability: The Institutional Roots of Low Party System Volatility in the Czech Republic, 1990–2009. *Czech Journal of Political Science (Politologický časopis), 17*(3): 227–241.
Dellmuth, L. M. (2011). The Cash Divide: The Allocation of European Union Regional Grants. *Journal of European Public Policy, 18*(7), 1016–1033.
Dellmuth, L. M., & Stoffel, M. F. (2012). Distributive Politics and Intergovernmental Transfers: The Local Allocation of European Union Structural Funds. *European Union Politics, 13*(3), 413–433.

Dimitrov, V., Goetz, K. H., & Wollmann, H. (2006). *Governing After Communism: Institutions and Policymaking*. Lanham et al.: Rowman & Littlefield.

Dimitrova, A. (2002). Enlargement, Institution-Building and the EUs Administrative Capacity Requirement. *West European Politics, 25*(4), 171–190.

Dimitrova, A., & Steunenberg, B. (2013). Living in Parallel Universes? Implementing European Movable Cultural Heritage Policy in Bulgaria. *JCMS: Journal of Common Market Studies, 51*(2), 246–263.

Dimitrova, A., & Toshkov, D. (2007). The Dynamics of Domestic Coordination of EU Policy in the New Member States: Impossible to Lock In? *West European Politics, 30*(5), 961–986.

Dimitrova, A., & Toshkov, D. (2009). Post-accession Compliance Between Administrative Co-ordination and Political Bargaining. *European Integration Online Papers, 13*, Article 19. http://eiop.or.at/eiop/texte/2009-019a.htm. Accessed Jan 2016.

Dimitrova, A. L. (2005). Europeanization and Civil Service Reform in Central and Eastern Europe. In F. Schimmelfennig & U. Sedelmeier (Eds.), *The Europeanization of Central and Eastern Europe* (pp. 71–90). Ithaca, NY and London: Cornell University Press.

Dimitrova, A. L. (2010). The New Member States of the EU in the Aftermath of Enlargement: Do New European Rules Remain Empty Shells? *Journal of European Public Policy, 17*(1), 137–148.

Döring, H., & Manow, P. (2014). *Parliament and Government Composition Database (ParlGov): An Infrastructure for Empirical Information on Parties, Elections and Governments in Modern Democracies*. Version 14/12–29 December 2014. Available at http://parlgov.org/. Accessed 27 Jan 2015.

Dotti, N. F. (2013). The Unbearable Instability of Structural Funds' Distribution. *European Planning Studies, 21*(4), 596–614.

Dotti, N. F. (2016). Unwritten Factors Affecting Structural Funds: The Influence of Regional Political Behaviours on the Implementation of EU Cohesion Policy. *European Planning Studies, 24*(3), 530–550.

Drevet, J.-F. (2000). Regional Policy in Central and Eastern Europe: The EU Perspective. In J. Bachtler, R. Downes, & G. Gorzelak (Eds.), *Transition Cohesion and Regional Policy in Central and Eastern Europe* (pp. 345–353). Aldershot et al.: Ashgate.

Druckman, J. N., & Roberts, A. (2007). Communist Successor Parties and Coalition Formation in Eastern Europe. *Legislative Studies Quarterly, 32*(1), 5–31.

Dusa, A. (2007). User Manual for the QCA (GUI) Package in R. *Journal of Business Research, 60*(5), 576–586.

Duverger, M. (1990). Caucus and Branch, Cadre Parties and Mass Parties. In P. Mair (Ed.), *The West European Party System* (pp. 37–45). Oxford: Oxford University Press.

EC. (2010). *The Financial Execution of Structural Funds.* Available at (accessed).

Ederveen, S., Gorter, J., de Mooij, R., & Nahuis, R. (2003). *Funds and Games: The Economics of European Cohesion Policy* (Occasional Paper No. 3). Brussels: ENEPRI. Available at http://aei.pitt.edu/1965/1/ENEPRI_OP3.pdf. Accessed 29 May 2017.

EE. (2003). Single Programming Document 2004–2006. *National Strategic Reference Framework.* Tallinn: Government of Estonia. Available at www.digar.ee/arhiiv/en/download/22611. Accessed 12 Feb 2016.

EE. (2007a). OP Economic Environment 2007–2013. *National Strategic Reference Framework.* Tallinn: Ministry of Finance, Estonia. Available at http://www.struktuurifondid.ee/public/inglisekeelsed_dokumendid/Modified_Economic_Environment_OP_070311.pdf. Accessed 12 Feb 2016.

EE. (2007b). OP Living Environment 2007–2013. *National Strategic Reference Framework.* Tallinn: Ministry of Finance, Estonia. Available at http://www.struktuurifondid.ee/public/inglisekeelsed_dokumendid/Modified_Living_Environment_OP_070311.pdf. Accessed 12 Feb 2016.

Ekiert, G., & Hanson, S. E. (Eds.). (2003). *Capitalism and Democracy in Central and Eastern Europe: Assessing the Legacy of Communist Rule.* Cambridge: Cambridge University Press.

Emmenegger, P. (2011). Job Security Regulations in Western Democracies: A Fuzzy Set Analysis. *European Journal of Political Research, 50*(3), 336–364.

Enyedi, Z. (2006). The Survival of the Fittest: Party System Concentration in Hungary. In S. Jungerstam-Mulders (Ed.), *Post-communist EU Member States: Parties and Party Systems* (pp. 177–202). Farnham and Burlington, VT: Ashgate.

Epstein, R. A., & Sedelmeier, U. (2008). Beyond Conditionality: International Institutions in Postcommunist Europe After Enlargement. *Journal of European Public Policy, 15*(6), 795–805.

European Commission. (2007). Cohesion Policy 2007–13: Commentaries and Official Texts. *European Union Regional Policy.* Brussels: European Commission, Directorate-General for Regional Policy. Available at http://ec.europa.eu/regional_policy/en/information/publications/legislation/2007/cohesion-policy-2007-13-commentaries-and-official-texts. Accessed 29 May 2017.

European Commission. (2013a). *Analysis of the Budgetary Implementation of the Structural and Cohesion Funds in 2013* (Commission Staff Working Paper). Brussels: European Commission, Directorate-General Budget. Available at http://ec.europa.eu/budget/library/biblio/documents/2013/sf_implem_rep_2013_en.pdf. Accessed 12 Feb 2016.

European Commission. (2013b, April 18). Cohesion Policy: Strategic Report 2013. *COM(2013) 210 final.* Brussels: European Commission. Available at http://ec.europa.eu/regional_policy/how/policy/doc/strategic_report/2013/strat_report_2013_en.pdf. Accessed 15 Mar 2017.

European Commission. (2016a). *Analysis of the Budgetary Implementation of the Structural and Cohesion Funds in 2016* (Commission Staff Working Paper). Brussels: European Commission, Directorate-General Budget. Available at http://ec.europa.eu/budget/library/biblio/publications/2016/AnalysisOfTheEuropeanStructuralAndInvestmentFundsIn2016_en.pdf. Accessed 20 June 2018.

European Commission. (2016b). *Innovation and Networks Executive Agency: TEN-T Programme 2007–2013*. Available at https://ec.europa.eu/inea/en/ten-t. Accessed 18 Feb 2016.

European Commission. (2017a). *Document for the Committee on Budgetary Control, European Parliament* (Commission Staff Working Paper). Brussels: European Commission, Directorate-General Regional and Urban Policy. Available at http://www.europarl.europa.eu/cmsdata/124722/Hearing%20Briefing_Absorption%20of%20funds%20July%202017%20resized%20with%20Adobe.pdf. Accessed 29 May 2017.

European Commission. (2017b). *My Region, My Europe, Our Future. Seventh Report on Economic, Social and Territorial Cohesion*. Brussels: European Commission, Directorate-General Regional and Urban Policy. Available at http://ec.europa.eu/regional_policy/sources/docoffic/official/reports/cohesion7/short_7cr_en.pdf. Accessed 20 June 2018.

Falkner, G. (2010). Institutional Performance and Compliance with EU Law: Czech Republic, Hungary, Slovakia and Slovenia. *Journal of Public Policy, 30*(1), 101–116.

Falkner, G., Hartlapp, M., Leiber, S., & Treib, O. (2004). Non-compliance with EU Directives in the Member States: Opposition Through the Backdoor? *West European Politics, 27*(3), 452–473.

Falkner, G., & Treib, O. (2008). Three Worlds of Compliance or Four? The EU-15 Compared to New Member States. *JCMS: Journal of Common Market Studies, 46*(2), 293–313.

Falkner, G., Treib, O., Hartlapp, M., & Leiber, S. (2005). *Complying with Europe: EU Harmonisation and Soft Law in the Member States*. Cambridge, MA: Cambridge University Press.

Falkner, G., Treib, O., & Holzleithner, E. (2008a). *Compliance in the Enlarged European Union: Living Rights or Dead Letters?* Aldershot and Burlington, VT: Ashgate.

Falkner, G., Treib, O., & Holzleithner, E. (2008b). Introduction: The Challenge of Implementation Research in the New Member States. In G. Falkner, O. Treib, & E. Holzleithner (Eds.), *Compliance in the Enlarged European Union: Living Rights or Dead Letters* (pp. 1–26). Aldershot: Ashgate.

Ferry, M., & Kah, S. (2017). *Research for REGI-Lessons Learnt from the Closure of the 2007–13 Programming Period*. Brussels. http://doi.org/10.2861/25187.

Fink-Hafner, D. (2005). Slovenia. *European Journal of Political Research, 44*(7–8), 1179–1187.

Fink-Hafner, D. (2006). Slovenia: Between Bipolarity and Broad Coalition-Building. In S. Jungerstam-Mulders (Ed.), *Post-communist EU Member States: Parties and Party Systems* (pp. 203–231). Farnham and Burlington, VT: Ashgate.

Fink-Hafner, D. (2009). Slovenia. *European Journal of Political Research, 48*(7–8), 1106–1113.

Fink-Hafner, D. (2012). Slovenia. *European Journal of Political Research Political Data Yearbook, 51*(1), 288–296.

Fink-Hafner, D. (2013). Slovenia. *European Journal of Political Research Political Data Yearbook, 52*(1), 217–222.

Fink-Hafner, D., & Krasovec, A. (2014). Slovenia. *European Journal of Political Research Political Data Yearbook, 53*(1), 281–286.

Fiss, P. C. (2011). Building Better Causal Theories: A Fuzzy Set Approach to Typologies in Organization Research. *Academy of Management Journal, 54*(2), 393–420.

Fortin, J. (2010). A Tool to Evaluate State Capacity in Post-communist Countries, 1989–2006. *European Journal of Political Research, 49*(5), 654–686.

Frank, K. (2012). Slovakia. *Expert Evaluation Network.* Bratislava: Slovak Academy of Sciences. Available at http://ec.europa.eu/regional_policy/sources/docgener/evaluation/pdf/eval2007/expert_innovation/2012_een_task2_sk.pdf. Accessed 29 May 2017.

Frank, K. (2013). Slovakia. *Expert Evaluation Network.* Bratislava: Slovak Academy of Sciences. Available at http://ec.europa.eu/regional_policy/sources/docgener/evaluation/pdf/eval2007/2013_een_task2_sk.pdf. Accessed 29 May 2017.

Frye, T. (2002). The Perils of Polarization: Economic Performance in the Postcommunist World. *World Politics, 54*(3), 308–337.

Frye, T. (2010). *Building States and Markets After Communism: The Perils of Polarized Democracy.* Cambridge: Cambridge University Press.

Gateva, E. (2013). Post-accession Conditionality—Translating Benchmarks into Political Pressure? *East European Politics, 29*(4), 420–442.

George, A. L., & Bennett, A. (2005). *Case Studies and Theory Development in the Social Sciences.* Cambridge, MA: MIT Press.

Gerring, J. (2008a). Case Selection for Case-Study Analysis: Qualitative and Quantitative Techniques. In J. M. Box-Steffensmeier, H. E. Brady, & D. Collier (Eds.), *The Oxford Handbook of Political Methodology* (pp. 645–684). Oxford: Oxford University Press.

Gerring, J. (2008b). The Mechanismic Worldview: Thinking Inside the Box. *British Journal of Political Science, 38*(1), 161–179.

Glusman, J. (2010). The Impact of Policy Implementation in Poland: Centralisation, Decentralisation and Recentralisation. In S. Milio (Ed.), *From Policy to Implementation in the European Union: The Challenge of a Multi-level*

Governance System (pp. 149–174). London and New York: Tauris Academic Studies.

Goetz, K. H. (2001). Making Sense of Post-communist Central Administration: Modernization, Europeanization or Latinization? *Journal of European Public Policy, 8*(6), 1032–1051.

Goetz, K. H., & Wollmann, H. (2001). Governmentalizing Central Executives in Post-communist Europe: A Four-Country Comparison. *Journal of European Public Policy, 8*(6), 864–887.

Grabbe, H. (2001). How Does Europeanization Affect CEE Governance? Conditionality, Diffusion and Diversity. *Journal of European Public Policy, 8*(6), 1013–1031.

Grabbe, H. (2014). Six Lessons of Enlargement Ten Years On: The EU's Transformative Power in Retrospect and Prospect. *JCMS: Journal of Common Market Studies, 52*(Annual Review), 40–56.

Greskovits, B. (1998). *The Political Economy of Protest and Patience: East European and Latin American Transformations Compared*. Budapest: Central European University Press.

Gross, M., & Debus, M. (2018). Does EU Regional Policy Increase Parties' Support for European Integration? *West European Politics, 41*(3), 594–614.

Grotz, F., & Weber, T. (2011). Regierungskoalitionen: Bildung und Dauerhaftigkeit. In F. Grotz & F. Müller-Rommel (Eds.), *Regierungssysteme in Mittel- und Osteuropa* (pp. 194–216). Wiesbaden: VS Verlag.

Grzebieluch, B. (2017). The Absorption of Structural and Cohesion Funds Under 2007–2013 Programming Period. *European Parliament Briefing*. Brussels: European Parliament, Policy Department D—Budgetary Affairs. Available at http://www.europarl.europa.eu/cmsdata/124722/Hearing%20Briefing_Absorption%20of%20funds%20July%202017%20resized%20with%20Adobe.pdf. Accessed 20 June 2018.

Grzymala-Busse, A. (2001). Coalition Formation and the Regime Divide in New Democracies: East Central Europe. *Comparative Politics, 34*(1), 85–104.

Grzymala-Busse, A. (2006). Authoritarian Determinants of Democratic Party Competition: The Communist Successor Parties in East Central Europe. *Party Politics, 12*(3), 415–437.

Grzymala-Busse, A. (2007). *Rebuilding Leviathan: Party Competition and State Exploitation in Post-communist Democracies*. Cambridge: Cambridge University Press.

Grzymala-Busse, A., & Luong, P. J. (2002). Reconceptualizing the State: Lessons from Post-communism. *Politics & Society, 30*(4), 529–554.

Gwiazda, A. (2009). Poland's Quasi-institutionalized Party System: The Importance of Elites and Institutions. *Perspectives on European Politics and Society, 10*(3), 350–376.

Gwiazda, A. (2013). The Europeanisation of Regional Policy in Poland: Did Political Parties Make a Difference? *East European Politics, 29*(2), 226–244.

Gyorine Szabo, G. (2014). How the Institutional System Charged with Regional Development Policy Actually Impact the Use of Cohesion Funds as Reflected by a Comparative Analysis of Poland and Hungary. *European Scientific Journal, 10*(19), 20–31.

Hagemann, C. (2017). How Politics Matters for EU Funds' Absorption Problems—A Fuzzy-Set Analysis. *Journal of European Public Policy*, 1–19.

Hartlapp, M., & Falkner, G. (2009). Problems of Operationalization and Data in EU Compliance Research. *European Union Politics, 10*(2), 281–304.

Haughton, T. (2014). Money, Margins and the Motors of Politics: The EU and the Development of Party Politics in Central and Eastern Europe. *JCMS: Journal of Common Market Studies, 52*(1), 71–87.

Haughton, T., Novotná, T., & Deegan-Krause, K. (2011). The 2010 Czech and Slovak Parliamentary Elections: Red Cards to the 'Winners'. *West European Politics, 34*(2), 394–402.

Haverland, M., & Romeijn, M. (2007). Do Member States Make European Policies Work? Analysing the EU Transposition Deficit. *Public Administration, 85*(3), 757–778.

Haverland, M., Steunenberg, B., & van Waarden, F. (2011). Sectors at Different Speeds: Analysing Transposition Deficits in the European Union. *JCMS: Journal of Common Market Studies, 49*(2), 265–291.

Hloušek, V., & Šedo, J. (2008). Tschechien: Konsolidierung des Parteiensystems bei anhaltenden Problemen der Mehrheitsbildung. In E. Bos & D. Segert (Eds.), *Osteuropäische Demokratien als Trendsetter? Parteien und Parteiensysteme nach dem Ende des Übergangsjahrzehnts* (pp. 91–103). Opladen and Farmington Hills: Verlag Barbara Budrich.

Holmes, L. (1997). *Post-communism: An Introduction*. Durham, NC: Duke University Press.

Horvat, A. (2005). *Why Does Nobody Care About the Absorption? Some Aspects Regarding Administrative Absorption Capacity for the EU Structural Funds in the Czech Republic, Estonia, Hungary, Slovakia and Slovenia Before Accession* (WIFO Working Papers). Wien: Österreichisches Institut für Wirtschaftsforschung. Available at http://www.wifo.ac.at/jart/prj3/wifo/resources/person_dokument/person_dokument.jart?publikation-sid=25750&mime_type=application/pdf. Accessed 29 May 2017.

HU. (2003). OP Environmental Protection and Infrastructure 2004–2006. *National Strategic Reference Framework*. Budapest: Ministry of Economy and Transport, Hungary. Available at http://www.inforse.org/europe/Structuralfunds/SF_docs/HU_SF_KIOP_en.pdf. Accessed 12 Feb 2016.

HU. (2007). OP Environment and Energy 2007–2013. *National Strategic Reference Framework*. Budapest: Government of the Republic of Hungary. Available at http://www.inforse.org/europe/Structuralfunds/SF_docs/SF_KEOP_07_13.pdf. Accessed 12 Feb 2016.

Hughes, J., Sasse, G., & Gordon, C. (2004). Conditionality and Compliance in the EU's Eastward Enlargement: Regional Policy and the Reform of Sub-national Government. *JCMS: Journal of Common Market Studies, 42*(3), 523–551.

Huntington, S. P. (1993). *The Third Wave: Democratization in the Late Twentieth Century.* Norman: University of Oklahoma Press.

Huszák, L. (2010). *Der Wettbewerb der Regionen: regionale Unterschiede in der Absorption der EU-Fördermittel: Eine empirische Analyse.* Frankfurt: Peter Lang.

Ikstens, J. (2007). Latvia. *European Journal of Political Research, 46*(7–8), 1012–1018.

Ikstens, J. (2008). Latvia. *European Journal of Political Research, 47*(7–8), 1039–1047.

Ikstens, J. (2010). Latvia. *European Journal of Political Research, 49*(7–8), 1049–1057.

Ikstens, J. (2011). Latvia. *European Journal of Political Research, 50*(7–8), 1035–1044.

Ikstens, J. (2012). Latvia. *European Journal of Political Research Political Data Yearbook, 51*(1), 175–186.

Ilie, L. (2011). *Romania's Roads to Nowhere* (Special Report). Bucharest: Reuters. Available at http://www.reuters.com/article/us-romania-infrastructure-idUSTRE74P0ZK20110526. Accessed 12 Feb 2016.

Jahn, D., & Müller-Rommel, F. (2010). Political Institutions and Policy Performance: A Comparative Analysis of Central and Eastern Europe. *Journal of Public Policy, 30*(1), 23–44.

Jasiewicz, K., & Jasiewicz-Betkiewicz, A. (2006). Poland. *European Journal of Political Research, 45*(7–8), 1231–1246.

Jasiewicz, K., & Jasiewicz-Betkiewicz, A. (2007). Poland. *European Journal of Political Research, 46*(7–8), 1063–1074.

Jasiewicz, K., & Jasiewicz-Betkiewicz, A. (2008). Poland. *European Journal of Political Research, 47*(7–8), 1096–1107.

Jasiewicz, K., & Jasiewicz-Betkiewicz, A. (2012). Poland. *European Journal of Political Research Political Data Yearbook, 51*(1), 243–256.

Joachim, J., Reinalda, B., & Verbeek, B. (2008). International Organizations and Implementation: Pieces of the Puzzle. In J. Joachim, B. Reinalda, & B. Verbeek (Eds.), *International Organizations and Implementation: Enforcers, Managers, Authorities?* (pp. 1–18). London: Routledge.

Jou, W. (2011). Left-Right Orientations and Ideological Voting in New Democracies: A Case Study of Slovenia. *Europe–Asia Studies, 63*(1), 27–47.

Jungerstam-Mulders, S. (2006). Parties and Party Systems in Post-communist EU Member States: Comparative Aspects. In S. Jungerstam-Mulders (Ed.), *Post-communist EU Member States: Parties and Party Systems* (pp. 1–22). Farnham and Burlington, VT: Ashgate.

Kaeding, M. (2006). Determinants of Transposition Delay in the European Union. *Journal of Public Policy, 26*(3), 229–253.

Kalvet, T. (2013). Estonia. *Expert Evaluation Network*. Tallinn: Ragnar Nurkse School of Innovation and Governance. Available at http://ec.europa.eu/regional_policy/sources/docgener/evaluation/pdf/eval2007/2013_een_task2_ee.pdf. Accessed 12 Feb 2016.

Karatchomakov, M. (2011). Bulgaria: The Deferred Crisis. In J. Jungmann & B. Sagemann (Eds.), *Financial Crisis in Eastern Europe: Road to Recovery* (pp. 64–107). Wiesbaden: Gabler Verlag.

Katz, R. S., & Mair, P. (1995). Changing Models of Party Organization and Party Democracy: The Emergence of the Cartel Party. *Party Politics, 1*(1), 5–28.

Katz, R. S., & Mair, P. (2009). The Cartel Party Thesis: A Restatement. *Perspectives on Politics, 7*(4), 753–766.

Kavas, D. (2010). Slovenia. *Expert Evaluation Network*. Ljubljana: Institute for Economic Research. Available at http://ec.europa.eu/regional_policy/sources/docgener/evaluation/pdf/eval2007/country_reports/slovenia.pdf. Accessed 12 Feb 2016.

Kavas, D. (2013). Slovenia. *Expert Evaluation Network*. Ljubljana: Institute for Economic Research. Available at http://ec.europa.eu/regional_policy/sources/docgener/evaluation/pdf/eval2007/2013_een_task2_si.pdf. Accessed 12 Feb 2016.

Kickert, W., & Randma-Liiv, T. (2015). *Europe Managing the Crisis: The Politics of Fiscal Consolidation*. London: Routledge.

Kiszelly, Z. (2008). Ungarn: Auf dem Weg zum Kartellparteiensystem. In E. Bos & D. Segert (Eds.), *Osteuropäische Demokratien als Trendsetter? Parteien und Parteiensysteme nach dem Ende des Übergangsjahrzehnts* (pp. 121–132). Opladen and Farmington Hills: Verlag Barbara Budrich.

Kitschelt, H. (1995). Formation of Party Cleavages in Post-communist Democracies: Theoretical Propositions. *Party Politics, 1*(4), 447–472.

Kitschelt, H. (1999). *Post-communist Party Systems: Competition, Representation, and Inter-Party Cooperation*. Cambridge: Cambridge University Press.

Kitschelt, H. (2001). Divergent Paths of Postcommunist Democracies. In L. Diamond & R. Gunther (Eds.), *Political Parties and Democracy* (pp. 299–323). Baltimore and London: Johns Hopkins University Press.

Kitschelt, H., Mansfeldová, Z., Markovski, R., & Toka, G. (1999). *Post-communist Party Systems: Competition, Representation, and Inter-Party Cooperation*. Cambridge: Cambridge University Press.

Kitschelt, H., & Wilkinson, S. I. (2007). Citizen–Politician Linkage: An Introduction. In H. Kitschelt & S. I. Wilkinson (Eds.), *Patrons, Clients and Policies: Patterns of Democratic Accountability and Political Competition* (pp. 1–49). Cambridge: Cambridge University Press.

Knill, C., & Tosun, J. (2009). Post-accession Transposition of EU Law in the New Member States: A Cross-Country Comparison. *European Integration*

Online Papers, 13, Article 18. http://eiop.or.at/eiop/pdf/2009-018.pdf. Accessed Jan 2016.

Kolarova, R., & Spirova, M. (2014). Bulgaria. *European Journal of Political Research Political Data Yearbook, 53*(1), 45–56.

König, K. (1992). The Transformation of a 'Real-Socialist' Administrative System into a Conventional Western European System. *International Review of Administrative Sciences, 58*(2), 147–161.

König, T., & Mäder, L. (2013). Non-conformable, Partial and Conformable Transposition: A Competing Risk Analysis of the Transposition Process of Directives in the EU 15. *European Union Politics, 14*(1), 46–69.

König, T., & Mäder, L. (2014). The Strategic Nature of Compliance: An Empirical Evaluation of Law Implementation in the Central Monitoring System of the European Union. *American Journal of Political Science, 58*(1), 246–263.

Kopecký, P. (2006a). Political Parties and the State in Post-communist Europe: The Nature of Symbiosis. *Journal of Communist Studies and Transition Politics, 22*(3), 251–273.

Kopecký, P. (2006b). The Rise of the Power Monopoly: Political Parties in the Czech Republic. In S. Jungerstam-Mulders (Ed.), *Post-communist EU Member States: Parties and Party Systems* (pp. 125–146). Farnham and Burlington, VT: Ashgate.

Kopecký, P., & Mair, P. (2012a). Conclusion: Party Patronage in Contemporary Europe. In P. Kopecký, P. Mair, & M. Spirova (Eds.), *Party Patronage and Party Government in European Democracies* (pp. 357–374). Oxford: Oxford University Press.

Kopecký, P., & Mair, P. (2012b). Party Patronage as an Organizational Resource. In P. Kopecký, P. Mair, & M. Spirova (Eds.), *Party Patronage and Party Government in European Democracies* (pp. 3–16). Oxford: Oxford University Press.

Kopecký, P., Mair, P., & Spirova, M. (2012). *Party Patronage and Party Government in European Democracies.* Oxford: Oxford University Press.

Kopecký, P., Meyer-Sahling, J.-H., Panizza, F., Scherlis, G., Schuster, C., & Spirova, M. (2016). Party Patronage in Contemporary Democracies: Results from an Expert Survey in 22 Countries from Five Regions. *European Journal of Political Research, 55*(2), 416–431.

Kopecký, P., & Spirova, M. (2011). 'Jobs for the Boys'? Patterns of Party Patronage in Post-communist Europe. *West European Politics, 34*(5), 897–921.

Kornai, J. (1995). *Das sozialistische System: Die politische Ökonomie des Kommunismus.* Baden-Baden: Nomos.

Kornai, J. (1996). Paying the Bill for Goulash Communism: Hungarian Development and Macro Stabilization in a Political-Economy Perspective. *Social Research, 63*(4), 943–1040.

Kostadinova, T. (2007). The Impact of Finance Regulations on Political Parties: The Case of Bulgaria. *Europe–Asia Studies, 59*(5), 807–827.

Krupavicius, A. (2005). Lithuania. *European Journal of Political Research, 44*(7–8), 1086–1101.

Krupavicius, A. (2007). Lithuania. *European Journal of Political Research, 46*(7–8), 1019–1031.

Krupavicius, A. (2009). Lithuania. *European Journal of Political Research Political Data Yearbook, 48*(7–8), 1022–1036.

Krupavicius, A. (2011). Lithuania. *European Journal of Political Research, 50*(7–8), 1045–1057.

Krupavicius, A. (2012). Lithuania. *European Journal of Political Research Political Data Yearbook, 51*(1), 187–200.

Krupavicius, A. (2013). Lithuania. *European Journal of Political Research Political Data Yearbook, 52*(1), 140–151.

Lackowska-Madurowicz, M., & Swianiewicz, P. (2013). Structures, Procedures and Social Capital: The Implementation of EU Cohesion Policies by Subnational Governments in Poland. *International Journal of Urban and Regional Research, 37*(4), 1396–1418.

Leonardi, R. (2005). *Cohesion Policy in the European Union: The Building of Europe*. Basingstoke: Palgrave Macmillan.

Leonardi, R. (2006). Cohesion in the European Union. *Regional Studies, 40*(2), 155–166.

Levitz, P., & Pop-Eleches, G. (2010). Monitoring, Money and Migrants: Countering Post-accession Backsliding in Bulgaria and Romania. *Europe–Asia Studies, 62*(3), 461–479.

Lewis, P. (2002). *Political Parties in Post-communist Eastern Europe*. London: Routledge.

Linek, L. (2007). Czech Republic. *European Journal of Political Research, 46*(7–8), 929–937.

Linek, L. (2008). Czech Republic. *European Journal of Political Research, 47*(7–8), 947–951.

Linek, L. (2011). Czech Republic. *European Journal of Political Research, 50*(7–8), 948–954.

Linek, L. (2012). Czech Republic. *European Journal of Political Research Political Data Yearbook, 51*(1), 76–81.

Linek, L. (2013). Czech Republic. *European Journal of Political Research Political Data Yearbook, 52*(1), 50–55.

Linek, L. (2014). Czech Republic. *European Journal of Political Research Political Data Yearbook, 53*(1), 92–103.

Linek, L., & Lacina, T. (2010). Czech Republic. *European Journal of Political Research, 49*(7–8), 939–946.

Linos, K. (2007). How Can International Organizations Shape National Welfare States? Evidence from Compliance with European Union Directives. *Comparative Political Studies, 40*(5), 547–570.

Lipset, S. M., & Rokkan, S. (1967). Cleavage Structures, Party Systems, and Voter Alignments: An Introduction. In S. M. Lipset & S. Rokkan (Eds.), *Party Systems and Voter Alignments: Cross-National Perspectives* (pp. 1–64). New York: The Free Press.

LT4. (2014). *Interview in Vilnius with Lithuanian Official on 7 May 2014.*

LT. (2004). *Single Programming Document for 2004–2006.* Vilnius: Government of Lithuania. Available at http://www.transp.lt/en/eu_support/stuctural_funds/single_programming_document. Accessed 12 Feb 2016.

LT. (2007a). OP Economic Growth 2007–2013. *National Strategic Reference Framework.* Vilnius: Government of Lithuania. Available at (accessed).

LT. (2007b). OP Promotion of Cohesion 2007–2013. *National Strategic Reference Framework.* Vilnius: Government of Lithuania. Available at https://www.google.de/url?sa=t&rct=j&q=&esrc=s&source=web&cd=2&cad=rja&uact=8&ved=0ahUKEwjJzJPOj6zLAhUL1SwKHXMFD9EQFg-glMAE&url=http%3A%2F%2Fwww.esparama.lt%2Fdocuments%2F42901%2F0%-2FOperational%2BProgramme%2Bfor%2BPromotion%2Bof%2BCohesion%2B-for%2B2007%25E2%2580%25932013%2Fdd445cb5-b9be-4fbe-ada5-13bbe-530a42c&usg=AFQjCNFmnHuKBauyvV0Zv7ZAIs8aQqKsRQ. Accessed 12 Feb 2016.

Lucaciu, L. O. (2012). Romania. *Expert Evaluation Network.* Bucharest: LIDEEA. Available at http://ec.europa.eu/regional_policy/sources/docgener/evaluation/pdf/eval2007/expert_innovation/2012_een_task2_ro.pdf. Accessed 12 Feb 2016.

Lucaciu, L. O. (2013). Romania. *Expert Evaluation Network.* Bucharest: LIDEEA. Available at http://ec.europa.eu/regional_policy/sources/docgener/evaluation/pdf/eval2007/2013_een_task2_ro.pdf. Accessed 12 Feb 2016.

LV. (2003). Single Programming Document 2004–2008. *National Strategic Reference Framework.* Riga: Government of Latvia. Available at http://www.esfondi.lv/upload/05-saistosie_dokumenti/spd_en_09112006.pdf. Accessed 12 Feb 2016.

LV. (2007). OP Infrastructure and Services 2007–2013. *National Strategic Reference Framework.* Riga: Ministry of Finance, Latvia. Available at http://www.esfondi.lv/upload/04-kohezijas_politikas_nakotne/op/3_op_2009-07-09_ENG.pdf. Accessed 12 Feb 2016.

Mahoney, J., & Goertz, G. (2006). A Tale of Two Cultures: Contrasting Quantitative and Qualitative Research. *Political Analysis, 14*(3), 227–249.

Mainwaring, S. (1999). *Rethinking Party Systems in the Third Wave of Democratization: The Case of Brazil.* Stanford: Stanford University Press.

Mainwaring, S., & Torcal, M. (2006). Party System Institutionalization and Party System Theory After the Third Wave of Democratization. In R. S. Katz & W. J. Crotty (Eds.), *Handbook of Party Politics* (pp. 204–227). London et al.: Sage.

Mainwaring, S., & Zoco, E. (2007). Political Sequences and the Stabilization of Interparty Competition: Electoral Volatility in Old and New Democracies. *Party Politics, 13*(2), 155–178.

Mair, P. (1997). *Party System Change: Approaches and Interpretations.* Cambridge: Cambridge University Press.

Malová, D., & Učeň, P. (2010). Slovakia. *European Journal of Political Research, 49*(7–8), 1154–1162.

Malová, D., & Učeň, P. (2011). Slovakia. *European Journal of Political Research, 50*(7–8), 1118–1129.

Malová, D., & Učeň, P. (2013). Slovakia. *European Journal of Political Research Political Data Yearbook, 52*(1), 208–216.

Maniokas, K. (2009). Conditionality and Compliance in Lithuania: The Case of the Best Performer. *European Integration Online Papers, 13*, Article 20. http://eiop.or.at/eiop/pdf/2009-020.pdf. Accessed 5 Jan 2016.

Maniokas, K., & Miseliuniene, A. (2013). Lithuania. *Expert Evaluation Network.* Vilnius: ESTEP. Available at http://ec.europa.eu/regional_policy/sources/docgener/evaluation/pdf/eval2007/2013_een_task2_lt.pdf. Accessed 12 Feb 2016.

Marek, D., & Baun, M. J. (2008). Conclusion. In M. J. Baun & D. Marek (Eds.), *EU Cohesion Policy After Enlargement* (pp. 248–269). Basingstoke: Palgrave Macmillan.

Markovic Hribernik, T., Kirbiš, M., & Vek, U. (2008). Institutional Regulation and the Effectiveness of Absorbing EU Funds: The Experiences of Ireland, Estonia and Slovenia. *Društvena istraživanja, 17*(6), 1219–1239.

Mastenbroek, E., & Kaeding, M. (2007). Transcending the Goodness of Fit. *Comparative European Politics, 5*(3), 342–343.

Mastenbroek, E., & Keulen, M. (2006). Beyond the Goodness of Fit: A Preference-Based Account of Europeanization. In R. Holzhacker & M. Haverland (Eds.), *European Research Reloaded: Cooperation and Integration Among Europeanized States* (pp. 19–42). Wiesbaden: Springer.

Mbaye, H. A. D. (2001). Why National States Comply with Supranational Law: Explaining Implementation Infringements in the European Union, 1972–1993. *European Union Politics, 2*(3), 259–281.

McCann, P. (2015). *The Regional and Urban Policy of the European Union: Cohesion: Results-Orientation and Smart Specialisation.* Cheltenham and Northampton: Edward Elgar.

McCubbins, M. D., & Schwartz, T. (1984). Congressional Oversight Overlooked: Police Patrols Versus Fire Alarms. *American Journal of Political Science, 28*(1), 165–179.

Medve-Bálint, G. (2017). Funds for the Wealthy and the Politically Loyal? How EU Funds May Contribute to Increasing Regional Disparities in East Central Europe. In J. Bachtler, P. Berkowitz, S. Hardy, & T. Muravska (Eds.), *EU Cohesion Policy: Reassessing Performance and Direction*. Abingdon: Routledge.

Medzihorsky, J., Oana, I.-E., Quaranta, M., & Schneider, C. Q. (2017). *Setmethods: Functions for Set-Theoretic Multi-method Research and Advances QCA. R Package Version 2.1*. https://CRAN.R-project.org/package=SetMethods.

Meyer-Sahling, J.-H. (2004). Civil Service Reform in Post-communist Europe: The Bumpy Road to Depoliticisation. *West European Politics, 27*(1), 71–103.

Meyer-Sahling, J.-H. (2006). The Rise of the Partisan State? Parties, Patronage and the Ministerial Bureaucracy in Hungary. *Journal of Communist Studies and Transition Politics, 22*(3), 274–297.

Meyer-Sahling, J.-H. (2008). The Changing Colours of the Post-communist State: The Politicisation of the Senior Civil Service in Hungary. *European Journal of Political Research, 47*(1), 1–33.

Meyer-Sahling, J.-H. (2009a). *Sustainability of Civil Service Reforms in Central and Eastern Europe Five Years After EU Accession* (Sigma Paper No. 44). Paris: OECD. Available at http://www.oecd-ilibrary.org/governance/sustainability-of-civil-service-reforms-in-central-and-eastern-europe-five-years-after-eu-accession_5kml60pvjmbq-en. Accessed 12 Feb 2016.

Meyer-Sahling, J.-H. (2009b). Varieties of Legacies: A Critical Review of Legacy Explanations of Public Administration Reform in East Central Europe. *International Review of Administrative Sciences, 75*(3), 509–528.

Meyer-Sahling, J.-H. (2011). The Durability of EU Civil Service Policy in Central and Eastern Europe After Accession. *Governance, 24*(2), 231–260.

Meyer-Sahling, J.-H., & Veen, T. (2012). Governing the Post-communist State: Government Alternation and Senior Civil Service Politicisation in Central and Eastern Europe. *East European Politics, 28*(1), 4–22.

Michelsen, J. (2008). A Europeanization Deficit? The Impact of EU Organic Agriculture Regulations on New Member States. *Journal of European Public Policy, 15*(1), 117–134.

Mikkel, E. (2006). Patterns of Party Formation in Estonia: Consolidation Unaccomplished. In S. Jungerstam-Mulders (Ed.), *Post-communist EU Member States: Parties and Party Systems* (pp. 23–47). Farnham and Burlington, VT: Ashgate.

Milio, S. (2007). Can Administrative Capacity Explain Differences in Regional Performances? Evidence from Structural Funds Implementation in Southern Italy. *Regional Studies, 41*(4), 429–442.

Milio, S. (2008). How Political Stability Shapes Administrative Performance: The Italian Case. *West European Politics, 31*(5), 915–936.

Milio, S. (2010a). Multi-level Governance and Implementation Performance: Lessons from Italy. In S. Milio (Ed.), *From Policy to Implementation in the*

European Union: The Challenge of a Multi-level Governance System (pp. 59–122). London and New York: IB Tauris.

Milio, S. (2010b). The Struggle to Implement European Union Policies: Political and Administrative Factors in the Member States. In S. Milio (Ed.), *From Policy to Implementation in the European Union: The Challenge of a Multi-level Governance System* (pp. 1–57). London and New York: IB Tauris.

Motyl, A. J. (2004). Communist Legacies and New Trajectories: Democracy and Dictatorship in the Former Soviet Union and East Central Europe. In Y. Brudny, J. Frankel, & S. Hoffman (Eds.), *Restructuring Post-communist Russia* (pp. 52–67). Cambridge: Cambridge University Press.

Mungiu-Pippidi, A. (2007). Is East-Central Europe Backsliding? EU Accession Is No 'End of History'. *Journal of Democracy, 18*(4), 8–16.

Muraközy, B., & Telegdy, Á. (2016). Political Incentives and State Subsidy Allocation: Evidence from Hungarian Municipalities. *European Economic Review, 89,* 324–344.

Myant, M., & Drahokoupil, J. (2012). International Integration, Varieties of Capitalism and Resilience to Crisis in Transition Economies. *Europe–Asia Studies, 64*(1), 1–33.

Nakrošis, V., & Gudžinskas, L. (2012). Party Patronage and State Politicisation in the Post-communist Countries of Central and Eastern Europe: A Game Theory Approach. *NISPAcee Journal of Public Administration and Policy, 5*(2), 89–120.

Noetzel, R., & Stumm, T. (1997). *Factors Influencing the Spending of Structural Money. A Discussion at the European and Member State Level, with Special Regard to the European Regional Policy.* Regional Policy Series. Luxembourg. Available at http://bookshop.europa.eu/en/factors-influencing-the-spending-of-structural-funds-money-pbQAREGIW24/. Accessed 9 Feb 2016.

Noutcheva, G., & Bechev, D. (2008). The Successful Laggards: Bulgaria and Romania's Accession to the EU. *East European Politics & Societies, 22*(1), 114–144.

Nunberg, B. (2000). *Ready for Europe: Public Administration Reform and European Union Accession in Central and Eastern Europe* (World Bank Technical Paper No. 466). Washington, DC: World Bank. Available at http://documents.worldbank.org/curated/en/2000/05/437136/ready-europe-public-administration-reform-european-union-accession-central-eastern-europe. Accessed 12 Feb 2016.

O'Dwyer, C. (2004). Runaway State Building; How Political Parties Shape States in Postcommunist Eastern Europe. *World Politics, 56*(4), 520–553.

O'Dwyer, C. (2006a). Reforming Regional Governance in East Central Europe: Europeanization or Domestic Politics as Usual? *East European Politics & Societies, 20*(2), 219–253.

O'Dwyer, C. (2006b). *Runaway State-Building: Patronage Politics and Democratic Development.* Baltimore: Johns Hopkins University Press.

Offe, C. (2004). Capitalism by Democratic Design? Democratic Theory Facing the Triple Transition in East Central Europe. *Social Research, 71*(3), 501–528.

Olejniczak, K. (2013). Mechanisms Shaping an Evaluation System—A Case Study of Poland 1999–2010. *Europe–Asia Studies, 65*(8), 1642–1666.

Olteanu, T. (2008). Rumänien: Vom Einparteiensystem zum Einheitsbrei. In E. Bos & D. Segert (Eds.), *Osteuropäische Demokratien als Trendsetter? Parteien und Parteiensysteme nach dem Ende des Übergangsjahrzehnts* (pp. 147–166). Oplanden and Farmington Hills: Verlag Barbara Budrich.

Pabriks, A., & Stokenberga, A. (2006). Political Parties and the Party System in Latvia. In S. Jungerstam-Mulders (Ed.), *Post-communist EU Member States: Parties and Party Systems* (pp. 51–67). Farnham and Burlington, VT: Ashgate.

Pedersen, M. N. (1979). The Dynamics of European Party Systems: Changing Patterns of Electoral Volatility. *European Journal of Political Research, 7*(1), 1–26.

Perkins, R., & Neumayer, E. (2007). Do Membership Benefits Buy Regulatory Compliance? An Empirical Analysis of EU Directives 1978–99. *European Union Politics, 8*(2), 180–206.

Pettai, V. (2004). Estonia. *European Journal of Political Research, 43*, 993–999.

Pettai, V. (2005). Estonia. *European Journal of Political Research, 44*(7–8), 1002–1007.

Pettai, V. (2006). Estonia. *European Journal of Political Research, 45*(7–8), 1094–1100.

Pettai, V. (2008). Estonia. *European Journal of Political Research, 47*(7–8), 962–968.

Pettai, V. (2010). Estonia. *European Journal of Political Research, 49*(7–8), 955–963.

Piattoni, S. (2001). Clientelism in Historical and Comparative Perspective. In S. Piattoni (Ed.), *Clientelism, Interests, and Democratic Representation: The European Experience in Historical and Comparative Perspective* (pp. 1–30). Cambridge: Cambridge University Press.

Piattoni, S., & Smyrl, M. (2003). Building Effective Institutions: Italian Regions and the EU Structural Funds. In J. Bukowski, S. Piattoni, & M. Smyrl (Eds.), *Between Europeanization and Local Societies: The Space for Territorial Governance* (pp. 133–156). Lanham et al.: Rowman & Littlefield.

PL. (2003a). *National Development Plan 2004–2006*. Warsaw: Government of Poland. Available at http://www.funduszestrukturalne.gov.pl/English/National+Development+Plan/. Accessed 12 Feb 2016.

PL. (2003b). OP Transport 2004–2006. *National Strategic Reference Framework*. Warsaw: Ministry of Infrastructure, Poland. Available at http://www.funduszestrukturalne.gov.pl/NR/rdonlyres/951EFC81-C785-461C-B4E9-28289B71DFA3/0/sop_transport_english.pdf. Accessed 12 Feb 2016.

PL. (2007). OP Infrastructure and Environment 2007–2013. *National Strategic Reference Framework*. Warsaw: Ministry of Regional Development, Poland. Available at http://www.pois.2007-2013.gov.pl/English/Documents_POIS/Documents/7122008_POIiS_ENG.pdf. Accessed 11 Mar 2016.

Pop, R., Doroftei, I. M., & Dimulescu, V. (2013). Risks of Corruption and the Management of EU Funds in Romania. *Romanian Journal of Political Sciences, 13*(1): 101–123.

Pop-Eleches, G. (2008). A Party for All Seasons: Electoral Adaptation of Romanian Communist Successor Parties. *Communist and Post-communist Studies, 41*(4), 465–479.

Pop-Eleches, G. (2010). Throwing Out the Bums: Protest Voting and Unorthodox Parties After Communism. *World Politics, 62*(2), 221–260.

Popa, A. (2012). The Impact of the Structural Funds in the Transformation Process of the New EU Member States. *L'Europe en Formation* (Vol. 364, pp. 161–179). Brussels: Centre International de Formation Européenne.

Pridham, G. (2007). Romania and EU Membership in Comparative Perspective: A Post-accession Compliance Problem?—The Case of Political Conditionality. *Perspectives on European Politics and Society, 8*(2), 168–188.

PRSG. (2001). *Political Risks Services Group. The International Country Risk Guide: Methodology*. Available at http://www.prsgroup.com/wp-content/uploads/2014/08/icrgmethodology.pdf. Accessed 20 Nov 2015.

Przeworski, A. (1995). *Sustainable Democracy*. Cambridge: Cambridge University Press.

Ragin, C. (1987). *The Comparative Method: Moving Beyond Qualitative and Quantitative Strategies*. Berkeley et al.: University of California Press.

Ragin, C. C. (2000). *Fuzzy-Set Social Science*. Chicago: University of Chicago Press.

Ragin, C. C. (2006). Set Relations in Social Research: Evaluating Their Consistency and Coverage. *Political Analysis, 14*(3), 291–310.

Ragin, C. C. (2008a). Qualitative Comparative Analysis Using Fuzzy Sets (fsQCA). In B. Rihoux & C. C. Ragin (Eds.), *Configurational Comparative Methods: Qualitative Comparative Analysis (QCA) and Related Techniques* (Vol. 51, pp. 87–121). London et al.: Sage.

Ragin, C. C. (2008b). *Redesigning Social Inquiry: Set Relations in Social Research*. Chicago: University of Chicago Press.

Ragin, C. C., & Fiss, P. C. (2008). Net Effects Versus Configuration: An Empirical Demonstration. In C. C. Ragin (Ed.), *Redesigning Social Inquiry: Fuzzy Sets and Beyond* (pp. 190–212). Chicago: University of Chicago Press.

Ragin, C. C., & Rihoux, B. (2008). *Configurational Comparative Methods: Qualitative Comparative Analysis (QCA) and Related Techniques*. London et al.: Sage.

Ram, M. H. (2012). Legacies of EU Conditionality: Explaining Post-accession Adherence to Pre-accession Rules on Roma. *Europe–Asia Studies, 64*(7), 1191–1218.

Ramonaite, A. (2006). The Development of the Lithuanian Party System: From Stability to Perturbation. In S. Jungerstam-Mulders (Ed.), *Post-communist EU Member States: Parties and Party Systems* (pp. 69–90). Farnham and Burlington, VT: Ashgate.

Regional Policy Glossary. (2015). *Financial Corrections.* Available at http://ec.europa.eu/regional_policy/en/policy/what/glossary/f/financial-corrections. Accessed 11 July 2015.

Rihoux, B., & De Meur, G. (2009). Crisp-Set Qualitative Comparative Analysis (csQCA). In B. Rihoux & C. C. Ragin (Eds.), *Configurational Comparative Methods: Qualitative Comparative Analysis (QCA) and Related Techniques* (pp. 33–68). London et al.: Sage.

RO. (2007a). OP Environment 2007–2013. *National Strategic Reference Framework.* Bucharest: Ministry of Environment, Romania. Available at www.posmediu.ro/ShowDocument.aspx?path=NFw1XDQucGRm. Accessed 12 Feb 2016.

RO. (2007b). OP Transport 2007–2013. *National Strategic Reference Framework.* Bucharest: Ministry of Transport, Romania. Available at http://old.fonduri-ue.ro/res/filepicker_users/cd25a597fd-62/Doc_prog/prog_op/5_POST/2_POST_Eng.pdf. Accessed 12 Feb 2016.

RO. (2009). Raportul Anual de Implementare 2008. *Annual Implementation Report.* Bucharest: Ministry of Transport, Romania.

RO. (2010a). A Formative Evaluation of Structural Instruments in Romania: Final Report. *Conducting Evaluations for the Period 2009–10.* Bucharest: Ministry of Public Finance, Romania. Available at http://ec.europa.eu/regional_policy/sources/docgener/evaluation/library/romania/1010_formative_nsrf_eval_en.pdf. Accessed 29 May 2017.

RO. (2010b). Raportul Anual de Implementare 2009. *Annual Implementation Report.* Bucharest: Ministry of Transport, Romania.

RO. (2011a). Raportul Anual de Implementare 2010. *Annual Implementation Report.* Bucharest: Ministry of Transport, Romania.

RO. (2011b). Second Ad Hoc Evaluation: Review of Investment in Transport and Environment Infrastructure: Final Report. *Conducting Evaluations for the Period 2009–10.* Bucharest: Ministry of Public Finance, Romania. Available at http://www.evaluare-structurale.ro/ro/list-viewreports-menu/details/8/31/rapoarte-evaluare-second-ad-hoc-evaluation-review-of-investment-in-transport-and-environment-infrastructure. Accessed 29 May 2017.

RO. (2012a). Government of Romania: Nota de Fundamentare HG nr.1200/04.12.2012. Available at http://gov.ro/ro/guvernul/procesul-legislativ/note-de-fundamentare/nota-de-fundamentare-hg-nr-1200-04-12-2012&page=738. Accessed 20 Dec 2015.

RO. (2012b). Raportul Anual de Implementare 2011. *Annual Implementation Report*. Bucharest: Ministry of Transport, Romania.

RO. (2013). Raportul Anual de Implementare 2012. *Annual Implementation Report*. Bucharest: Ministry of Transport, Romania.

RO. (2014). Raportul Anual de Implementare 2013. *Annual Implementation Report*. Bucharest: Ministry of Transport, Romania.

RO. (2015a). *Government of Romania: General Transport Master Plan, Approved by the Government*. Available at http://gov.ro/en/government/cabinet-meeting/general-transport-master-plan-approved-by-the-government. Accessed 18 Feb 2016.

RO. (2015b). *Ministry of EU Funds*. Romania: Prezentare MFE. Available at http://www.fonduri-ue.ro/minister/prezentare. Accessed 18 Feb 2016.

RO1. (2015). *Interview in Bucharest with Romanian Official on 15 June 2015.*

RO2. (2015). *Interview in Bucharest with Romanian Official on 20 June 2015.*

Rohlfing, I. (2012). *Case Studies and Causal Inference: An Integrative Framework*. Basingstoke: Palgrave Macmillan.

Roper, S. D. (2006). The Influence of Party Patronage and State Finance on Electoral Outcomes: Evidence from Romania. *Journal of Communist Studies and Transition Politics, 22*(3), 362–382.

Rouban, L. (2003). Politicization of the Civil Service. In B. G. Peters & J. Pierre (Eds.), *Handbook of Public Administration* (pp. 310–320). London et al.: Sage.

Rybar, M. (2006). Old Parties and New: Changing Patterns of Party Politics in Slovakia. In S. Jungerstam-Mulders (Ed.), *Post-communist EU Member States: Parties and Party Systems* (pp. 147–176). Farnham and Burlington, VT: Ashgate.

Rybar, M. (2008). Slowakei: Vom Regimekonflikt zur Dominanz der sozi-oökonomischen Konfliktlinie. In E. Bos & D. Segert (Eds.), *Osteuropäische Demokratien als Trendsetter? Parteien und Parteiensysteme nach dem Ende des Übergangsjahrzehnts* (pp. 105–120). Opladen and Farmington Hills: Verlag Barbara Budrich.

Rybář, M., & Deegan-Krause, K. (2008). Slovakia's Communist Successor Parties in Comparative Perspective. *Communist and Post-communist Studies, 41*(4), 497–519.

Rynck, S. D., & McAleavey, P. (2001). The Cohesion Deficit in Structural Fund Policy. *Journal of European Public Policy, 8*(4), 541–557.

Sagemann, B., & Reese, P. (2011). The Great Subprime Credit Crisis and Its Impact on Eastern Europe. In J. Jungmann & B. Sagemann (Eds.), *Financial Crisis in Eastern Europe* (pp. 21–63). Wiesbaden: Gabler Verlag.

SAR. (2011). Morti de foame, cu banii in buzunar. *Raport SAR*. Bucharest: Societatea Academica din Romania. Available at http://sar.org.ro/morti-de-foame-cu-banii-in-buzunar-autoritatile-romane-sunt-depasite-de-sarcina-de-a-cheltui-15-milioane-euro-pe-zi/. Accessed 12 Feb 2016.

Sasse, G. (2008). The Politics of EU Conditionality: The Norm of Minority Protection During and Beyond EU Accession. *Journal of European Public Policy, 15*(6), 842–860.

Scherpereel, J. A. (2010). EU Cohesion Policy and the Europeanization of Central and East European Regions. *Regional and Federal Studies, 20*(1), 45–62.

Schimmelfennig, F. (2001). The Community Trap: Liberal Norms, Rhetorical Action, and the Eastern Enlargement of the European Union. *International Organization, 55*(1), 47–80.

Schimmelfennig, F., & Sedelmeier, U. (2005a). Conclusions. The Impact of the EU on the Accession Countries. In F. Schimmelfennig & U. Sedelmeier (Eds.), *The Europeanization of Central and Eastern Europe* (pp. 210–228). Ithaca, NY: Cornell University Press.

Schimmelfennig, F., & Sedelmeier, U. (2005b). Introduction. Conceptualizing the Europeanization of Central and Eastern Europe. In F. Schimmelfennig & U. Sedelmeier (Eds.), *The Europeanization of Central and Eastern Europe* (pp. 1–28). Ithaca, NY: Cornell University Press.

Schimmelfennig, F., & Winzen, T. (2017). Eastern Enlargement and Differentiated Integration: Towards Normalization. *Journal of European Public Policy, 24*(2), 239–258.

Schneider, C. Q., & Rohlfing, I. (2013). Combining QCA and Process Tracing in Set-Theoretic Multi-method Research. *Sociological Methods & Research, 42*(4), 559–597.

Schneider, C. Q., & Rohlfing, I. (2016). Case Studies Nested in Fuzzy-Set QCA on Sufficiency: Formalizing Case Selection and Causal Inference. *Sociological Methods & Research, 45*(3), 526–568.

Schneider, C. Q., & Wagemann, C. (2007). *Qualitative Comparative Analysis (QCA) und Fuzzy Sets: Ein Lehrbuch für Anwender und jene, die es werden wollen*. Opladen and Farmington Hills: Verlag Barbara Budrich.

Schneider, C. Q., & Wagemann, C. (2010). Standards of Good Practice in Qualitative Comparative Analysis (QCA) and Fuzzy-Sets. *Comparative Sociology, 9*(3), 397–418.

Schneider, C. Q., & Wagemann, C. (2012). *Set-Theoretic Methods for the Social Sciences: A Guide to Qualitative Comparative Analysis*. Cambridge: Cambridge University Press.

Schraff, D. (2014). Buying Turnout or Rewarding Loyalists? Electoral Mobilization and EU Structural Funding in the German Länder. *European Union Politics, 15*(2), 277–288.

Schwellnus, G., Balázs, L., & Mikalayeva, L. (2009). It Ain't Over When It's Over: The Adoption and Sustainability of Minority Protection Rules in New EU Member States. *European Integration Online Papers, 13*, Article 24. http://eiop.or.at/eiop/pdf/2009-024.pdf. Accessed Jan 2016.

Sedelmeier, U. (2008). After Conditionality: Post-accession Compliance with EU Law in East Central Europe. *Journal of European Public Policy, 15*(6), 806–825.

Sedelmeier, U. (2009). Post-accession Compliance with EU Gender Equality Legislation in Post-communist New Member States. *European Integration Online Papers, 13*, Article 23. http://eiop.or.at/eiop/texte/2009-023a.htm. Accessed Jan 2016.

Sedelmeier, U. (2012). Is Europeanisation Through Conditionality Sustainable? Lock-in of Institutional Change After EU Accession. *West European Politics, 35*(1), 20–38.

Segert, D. (2007). Postsozialismus–Spätsozialismus–Staatssozialismus. Grundlinien und Grundbegriffe einer politikwissenschaftlichen Postsozialismusforschung. In D. Segert (Ed.), *Postsozialismus: Hinterlassenschaften des Staatssozialismus und neue Kapitalismen in Europa* (pp. 1–23). Wien: Braumüller.

Segert, D. (2008). Parteien und Transformation in Osteuropa nach dem Ende des Übergangsjahrzehnts. In E. Bos & D. Segert (Eds.), *Osteuropäische Demokratien als Trendsetter? Parteien und Parteiensysteme nach dem Ende des Übergangsjahrzehnts* (pp. 11–32). Opladen and Farmington Hills: Verlag Barbara Budrich.

SGI. (2014a). Policy Performance and Governance Capacities in the OECD and EU. *Sustainable Governance Indicators*. Gütersloh: Bertelsmann Stiftung. Available at https://www.bertelsmann-stiftung.de/fileadmin/files/BSt/Publikationen/GrauePublikationen/Policy_Performance_and_Governance_Capacities_SGI2014_Overview.pdf. Accessed 29 May 2017.

SGI. (2014b). *Sustainable Governance Indicators 2014 Codebook*. Available at http://www.bertelsmann-stiftung.de/bst/en/media/xcms_bst_dms_37442__2.pdf. Accessed 24 Sept 2014.

Shefter, M. (1994). *Political Parties and the State: The American Historical Experience*. Princeton: Princeton University Press.

SI. (2003). *Single Programming Document 2004–2006*. Ljubljana: Government of Slovenia. Available at http://www.eu-skladi.si/other/programski-dokumenti/epd. Accessed 12 Feb 2016.

SI. (2007). OP Environmental and Transport Infrastructure Development for the Period 2007–2013. *National Strategic Reference Framework*. Ljubljana: Ministry of Infrastructure, Slovenia. Available at http://www.mzip.gov.si/en/areas_of_work/investment_monitoring_and_finance_division/program_period_2007_2013/. Accessed 12 Feb 2016.

SI. (2016). *OP Environmental and Transport Infrastructure Development 2007–2013*. Ljubljana: Ministry of Infrastructure, Slovenia. Available at http://

www.mzi.gov.si/en/areas_of_work/investment_monitoring_and_finance_division/program_period_2007_2013/. Accessed 12 Feb 2016.

Siegel, S.N. (2006). *Law and Order in the European Union: Explaining Variations in Compliance with the European Community Treaty* (Discussion Paper SP IV 2006-303). Berlin: Wissenschaftszentrum Berlin für Sozialforschung. Available at http://www.ssoar.info/ssoar/bitstream/handle/document/11351/ssoar-2006-siegel-law_and_order_in_the.pdf?sequence=1. Accessed 12 Feb 2016.

Sikk, A. (2012). Estonia. *European Journal of Political Research Political Data Yearbook, 51*(1), 90–95.

Šipikal, M. (2014). *Political and Administrative Barriers of Cohesion Policy Implementation in Slovakia*. Paper Presented at the Conference of the Regional Studies Association 4 June 2014, Prague, 05.06.2014.

SK. (2003). OP Basic Infrastructure 2004–2006. *National Strategic Reference Framework*. Bratislava: Ministry of Construction and Regional Development, Slovakia. Available at (accessed).

SK. (2007a). OP Environment 2007–2013. *National Strategic Reference Framework*. Bratislava: Ministry of Environment, Slovakia. Available at http://www.nsrr.sk/en/operational-programmes/environment/. Accessed 12 Feb 2016.

SK. (2007b). OP Transport 2007–2013. *National Strategic Reference Framework*. Bratislava: Ministry of Transport, Slovakia. Available at http://www.nsrr.sk/en/operational-programmes/transportation/. Accessed 12 Feb 2016.

Spendzharova, A., & Versluis, E. (2013). Issue Salience in the European Policy Process: What Impact on Transposition? *Journal of European Public Policy, 20*(10), 1499–1516.

Spirova, M. (2005). Political Parties in Bulgaria: Organizational Trends in Comparative Perspective. *Party Politics, 11*(5), 601–622.

Spirova, M. (2007). Bulgaria. *European Journal of Political Research, 46*(7–8), 901–908.

Spirova, M., & Kolarova, R. (2010). Bulgaria. *European Journal of Political Research, 49*(7–8), 909–918.

Stan, L. (2013). Romania. *European Journal of Political Research Political Data Yearbook, 52*(1), 196–207.

Stan, L., & Zaharia, R. (2007). Romania. *European Journal of Political Research, 46*(7–8), 1082–1095.

Stan, L., & Zaharia, R. (2008). Romania. *European Journal of Political Research, 47*(7–8), 1115–1126.

Stan, L., & Zaharia, R. (2009). Romania. *European Journal of Political Research, 48*(7–8), 1087–1099.

Stan, L., & Zaharia, R. (2010). Romania. *European Journal of Political Research, 49*(7–8), 1139–1153.

Stan, L., & Zaharia, R. (2011). Romania. *European Journal of Political Research, 50*(7–8), 1108–1117.

Stark, D. (1990). Privatization in Hungary: From Plan to Market or From Plan to Clan? *Eastern European Politics and Societies, 4*(3), 351–392.

Steunenberg, B., & Toshkov, D. (2009). Comparing Transposition in the 27 Member States of the EU: The Impact of Discretion and Legal Fit. *Journal of European Public Policy, 16*(7), 951–970.

Stone, R. W. (2002). *Lending Credibility: The International Monetary Fund and the Post-communist Transition*. Princeton: Princeton University Press.

Stykow, P. (2006). *Staat und Wirtschaft in Russland: Interessenvermittlung zwischen Korruption und Konzertierung*. Wiesbaden: VS Verlag.

Šumpíková, M., Pavel, J., & Klazar, S. (2004, May 14). *EU Funds: Absorption Capacity and Effectiveness of Their Use, with Focus on Regional Level in the Czech Republic*. Paper presented at the The 12th NISPAcee Annual Conference 'Central and Eastern European Countries Inside and Outside the European Union: Avoiding a New Divide', Vilnius.

Surubaru, N.-C. (2017a). Administrative Capacity or Quality of Political Governance? EU Cohesion Policy in the New Europe, 2007–13. *Regional Studies, 51*(6), 844–856.

Surubaru, N.-C. (2017b). Revisiting the Role of Domestic Politics: Politicisation and European Cohesion Policy Performance in Central and Eastern Europe. *East European Politics, 33*(1), 106–125.

Szczerbiak, A. (2006). Power Without Love? Patterns of Party Politics in Post-1989 Poland. In S. Jungerstam-Mulders (Ed.), *Post-communist EU Member States: Parties and Party Systems* (pp. 91–124). Farnham and Burlington, VT: Ashgate.

Szczerbiak, A. (2008). The Birth of a Bipolar Party System or a Referendum on a Polarizing Government? The October 2007 Polish Parliamentary Election. *Journal of Communist Studies and Transition Politics, 24*(3), 415–443.

Terracciano, B., & Graziano, P. R. (2016). EU Cohesion Policy Implementation and Administrative Capacities: Insights from Italian Regions. *Regional & Federal Studies, 26*(3), 293–320.

The Economist. (2014). *Poland's Second Golden Age: Europe's Unlikely Star (Published 28 June 2014)*. Available at http://www.economist.com/news/leaders/21605910-poland-just-had-best-25-years-half-millennium-its-transformation-remains. Accessed 20 Jan 2016.

The Independent. (2006, September 19). *Budapest Rioters Storm TV Station in 'Lying PM' Protest*. Available at http://www.independent.co.uk/news/world/europe/budapest-rioters-storm-tv-station-in-lying-pm-protest-416640.html. Accessed 27 Oct 2015.

Thomson, R. (2007). Time to Comply: National Responses to Six EU Labour Market Directives Revisited. *West European Politics, 30*(5), 987–1008.

Thomson, R. (2009). Same Effects in Different Worlds: The Transposition of EU Directives. *Journal of European Public Policy, 16*(1), 1–18.

Thomson, R. (2010). Opposition Through the Back Door in the Transposition of EU Directives. *European Union Politics, 11*(4), 577–596.

Tiemann, G. (2008). Cleavages' oder, Legacies'? Die Institutionalisierung und Struktur des politischen Wettbewerbs im postsozialistischen Osteuropa. In E. Bos & D. Segert (Eds.), *Osteuropäische Demokratien als Trendsetter? Parteien und Parteiensysteme nach dem Ende des Übergangsjahrzehnts* (pp. 33–53). Opladen and Farmington Hills: Verlag Barbara Budrich.

Toshkov, D. (2007). Transposition of EU Social Policy in the New Member States. *Journal of European Social Policy, 17*(4), 335–348.

Toshkov, D., Knoll, M., & Wewerka, L. (2010). *Connecting the Dots: Case Studies and EU Implementation Research* (Working Paper No. 10/2010). Vienna: Institute for European Integration Research (EIF). Available at https://eif.univie.ac.at/downloads/workingpapers/wp2010-10.pdf. Accessed 12 Feb 2016.

Tosun, J. (2014). Absorption of Regional Funds: A Comparative Analysis. *JCMS: Journal of Common Market Studies, 52*(2), 371–387.

Trauner, F. (2009). Post-accession Compliance with EU Law in Bulgaria and Romania: A Comparative Perspective. *European Integration Online Papers, 13*, Article 21. http://eiop.or.at/eiop/pdf/2009-021.pdf. Accessed Jan 2016.

Treib, O. (2004). *Die Bedeutung der nationalen Parteipolitik für die Umsetzung europäischer Sozialrichtlinien*. Frankfurt and New York: Campus Verlag.

Treib, O. (2014). Implementing and Complying with EU Governance Outputs. *Living Reviews in European Governance, 9*(1). http://www.europeangovernance-livingreviews.org/Articles/lreg-2011-1/ (cited version from August 2014).

Vachudova, M. A. (2005). *Europe Undivided: Democracy, Leverage, and Integration After Communism*. Oxford: Oxford University Press.

van Biezen, I. (2003). *Political Parties in New Democracies: Party Organization in Southern and East-Central Europe*. Basingstoke: Palgrave Macmillan.

van Biezen, I. (2005). On the Theory and Practice of Party Formation and Adaptation in New Democracies. *European Journal of Political Research, 44*(1), 147–174.

Van Evera, S. (1997). *Guide to Methods for Students of Political Science*. Ithaca, NY: Cornell University Press.

Vanags, A., & Skruzkalne, K. (2012). Latvia. *Expert Evaluation Network*. Riga: Baltic International Centre for Economic Policy Studies. Available at http://ec.europa.eu/regional_policy/sources/docgener/evaluation/pdf/eval2007/expert_innovation/2012_een_task2_lv.pdf. Accessed 12 Feb 2016.

Vanhuysse, P. (2006). *Divide and Pacify: Strategic Social Policies and Political Protests in Post-communist Democracies*. Budapest: Central European University Press.

Varnagy, R. (2011). Hungary. *European Journal of Political Research, 50*(7–8), 991–998.

Varnagy, R. (2012). Hungary. *European Journal of Political Research Political Data Yearbook, 51*(1), 129–135.

Varnagy, R. (2015). Hungary. *European Journal of Political Research Political Data Yearbook, 54*(1), 133–140.

Vazac, R. (2011). Czech Republic: Crisis Postponed—Navigation to Recovery. In J. Jungmann & B. Sagemann (Eds.), *Financial Crisis in Eastern Europe: Road to Recovery* (pp. 109–175). Wiesbaden: Gabler Verlag.

Verheijen, A. J. G. (2000). *Administrative Capacity Development: A Race Against Time?* (Working Documents W 107). The Hague: Scientific Council for Government Policy. Available at http://www.wrr.nl/fileadmin/nl/publicaties/DVD_WRR_publicaties_1972-2004/W107_Administrative_capacity_development.pdf. Accessed 12 Feb 2016.

Verheijen, T. (1999). Civil Service Systems in EU Candidate States: Introduction. In T. Verheijen & A. Kotchegura (Eds.), *Civil Service Systems in Central and Eastern Europe* (pp. 85–91). Cheltenham: Edward Elgar.

Verheijen, T. (2007). *Administrative Capacity in the New EU Member States: The Limits of Innovation?* (World Bank Working Paper No. 115). Washington, DC: World Bank. Available at http://elibrary.worldbank.org/doi/abs/10.1596/978-0-8213-7155-8. Accessed 12 Feb 2016.

Wasilewski, J. (1990). The Patterns of Bureaucratic Elite Recruitment in Poland in the 1970s and 1980s. *Soviet Studies, 42*(4), 743–757.

Way, L. A., & Levitsky, S. (2007). Linkage, Leverage, and the Post-communist Divide. *East European Politics & Societies, 21*(1), 48–66.

Whitefield, S. (2002). Political Cleavages and Post-communist Politics. *Annual Review of Political Science, 5*(1), 181–200.

World Bank. (2010). Romania: Transport Sector: Final Report. *Functional Review*. Washington, DC: World Bank. Available at http://documents.worldbank.org/curated/en/2010/10/17055950/romania-functional-review-transport-sector. Accessed 29 May 2017.

World Bank. (2015). *World Bank Governance Indicators: Government Effectiveness*. Available at http://info.worldbank.org/governance/wgi/pdf/ge.pdf. Accessed 20 Dec 2015.

Zhelyazkova, A., Kaya, C., & Schrama, R. (2017). Notified and Substantive Compliance with EU Law in Enlarged Europe: Evidence from Four Policy Areas. *Journal of European Public Policy, 24*(2), 216–238.

Zubek, R. (2005). Complying with Transposition Commitments in Poland: Collective Dilemmas, Core Executive and Legislative Outcomes. *West European Politics, 28*(3), 592–619.

Index

C. Hagemann, *EU Funds in the New Member States*, Palgrave Studies in European Union Politics, https://doi.org/10.1007/978-3-030-02092-7

B

C

N

O

Kolibri 360 GmbH
Ferdinand-Jühlke-Straße 7
99095 Erfurt, Deutschland
produktsicherheit@kolibri360.de